Bootleg

BOOTLEG

The Secret History
of the
Other Recording Industry

CLINTON HEYLIN

St. Martin's Press
New York

To sweet D.
Welcome to the machine

ISBN 0-312-13031-7

First published in Great Britain by the Penguin Group

First Edition: June 1995
10 9 8 7 6 5 4 3 2 1

Contents

Prologue

In the summer of 1969, in a small cluster of independent LA record stores, there appeared a white-labelled two-disc set housed in a plain cardboard sleeve, with just three letters hand-stamped on the cover – GWW. This was *Great White Wonder*, a motley collection of unreleased Bob Dylan recordings, culled primarily from home sessions in Minneapolis in 1961 and Woodstock in 1967. It was the first rock bootleg, and it spawned an entire industry.

For twenty-five years now the bootleggers have persevered, even occasionally thrived. They continue to be a thorn in the side of an industry grown bloated by its own excess. Throughout these years they have reflected the best and worst of legitimate releases. The bootleggers are the ultimate free-marketeers, giving fans what they want – and to hell with the wishes of the artist or record company.

Bootleg collectors the world over will remember their initial 'hit' – that first time they stumbled upon a stall or store selling albums you weren't supposed to be able to buy – and the charge that first blast of illicit vinyl gave them. For me it was as a thirteen-year-old would-be obsessive that I learnt of a seedy little porn shop in the nether regions of central Manchester, free-standing in the centre of an area modelled on Dresden *circa* 1945. It was a Sunday and the store was closed, but a friend and I bussed into town just to confirm that this really was a purveyor of hot wax. Sure enough, sellotaped in the window were three of their more attractive artifacts, with titles at once cryptically enticing – *LiveR Than You'll Ever Be*, *Seems Like a Freeze Out, Yellow Matter Custard* – huh?

Returning the following Saturday, oblivious to the well-endowed German ladies thrusting out from the covers of magazine upon magazine, I edged my way to the back of the store and two cardboard boxes. I was searching for one item in particular – Bob

Dylan at the Royal Albert Hall. Having read a description of the events one night in 1966 when Dylan scrambled the synapses of an entire generation, how could I fail to be intrigued?

'Sorry, we're out of stock on that one. We'll be getting some more, though.'

I furtively flicked through whatever quasi-definitive Dylan bootleg guide I had along for the ride. It recommended one they did have, *Talkin' Bear Mountain Picnic Massacre Blues*. Great title. And I loved the lyrics I'd read in *Writings and Drawings*. It had a proper cover, t'boot. 'I'll take it.'

'Two quid, to you, lad.'

My most recent legitimate acquisition – Mr Bowie's *Aladdin Sane* – had required a seemingly hefty £2.19, courtesy of Boots the Chemists.

After all the scaremongering that accompanied bootlegs in the early seventies (and even today), I was pleasantly surprised to discover that the sound quality of this new addition to my Dylan collection (which numbered exactly two collections of *Greatest Hits*) was perfectly good – a bit of hiss that was largely lost on my parents' Grundig gramophone, but pretty damn fine (little did I know it was actually a Berkeley Records edition of an original Trade Mark of Quality bootleg and that TMQ's version was hiss-free).

By the time I established that the acquisition of these items carried considerable kudos among the record-swapping fraternity at school, I was a teenage bootleg junkie.

In those days there was no real way of knowing what one was buying. Bootleggers were (and are, though no longer for the same reasons) notoriously vague about the sources of their material. My friendly neighbourhood bootleg dealer was generous enough to let me take 'items' home to decide if I wanted them. Though funds were tight, I bought what I could. Soon enough he had moved to new premises and the German ladies had been shunted to the back shelf – in two cardboard boxes. The albums kept multiplying. The 'above board' record store across the road did not appreciate all the punters who came in asking if they sold bootlegs and decided to make a phone call. One Saturday I saw a new Dylan bootleg, *Joaquin* (pronounced 'walkin'', as in 'she's a . . .') *Antique*, the first to feature outtakes from his recent return to form, *Blood on the Tracks*. The official album had been out all of six weeks. I was broke and prices had by now nudged up to £2.60. I was obliged to return the following weekend, money now in hand, intent on buying this exciting new platter. There was no stock. Indeed there was no window. Orbit Books was no more.

Twenty years later, I'm sitting in an upmarket Chinese fry-up joint trying to tape an interview with one of the central figures in the eighties 'Boot Biz' over a cacophony of sizzling fat. 'Eric Bristow' – his chosen pseudonym – despite a healthy American tan, has not lost his broad Lancastrian accent. He is telling me about this great shop in Tibb Street, Manchester, where he first started buying bootlegs . . .

Everyone's stories are different, yet the song remains the same. *BOOTLEG* is as much an excuse to collect all those tall tales as an attempt to provide a layman's account of the contradictory constructs that have been mounted to stamp out an industry that has proved to be remarkably resilient. Bootlegs are here to stay because the appeal of hearing music that has not been authorized or sanitized by the artist will always be an enduring one.

BOOTLEG is, above all, a celebration. Despite many shoddy titles, shameful practices and cowboy practitioners – who have been responsible for much that is bad and ugly – I believe bootlegs have been a positive influence on the music. They have reminded fans that rock & roll is about 'the moment', that you might have to wade through static, pops, crackles, bad nights and worse tapes to find one clear moment, but no record company can capture each and every one worth preserving; that the record companies cannot lock music up in neat little boxes and say, 'This is what you may listen to.' Hopefully the bootleggers have also freed an awful lot of music that the artists themselves might not have 'approved' for release. But then, never trust the artist, trust the tale.

Clinton Heylin – *June 1994*

Introduction: A Boot by Any Other Name . . .

The Privateering Stroke so easily degenerates into the Piratical, and the Privateering Trade is usually carried on with an Unchristian Temper, and proves an Inlet into so much Debauchery and Iniquity.[1]

Though rock bootleg albums are the bouncing babies of illicit trade, the impetus for bootlegging most forms of popular art has a hoary ol' tradition dating back at least as far as Shakespeare. The line between 'the privateering stroke' and the 'piratical' has remained blurred throughout its 400-year history.

The word *bootleg*, as fans of gangster movies are well aware, originally referred to the sale of illicit booze (generally the moonshine variety). The expression, which became current late in the nineteenth century, came from the apparently common practice of carrying a bottle of whiskey or the like in the leg of one's boot, presumably in the interests of avoiding detection. (Appropriately, this is also a popular method of smuggling tape-recorders into rock gigs.) Its transference to the musical world dates from the prohibition era, when the word was in common currency. Around 1929, the showbiz journal *Variety* referred to a 'huge market' for what it called 'bootleg disk records'. What *Variety* was referring to were not so much bootleg albums, in the sense now understood by the term, but 'pirate' albums – i.e. illegal copies of legitimate releases.

So how is a bootleg album different from a *pirate* or *counterfeit* album? Certainly the record industry has gone to great pains to imply that there is very little difference between a pirate and a bootleg album, often interchanging the terms at will. Indeed the standard American textbook, *This Business of Music*, makes no real distinction, the bootlegger being simply branded one particular type of pirate:

Piracy in the record business applies to the unauthorized duplication of tapes or records sold openly as manufactured without permission of the record company ... The counterfeiter and the pirate ... are obviously misappropriating the services of the artist and a product owned and paid for by a legitimate manufacturer. Both benefit at the expense and detriment of record companies, performing artists, music publishers, unions and the federal and local governments. The counterfeiter and the pirate fail to pay the recording costs incurred by the record company, and they steal the profits which might otherwise accrue to the record company. Detriment to the artist results from inferior-quality recordings manufactured by the counterfeiter or pirate and from the non-payment of artist royalties.[2]

Already black and white must turn to shades of grey. Most so-called 'bootlegs' manufactured in the world in 1993 had full 'mechanical' royalties paid to the artist concerned, via the usual copyright-house channels. Likewise, most bootlegs, taped from the audience using sophisticated portable domestic tape-recorders, incur no recording costs to anyone but the taper, who may or may not be in direct cahoots with the bootlegger. So much for the standard definition of piracy!

Bootleg albums, transferred from tape to vinyl or CD, exist as product only when the bootlegger undertakes to create the artifact. The transfer from non-commercial bootlegs (tapes) to commercial bootlegs (LPs or CDs) changes the form, not the substance. The notion that a bootleg exists in direct competition to the product peddled by legitimate record companies is absurd. It certainly gets short shrift from bootleggers themselves:

Lou Cohan [a bootlegger]: I get very angry when I see people saying the word 'bootleg' when, in fact, what they mean is 'counterfeit' or 'pirate'. I am against counterfeiting, I am against pirating legitimate releases of the record company, but if anybody thinks that if I have purchased every single Rolling Stones album in existence, and I have bought all the Rolling Stones albums that have been released in England, France, Japan, Italy and Brazil, that if I have an extra one hundred dollars in my pocket, instead of buying a

Rolling Stones bootleg I am going to buy a John Denver album or a Sinead O'Connor album, they're retarded![3]

An essential element of creativity separates the bootleggers from their piratical cousins – those who copy official material but make no attempt to pass their product off as the original – and counterfeiters – who are trying to replicate official product, presumably with the intention of hoodwinking the public. And like the rock artists they emulate, some bootleggers produce good art, some bad.

Tom Schultheiss, in his account of the early history of bootlegging, makes a useful distinction by labelling bootlegs 'performance piracy', that is to say, 'the creation of unauthorized recordings not from pre-existing ones, but from unauthorized taping of live performances or radio and TV broadcasts, or utilization of stolen tapes from unreleased studio sessions'.[4]

The distinction between bootlegs and pirate albums should be clear-cut: bootlegs are primarily designed to be collectors' items. They are bought by ultra-keen fans, not those looking for a cut-price alternative to pukka product. And yet if there are deleted or impossible-to-find cuts on legitimate releases somewhere in the world, then bootleggers have considered these fair game for anthologizing (indeed the pirating of long-deleted independent singles on 'anthology' albums of the *Nuggets* variety has long been a mini-industry in itself). Often, bootlegs are actually hybrids comprising bootleg material interspersed with 'pirated' official cuts. Such instances were relatively common in the days of vinyl, less prevalent in the modern CD era. Thus bootleggers commit a form of piracy in catering to hardcore collectors, while official companies choose to ignore this area or are simply unaware of the latent demand.

In the collectors' marketplace the normal rules of commerce do not apply. Here, consumers are quite happy to pay considerably more than the price of an official album to purchase alternative takes of songs they already own multiple versions of, or hear a series of false starts and incomplete takes of a song already released in a finished, 'definitive' form. (Two good examples are the sessions for The Beatles' 'Strawberry Fields Forever' and The Beach Boys' 'Good Vibrations'. Both have been heavily bootlegged and, while quite fascinating to hear, remain ancillary to the perfection of the finished 45s.)

The criteria for what makes a good bootleg are entirely distinct from what might make a good official release. It becomes a form of rock archaeology, where the quest for revelation often subverts any search for aesthetic content. It is assumed that the multiple layers of backing tracks for 'Good Vibrations' reveal Brian Wilson's working processes at a time when his productions were becoming increasingly complex. It is this insight that bootleg collectors seek. Of course, they require a considerable backdrop of accumulated knowledge before venturing into the murky waters of bootlegging, knowledge usually acquired by purchasing the entire official corpus ('rarities' included) and reading the requisite fanzines.

Bob Walker [editor *Hot Wacks*]: [Collectors] know not all live performances are good and not all bootlegs are high quality. You [may] get a person not knowing what to expect picking up a piece of bad product and being turned off forever, whereas a knowledgeable person knows that this could very well have been recorded in the men's washroom at the back of the arena but that's OK because it has a version of this song that has never been played before and that's fine.[5]

If studio outtakes – meaning unreleased songs – and alternative takes represent something of a holy grail to the collector, the rock bootleg market, much like the jazz bootleg market, is largely fuelled by tapes of live performances. These are generally complete live performances, bum notes and all – something legitimate record companies have often baulked at releasing – captured crudely from the audience or perhaps from an unmixed 'board' tape. To a Stones collector *LiveR Than You'll Ever Be* is a more authentic take on the Stones live '69 than *Get Your Ya-Ya's Out*, with its retinue of post-production credits.

The Beatles excepted, European bootleggers prefer – particularly in the modern copyright minefield – complete, just-as-it-was live performances by the rock pantheon. There is virtually no crossover into soul, funk or rap. Until recently, with the advent of what have been dubbed 'protection gap' bootlegs (i.e. bootlegs that are legitimate, though unauthorized, releases in the country of origin but are generally illegal when exported), the more lightweight, ephemeral forms of AOR Poprock (the Dire Straits and Simply Reds of this world) had been largely immune from the bootleg virus. Ironically, it has been these bands who have objected most strongly to the unauthorized release of their live performances.

According to an article in the *LA Times* in 1986, 'There . . . are virtually no bootlegs of popular black artists, even those with large crossover audiences, such as Prince and Michael Jackson.'[6] Actually the *LA Times* could not be more off beam citing Prince as an unbootlegged performer. He has been the most bootlegged of all eighties artists and was unwittingly responsible for probably the best-selling bootleg of all time, the legendary *Black Album*. But with few exceptions, the dinosaurs rule in this kingdom. Even with the switch to CD in the last five years, the five most bootlegged artists remain The Beatles, Led Zeppelin, The Rolling Stones, Bob Dylan and Bruce Springsteen. If the new kids on the block – REM, Guns'n'Roses and U2 – are making some headway, the flood of product from the Old Guard carries on unabated, irrespective of any exciting new source material or the vagaries of fashion.*

Within this context, bootlegs can be seen as the product of an entirely separate record industry. The crossover between bootlegs and 'in print' official product verges on the non-existent, save for the few instances where the legend status of a particular bootleg has warranted official release (for example Bowie's *Ziggy's Last Stand*, Dylan's *Basement Tapes*, The Buzzcocks' *Time's Up*). Though the record industry has worked hard to suggest its activities should encompass all forms of music – whether or not it was recorded (or even copyrighted) by one or more of its 'employees' – the notion

---

* Bootleggers have been as prone to fads as their official counterparts. Witness the Japanese-driven flood of King Crimson CDs that occurred in 1990–91, when for a short time there seemed no end to the demand for this previously overlooked dinosaur of prog-rock, a demand which prompted Robert Fripp to compile his own boxed-sets of Crimson live performances.

that bootlegs 'cost' the record industry 'income' does not hold up to the most cursory examination. The bootleggers operate from within cracks too small for the Biz to edge into, surviving on margins and sales that corporate economics could not withstand. As one seventies bootlegger told *Who Put the Bomp*'s Greg Shaw:

The industry may be losing $200 million a year, but if so, 99 per cent of it is to tape piracy. They're talking about Mafia plants that turn out millions of Donna Summer 8-tracks and sell them to rackjobbers in New Jersey for 3 cents less than they'd pay Polygram, or some shit like that. But it's no easier to bust those guys for this than for anything else, so they come after us. For one thing, the average run on a bootleg album is no more than 2,500. Some only 500. A really good-selling title can go as high as 10,000 . . . The record company loses no sales because the record was never in their catalogue, and never would have been.[7]

It should be apparent that bootlegging, by its very nature, qualifies as disorganized crime, that there is no conspiracy, no 'Mr Big', just people operating in a twilight of insatiable demand for a lot of pleasure and a modicum of profit. The figures provided by the Recording Industry Association of America (RIAA) and the British Phonographic Industry (BPI) seem deliberately distorted to imply a problem on a far greater scale than reality suggests. Much like the bogeymen of home-taping, the big-time bootlegger is an invention of an industry in search of a technological scapegoat to explain diminishing profits, due in truth to corporate insensitivity.

Lou Cohan: The figures they gave at the time of [my] 1976 bust, like they confiscated 250 million dollars worth of bootlegs, is totally ridiculous. I was manufacturing 2,500, 3,500, at the most 4,000 of a particular bootleg of a particular artist and selling them wholesale at a dollar, a dollar and a quarter, at the most a dollar fifty each. They would retail for, what? Five bucks? Seven bucks in a record store. So where RIAA gets this 200 million, 250 million dollar figure from is beyond me. They're jerking off the record companies.[8]

Artifacts

1 Prehistory: From the Bard to the Blues

THE

Tragicall Historie of

HAMLET

Prince of Denmarke

By William Shake-speare.

As it hath beene diuerse times acted by his Highnesse ser-
uants in the Cittie of London : as also in the two V-
niuersities of Cambridge and Oxford, and else-where

At London printed for N.L. and Iohn Trundell.
1603.

It was a witty and a truthful rejoinder which was given by a captured pirate to Alexander the Great. The king asked the fellow, 'What is your idea, in infesting the sea?' And the pirate answered with uninhibited insolence, 'The same as yours, in infesting the earth! But because I do it with a tiny craft, I'm called a pirate: because you have a mighty navy, you're called an emperor.'[1]

In the ancient world, the only permanent forms of art were visual – the written word, the ivory sculpture, the painted canvas. The original 'bookleggers' appointed themselves to disseminate religious or politically subversive tracts, anything which challenged the accepted canon. The booklegger generally sought to set himself apart from the pirate. Of course, the motives of early bookleggers were not tainted by financial considerations. When the written word was truly written, an author's publishing rights were of no consequence.

Only with Gutenberg's invention of the printing press did the possibility of a wide dissemination of the printed word become a reality. Inevitably, from the early days of Caxton's press in England, the most powerful of vested interests sought to regulate what could and could not be printed. Initially the Crown, like the Church before it, was more concerned with censorship than the profits that might be made from licensing 'the right to copy'. Given the climate that existed in the aftermath of the Hundred Years' War and the War of the Roses, the king's servants sought to ensure that what came off the printing presses did not create political turmoil. In this they were singularly unsuccessful.

By the time that Shakespeare was writing his plays at the end of the sixteenth century, political pamphleteers had long operated as a check on the extremes of government, reflecting popular perceptions and criticisms of policy in an anonymous manner designed to ensure that the writer stayed attached to his pen and not the scaffold. But the printing presses were also beginning to publish contemporary works of drama, in both authorized and unauthorized forms. The most revered of contemporary playwrights, Ben Jonson, oversaw the publication of all his plays. However, it was piratical Elizabethan and Stuart publishers who were first to publish the plays of William Shakespeare, albeit in unauthorized form. These bookleggers were the first generation of privateers catering to a public demand for texts of performances they had enjoyed and wished to re-enact in their minds.

William Shakespeare, though a successful playwright, was not considered the prodigious genius that Jonson was and, for reasons we will never know, chose not to authorize published versions of his plays.* Quite probably, Shakespeare believed that the plays were written for the stage and the stage alone and was unconcerned with overseeing their publication (though it is presumed by some scholars that he gave his tacit blessing to some of the 'good' quartos published to counteract piratical 'bad' quartos of plays like *Romeo and Juliet* and *Hamlet*). Clearly, Dr Johnson believed this when he wrote in 1756:

[Shakespeare] sold [his plays], not to be printed, but to be played. They were immediately copied for the actors, and multiplied by transcript after transcript, vitiated by the blunders of the penman, or changed by the affectation of the player ... and printed ... from compilations made by chance or by stealth out of the separate parts written for the theatre.[2]

Though the 'good' quartos were all published after the requisite registration with the Stationers' Company, absence of registration was not always evidence of piratical intent, just as 'simultaneous entrance and transfer' (i.e. registration) was not in itself evidence of honest dealing.

The 'bad' quartos that were published are presumed to come from transcriptions made in the audience at the Globe Theatre, the

---

* Though 'good' quartos of fourteen of his plays were published before the first collected edition in 1623, there is no evidence that any of these were published with Shakespeare's blessing. Five 'bad' quartos, along with editions of *Richard III* and *King Lear*, almost certainly were not.

sixteenth-century equivalent to taping a rock concert (though reference to a player's or prompter's copy may well have helped produce the early quartos of *King Lear* and *Richard III*). Three systems of shorthand were in existence in the Elizabethan era, though stenography came last, in 1602. In the case of one play, *Pericles* (1608), the text has come down to us only in a surreptitious edition comprising what may well be a shorthand report. Some of the other quarto editions drawn from 'shorthand reports' were wildly off the mark; witness Hamlet's most famous soliloquy as first published:

> To be, or not to be; ay, there's the point
> To die, to sleep, is that all? Ay, all;
> Not, to sleep, to dream. Ay, marry, there it goes,
> For in that dream of death, when we awake
> And borne before an everlasting judge
> From whence no passenger ever returned.[3]

Shakespeare also seems to have resisted preparing any approved version of his complete works. Only after his death did John Heminge and Henry Condell attempt to collect all of the plays into what has become known as the First Folio. In some instances, they relied on previous quarto editions, notably for *Troilus and Cressida* and *Henry IV Part Two*, but there are clearly plays in the First Folio where they did not have access to a prompter's copy or Shakespeare's own manuscripts or 'foul papers' (i.e. early drafts). In certain instances – *Richard III* and *King Lear* – it would appear that the Folio versions were set up from quarto editions but with reference to manuscript versions (in the case of *King Lear*, the Folio is presumed to derive from a revised 'playhouse manuscript', while the quarto edition of *Lear* appears to derive from a 'stolen report').

In fact, the First Folio of 1623 was not the first attempt to collect Shakespeare's plays. A publisher by the name of Thomas Pavier attempted such a venture in 1619 but had published barely a quarter of the plays when a letter from the Lord Chamberlain to the Stationers' Company bid them 'to take order for the stay of any further impression of any of the plays or interludes of His Majesty's servants without their consents'. The 'approved' 1623 folio killed off the need for pirated editions.

That Shakespeare did not even sanction the posthumous publication of his plays suggests that, like many artists, he was the last person to have a perspective on his own work. For seventeenth-century bookleggers, no doubt a mercenary motive lay behind their endeavours. Nevertheless, their publication of Shakespeare's plays – if just for the fact that they showed there was a demand for textual versions – may well have saved England's finest body of drama from oblivion.

The proliferation of printing presses and the popular demand for drama, aligned to an ever-increasing literacy among the artisan classes, meant that in the late seventeenth century – for the first time – it was possible to earn a successful living as a writer. As such, writers as well as publishers began to lobby for an act of parliament to regulate the 'right to copy'.*

Britain's first copyright act in 1709 was intended to clamp down on pirate editions, though it would have offered little protection to the likes of Shakespeare (unless he had chosen to register his plays). It sought to guarantee the rights of legitimate publishers, whose licences were granted by the Crown. In the troubled times that followed the overthrow of England's last Papist king, James II, the issue of political censorship was again behind such legislation.

As one of the first countries to introduce a formal copyright statute, the Anglo-Saxon attitude towards authors was always firmly based around the pragmatic notion of 'ensuring he received his due' rather than more censorial rights (i.e. the right to publish in the first place), which devolved to the Crown and/or government first, the 'producer' (in the eighteenth century, the publisher)

---

* The US Copyright Office defines copyright as 'literally . . . the right to copy . . . [i.e.] that body of exclusive rights granted by statute to authors for protection of their writings. It includes the exclusive right to make and publish copies of the copyrighted work, to make other versions of the work, and . . . to perform the work in public.'[4]

second, and the author a poor third. Theirs was not considered to be a 'natural right' in their work, but rather a statutory right, designed to foster creativity. The lack of any provision in the 1709 act for unpublished works also smacked of pragmatic common sense:

There is an important public-interest consideration underlying the entire copyright system: authors and other exploiters of copyright material are given rights partly to provide an incentive for creativity . . . The creation of exclusive rights, however, represents one side of the coin: the right to exploit the protected works and to obtain appropriate rewards for their use. But that may not reflect satisfactorily the other side of the coin: the public interest may not be satisfied if the copyright owner is not prepared to make his works available to the public, whether at all, at a reasonable cost, or subject to reasonable conditions.[5]

It was not until the nineteenth century that Victorian fascination with popular personalities began the cult of authorship (soon transferred to film stars and eventually rock stars). In the early years of the Industrial Revolution, it was not considered relevant who the author of a particular tract or racy serial might be. Many were published anonymously or under pseudonyms. There was a general fascination with folk tales and popular mythology. Many literary figures spent their time tracking down and documenting 'public domain' material in danger of being lost to the world due to the huge demographic changes the Industrial Revolution was wreaking on 'traditional life'. Thus it was that someone like Francis Child, probably the first meticulous archivist of popular musical traditions, came to publish his eight volumes of *English and Scottish Popular Ballads*, collected from manuscript collections and private books scattered throughout Britain.

The world was changing, and profit and progress were the new arbiters of 'popular genius'. In 1886 emissaries from all the major European states gathered in Berne, Switzerland, to thrash out what they hoped would be a universal copyright agreement to protect the interests of not just the authors but also the publishers who made their work accessible to an ever-expanding mass audience.

The Berne Convention was just the beginning of an ongoing process whereby publishers and 'producers' have extended copyright into every realm of 'creativity'. It established copyright in a published work that ran until fifty years after the death of the author. As one modern critic of the Berne Convention has observed, this was 'because it suited the interests of the publishers, [not] because it encouraged the production of new works'.[6]

The delegates' declared intention at Berne was to ensure an appropriate balance between copyright holder and public interest, 'based on the quasi-mystical concept of protecting the rights of authors in their works'. Yet the balance was already tilting the publishers' way. The most significant aspect of the Berne Convention was the reciprocal copyright protection between signatories. Under the convention, a signatory had to guarantee the same treatment to authors of other signatories as they accorded their own citizens.

But the Berne Convention was not adopted by all industrial countries. There was one very significant abstention, the United States, who received considerable condemnation at the time for 'sitting on the fence'. In a particularly vitriolic editorial in London's *Musical Times*, America was accused of continuing 'to walk alone in the path of self-interest and dishonesty'. This dose of bile stemmed from the sheer volume of sheet music published in the US without licence or copyright and then exported to countries where they breached copyright. In a previous *Musical Times* editorial it had been suggested that some 90 per cent of the sheet music imported from the US were 'piratical reprints'. In the late nineteenth century, America was the home of sheet-music 'piracy', and the European market her intended target. The *Musical Times* editorial bluntly asserted that this was the true reason why the US had chosen to attend, but not adopt, the Berne Convention.

By the second half of the nineteenth century, the copyrighting of something as intangible as music had become an important issue. Though the ability to record a performance was still some years away, sheet music had become an extremely popular form of printing. The Victorian family unit's habit of sitting around a piano singing songs, and the popularity of recitals and music halls, had created a substantial demand for hard copy musical notation.* Since the music publishers paid royalties and produced some highly ornate sheet music (while raking off considerable profits for themselves) the price of a legitimate libretto was often prohibitive. This left a wide enough breach for cheap, mass-market copies, one quickly filled by small-time entrepreneurs. James Coover's study of sheet-music piracy in Victorian England provides many parallels with more modern copyright conflicts:

> For twenty five years [between 1881 and 1906], the music publishers in Britain warred with those who copied music illegally and struggled with a government irresolute about helping to suppress those crimes ... The reciprocal mistrusts and sometimes open dislike between music-sellers and publishers; the determination of those publishers to protect a status quo against all persuasions; the guile and arrogance of the pirates, and the curious group which made excuses for their piracy; the proliferation of protective associations put together by publishers, retailers, and even the pirates ... the apparent indifference of the public to most of these events, and in reverse, the publishers' indifference to the public's interests ... the enmity aroused by a traditional system of pricing music to wholesalers, professionals, retailers, schools and public – [created] a system displeasing to just about everyone.[7]

In fact, the public were hardly indifferent to the plight of the pirates, who enjoyed considerable popular support. They were widely viewed as a necessary check on unscrupulous profiteering by the music publishers. Many argued that 'cheap reprints [of sheet music] were helping to satisfy the needs of a great mass of people who could not afford legitimate prints – whose prices, many times, the publishers kept artificially high.'[8] All the while, music publishers continued to petition for new copyright laws.

By the turn of the century, hawkers who sold pirated sheet music on the streets were fast becoming a dying breed. As publish-

---

* Publishers were not solely interested in selling sheet music. They also hoped to license the rights to publicly perform works they held in copyright.

ers pushed for punitive penalties, the pirates could only respond with sly digs at music publishers' expense. A 1902 broadside entitled 'An Occupation Gone' mourned the passing of these hawkers:

> Weep! for they take my goods away;
> 'Tis sad and strange as if today
> The partridge on the hawk should prey,
> To see musicians rob the hawker.
> So, pillaged, plundered, sacked, I walk
> The streets – nay, cease from vulgar talk,
> Don't, don't say 'Walker!'
>
> The public trust in me was placed,
> And so with high and cultured taste
> In music one and all were graced,
> But now, oh! how the news must grieve you.
> My trade is gone, and I must say
> In truth 'Goodbye, my Dolly Gray,
> For I must leave you.'
>
> Cheap was sweet 'Down the Vale' I know,
> And cheap that moving strain 'Oh, Flo!'
> At twopence each I let them go,
> For mine was never once a high rate.
> But woe for us! it's woe, I vow,
> I, erst your benefactor, now
> Am dubbed a pirate.[9]

In 1906, the music publishers finally got their way: a new copyright act. This was despite a sturdy defence of the pirates by some members of Parliament. The Hon. Mr Harwood laid the blame for the so-called 'disease of piracy' at the door of the music publishers, given 'that the whole trade of music publishing [is] rotten . . . in fact one of the most outrageous examples of a trust'. The 1906 Act, designed 'to amend the law relating to Musical Copyright', was a paragon of economy, running to just two pages (compared with the 230 pages required for the 1988 Copyright Act). It stated that:

Every person who prints, reproduces or sells, or exposes, offers, or has in his possession for sale, any pirated copies of any musical work, or has in his possession any plates for the purpose of printing or reproducing pirated copies of any musical work, shall (unless he proves that he acted innocently) be guilty of an offence punishable on summary conviction, and shall be liable for a fine not exceeding £5, and on a second or subsequent conviction to imprisonment with or without hard labour for a term not exceeding two months or to a fine not exceeding ten pounds.[10]

By 1906, though, technology was rolling on and a full revision of UK copyright was required. Rights for recorded performances were already becoming an issue. Though it dates from a mere five years after the 1906 revision, the British Copyright Act of 1911 provided protection not only for printed copies of any musical work but also for sound recordings throughout the entire British Empire (a substantial part of the world market in 1911).

Even America was awakening to the need to provide a more sturdy defence of copyright. After all it was here, in 1877, that Edison had first proved sound could be reproduced mechanically, in one fell swoop dissolving the division between performance art and more permanent media.

At this stage it was principally piano rolls – a series of holes on a hard card roll that mechanically reproduced music on a piano – which were prone to piracy. Recorded music was barely at the teething stage. This didn't stop early record manufacturers seeking protection under Article I, Section 8 of the American constitution, which gave 'authors and inventors ... exclusive right to their respective writings and discoveries.'

Unfortunately for the manufacturers, a 1908 Supreme Court hearing judged that a composer had no legal right to control sound recordings of their works as they could not submit the requisite 'copies' to the Library of Congress ('mechanical reproductions' did not qualify as 'copies' of writings or discoveries). A more serious blow came the following year, with the most substantial revision of American copyright law in 119 years. In this, Congress chose to uphold the Supreme Court's judgement, ruling that 'records are not literary or artistic creations, but mere uses or applications of creative works in the form of physical objects.' The only rights granted a composer under the 1909 Copyright Act were:

(i) the exclusive right to perform their songs;
(ii) the exclusive right to record their songs if written copies, i.e. sheet music, had been duly copyrighted.

Given that 'there was no visible expression of creative effort within the grooves of a record', the only legal recourses open to record manufacturers were via state laws, which were Byzantine and contradictory. Ironically, record labels and liner notes were considered 'visible expressions of creative effort', and were thus eligible for copyright. It seemed that, for the moment at least, the US was determined to exist in a limbo, paying mere lip service to the principle of protection for writers and inventors expressed in its constitution.

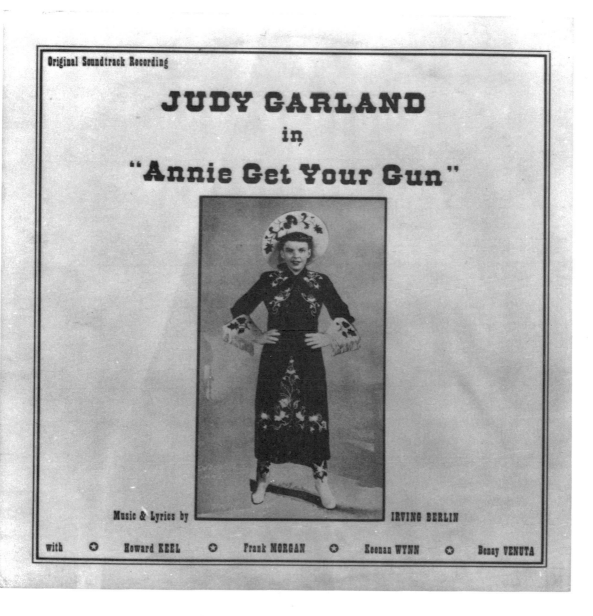

Original Soundtrack Recording

JUDY GARLAND

in

"Annie Get Your Gun"

Music & Lyrics by   IRVING BERLIN

with   ✪   Howard KEEL   ✪   Frank MORGAN   ✪   Keenan WYNN   ✪   Benay VENUTA

We 'pirates' – if you must call us that – are the custodians of vocal history and we're doing a damn good job of it – a job you can't expect record companies to do because they're not in business for that.[1]

By the time the 1909 Copyright Act had passed through Congress, the man once dubbed the Father of Bootlegging, Lionel Mapleson, had already accumulated his impressive collection of assorted arias from the 1901, 1902 and 1903 seasons at New York's Metropolitan Opera House. Mapleson had been given a phonograph recorder by Thomas Edison himself and, as librarian at the Metropolitan, had proceeded to record snippets of operas (he could only record a couple of minutes at a time due to the crudity of the equipment). At first, Mapleson concealed the phonograph in the prompter's box. Unfortunately, the large horn needed to collect the sound protruded from the box, obstructing the view of certain paying customers. After some complaints Mapleson rigged up the phonograph on the catwalk, just behind the proscenium arch, high above the stage with the horn hanging below, concealed by the scenic borders.[2]

Though the Mapleson cylinders have been described as 'probably the worst-sounding collection of live performances ever recorded on phonograph cylinders, thus setting the standard for most subsequent bootleg recordings',[3] they are now considered to be vital historical documents, providing performances that would otherwise have been lost, from the dawn of the recording era. James Hinton, writing in *High Fidelity* magazine in the early sixties, exactly captured the fascination with hearing such arcane recordings:

[The sense is one] of listening from backstage, through a door that keeps suddenly opening and closing, to bits and pieces of performances. The vantage point is at a little distance from the singers, and they seem to be heard through a certain amount of backstage clatter; sometimes they move out of line of hearing, and sometimes the noise obscures the voices. But mostly, they can be heard quite well enough for the listener to get a very definite sense of personalities and occasionally of the full impact of virtuosity that, in terms of the opera house today, is quite literally beyond the wildest imagination.[4]

If American copyright law was lagging behind the demands of new technology from the very outset of the twentieth century, it is understandable that the legislators had problems defining what was 'visible' and 'original' about the sounds coming from the likes of Afro-American musicians, with their improvisational bent and unique rhythmic skills. It was left to others to notate such 'rhythmic skills'. Following the example set by Francis Child's collection of English and Scottish ballads, American folk archivists began to uncover and transcribe previously undocumented folk and blues songs. Ironically, this made them the authors in the eyes of the law, even though the pioneering work of collectors like Carl Sandburg and Alan and John Lomax was largely philanthropic. Yet the question of when and how material passed into public domain was to remain an issue beyond the demise of vinyl.

The 1909 Act may have dispirited US manufacturers, but they were tenacious in their attempts to test the law in the courts of the land. Between 1925 and 1951, there were some thirty-one bills introduced and reintroduced into Congress attempting to extend copyright to sound recordings. However, there remained an irritating, but tolerable, degree of record piracy and counterfeiting, even if most infringements were too small to justify an expensive law suit. Though no court decision between 1909 and 1955 actually rendered 'the copyrightability of sound recordings', the industry did not prove entirely powerless. There remained two principal means of legal redress, 'common law copyright' and 'unfair competition':

'Common law copyright' in a sound recording asserts that, as an 'original intellectual creation,' recorded performances are protected under law against unauthorized use as long as they remain 'unpublished' . . . 'Unfair competition' recognizes property rights in authorized sound recordings as business assets, protecting the investor against misappropriation by others who may seek to make unfair use of the money, time, skill and effort expended by the manufacturer of the recording.[5]

It was the advent of further new technology, and the increase in radio broadcasting after the Second World War, that finally upped the ante, creating piracy's twin brother – the commercial bootlegger. Very little unauthorized, previously unreleased material had percolated into circulation in the early years of the phonograph. Most transgressions of a performer's legal and moral rights took the form of direct piracy. Access to unreleased recordings was very limited and the technology required to duplicate studio tapes or make one's own live recordings lay well outside the bounds of mass consumption. But the times were a-changin', and the late forties saw a widespread availability of reel-to-reel tape recorders, which were becoming increasingly compact and inexpensive. There were even portable battery-operated machines that afforded the opportunity for 'field' recordings.

The incidence of counterfeiting and commercial piracy had also dramatically increased in the first years of peace. The record pirates had begun to change the emphasis of their activities from what might be termed 'rarities' (i.e. long-deleted items) and classics to the pirating of contemporary hit singles. This resulted in a new resolve by the recording industry, reflected most evidently in the formation in 1951 of the Recording Industry Association of America.

The RIAA had a brief to stamp out all forms of piracy. Unfortunately, the commercial pirates were no longer a band of disorganized, small-time pre-war profiteers. The Mafia had begun to realize that there was a good mark-up in pirating hit singles. Even a newly galvanized record industry was not geared up to fight such a formidable lawbreaker:

'Eric Bristow' [a bootlegger]: The reason that counterfeit records were created in the first place is that the Mafia have traditionally controlled everything with a slot in it, since day one. Cigarette machines, food vending machines, casino gambling machines, one-arm bandits, everything with a slot, because they learned early on that there's no real way of knowing how much money you've taken on a pinball machine. It's a Laundromat. All their drug and prostitution and big crime money can be laundered through a few thousand pinball machines, because how can you tell whether it took $5 or $5,000? So the Mafia took over the slot machines, and they learned quickly that jukeboxes were a really popular thing in the fifties, made them a lot of money, 'cause they controlled all the slots. But they didn't like having to buy the records to put in them. So they made their own. Every time a new record came out, they knocked it off and put it in 20 or 30,000 jukeboxes across America and that was how it ended up becoming a big Mob-controlled thing.[6]

With the much-publicized formation of the RIAA, the industry needed a more digestible scapegoat for the evils of piracy. For a brief period in the early fifties, before it was diverted by the onset of rock & roll and the lurid details of 'payola', the record industry seized upon bootleg albums as a way of highlighting the lack of adequate copyright protection for 'recorded music'. Two cases in 1951–2 suggested that bootlegging could yet become a major issue. Though the rock bootleg was still some eighteen years away, other musical genres were not immune to the collector mentality. In 1951 the area where the greatest body of accessible, unreleased recordings existed was classical music. It was in this field that the first case of 'accidental' bootlegging received national attention and brought great embarrassment to America's largest record label.

Classic Editions had released a recording of Verdi's *A Masked Ball* purportedly made in Italy by Maria Caniglia, Carlo Tagliabue, and Cloe Elmo. In fact, it was a 1947 broadcast by the Metropolitan Opera Company, starring Daniza Ilitsch, Jan Peerce, Leonard Warren, and Margaret Harshaw. The *faux pas* was unveiled by Irving Kolodin in the *Saturday Review*, and Classic Editions were quick to insist that the release was a mistake and would be withdrawn. The whole affair was a great embarrassment to RCA, for it turned out that the discs had actually been manufactured by their own custom pressing division, and RCA had exclusive contracts with Jan Peerce and Leonard Warren.

Though Classic Editions claimed that their 'bootleg' was an honest error, there were more brazen labels waiting in the wings, prepared to carve out their own niche in the marketplace. None was more brazen than the Wagner-Nichols Home Recordist Guild. Wagner-Nichols had recorded at least twenty Saturday matinée performances during the 1949–50 season at the Metropolitan Opera House, each broadcast in their entirety by the American Broadcasting Corporation. Wagner-Nichols were not unduly concerned by legal niceties, openly advertising and retailing the records, clearly identified as 'off-air' recordings from the Metropolitan. When the Metropolitan Opera House, ABC and Columbia Records – who held the 'mechanical' rights to Met performances – brought suit against Wagner-Nichols, the 'Guild' fought for the right to release these 'unissued' recordings. The case brought national attention to 'a new form of piracy':

Charging unfair competition, the plaintiffs ... sought an injunction to prevent Wagner-Nichols from further recording, advertising, selling, or distributing such records. Wagner-Nichols maintained that they were not competing with the plaintiffs since they had not attempted to palm their records off either as Columbia Records or official Met recordings, and further held that everybody concerned had abandoned property rights in the performances when they were broadcast. The New York court granted the injunction and in doing so set an important precedent because this interpretation of unfair competition has been very useful to record companies in combating pirates ever since ... In a legal commentary, The New York Supplement, 2nd Series, said: 'The modern view as to the law of unfair competition does not rest solely on the ground of direct competitive injury, but on the broader principle that property rights of commercial value are to be and will be protected from any form of commercial immorality.'[7]

Unfair competition was to become a favourite means of counteracting infant bootleggers. But the judgement against Wagner-Nichols did little to dissuade determined collector/bootleggers, more concerned with the art of it all than bringing the record industry to its knees. The Wagner-Nichols case had also illustrated the ease with which radio broadcasts could be put out – maybe not with impunity but with expensive civil action (and minimal damages) the only legal recourse.

'Popular' music was also becoming susceptible to the bootleg virus. Collectors of the blues had for some time been pirating obscure pre-war 78s, issued in minuscule numbers on local labels and long impossible to find in their original form. Jazz buffs had also begun pirating certain long-deleted artifacts, though they tended to prize live performances over and above recordings achieved in a studio. As a music founded on improvisation, each jazz performance was intrinsically unique (if not necessarily inspired). Jazz was an obvious medium for someone smitten by the bootleg mentality.

Sure enough, Dante Bolletino formed his little Jolly Roger label in 1950 and began issuing pirate and bootleg jazz material. With 'bravado worthy of any buccaneer', he had his records manufactured by the RCA custom pressing department. Bolletino would later insist that his primary motivation had been anger at RCA and Columbia for failing to reissue early 78s of jazz masters like Louis Armstrong, Jelly Roll Morton and Bessie Smith. His chosen route seemed the only way to force their hand. Bolletino's label also did not keel over when Columbia made their initial legal threats. When Columbia, in tandem with Louis Armstrong, alleged unfair competition and invasion of property rights, Bolletino maintained that recorded performances could not be copyrighted. Though Bolletino wanted to fight the case, he soon realized the sheer weight of corporate clout that Columbia could mount against him:

Dante Bolletino: My lawyer insisted that we had a good case and could win, but I knew the record companies would feel they couldn't afford to lose and would throw in everything they had. I was only twenty-three at the time and didn't have the money for a long, expensive court case, so I settled. But afterwards the big companies began to reissue more jazz records, so maybe I accomplished something after all.[8]

Bolletino was thus the father of commercial jazz bootlegging, a form that has remained a perennial for nearly half a century.

Indeed a 1974 *Billboard* feature on bootlegging claimed that, 'jazz is the genre that seems to be bootlegged the most,' further noting that, 'accessibility to jazz product has [always] been relatively easy, [being] taken from tapes of rehearsals, live performances at theatres and hotels, radio broadcasts and record sessions.'

'Accessibility' has always been the key to putting out bootlegs. Unlike pirates, bootleggers are required to seek out arcane, long-lost recordings. Though the easiest, and best-quality, sources were usually radio broadcasts, jazz collectors went to considerable lengths to preserve many live recordings themselves. Perhaps the most famous instance of a jazz buff's archival bent was Dean Benedetti who, in the late forties, taped literally hundreds of Charlie 'Bird' Parker solos during a two-year spate of appearances in New York.

Collectors remained no less prevalent in classical circles. The bootlegging of operatic performances continued to generate the largest area of growth in the decade before rock bootlegs stole headlines and shook up executives. Opera bootleggers displayed a commendable ingenuity when it came to accessing 'classic' performances of their favourite operas. Those who were issuing performances from the thirties and forties were getting their master tapes from collectors. They in turn had managed to obtain dubs of most 'acetate air-checks' (a perishable shellac record cut by the radio networks at the time of a live broadcast) made by those networks broadcasting operatic performances. Only in the forties did the miniaturization of tape recorders make it increasingly common for concert- and opera-goers to tape performances they attended, to have either as a souvenir or as something to swap with other tape collectors.

It was a privateer 'opera lover', Steven E. Jones, who began the commercial bootlegging of operas in earnest. Jones had obtained a large number of 'acetate air-checks' of matinée broadcasts from the thirties and forties and began, in the late fifties, to issue them on his Golden Age of Opera label. It was the Metropolitan Opera House (again!) that provided the bulk of GAO's product, and yet again Met lawyers had to track the bootlegger down and extract a

promise that he would 'cease and desist' selling Met recordings. Jones gave up without much of a fight. The role of outlaw did not suit him. His lack of knowledge of performers and conductors, plus the poor mastering and cheap pressings he used for the Golden Age of Opera series, suggested that his interest in opera was not entirely philanthropic.

By the time Jones called it quits in the early sixties he had already been superseded by a second generation of privateers, 'younger men with greater technical knowledge who were more fastidious about the quality of the sound they would commit to records'.[9] These bootleggers maintained a considerably lower profile and accessed their source material far more covertly. One, who went by the name of Roland Ernest, seemed able at will to obtain high-quality recordings of any Carnegie Hall concert he so desired. He even managed to release some genuine stereo recordings in the early sixties, when stereo technology was new and assumed to be inaccessible to the bootleg fraternity.

Ernest's greatest coup was perhaps the most famous opera bootleg of them all: Caballé's American debut in Donizetti's *Lucrezia Borgia*. (Though it sold very well, Ernest's collector friends poured scorn on RCA claims that he had sold 30,000 copies.) Sadly, Ernest's devotion to producing high quality product, whatever the logistics and cost, proved his undoing. He apparently ended up driving a taxi in New York for a living, having lost his money issuing such obscure titles as Hindemith's *Cardillac* (of which he managed to sell less than a hundred copies). The quality of Ernest's source tapes, mastering and pressings were certainly ahead of their time.

His successors sought to match the one remaining bastion of legitimate record manufacturers – professional packaging. In 1966, a boxed-set of *La Traviata* with Bidu Sayao signalled the beginning of a packaging revolution much like the one augmented by Dario Soria in the early 1950s with Angel Records' de luxe editions featuring complete libretti and tastefully artistic covers.

The producer of *La Traviata* and another dozen releases of singers 'no longer before the public', insisted when interviewed by

Stereo Review that, 'all my albums are issued with the permission of the major artists involved, and all are autographed. I reach an agreement with the singers on the size of the edition, usually about two hundred, and they get as many free copies as they wish for their friends. I also send a free copy to the Library of Congress. The others are offered first to libraries and archives at a special institutional price not much more than actual cost, and I sell the remaining sets to collectors I know at $5 per disc or $12.50 for a three-disc set. I place a few with private dealers, but I prefer not to sell through record stores. My editions are really limited, and when they are sold out, I don't repress.'10

He was not the only mid-sixties classical bootlegger whose work met such exacting standards. Among the cognoscenti of classical collectors, there was clearly a demand for quality presentations. These collectors were tired of cheap pressings and poor artwork. As the man behind the BJR label observed, '[The bootleggers] don't compete with record companies. Callas recorded *Norma* and *Tosca* twice for Angel. Anybody who buys ours will already have both commercial versions ... [Ours is] a labour of love. We work slowly and produce few albums. Quality is what we strive for, and it's often hard to achieve with some of these old tapes. We do what we can to correct fluctuations of pitch and drops in volume, but we never doctor a sour note if the singer sang it that way. We want to document what really happened.'11

These opera bootleggers were clearly operating in a commercial twilight where demand was measured in hundreds. Producing obscure versions of lengthy operas in increasingly exotic boxed-sets was never going to be a mass-market exercise. After bringing out a complete version of Wagner's *Ring* cycle by Furtwängler, one opera bootlegger swore, 'I would never attempt anything so arduous as *The Ring* again. The tapes were copies of acetate discs, and the endless hours of removing ticks and pops have aged me ten years. EMI and DGG had dickered over this *Ring* for years and finally pronounced it a dead issue, but I knew Furtwängler's widow wanted the performances on records, so I decided to issue them.'12

Such dedication, in the face of minimal sales, guaranteed that a slimmed-down sixties record industry would turn a blind eye to the activities of these classical bootleggers. After all, this was a time when a considerable expansion in the pop-music field was shifting the demographics of the industry irrevocably. The legitimate companies could barely maintain their profit margins on classical product that concentrated on the more popular end of the spectrum. It was rock music that made the industry profitable in the mid-to-late sixties, and bootleggers seemed oblivious to such decadent sounds.

The other expanding market for bootleg records was another niche almost entirely overlooked by legitimate producers – nostalgia. In the nostalgia game, sourcing tapes was not difficult. There was a vast archive of radio performances by movie stars and crooners from the thirties and forties, singing their hit songs, telling favourite routines or re-enacting famous roles. Also, because of the contractual and logistical problems involved in issuing genuine soundtracks to famous Hollywood musicals, most so-called 'soundtrack' albums were re-recordings of the same material under studio conditions (often with an in-house orchestra). The results were usually unsatisfactory. Many collectors wanted the original film soundtracks on record.

Though the legal position *vis-à-vis* 'air-check acetates' was not clear-cut, movie soundtracks clearly breached the copyright of the film company in question. Yet theirs was a different sector of America's gargantuan entertainment industry, and the film studios were unconcerned by the practice (save for the rare instances when bootleggers dug up unreleased soundtrack material). One exception was *Annie Get Your Gun*, which was issued in the early seventies by a bootlegger not unconnected with the birth of rock bootlegs. He had secured a pre-production tape of MGM's *Annie Get Your Gun* soundtrack, recorded with the original actress assigned to play the lead role – Judy Garland. Betty Hutton was only given the starring role after Garland broke down as filming was about to commence. The original Garland version of the soundtrack had long been thought lost, but three weeks after MGM apparently destroyed their master reels, a bootleg edition of Garland's version was in collectors' stores.

Many labels preferred to specialize in transcriptions of radio shows. Memorabilia, a California-based operation, developed a series called When Radio Was King, and were perhaps the best known of the labels catering to the nostalgia market. However, the sound quality of their releases was often quite poor. Many were derived from old reel-to-reel tapes which were shedding their oxide, resulting in sound 'drop-outs'. These tapes, in turn, often derived from acetate recordings made at the time of the broadcast (these acetates had a very limited life, perhaps a dozen plays before they would start to audibly deteriorate). Clearly the commercial release of these tapes in a pre-digital age (when 'cleaning up' tapes was not the computer-generated industry it is now) was not even an issue.

Aside from quasi-legitimate labels specializing in nostalgia, usually operating from anonymous PO boxes, the sixties also saw a whole series of releases under the guise of 'fan club only'. Assorted Frank Sinatra fan clubs had been pressing very limited editions of Sinatra performances from the late fifties on (though it was considered inadvisable to bootleg Sinatra commercially). The presumed legal 'right' to issue this material on a non-profit basis 'to subscribers only' had never been tested in the courts, and these recordings were invariably live performances. As late as February 1970

a number of such clubs [were still] devoted to preserving the work of a particular artist or to sharing collections of a particular kind of music . . . It is widely believed among members of these clubs that if the edition is one hundred copies or less and the records are sold or distributed only among members, without profit, the clubs are free to ignore copyright and reproduce whatever they like for their private use – old 78s or excerpts from radio programmes. Club records are usually stamped 'Private Recording Not For Sale', or 'Limited Edition Not For Sale'. But club records, which usually feature very rare and sought after performances, have a way of turning up in some record stores, where they are sold to the public for profit. And it often appears that the 'limit' to the edition is whatever the traffic will bear.[13]

The record shops in New York's Greenwich Village in the late sixties were stuffed with opera bootlegs, jazz bootlegs, radio transcripts, blues anthologies with dubious antecedents, and even 'original' soundtracks to movies that had no commercial soundtrack. Yet bootlegging remained an underground phenomenon, little discussed in the media and tacitly ignored by the record companies. The economics of bootleg production operated as the most obvious constraint on their mass-marketability:

If his packaging is simple, [a bootlegger] may be able to produce a small edition of a two-disc opera for as little as $1,000 to $1,500, and if he sells 100 or 150 copies at $10 each, he breaks even. The break-even point for a commercial company is 5,000 to 6,000 copies. Thus, a pirate or privateer can afford to issue connoisseur repertoire that would be financially disastrous for a major company.[14]

Of course, if a bootlegger could sell 5,000 or 6,000 copies of an album without incurring the costs of libretti and sleeve-notes (as classical collectors now demanded), and without the payment of royalties, then the economics became completely different. But the only musical genre where official records sold in hundreds of thousands was rock music. And there were no rock bootlegs.

3 The First Great White Wonders

Dub [a bootlegger]: [*Great White Wonder*] was just this phenomenon. All of a sudden we just started having fistfuls of money. We didn't realize what we had gotten into.[1]

It seems remarkable, in the light of bootleg activity in jazz, blues and opera – and the proven commercial demand for the icons of sixties rock – that it took until 1969 for rock bootlegs to become a reality. The existence of a number of admittedly lo-fi audience tapes recorded before the first rock bootleg, *Great White Wonder*, clearly suggests that the idea of taping a rock show was not lost on everyone in the sixties. Likewise, the rapid emergence of a bootleg collecting circuit built around the success of *Great White Wonder* suggests a considerable latent demand. Yet it was the strangest confluence of supply and demand that resulted in the *Great White Wonder* phenomenon, for phenomenon it certainly was, and it was all bound up with the increasing mythology that circled around the skull of one Mr Dylan.

The central role of Dylan in rock bootlegging highlights a marked difference between 'demand for bootlegs' and commercial sales. In Dylan's case, people seemed to take the vagaries of his chameleon twists quite personally. In 1968 – despite the dramatic resurrection Dylan achieved with his first post-accident album, *John Wesley Harding* – people began to hanker for something closer to the 'old' Dylan (meaning the *Highway 61 Revisited/ Blonde on Blonde* Dylan). At the same time it became apparent that *John Wesley Harding* was not the only 'new' material he had recorded in the eighteen months since he tumbled from his motorcycle in July 1966.

Suddenly Manfred Mann, Peter, Paul and Mary, Julie Driscoll and the Trinity and other assorted Dylan-sanitizers were in the charts with the new Dylan songs that seemed much more like the 'old'

Dylan, the one that preferred to burn at the altar rather than offer up ribald little morality tales. When The Band and The Byrds divided up half a dozen more Dylan cuts on 'countryfied' albums, it became apparent that something had gone down before *John Wesley Harding* – a bridge between *Blonde on Blonde* and Country Bob.

The late sixties were perhaps the great era of American popular radio. The great AM/FM divide had yet to create rigid programming, and radio stations – particularly hip 'coast' stations – were keen to be seen to be on the cusp of a happening scene.

Michael O [a bootlegger]: In the sixties they would get advance copies of artists' songs, and they would start airing them weeks or even months before they were released. In fact, that got to be part of listening to the radio, at least in LA, in the sixties – hearing all the hits before they came out.[2]

The material that had led to such an onslaught of unreleased Dylan came from a fourteen-song acetate of publishers' demos, recorded by Dylan and the as-yet-unchristened Band in the basement of The Band's home in Woodstock in the summer of 1967, several months before *John Wesley Harding*. Inevitably the wide dissemination of this acetate – at least within the music industry – created a furore. To further rub salt in frustrated Dylan fans' wounds, after two years starved of new Dylan, in June 1968 *Rolling Stone* ran a cover story on these 'basement tapes'. The title of the article? 'The Missing Bob Dylan Album'. When it became apparent that Dylan's versions were not about to be released, something had to give.

Michael O: We just assumed it was his next album and got very excited 'cos they played 'This Wheel's On Fire' relentlessly on KPPC-FM, the LA underground FM station. It sounds perfect for coming after *Blonde on Blonde* ... I was fifteen at the time. I called the radio station constantly saying, 'Where'd you get the tape? Where'd you get the tape? I want the tape ...' I finally got a sympathetic ear ... It was a record store called Records and Supertape, on Peco, that had gotten a tape, and was selling them for $5 a reel, at $7\frac{1}{2}$ ips . . . So I got the tape, and I thought, 'This is great. It'd be great to do a record of this. You can do that, can't you?' I would go to record stores – it was the psychedelic era and people did a lot of goofy things to break the rules – and I went around and was told, 'No, that's copyrighted, there's no way, forget about it.' So I forgot about it.[3]

Though Michael O was dissuaded from releasing the basement tapes, its very inaccessibility merely stoked up demand. Dylan's motives in choosing to disseminate these remarkable recordings in such a scattershot way has often been questioned. Perhaps he genuinely never anticipated the interest there might be in 'new' Dylan (particularly if it sounded like 'old' Dylan). After being marketed by CBS under the immortal catch-phrase 'Nobody sings Dylan like Dylan', he could hardly complain when legions of Dylan fanatics wanted to hear his version of 'This Wheel's On Fire', not some drippy English hippy's.

Then there was suddenly a new official Dylan album, *Nashville Skyline*, and attention temporarily shifted to what 'the master' had to say in 1969, as Vietnam escalated to berserk proportions and the country turned its back on the radical changes this decade had wrought. 'Oh me, oh my, love that country pie,' is what Dylan appeared to wish to say. Oh dear. *Nashville Skyline* seemed like the ultimate slap in the face to many of his fans. The radio stations reverted to playing Dylan's old songs within days of the release of *Nashville Skyline*. Meanwhile the likes of Greil Marcus kept referring to a mountain of unreleased Dylan tapes in *Rolling Stone*. A meeting of minds (and wallets) like the one between rock's original bootleggers, 'Dub' and Ken, in Los Angeles seemed inevitable.

Dub: Ken and I worked for a major record distributor here in LA. We were returning some tapes that hadn't sold – I think they were 4-track Donovan tapes – and we had both been acquiring some unreleased tapes of Bob Dylan. We were both real hardcore Dylan fans, and we started talking. We were saying, 'Wouldn't it be fun to make a record of this stuff and to put it out' . . . 'cos Dylan had just done *Nashville Skyline*, which was a disaster commercially . . . We had piles of 'em at the distributor, nobody wanted it. So Ken says, 'I know someone who might be willing to put up the money for this.' So we talked to this man, who I'll call the Greek, and he agreed to put up the initial capital to get the records pressed. I'm not sure how many we pressed originally, it was either 1,000 or 2,000, but the originals are just a white cover and a white label, there's nothing on them. And the album did not have a title at that time. I had this other friend, Patrick . . . I approached him because Ken and I were known in the business and couldn't go in the stores and sell these [albums] ourselves . . . At the time he was a deserter from the army . . . and he needed money and I said, 'We're doing this bootleg Dylan thing, why don't you take 'em around? I'll go round with you and show you where the stores are, you take 'em in and see if you can sell them . . .' I think originally we sold them for eight to twelve dollars each . . . we thought we could sell a few and make a little money. We had no idea what was going to happen.[4]

The anonymous album did not stay nameless for long. Unwittingly, Ken and Dub had founded an industry, and it required a name.

Dub: One of the [first] customers we had was the *LA Free Press*, which was the LA counterpart to the *Village Voice* in New York . . . They had bookstores in LA. One of 'em was on Fairfax, and we went to their office and we talked to this woman who was from Brooklyn in New York, this Jewish woman . . . and explained that we had this underground Dylan album and [asked], 'Would you like to carry it in your store?' And she just loved the idea, she goes 'This is great. We'll put ads in our newspaper saying that we have this unreleased Bob Dylan album . . .' We were real excited about this, 'cos this was the first time that someone could actually advertise it and stir up some shit . . . It was the mentality of the time, the Vietnam war. There was such an anti-establishment feeling in the air . . . We were in there talking to her and she says, 'You know, we have to call this album something . . . Why don't we call it . . . how about *Great White Wonder*?' And we looked at her and we said, 'That's fine . . . we'll call it *Great White Wonder*.' So we went out and had a rubber stamp made that said 'GWW' and started stamping the fronts of the covers. I don't think that she meant that Dylan was the great white wonder or anything, but we thought, 'That sounds a little weird. let's do it!'[5]

Considering it is such a legendary artifact, *Great White Wonder* is something of a mess. Dub and Ken had established a dubious format – cut'n'paste bootlegs – choosing to compile the double-album from multiple sources (rather than just putting out the basement tapes, clearly at the heart of the demand). They thus cursed other bootleggers with the task of filling in gaps around them. Sides one and three of *Great White Wonder* were entirely given over to songs from an informal ninety-minute session Dylan recorded in the apartment of an old girlfriend, the 'real' 'Girl from the North Country', in Minneapolis in December 1961, while side two was a cut-up of miscellaneous studio outtakes. However, it was the seven basement-tape cuts that filled up the end of side two and all of side four which caused the greatest fuss.

The west coast radio stations were first to pick up on *Great White Wonder*. Five radio stations – KCBS in Santa Barbara, KNAC in Long Beach, KRLA in Pasadena and KMET-FM and KPPC-FM in Los Angeles – immediately began playing the album. KRLA was the first. Unconcerned with legal niceties, these LA radio stations were quite willing to fuel demand for both *Great White Wonder* and the spate of bootlegs that soon followed its metal-stamped heels.

Dub: The first time *Great White Wonder* was played on the radio was on a station in Pasadena, a small station ... I knew one of the DJs there and Patrick and I went over there and he played it on the air. That was probably July '69 ... I remember when *Stealin'* came out I was in Hollywood right near Capitol Records and I turned the radio on and it was a track from *Stealin'* and the guy said, 'That's from a new Dylan album called *Stealin'* and that's what it was, folks, stolen!'[6]

The press soon picked up on this 'unauthorized' Dylan artifact. In September *Rolling Stone*, *The Wall Street Journal* and the *LA Herald Examiner* all ran stories on the first rock bootleg. In November 1969, *Rolling Stone* published a six-page article by

Greil Marcus, entirely devoted to unreleased Dylan recordings. This was not about to temper demand for more Dylan bootleg albums. It seemed that the only real option available to Columbia was to release the material itself. Indeed *Entertainment World* noted as much: 'The success of *The Great White Wonder* [could] inspire Columbia and other manufacturers to look to their vaults so that significant material such as this will be more readily and legally available to the consumer.'[7]

Though *Entertainment World* seemed to consider *Great White Wonder* to be 'significant material', CBS proved remarkably unwilling to respond to the obvious demand (though Dylan's next album, *Self Portrait*, was interpreted by many, Greil Marcus included, to be his idea of an official bootleg). British journalist Richard Williams went as far as to ask the Managing Director of CBS-UK why they would not release Dylan's unreleased recordings:

His reply was . . . 'One always ought to respect the artist's wishes, at least until he's dead.' . . . When he's dead, it's not unreasonable to suppose that CBS will waste no time in putting out a whole series of Dylan Memorial Albums, chronicling every last cough and splutter. Well, I don't want to wait that long to know about Bob Dylan. And you can't know about him unless you've heard most of the hundred-odd unreleased demos, bad takes, unreleased songs, and concert and club recordings which have so far been bootlegged.[8]

Whatever uncommon scruples Columbia displayed by 'respect-[ing] the artist's wishes', they were largely lost on rock fans, delighted by the unauthorized nature of *Great White Wonder*. The political climate in the summer of 1969 was also bound to make Dub and Ken counter-culture heroes, particularly when they made statements (to *Rolling Stone*) like, 'We're just liberating the records and bringing them to all the people, not just the chosen few.'

Great White Wonder, though, was already beyond Dub and Ken's command. What a couple of outlaws could do, others could always redo. The venture was too lucrative, and *Great White*

Wonder too easy to copy, for the field to remain unsullied by counterfeit bootlegs for long.

Two Los Angeles record store owners, Norton Beckman and Ben Goldman, had witnessed first-hand the seemingly insatiable demand for *Great White Wonder*. When they decided to rebootleg the album, though, they discovered that the wheels of the law had begun to grind. Quickly slapped with an injunction by Columbia and Dylan, they were required to deliver up 'all disks and tapes embodying or including any performance of any part of the following copyrighted musical compositions: "Living the Blues", "Tears of Rage", "This Wheel's On Fire", "Mighty Quinn (Quinn the Eskimo)", "I Shall be Released", "Open the Door, Homer", "Nothing was Delivered", and "Too Much of Nothing", [all] recorded without the consent or authorization of Dylan, including but not limited to any and all copies of the record album referred to as *The Great White Wonder*.'⁹

These piratical bootleggers proceeded to give Dub's name to Columbia's lawyers – believing that it was his girlfriend who had put Columbia's lawyers on their trail. It seemed that the shit was about to hit this particular fan. Columbia were convinced that the law was on their side. Their deposition to the court in the Beckman–Goldman case stated that *Great White Wonder* was 'a simple case of piracy of Dylan's private musical performances for defendants' profit, and a brazen disregard of the Copyright Act provisions respecting recording licences, copyright royalties and elementary fair play'.¹⁰

But Columbia were about to discover that stemming the tide was no easy matter. Though they had the name of one of the original bootleggers, they had no address, and thus no means of serving a writ. When Dub and Ken let it be known that they had hightailed it to Canada to 'open a gas station', Columbia took the grapevine at its word. Yet Columbia needed to be seen to be doing something. The only question was what.

Though their lawyers had been very specific about the breach of 'copyrighted musical compositions' from the basement tapes on *Great White Wonder*, Columbia's lawyers failed to act on the most flagrant breach of copyright on *Great White Wonder*, the studio recordings that kick off side two. These derived from Columbia sessions, and one song – 'If You Gotta Go, Go Now' – had been released as a single in Europe. They had also seemingly overlooked the more numerous recordings from December 1961 found on the *GWW* set. These would only have served to highlight a certain weakness in American copyright law. The December 1961 songs had two major flaws as regards any legal claim by Columbia and/ or Dylan:

(i) Columbia were not at all sure that this 'Hotel Tape' was made after Dylan formally signed to CBS. Even if it was recorded after the CBS deal (as indeed it was), they could have trouble proving that the contract was valid in court. Dylan had been a minor when he had signed it.
(ii) The songs were largely traditional or 'public domain', and Dylan had never copyrighted his arrangements of these songs.

Any claim on Columbia's behalf relating to the basement-tape material was equally tarnished. The songs had not been recorded in a Columbia studio, Dylan was 'between contracts' when the recordings were made, and the members of The Band accompanying Dylan had yet to sign a record deal. Because Dylan was not in anyway identified on the cover of *Great White Wonder*, even the question of appropriating the artist's name and likeness did not arise. This could have been a legal issue, since when a record company signs a contract with a performer, it not only acquires all rights relating to the singer's musical services but also the exclusive right to use his or her name and likeness to promote the sale of records.

Dub and Ken were not about to give up creating further artifacts in this new, exciting medium. By the time they restarted operations – confident that Columbia's legal threats had come to naught – they had adopted a disclaimer used by some Chicago-based cassette-pirates to take advantage of America's lax copyright laws. For their first few post-*GWW* efforts, Dub and Ken provided yellow stickers which proudly proclaimed:

No relationship of any kind exists between [this manufacturer] and the original recording company, nor between this recording and the original recording artist. This tape is not produced under a licence of any kind from the original recording company nor the recording artist(s) and neither the original recording company nor artist(s) receives a fee or royalty of any kind from [this recording]. Permission to produce this album has not been sought nor obtained from any party whatsoever.[11]

Dub: They could sue us for name and likeness or not paying royalties or something like that, but there was no actual law against what we did.[12]

The year before *Great White Wonder*, California state had attempted to pass a new law against phonograph-record piracy (based on one already passed in New York), making 'piracy' into a misdemeanour. But a band of Californian tape duplicators decided to take the matter to the Federal Court, challenging the constitutionality of California's new law. While the matter was in the hands of three Federal judges, enforcement of the law had to be suspended, pending a decision. As such, the Golden State's climate in the summer of 1969 clearly favoured the bootleggers.

But then as long as the identity of the bootleggers remained unknown, any suits could only be directed against those at the retail end of the chain and, according to a San Francisco attorney whom *Rolling Stone* consulted on the legalities of the bootleg trade,

The worst that can happen is that the bootleggers, and record stores, will be enjoined by the courts from continuing their trade. If they refuse to cease and desist, they can be held for contempt of court. The plaintiff can also sue, as Columbia has done, for the amount of money they think they lost. This figure . . . is usually just picked out of the air, since the companies can't really set a precise figure. And to sue each record store for their sales would only amount to a couple hundred dollars per store . . . To prevent any store from bootlegging at all, each store has to be enjoined separately.[13]

In America in 1969, the only copyright-holder who had any rights on a Federal level was the songwriter. Only composers could bring action for the misappropriation of 'unreleased' recordings on the grounds of 'right of first publication' and 'exclusive mechanical recording right'. The performer and the producer-manufacturer (that is any record company holding an exclusive contract with said performer) could not bring any suit for Federal copyright violation. So even if Columbia had managed to catch up with Dub and his partner, they would have had little chance of stopping them releasing Dylan's interpretations of traditional songs (i.e. most of his early recordings).

In fact, copyright protection for unreleased recordings under the Universal Copyright Convention – the only international convention that the US subscribed to – also verged on the non-existent:

> While under the Berne Convention no formalities such as deposit, notice, registration, or fee are required to obtain copyright protection, for UCC, the symbol © and the name of the copyright proprietor and the year of first publication must be shown in all copies in such a manner and location as to provide reasonable notice of a claim of copyright.[14]

At this point the official companies were still hoping that Dylan's 'bootlegability' was an isolated problem – certainly a 'rock' bootleg of anyone outside 'The Big Three' (Dylan, The Beatles, The Rolling Stones) did not seem a commercial proposition. Though Dylan could never claim to be a comparable seller to The Beatles or Stones – as a singles artist he was a non-starter, and neither of his post-accident albums, *John Wesley Harding* and *Nashville Skyline*, had made number one – the level of fanaticism he inspired was without parallel. There was also a substantial number of unreleased Dylan songs circulating among a small but growing cabal of tape-collectors. *Great White Wonder* was not destined to be the one and only Dylan bootleg:

> Henry Brieff, executive director of the RIAA, estimate[d] the pirates could have cleared as much as $6 an album. If that's true, they have cleared $30,000 to $43,800. That could be [more than] enough incentive to encourage competition in the Dylan-pirating field, and perhaps it already has.

There are reports that a pirated Dylan album, entitled *Troubled Troubador*, is now on sale in Chicago.[15]

In fact, *Troubled Troubador* was not the second Dylan bootleg. The second Dylan title, and surely the rarest of all Dylan bootleg albums, came in a blank white sleeve with a pen drawing of a flower on each copy, drawn by the bootlegger's girlfriend. For this reason it became known as *Flower*. Having bought *Great White Wonder* when it first appeared, Michael O had been distinctly unimpressed by the sound quality of Dub's basement-tape material:

Michael O: [My original tape] was good. I immediately said 'This is ridiculous. My basement tapes sound so much better, I'm gonna do it,' so I went to a record store called The Auditory Odyssey in the Valley, and I said [to the owner], 'Give me some money and we'll make a couple of hundred of these . . .' So he gave me some money. I didn't know any better about where to get them mastered, so I took 'em to Capitol Records 'cos there was an engineer who worked in a little valley studio by me who also worked at Capitol, and I said 'Will you make a record of this for me?' and he said 'Sure.' I guess they just don't notice what you're doing at Capitol. He came back with a master. Because *Great White Wonder* had used some of the basement-tape songs and I had collected others off the radio I made a decision . . . I let the first seven songs [from the basement tapes] run on my side one and then I made side two some different things. I didn't know where to get it pressed so I took it to Monarch Records Pressing, who press CBS . . . and a week later I picked 'em up, my two hundred records, I was jazzed and I started taking 'em to record stores . . . Somebody bought ten, and somebody bought twenty, and then Aron Records bought a hundred, and I thought 'Wow!' I was wholesaling for $2.75 or $3.25, so all of a sudden I have $500 . . . I thought 'This is great. I'm gonna keep doing this.'[16]

Though Michael O had only pressed 200 copies of *Flower*, the young bootlegger's decision to have them made at Columbia's pressing plant might qualify as indiscreet.

Michael O: I got home and my mother was staring at me because she'd had a call from Columbia Records, who wanted to talk about her son ... and I'm sixteen, I'm scared to death ... She said, 'You have to go and see the man at Monarch because you're in big trouble ...' So I went with my uncle and we got in there and the guy who ran Monarch was this old guy, like a cigar-chomping guy – terrifying to me – and he said, 'What's on these records?' and I said, 'Well, music and singing ...' and he said, 'Who's the artist?' and I went, 'Well ...' 'Is it Bob Dylan?' and I said, 'Yeah, I guess so' ... He told me, 'Oh, you have to give me the stampers and buy back the records or you're gonna be in tremendous trouble ...' and I believed him. So I went back to Aron Records and bought like seventy-five back, and took them back to him. He told me I had narrowly avoided going to jail, and I wasn't sure if he had a point ... [but] somehow it just faded away.[1/]

If Columbia thought that they had dented the enthusiasm of our young Californian tyke then they were mistaken. Before the year was out he was to produce one of the most famous rock bootlegs. Meanwhile another young Dylan nut in Burbank, a true obsessive, with pictures of Dylan plastered all around his dark bedroom, had finally put out a basement-tapes-only release. His ten-track *Troubled Troubador* was again housed in a blank sleeve (the TT matrix number was the only real clue as to its 'working' title). Retailers were beginning to label albums themselves to distinguish them, and the title *Troubled Troubador* stuck. *Troubled Troubador* was the best-quality rock bootleg to date, but again the bootlegger omitted four basement cuts already featured on *Great White Wonder*.*

Despite the omissions, *Troubled Troubador* still partially duplicated *Great White Wonder*. This seemed to have no effect upon consumer demand. Indeed one shrewd retailer began packaging *Great White Wonder* and *Troubled Troubador* together, dubbing them *Bob Dylan Approximately* and making people buy *Great White Wonder* all over again for the extra material. Emanuel

---

* It would take until 1971 for the Europeans to issue the first 'complete', fourteen-song basement-tape bootleg, *Waters of Oblivion*.

Aron, of Aron Records, one of the central retail outlets for early bootlegs, was quick to recognize a lack of discrimination by his customers:

The hell of it is, some of them are juggling tapes; they're taking the same tapes and mixing them up, including some songs on one album, some of the same but some different on others, and selling them as different LPs. They are different, of course, but only slightly. The odd thing is, it doesn't seem to matter. They all sell.[18]

The bootleg phenomenon was already spreading beyond California's sunny climes, at least at a retail level. Chicago and New York were now major outlets. Though the East Coast was surprisingly slow to enter the manufacturing fray, the early Dylan bootlegs were all freely available in Greenwich Village. The first genuine East Coast Dylan bootleg was a fairly lo-fi production entitled *A Thousand Miles Behind*. Once again, the only artist identification was the *GWW* moniker on a hand-stamped cover. A nice compilation of already bootlegged Dylan cuts called *The Best of Bob's Bootlegs* was also almost certainly pressed on the East Coast.

Canadian retailers had also got in on the act early, ineffectual fines being the sole legal restraint on Canadian bootleggers. However, Canadian pressing plants were (and are) few and far between and tended to be closely regulated by the record companies. The proliferation of titles and – in the cases of *Great White Wonder* and Dub and Ken's second Dylan title, *Stealin'* – copies of the original bootlegs, was creating its very own microcosm of free-market forces. As *Rolling Stone* observed:

Everybody's getting into the act. People are going out and buying an 'underground' album, then pressing a few thousand copies for themselves. All five albums on the market today are being distributed by at least three different producers, and competition is driving the price down.[19]

Though the quality of *Great White Wonder* in its original form had been quite good, the patently inferior rebootlegged versions and poor-quality releases like *A Thousand Miles Behind* and the first bootleg version of Dylan's August appearance at the Isle of

Wight were giving bootlegs a bad name. Dub and Ken, though, were still leading the way with two quality Dylan titles. *Stealin'* and *GWW Sings The John Birch Society Blues* illustrated just how much important Dylan material remained unreleased. Both represented a significant advance in sound quality on *Great White Wonder* and came with two-colour printed labels and full track information.

Stealin', in particular, with its concentration on studio outtakes from 1964–5, was an exemplary release, showing the medium's true potential. Meanwhile, *John Birch Society Blues* concentrated on Dylan's acoustic Columbia sessions. With *Stealin'* and *John Birch*, Dub and Ken were also rubbing Columbia's face in it. This time there was no question who wrote most of the songs – Mr R. Zimmerman – and who paid for the sessions they derived from – Columbia. The fact that both albums were disarmingly close to official quality made these releases particularly galling. If *Stealin'* was quickly rebootlegged, the indiscriminate frenzy that had greeted *Great White Wonder* was already starting to abate.

In the winter of 1969–70 Columbia's vaults must have seemed positively porous (though the 'raid' on Columbia's Dylan tapes had actually occurred some time before the advent of bootleg vinyl). Dylan bootleggers had been able to concentrate on unreleased songs, not alternative versions of compositions already commercially released.

It seemed obvious that similar-quality studio material by The Beatles would have at least as great a sales potential as the better Dylan boots. However, EMI and The Beatles had been far more astute about who might have access to their recordings, and the band far less prolific in the song department.

There was one Beatles 'item' in particular that the world was eagerly awaiting. Throughout 1969 there had been many column-inches devoted to the much-delayed album from the so-called 'Get Back' project. Predating the recently released *Abbey Road* in both conception and execution, an album from January 1969 sessions had originally been planned as the follow-up to *The White Album*. The original concept was a record that replicated the easy informality of The Beatles' debut LP, *Please Please Me*. It was to have been called 'Get Back and 12 Other Songs'. The cover was to have been a contemporary take on their famous pose from 1962 when four cherubic faces first looked over the balcony of EMI's Manchester Square HQ. *Get Back* was intended to abandon the indulgent conceits evident on *Sgt Pepper* and the Beatle-backed-by-three-friends sound on *The White Album*. This time they would rehearse the songs at Twickenham film studios and 'cut' them live at Abbey Road studios. Lennon was to later claim that he always wanted this original version released:

John Lennon: I thought it [would have been] good to let it out and show people what had happened to us ... The bootleg version is what it was like.[20]

In fact the Twickenham sessions were conceived in a similar way to Dylan and The Band's basement-tape sessions, being an attempt to get back to writing and recording songs informally and spontaneously, playing some old favourites and generally acting like a band.* However, George Martin's attempts at putting together a properly sequenced record seemed bedevilled. After several unsatisfactory attempts Phil Spector was brought in to give the project fresh impetus. Spector, though, did not share Lennon's notion of documenting The Beatles' fragmentation on record and he attempted to 'clean up' the tapes, adding a syrupy 'Across the Universe' to an album that was originally a cry of self-assertion by a band rapidly derailing before unknowing eyes. He also deleted the smattering of half-formed rock & roll covers that had best typified the spirit the Fab Four had been trying to get back to.

Spector's patchwork repairs took some considerable time. Since Martin had produced several test pressings in his quest for an album which met with all four Beatles' approval, it was inevitable that tapes of these would eventually pass into the public domain. By the autumn of 1969, fans had come to believe that *Get Back and 12 Other Songs* might never happen.

---

* The Beatles actually ran through a couple of the basement-tape songs at the Twickenham sessions.

Once again, the Californian FM radio stations were to the fore in breaking the Martin tapes, which they began to promote as the next Beatles album. Within weeks the first bootleg version of *Get Back* was available in Berkeley, pressed (in LA, as there were no plants in San Francisco) by an unknown small-time entrepreneur. The demand for this projected album was bound to be vast, and Michael O, who had learnt a few important lessons from his experiences with his first Dylan bootleg, set about rebooting the San Franciscan *Kum Back*:

Michael O: All of a sudden everybody was playing *Let It Be* [*sic*] . . . In the meantime my record-store owner friend, who was older than me, said, 'I think we could do this a lot better. I think we could figure out a smart way to do it . . . go figure it out.' We found a place called Rainbow Records. My friend came back and said, 'I think Rainbow is the place where *Great White Wonder* is getting done.' We got the impression that things would be safer there . . . And all of a sudden the first bootleg copy appeared in San Francisco, *Kum Back*. I immediately flew up to Berkeley to buy a copy, within two days, and it was all in the wrong order – for some reason I was already aware of what the order should have been. So we slapped it together [in the correct order] real quick and the record-store owner [gave us] a bunch more money and we pressed 3,000 . . . we had 'em all sold in days. We pressed up another 2,000 and I think we finally pressed 1,000 more before it got copied. We got sophisticated fast, we knew that it would get copied and we would be out of business . . . We still couldn't print covers, but we wanted to be the first to have a picture on the cover. I devised doing the insert . . . We didn't know how to get shrinkwrapping, except to get 'em sealed . . . and we thought that would look better any way. We put it out on Lemon Records . . . In three weeks the copies appeared and they were cheap – we priced ours high, we were smart – and we were pretty much out of business. So we split up the money. This is '69, I was seventeen and I got half. I got $4,000 for three weeks' work.[21]

The Lemon Records version of *Get Back* became the first of many bootlegs to have wildly outlandish sales figures attributed to them by the media. A feature in *Entertainment World* in March 1970 claimed six-figure sales for Michael's humble effort:

The most widely distributed [version of *Get Back*], with a reported 100,000 copies in the Los Angeles and New York markets, was produced by Lemon Records. Its producers' sense of humour and bravado far surpasses that of any other underground packagers. Pasted on the traditionally blank jacket is a black and white photo of The Beatles filming and recording on a rooftop. The picture is accompanied by a hand-drawn outline of a lemon and the caption: 'We wish to thank all the people connected, both directly and indirectly, with this project and its fulfilment. And a warm thank you to the Bailey Brothers for their assistance.' The note is signed 'John'.[22]

Soon enough fans realized that this *Get Back* was not the album scheduled for April release by Capitol. Now that Spector had finally completed his work, the 'sanitized' nature of *Let It Be* – as it was now titled – ensured a long-term market for the original *Get Back*. Indeed it would be one of the first bootlegs to appear on CD.

Apple had managed to nip an earlier Beatles-related bootleg in the bud by doing what they did not do with *Let It Be*. *Live Peace in Toronto*, probably the first non-Dylan rock bootleg, quickly disappeared from the stores when Apple Records released the official version before Christmas 1969, undercutting the bootleg and producing a considerably more hi-fi experience. (Ironically, the original bootleg was a far more accurate document of the actual event, as Yoko Ono's vocals on the 'rock & roll side' were drastically mixed down.) Apple had unwittingly come up with the most successful tactic for killing bootlegs at birth – releasing the item officially. Other record companies were slow to follow their example. Indeed when London Records attempted to compete with the first Rolling Stones bootleg by releasing a 'superior' product, fans and critics alike concluded that theirs came a poor second.

Despite the high media profile given to rock bootlegs, less conspicuous pirates of popular music were largely unaffected by the fall out from *Great White Wonder* and its progeny. On the East Coast bootleggers were sticking to 'low exposure' product:

Piracy of classical records has become almost an above-ground industry. Piracy in the classical field is so accepted that a *New York Times* reviewer once chided a big recording company in print for altering what was supposed to be a recording of a concert performance. A pirated recording of the concert was more authentic, he wrote. Montserrat Caballé, the Spanish soprano, is quoted in the current issue of *Stereo Review* as saying: 'Many people come back to speak to me after a performance, and I have noticed that more and more of them carry briefcases or small suitcases, and I sometimes get the impression that everyone in the audience is recording the performance.' It's easy to buy a pirated classical record. Whereas a reporter had to visit several record stores to find one that had the new Dylan record.[23]

In their first flush, rock bootlegs had confined themselves to unreleased studio material. However, clearly there was a finite amount of studio material that could be accessed, particularly when it came to bands like The Beatles and The Stones. It was equally rare for such bands to do soundboards of their own shows, and rarer still for such tapes to pass into collectors' hands. Dylan had recently played his one-and-only paid appearance since his fabled motorcycle accident. The Beatles were no more, and had not played a paid concert since 1966. Only The Stones were still a touring band. When it was announced that The Stones (with new guitarist Mick Taylor) were beginning their autumn 1969 tour of America on the West Coast, one bootlegger's thoughts turned to producing an ultimate souvenir of The Stones in concert:

Dub: At the time there was no problem getting into concerts to tape things 'cos it had never been a problem before. So you can thank us for the problems you have going into concerts with a tape recorder now ... ! After we did *Stealin'* and *John Birch* ... a friend of mine who was in the business and was a Dylan fan and also a Rolling Stones fan approached me and said, 'The Stones are ... going to be here on the West Coast. Would you like to tape some of the concerts and do an album?' And I thought, 'Sure! This is the next step' ... Because I had the money I went out and bought state-of-the-art equipment, because I had to do a good audience recording. What I used was a Sennheiser 805 'shotgun' microphone and a Uher 4000 reel-to-reel tape recorder, which was real small, 7½ips, 5" reels. We taped six Stones concerts on the West Coast, two in LA, two in Oakland, one in San Diego and one in Phoenix. The one we used, which became *LiveR Than You'll Ever Be*, was the second Oakland show. It was taped between two and five in the morning.[24]

Though jazz and opera buffs had been using this sort of equipment for years, rock & roll concerts were rarely targeted by audiophiles aiming for the best fidelity possible.* Dub's decision to use quality microphones and record at 7½ inches per second, on the best portable reel-to-reel on the market, combined with Oakland Coliseum's surprisingly fine sound, resulted in a recording which surprised everyone.

LiveR Than You'll Ever Be is a remarkable document of the originators of rock & roll's toughest guitar sound. Taylor's tasteful fills mesh perfectly with the cut'n'thrust of 'Keef'. It was these shows that really staked their claim to the tag 'greatest live rock & roll band in the world', something that could only apply during the Taylor years. Dub's 'shotgun' caught the soul of The Stones in performance as they found new depths to a rare 'Prodigal Son', Robert Johnson's 'Love in Vain', a positively chilling 'Midnight Rambler' and seven further slices of Stones *circa* '69.

The rush release of *LiveR Than You'll Ever Be* before Christmas (the show having been on 9 November), while the memory of the tour – and its Altamont aftermath – was still news, forced ABKCO to issue a press statement that tapes (i.e. board tapes) were made at concerts in Baltimore and New York but that 'no tapes were recorded on the West Coast'. In January 1970, though, *Rolling Stone* ran Greil Marcus's hyperbolic review of *LiveR*, thus passing into rocklore the myth of an Oakland soundboard:

---

* What sixties tapes reside in collectors' circles were mostly recorded on primitive cassette recorders. Cassette recorders were first introduced by Phillips in 1964, though it would be a good decade before cassette technology produced any real sonic range or a tolerably low level of hiss.

The sound quality is superb, full of presence, picking up drums, bass, both guitars and the vocals beautifully. The LP is [also] in stereo [*sic*] . . . From a little hide-away microphone in someone's lap? Not too likely. So these may in fact be tapes that were made on stage by someone involved in setting up The Stones' own sound system . . . It captures every thrill of The Stones live on stage, 1969 . . . The turn-around violence of their sound, the ripping hardness of the guitars, and the energy of the rhythm section is all here . . . It is the most musically exciting record I have heard all year, fully the equal, in its own way, of *Let It Bleed*, and in some ways better. All qualifications aside, it is the ultimate Rolling Stones album.[25]

Marcus's speculations upon the album's original source made ABKCO and London even more paranoid about who might be behind such a fine-sounding live document. Dub Nutter, the Los Angeles attorney given the task of handling London Records' lawsuit over the bootleg album – a lawsuit that lacked just one vital ingredient: a defendant – admitted that, 'we frankly don't know who did it, but we believe they bootlegged into the public address system itself.'[26]

There was even speculation that the bootlegger had had the cooperation of The Stones. It was common knowledge in the industry that The Stones' relationship with Decca (and, in turn, London Records) had long passed breaking point. There had been a series of major disagreements, the most substantial of which – the graffiti-strewn 'toilet' cover for *Beggars Banquet* – had involved recalling an album sleeve approved by The Stones. The Stones had already decided to leave the label after they delivered one final album – a live collection from their US tour – and one single. The single they delivered, 'Cocksucker Blues', was so obscene that it could never be released.* What better way to deflate the potential demand for Decca's album of their US tour than to pre-empt it with a bootleg version? Certainly when the official version

---

* English bootleggers eventually issued the single, in the late seventies, with the original 1970 version of 'Brown Sugar' – with Eric Clapton on slide-guitar – as its flipside. This would have been the official version of 'Brown Sugar' if the inclusion of Clapton on the cut had not created its own problems.

eventually hit the racks, after overdubbing and rejigging in the studio had destroyed some of that authentic live feel, *Get Your Ya-Ya's Out* lacked the vitality and freshness evident at the outset of the tour, captured faithfully by Dub's Sennheiser microphone.

Dub: We loved it when they said that *LiveR* was recorded on a multi-track backstage and all that stuff . . . we got a big kick out of that one. It was just the Sennheiser shotgun pointed at the PA system. Usually I would point it at the drum set. I wanted to get the cymbal sound and usually the PA would fill in around it and generally it was so directional that it would go over people's heads, so it didn't pick up too much audience. It was the perfect mike for that purpose. I had it anodised black . . . so it wouldn't reflect light and couldn't be seen in the dark.[27]

If there was never any real evidence implicating the Stones in the production of *LiveR Than You'll Ever Be*, they did not go out of their way to condemn the release. When some copies were brought up to KSAN radio station in San Francisco, Sam Cutler, The Stones' road manager, having listened to it, ended up buying six copies, one for himself, the remaining five for The Stones themselves. In subsequent years both Jagger and Richards were to be ardent bootleg collectors, and various statements in the press suggested that they always encouraged such documentation.

LiveR was one instance where Ken was not Dub's partner in crime. Dub had enlisted the help of 'a big-time legitimate recording engineer', who did some in-house tinkering with the tapes as well as partially financing the release. To further rub salt in the record company's wounds, they pressed the album at one of the plants usually utilized by London.

Dub: The discs were delivered to us in London boxes! The people at the plant didn't want anyone to know what the records were, of course.[28]

LiveR Than You'll Ever Be established a demand for well-recorded audience bootlegs, a revelation at least as significant as the initial success of *Great White Wonder*. Of course, bootleggers required not just the (financial) means and motives, but also the opportunity. It was the casual attitude of LA pressing plants that ultimately explains why California remained the hub of bootlegging throughout the vinyl era – even when state anti-piracy laws were tightened up in the late seventies. Many local pressing plants were unconcerned about the legalities of what they were doing. Given the sheer number of plants that existed in the Golden State it was always going to be possible to find one that didn't ask too many questions.

Dub: We would talk to people and find out who was cool and who wasn't. This [one] plant was owned by this old guy who was an alcoholic and just wanted cash and didn't care. They made a lot of money from us and a lot of people came there. The word got out. They were pressing for everybody. We'd all run into each other at the plant . . . People'd pick up the wrong box, and get somebody else's records.[29]

As one employee of the James Lee Record Processing Company told the press at the time of the initial goldrush, 'We've had lots of stuff come through here that's later turned up stolen or dirty, but we don't know that. We don't play the records when we get them, because if we do that we have to be responsible.'[30] When Columbia's private detective went down to the S&R plant in Gardena – where *Great White Wonder* had been rebootlegged – to advise them to 'cease and desist', he was informed that they would stop when a court told them to stop.

The record companies were still fumbling in the dark. Weak anti-piracy laws made it very difficult for the record companies' investigators to search a plant for illegal 'stampers' and 'mothers'.* In fact, most bootlegging was being done right under their noses. In 1969 Capitol was the only major label to have its own pressing plant in California. All the others used independents, just like the bootleggers.

While the release of *LiveR Than You'll Ever Be* showed the

---

* An acetate of the original recording would be used to create metal discs, termed 'mothers' or 'masters', from which would come the 'stampers', which would be used, in turn, to press the actual albums.

potential for 'souvenir' bootlegs – Dig it! Hear the tour you just attended! – Dub needed the sort of distribution network that would put copycats out of business through sheer organization. As the only bootlegger producing multiple titles – three Dylans and a Stones title to date, and with a slew of new titles planned – Dub was the one bootlegger in a position to put the sale of these items on a sounder financial footing.

Dub: We had been in contact with these two guys who were managers of a major American group. We were actually in there working on *LiveR* when they were recording their [first] album, and their managers became our distributors for North America and Canada. We had an agreement with them not to bootleg their group, which we didn't. That stuff was shipped all over the country. We would go down to the airport here at LA International, and one of these guys would bribe one of the porters and we would have cartons and cartons of records, not just *LiveR* – most of them were *LiveR* though – and he would put them on the planes as luggage, and he would put all the claim cheques in one of the boxes and put Xs on it and then his partner at the other end would look for the box with the Xs and pull out all the claim cheques.[31]

The demand for *LiveR* exceeded any previous title, partially because there was no real attempt to copy the Lurch Records edition (on which The Stones were identified simply as 'The Greatest Group on Earth'). Before *Get Your Ya-Ya's Out*, *LiveR* was the essential document of The Stones live, bootlegs were news and, to quote Andrew Loog Oldham, The Stones' early mentor, there was no such thing as bad publicity. After all, this was the late sixties and California was the home of the counter-culture. Displays of corporate mentality – 'bootlegs deprive me of royalties and take away my control' – held little kudos with the fans. For now, the few bands to be bootlegged steered clear of any overt anti-bootleg statements. And there was still considerable prestige to being bootlegged.

Dub: In my opinion bootlegs were the greatest promotional tool ever invented. I think that people like Pete Townshend who saw the wisdom in bootlegs and encouraged people to bootleg them, I think that's smart! . . . We never sold large enough quantities to hurt . . . *LiveR* sold a lot, it would be tens of thousands, not 200,000 or anything like that, but over a period of six years, seven years.[32]

Dub now realized that his outlaw activities were attracting the interest of more organized criminals, prepared to offer their own, more sophisticated distribution services – as well as providing a cast-iron (or perhaps concrete) guarantee that no one would reboot-leg Dub's titles.

Dub: We were actually approached by the Italians one time. In 1970. They wanted to go into business with us, our Italian friends from the island over there. I stayed away from that. That kinda scared me. They saw we were into something and they were interested in such things, but my gut told me to stay away from that and I did. I'm sure we could have been bankrolled very generously but . . . getting out of business with those people doesn't happen.[33]

It wasn't just the criminal element who were starting to take a serious interest in Dub and his kin's activities. The record companies had decided that the fun had gone on long enough. But in order to stamp out this particular nest of Californian ants, they were going to have to change laws. Whatever the relative sales of rock compared with jazz, classical and nostalgia bootlegs – and the differential was not actually that great – the record companies saw Zeppelin selling hundreds of thousands of their studio albums and translated this into commensurate sales for their live bootlegs. They turned to the media to aid them in a sustained campaign of misinformation, designed to distort the 'failings' of bootleg producers. Firstly, KSAN in San Francisco put out a story that bootlegs had a lifespan of maybe twenty playings because the top layer of vinyl was so thin that it would be quickly scraped off by the stylus, a myth subsequently reiterated by *Rolling Stone* and *Life*. Though most of the early bootlegs did suffer from poor vinyl quality, this story was more transparent than any bootleg. When this brand of scaremongering failed to produce any discernible downturn in demand, the industry wheeled out various 'authorities' predicting the demise of the record industry 'as we know it':

Joe Smith [vice-president of Warner Brothers]: If bootlegging were to continue indefinitely the entire structure of the music business as we know it would be absolutely destroyed. There would be a chaotic period of nobody willing to pay for anything.[34]

Paranoia about the 'damaging impact' of bootlegs seemed contagious. Columbia told *Rolling Stone* that *Self Portrait*, Dylan's follow up to *Nashville Skyline*, had been rush released 'following the discovery that copies of many of the tapes used on the album had been stolen from Columbia's vaults'. In fact only two outtakes from *Self Portrait* ever circulated among Dylan collectors, and these were written about in *Rolling Stone* three months before the album's release. Likewise, sales of Elton John's live album *11–17–70* were reportedly heavily hit by an East Coast bootleg version preceding the official album by several weeks (the concert in question had been a radio broadcast). In fact, the main reason that Elton fans sought out the bootleg – and were disappointed by *11–17–70* when it finally made it to the shops – was the fact that the bootleg featured the complete one-hour broadcast, not the forty-minute single-album version that DJM, in their infinite wisdom, deemed fit for public consumption. The record companies could not begin to compete with live bootlegs until they recognized their intrinsic appeal. Record company press pronouncements suggested that they were a long way short of understanding fans and collectors.

When tall tales did nothing to change consumer attitudes, certain 'majors' directly threatened retailers who were selling bootlegs. When a store owner in LA was given a warning by his Warner rep., he reported the incident to *Rolling Stone*:

Steve Gabor [retailer]: I was instructed by the Warner Elektra–Atlantic group that if I carried a single bootleg, they wouldn't sell me any more records. They were unwilling to put this in writing.[35]

The problem with such a bare-faced threat was that it was, and is, illegal – a clear violation of Federal anti-trust laws. And frankly, at this point, there were too many independent record stores and the record companies needed these stores to push their product. The last thing they needed was stores selling bootlegs exclusively. Such stores would then be in direct competition with dispensers of official product.

Piecemeal legal threats temporarily worked in New York's East Village, where rock bootlegs were a small part of their business and the stores were not looking to rock the boat (otherwise the labels might start investigating the legality of various rockabilly, blues and jazz anthologies these stores were openly selling). Also, New York's anti-piracy laws gave the Biz lawyers powers yet to be established in the Golden State.

Only by changing federal law (meaning the Copyright Act of 1909) could legitimate manufacturers have any hope of curtailing bootlegs and, more importantly, the large-scale counterfeiting of hit albums (which was once again on the increase). However, the cumbersome American political system meant that progress in this department had been fitful. As long ago as 1955 the copyright office had been asked to submit proposals for a new copyright act. It had taken ten years for those proposals to be submitted to the House of Representatives. When they finally arrived, there was considerable controversy over the Bill's provisions for copyrighted material played on jukeboxes, community antenna TV and educational TV. Such disputes served to further delay the Bill's passage. When it was introduced into Senate in 1968 by John L. McClellan, becoming known as the McClellan Bill, it was immediately killed for that session. Reintroduced in 1969, the Bill failed to pass. The record industry found itself back at the starting block.

If they were ever to get the McClellan Bill passed, it was in the industry's interests to exaggerate the damage that this new beast, the rock bootleg, was doing to the God-fearing, tax-paying record industry, indeed to corporate capitalism itself. The considerable publicity bootlegs had generated in the winter of 1969–70 became a useful weapon in a battle only marginally connected to the real issues raised by bootlegs. In fact, the McClellan Bill was essentially an anti-piracy bill (the RIAA was still primarily concerned with infringements relating to commercially released recordings).

The international community was not so slow to recognize the growing threat of large-scale piracy of phonograms and cassettes, and American government representatives were among those attending a 'Convention for the Protection of Producers of Phonograms Against Unauthorized Duplication of Their Phonograms' held in Paris in March 1971. The convention resulted in a brief to design and produce a treaty that would establish a network of international legislation to defeat piracy on a worldwide basis. On 29 October 1971, representatives of fifty nations met in Geneva, Switzerland, to consider the resultant treaty. However, only twenty-three countries signed the Geneva Convention, which obliged any signatory country to ban the sale of pirated discs and tapes and to ensure that no such product was imported from, or exported to, signatory countries.

Though the US had been one of the forty countries involved in drafting the Geneva Convention, without a revised copyright act it was not in a position to implement many of the relevant clauses. The US would not, indeed could not, become a signatory until March 1974. However, their acceptance of the principles expressed in the Geneva Convention suggested a renewed determination to finally force through the McClellan Bill.

The presence of the US may have been vital to the success of the convention, but it had produced some rather ill-informed 'experts'. In an attempt to taint bootlegs, one of their 'experts' reported that, according to their calculations, 'about 90 per cent of the bootleg trade is in pop music'. Alan Ladd, head of the American delegation to Geneva, further alleged that 'Mafia money was now behind some bootleg sources.' Presumably the use of the M word was intended to cause ripples in Washington.

The industry's continued belief that bootleggers were exploiting a hole in copyright protection which, once filled, would signal an end to this brand of 'performance piracy' was to prove naïve and fallacious. The bootleggers were just beginning to realize the potential of the medium. And for Dub and Ken the time had come to establish their own trademark – a trademark of quality.

4 All Rights Reserved, All Wrongs Reversed

Albums of The Band's concert at Pasadena Civic Auditorium and Dylan's live performance at the Isle of Wight have been rejected by most youthful buyers because of the poor quality of the original tapes. Said one young girl of The Band album: 'It sounds like something my kid brother made in the second row with his home tape recorder. At the beginning of one number, you can hear someone yell "Get your hand off the mike!"'[1]

The record industry's campaign of misinformation had been given some credence by charlatans, incompetents and tone-deaf entrepreneurs now chasing the latest bandwagon. The record industry's best weapon was poor product from bootleggers. By the spring of 1970 some degree of calm had descended. That hole in time when any bootleg, however shoddy, seemed to be snapped up, was over. Either bootleggers were going to have to cater to the collectors, to whom the music was more important than its artifact value, or bootlegs would become a historical curio, one more neutered 'threat' in a twenty-year battle for copyright reform. The merchants of grey-area economics were dropping from the bandwagon. Perhaps the serious bootleggers could get their hands on the wheel.

If the wind seemed to be going out of the pirates' sails in the summer of 1970, the independent youth responsible for Lemon Records' solitary release had a hot new platter to peddle – quite probably the most dramatic live rock album ever recorded. Prior to Michael O's landmark release, the only commercially available evidence of Dylan's pre-accident, post-amphetamine stage-self, accompanied by his own set of Hawks, was one apocalyptic rendition of 'Just Like Tom Thumb's Blues' filed away on the b-side of *Blonde on Blonde* single No. 3. Greil Marcus's description of Dylan and the Hawks' live sound, though, in a November 1969 *Rolling Stone* article, stoked up demand for audio evidence of Bobby D. *circa* 1966:

The sound they produced was stately, extravagant, and visionary – there is nothing with which to compare it in all of Dylan's recordings. At the bottom of that sound was a rough, jerking marriage of blues and honky tonk, but over that were grafted the sort of echoes that come from the music box of a circus merry-go-round.[2]

In temporary retirement after the success of *Get Back*, Michael O had seen many clowns getting in on the game. But he lacked the sort of source tapes he could turn into an album – until an Englishman named Alan came through this particular door of opportunity:

Michael O: Alan wandered into our record store . . . He was a very flash-dressed English person walking into a hippy store, and he said he had some tapes and had no clue as to how to get them pressed up. So of course I said, 'I do. What have you got?' and he said, 'I've got lots and lots. Why don't you come over and hear them?' So we drove over to this huge rented house in Laurel Canyon where he was living with an American friend who was a rock photographer . . . and he puts on this acetate of [Dylan at the] Royal Albert Hall. Side two starts with 'Leopard Skin Pillbox Hat' . . . and we said, 'God, where did you get this?' . . . He had The Beatles at the Bowl, that's where that came from originally, he had the Beatles' Decca Audition [tape] and he had some Who stuff. My understanding of where all this came from was an engineer at a very popular pressing plant. There were no cassettes in those days. If an artist wanted [to hear] his music he had an acetate made, they would leave 'em with him and he would run off tapes for himself. *Royal Albert Hall* came from Dylan's people. After the show [they] wanted to have a reference disc of one of the shows to be able to play on the road, 'cos you can't really carry a reel-to-reel about, and that kind of jives with what I heard about them wanting to go home and hear the things because they couldn't believe people were booing.[3]

The Dylan tape was not only of stupendous quality, but contained music seething with the fury of a man done wrong, and raging at the world for it. As the final denouement, it even had Dylan being called a Judas, before he launches into the ultimate

'Like a Rolling Stone' with the barked command to his band, 'Play fucking loud!' Alan, though, was uncertain whether he really wanted such a sensitive document out on the street.

Michael O: He flew back to England immediately. He was a nervous type ... he kept going on and off [the boil] with [the tape], and I didn't know him. I'd called him back and he'd say he wasn't going to do it. So, of course, I thought I was never going to hear that tape again ... I would persuade him and then he'd call back and say I can't do it, the potential for trouble is too great ... We went back and forth for a week and a half, and as he was due to go back to England, he left the tapes here with the American friend. I called the American friend and he said, 'Alan can't make up his mind. He should do it, let's do it.'[4]

Michael felt that the contents warranted something a little more extravagant than the stamped cover that was still the norm on bootlegs. After the success of the picture insert on *Get Back*, Michael wanted to give *Royal Albert Hall* a printed sleeve. Since a conventional album cover would require the services of a sleeve manufacturer (and these were all in the pockets of legitimate companies), the cover was a single 15″ × 24″ sheet of card, folded twice. With two photos from Daniel Kramer's Dylan photobook, the effect was really quite professional – particularly when shrink-wrapped. With gold *Royal Albert Hall* labels and full track separation,* *Royal Albert Hall* made for a highly attractive package – and the contents were quite simply devastating!

Michael O: This was the first printed cover bootleg. All in mono, four songs on one side, four on the other ... My hippy friend's conceptual take was that we should call the record label 'Necessary Records' because records like this were necessary for people to hear. In the end we called the label *Royal Albert Hall*, because we thought the pressing plant would think the label was 'Royal' and the artist was Albert Hall.[5]

Sadly, though, the engineer had not done a good job EQing the tape and had, in Michael's words, 'squash[ed] it to death', so it

---

* Most bootleggers did not 'groove' their records to indicate the start of each track.

sounded more like a bootleg than a legitimate release. The whole presentation, and general attention to detail, had been designed to make the album transcend a bootleg-buying market. The music was certainly of interest to any fan who liked his rock & roll close to the edge. But the bootleg bubble had burst and Michael's distribution outside of LA was non-existent.

Michael O: We went out and did the sales thing again like we did with The Beatles, but the fad had peaked a little and people weren't interested in buying more than a few. A couple of stores bought seventy-five but mostly it was tens and twenties. It was slow going and then it was bootlegged itself, just as quickly as *Get Back*, but we had only managed to get through 1,000 copies. So from that point on it was a bootleg of a bootleg.[6]

This was an ironic turn of events. Michael had rebootlegged a Berkeley original of *Get Back* and now the first 'copy' of *Royal Albert Hall* was San Franciscan in origin. *Looking Back*, though, was a double-album, combining Michael's electric set with one side of acoustic 1966 material (from a show in Dublin) and, rather incongruously, part of Dylan's first show at the New York Town Hall in 1963 (credited to Berkeley Community Theatre, presumably in the hope of enticing locals to dig into their pockets).

Unbeknownst to Michael, his *Royal Albert Hall* had been pressed at the plant now used by Dub and Ken, and it eventually reappeared in Michael's covers but with Ken's Smokin' Pig labels, suggesting that at some point Ken had gained access to Michael's artwork (and quite possibly his stampers).

Michael O: This was not done at Rainbow. We found another pressing plant and the woman who ran it was an alcoholic, and was always drunk, and it turned out that it was the same place that Dub was already at. He had already moved to the coloured vinyl phase ... At that plant it was possible to pilfer somebody else's plates.[7]

Michael was disheartened by the whole episode. Having issued surely *the* most cataclysmic performance of rock's most bootlegged artist, he hadn't shifted anything like the numbers he had expected,

had been rebootlegged twice and was being totally out-
distributed.

Michael O: I got all artistic on the cover, and because it was selling slow, it
didn't generate the kind of money that *Get Back* did, so when [Alan] got
back to the States hoping for a big payoff, I had a few hundred dollars for
him and some pressings. He went back to England again almost
immediately.[8]

The muted response to Michael's *Royal Albert Hall* was largely
unique to California. When the album was repressed under Michael's
auspices and exported to the UK, housed in a more traditional
hand-stamped cover (with a cryptic new moniker, *In 1966 There
Was*), it was quickly revered by fans and critics alike. After the
release of *Self Portrait*, *In 1966 There Was* explained why anyone
had ever listened to crooning Country Bob. *Royal Albert Hall*
remains one of that very rare breed of bootlegs – a perennial.
Second-generation copies continued to sell year in, year out, and,
appropriately enough, in 1988 it became the second Dylan bootleg
CD.

Michael's artistic bent had proved his undoing. The economics
of bootlegs only remained attractive when costs were low and
turnover was good. Printed covers would be a no-no for some time
yet. The truth to tell, a cover like the one for *Royal Albert Hall*
probably cost more to manufacture than the albums. The other
bootleggers could copy such an intrinsically 'clean' recording with
minimal quality loss and have their low-budget versions on the
streets within weeks.

Meanwhile, whatever predictions had been made about the
'bootlegability' of acts outside the Big Three – and there had been
many – it was really only a matter of time before the new kids on
the block got their very own bootleg platters. At the start of 1970
came a compilation of Crosby, Stills, Nash and Young live, taken
from shows at Big Sur and the LA Forum. CSNY were big news,
and their first studio album since Neil Young hooked up with
his Springfield cohort Mr Stills was eagerly awaited. *Wooden
Nickel* was well-received, not just by the fans.

Graham Nash: When *Wooden Nickel* came out, we were really pleased that it was out ... If Neil had been anti-*Wooden Nickel* he would have found some way to put a stop to it. But Neil's up there with the most rebellious of people, and we didn't think that it would put a serious dent in our money-making capabilities.[9]

The end of the sixties was to mark a significant shift in rock audiences' allegiances. If Dylan remained revered out of all proportion to his sales, the bands coming out of England's 'second generation' r&b boom, and California's own crop from the Summer of Love, gave fans a new set of icons. Dub, back in partnership with Ken, felt that the new English bands were creating the bigger stir and worked very hard to convince Ken that they should put out a Jethro Tull title. Tull were still building up their audience base when Dub put out *My God*. However, it was Dub's LA Forum recording of England's hardest working prog-rockers, Led Zeppelin, which confirmed that the tide was turning. The Big Three was now the Big Four.

Dub: I remember seeing Zeppelin in '68 at the Rose Palace in Pasadena. They were third on the bill ... there were a couple of hundred people there. Then they had gotten big and when they came back later we taped the Forum Concert. [*Blueberry Hill*] we really rushed out in two weeks ... 'cos we wanted that out while they were still on tour.[10]

It was the incredible speed with which Dub and Ken managed to get *Blueberry Hill* out that gave it its remarkable impetus. On the streets before *Led Zeppelin III*, *Blueberry Hill* captured Zeppelin already extending beyond the prototypes recorded for their third album. The highlight of the two-hour set is a scintillating 'Since I Been Loving You'. The furore *Blueberry Hill* created, and the thinly veiled threats of Zep's overbearing manager, Peter Grant, to seek and sort out the perpetrators, only furthered the demand. Any witness to Zeppelin's '69 shows knew that here was a band best heard live. *Blueberry Hill* also boasted Dub and Ken's first cover, a two-colour insert along the lines of Lemon Records' *Get Back*. Theirs, though, was considerably more surreal, a melange that seemed to cross Hieronymus Bosch with Terry Gilliam and George Dunning's 'Yellow Submarine'.

The idea that a bootlegger could put out a show within three weeks of the event was a terrifying idea – at least for the record companies. With the 'targeting' of retailers, the need for pre-release hype and slotting into schedules, they couldn't hope to compete with such efficiency. Bootleggers were bound only by the pressing plant's turn-round time, and the minimal effort required to EQ the original audience tape. Corporate wheels ground far more slowly. Of course, the demand for 'souvenir' bootlegs was bound to be more ephemeral than for stalwarts like *Stealin'*, which would continue to sell and sell, but on a simple turnover basis they represented the way ahead.

Blueberry Hill came at the very end of the season of hype as regards rock bootlegs. Though there were signs that the honeymoon was over, *Blueberry Hill* broke many of the remaining bootleg taboos – all the while threatening to be almost as great a success as *LiveR Than You'll Ever Be*. It was an audience tape and, though superior to most contemporary recordings, it was several notches down from *LiveR*. Led Zeppelin were also just eighteen months (and two albums) old. *Blueberry Hill* was 110 minutes of solid noise scrunched on to a double album and, for the first time, Dub and Ken had to compete with a superior version. Rubber Dubber, California's latest bootlegger, had put out his own recording of the same show at a 'recommended retail price' of $6 (the price was stamped on the cover), and his tape surpassed Dub's own commendable efforts. Ironically, the LA Forum show in question was not an example of Zeppelin firing on all cylinders. Though *Blueberry Hill* remains a legendary title among Zep aficionados – there are at least three CD editions of the album – the band already sound slightly jaded. Their penchant for indulgence was beginning to eat at the roots of their brand of hard rock. Even the Led Zeppelin tape-collectors' guide observes:

[Though] it is . . . full of surprises and rarely played songs . . . the playing is merely average at certain points. Page's fingers are a little sticky and he performs a rather lazy concert.[11]

A far better performance, and probably the first Zeppelin bootleg if the truth be told, was a single album from the first show of their spring 1970 US tour. Entitled *Pure Blues Live*, it caught Zeppelin six months before Dub and Rubber Dubber, and, despite Plant's sore throat, *Pure Blues* was a demonic display of Zep mid-flight (and for many years it was the only vinyl source of a live 'We're Gonna Groove'). The forty-minute tape, recorded in Vancouver, is frequently cited as an FM broadcast. Yet no tape of the broadcast, save for the vinyl version immortalized on *Pure Blues*, has ever circulated among collectors. In reality the bootleg came from an incomplete soundboard tape and was almost certainly produced first-hand by someone at the venue who had access to the PA system, a rare one-off example of private enterprise in British Columbia. The bootleg itself, with a simple hand-stamped cover, boasted an exemplary vinyl pressing and was only ever distributed in the North-West.

It was almost certainly pressed in very limited numbers in Seattle, where there were a couple of independent pressing plants and a small but solid retail market for bootleg product. *Pure Blues*, simply because of its North-West origins and exclusive pressing, was largely unknown at the time *Blueberry Hill* was giving Peter Grant palpitations. It needed a more mainstream release to achieve legend status. When one assiduous collector/taper moved from Seattle to Los Angeles in the spring of 1971, he took his copy of *Pure Blues* with him.

Deke: [Back in '71] I went out to the La Marada swap-meet. It was just a regular swap-meet. I'm out there with my Dad and I'm whining to my Dad, 'Oh shit. I'm not gonna know where to find bootleg albums.' All of a sudden there's a guy with a spot and the whole spot's nothing but bootleg covers laid out on a sheet, and there's thirty-five different bootlegs sitting there and this guy with a US army jacket, a white t-shirt, long hair and a beard, and I go up and I go, 'Wow, I collect these things. By the way I have a few rare things. I'm from Seattle. I got this Led Zeppelin thing called *Pure Blues* that you don't have here. It's real high quality. It's better than this *Blueberry Hill* you got.' I got his phone number and ended up bringing him the album.[12]

The long-haired ex-Marine was Ken, still involving himself in a little first-hand retailing. *Pure Blues* soon became *Mudslide*, TMQ's second Zeppelin title, and 'Deke' was later to become a useful source of first-generation audience recordings for Ken when he was no longer able to rely on Dub. *Pure Blues* was one of the better examples of left-field one-off bootlegs. Many such 'vanity' releases were just that, stripped of any aesthetic value by poor source material, corner-cutting and lousy presentation.

Though Dub was the only bootlegger, apart from Rubber Dubber, to display attention to detail on a steady run of titles, he did not benefit from the kudos lavished upon Rubber Dubber. Each of Dub's albums had its own label (be it Lurch, Winklhofer or Blimp).

Dub: I would EQ everything. It was all taped at high speed, then I'd use Dolby, and later DBX, and I had Ampex studio machines and Revox, everything was state of the art, 15 ips, whatever was available at the time ... The weak point in our records was the pressings, we couldn't get state of the art pressings at that time. We couldn't get the best vinyl.[13]

Dub did not want to make it clear that Har-Kub, Lurch and Blimp were all guises of the same bootlegger. But the spring of 1970 had brought with it his first serious rival – the notorious Rubber Dubber. Rubber Dubber was not so coy. Indeed his flair for self-promotion seemed like a recipe for trouble.

Rubber Dubber went as far as sending review copies of his early releases to *Rolling Stone*. He even attempted to place an ad in the *Stone*, though this 'voice of the counter-culture' refused to accept the advert, and its senior editor, Ralph J. Gleason, dismissed him in a front-page editorial as just another 'quack Robin Hood'. In fact, this 'quack Robin Hood' was the son of an organized crime family in Dallas who, not wishing to join the family business, had joined naval intelligence. His first flirtation with rock & roll came when he went out on the road with one-hit wonders Paul & Paula and, when Paul experienced a 'road to Damascus' experience akin to his namesake, was obliged to 'become' Paul for the remainder of the tour.

Whatever *Rolling Stone*'s opinion of this small-time entrepreneur, there is no doubt that, in the eighteen months preceding the autumn 1971 passage of the McClellan Bill, Rubber Dubber was responsible for some of the very best bootlegs on the streets. His releases tended to be double albums and all originated from his own audience tapes, which were often remarkable quality and usually derived from shows at LA's Inglewood Forum. Indeed, according to one source, Atlantic Records were considering approaching the Dubber for his tapes of CSNY, 'a model of recorded clarity . . . [and] one of the group's rare "on" nights'. Legend has it that his recordings were so impressive (at least for the early seventies) because he circumvented smuggling in a tape-recorder altogether:

The [record] companies, in order to show their concern, erected airport-style metal detectors at the exits at concerts in the Los Angeles area in hopes they'd erase any tapes made during the performance. But [Rubber Dubber] had never been so crude as to take a tape recorder into a concert hall. He smuggled microphones with tiny built-in FM transmitters that beamed the signal into a truck parked a quarter of a mile away.[14]

Rubber Dubber covers began as 'traditional' rubber-stamped white sleeves with a simple 'Yours truly, Rubber Dubber' in the bottom right-hand corner. However, they became increasingly ornate (the CSNY double-set came with a two-colour mock 'American flag' design), and a 'recommended retail price' – $6 per double album – stamped on each album.

Uninterested in recycling previous releases, his titles were often only single pressings and, despite some extravagant sales claims on his behalf, they were mostly limited to a couple of thousand copies. The reputation Rubber Dubber titles quickly garnered ensured that each release was snapped up by established customers. Unfortunately, Rubber Dubber also allowed himself to become

something of a darling to the underground press. Here was a bootlegger with his own sardonic little moniker, quite prepared to justify
the morality of what he was doing to an ambivalent media:

Rubber Dubber: Our goal is very simple. We want to put the record
companies out of business by simply giving the fans what they want and at
the same time not screwing the performer ... We use only the finest
materials and only charge six bucks for a two-record set. We sell them
to the stores for $2.75, and out of that has to come the salaries and
the overhead ... We record concerts played into the free air to a
paying audience – including us – and for every record we sell, we put
25c into an escrow fund payable to the artist himself, not to any of the
parasites that surround him. That quarter covers the publisher's fees and
the artist's royalties, and any artist can pick up his cash by contacting us
through one of our salesmen at any store where Rubber Dubber records
are sold.[15]

Unlike Dub and other rivals, Rubber Dubber had managed to
acquire his own pressing facility. In fact he had converted a rubber
swim fin press into a record press, which was housed at a farm in
Oregon, making detection by the authorities more than a little
problematic. However, the mastering and what little mixing was
required were carried out in Los Angeles, where, according to the
Dubber himself, he employed (part-time) some thirty people 'who
do everything but press the records'. Because he had his own
pressing facility, Rubber Dubber's releases did not contain that tell-
tale groove on the outer edge of the record label that all other
bootlegs coming out of LA seemingly carried, the result of convert-
ing old 10″ presses to take 12″ albums (this should have tipped off
the authorities to the fact that pretty much everything was coming
out of one plant).

Unfortunately, when a fire seriously damaged the Oregon farm
plant, Rubber Dubber was forced to relocate the entire operation
to LA. Though some of the machinery was salvaged and moved as
well, the demand for Rubber Dubber product was such that, in
order to keep up with demand, some orders had to be farmed out
to the pressing plants of LA. Rubber Dubber was also acquiring a

media profile, which was not necessarily good for business. Not only was he written up in *Rolling Stone* and *Esquire* but, because of his pricing system and the speed with which he turned his titles around, he above all others was perceived as threatening to the industry. When Mr Dubber's media profile ran to an extensive interview in *Rolling Stone* in the summer of 1971, he signed his own warrant.

Dubber was not unaware of the mounting pressure to nail him. When the Senate finally passed the McClellan Bill in August 1971, he knew time was running out and began to unload all the remaining Rubber Dubber stock before the watershed of 15 February 1972, the point at which the Bill became law. On 9 September 1971, an informer in the Rubber Dubber set-up showed up with a few friends, 'some private detectives from the Kinney Corporation [owner of the Warner Brothers and Atlantic labels, both of which had had artists Rubber Dubbed] and a handful of US marshals'. Thankfully Rubber Dubber, expecting a bust at any moment, had already moved almost everything incriminating (like the actual presses) out of the office. When the marshals arrived Rubber Dubber's lawyer was on hand to point out that the anti-bootleg law did not go into effect until February 1972.

Nevertheless, the marshals confiscated boxes of alleged contraband, and the Kinney Corp., professing to represent the late Jimi Hendrix, Jethro Tull, Led Zeppelin, Van Morrison and CSNY, brought suit against Mr Dubber (and seventeen John and Jane Does) alleging 'unfair competition and interference with contractual relationships'. A few days later, the judge threw out all the charges and instructed the officers to return the boxes and empty album covers that they had confiscated. Meanwhile one of Dubber's employees had gone to Warners in LA and stamped the Rubber Dubber trademark all over the (recently painted) walls of the executive loo. Despite such bravado, the heat was quite enough to convince the Dubber to call it quits – though not before he and his partner Jack unloaded most of their backstock. On the day that the McClellan Bill kicked in, Dubber was interviewed by ex-*Rolling Stone* editor Ed Ward about his halcyon days:

Rubber Dubber: [When] something gets that big . . . it just gets out of hand. But I don't really believe that we got busted for making records of live concerts of rock & roll groups . . . I don't believe that's what got them so uptight. They were just angry because we found a way to make capitalism do something it wasn't supposed to do. And we had fun doing it. And THAT'S what made them mad.[16]

Though Rubber Dubber never re-entered the bootleg biz – leaving the legend largely intact to this day – rock bootlegging was not to be his last brush with the authorities. After years of living outside the law, he is now languishing in a New Mexico jail on a trumped-up Murder One rap, an unfitting end for the great Dubber.

What Rubber Dubber had proven was that a bootlegger who acquired his own trademark, and maintained the quality of his product, was endorsing all of his releases. The mark of Rubber Dubber on an album stood for a certain standard. By the time Rubber had dubbed his last, the most famous bootleg label of them all had created its own trademark.

A switch to coloured vinyl in 1971 at last gave Dub's product a uniform identity. The best vinyl was virgin vinyl, but the small independent pressing plants rarely used it, and there was no real way of ensuring a quality pressing as long as it was on black vinyl. On the other hand, coloured vinyl – where any imperfection would be clearly visible – was always virgin. Dub's use of coloured vinyl, debuting with two brand-new Dylan titles (*Seems Like A Freeze Out* and *Talkin' Bear Mountain Picnic Massacre Blues*), identified Dub and Ken's product (now also emblazoned with a large '1' and '2' on the record labels) as well as improving the general quality of their pressings.* Coloured vinyl only made Dub hanker after some further stamp of authentification.

Dub: I had always been a perfectionist. Whenever I did a record I wanted it to be as good as possible, soundwise [and] technically. The pressings you

---

* Confusion was still possible. When, some time in 1971, Michael O had a special edition of *Royal Albert Hall* made for the UK, with the last two cuts in full-blown stereo, he used coloured vinyl and stock labels lying around the pressing plant – *voilà*, a British TMQ album.

got were not the best in the world but that's all you could get at the time. The best American pressings were made by Columbia Records and obviously we couldn't go to them . . . So I wanted to establish an identity for the label, this would be '70, '71 . . . I was at my bank one day and I was looking through this book that showed all these different things you put on your cheques, all these little symbols and pictures and everything. And they had a whole section for ranchers and farmers and they had livestock. They had cows and chickens and pigs. I just thought 'God! A pig! What a great symbol!' I had them give me a lead cut of the pig . . . [And then] I thought, 'What's it gonna be called?' . . . and I was lying in bed, half-awake . . . I wanted to say what our label was . . . and it just popped into my head, 'Trade Mark of Quality'! 'Cos I wanted a trademark . . . So I took a cut of the pig and I went to a label maker and I said, 'I want a pig here and a round circle that says "Trade Mark of Quality" and I want you to make ten or twenty thousand stickers, and I want 'em in day-glo colours,' and we started putting 'em on the records. I wanted to differentiate us from the other bootleg labels.[17]

Dub was able to give his new label the best bootleg catalogue in America. With TMQ's formation, all pre-TMQ releases were assigned numbers in the 71000 series in approximately chronological order. Though the first real TMQ release was Frank Zappa's *200 Motels*, 71001 was Dylan's *Stealin'*, 71002 *John Birch Society Blues*, 71003 *LiveR Than You'll Ever Be* and so on. Dub's two double-sets to date – *Great White Wonder* and *Blueberry Hill* – kicked off the 72000 series. All subsequent repressings carried a TMQ sticker and a 'pig' label. Dub also persevered with coloured vinyl, at least for first 'runs'.

The new label, though, had a problem most bootleggers encounter a couple of years after entering the business – coming up with material to equal their early releases. In Dub's case these earlier releases were pre-TMQ, but the song remained the same. Dub and Ken's first six Dylan bootlegs – *Great White Wonder, Stealin', John Birch Society Blues, While The Establishment Burns, Seems Like a Freeze Out* and *Talkin' Bear Mountain Picnic Massacre Blues* – comprised five 'original' titles (*While the Establishment Burns* was a copy of the second volume of *Looking Back*, though

TMQ's version may well have been from a source tape) and are five of the most revered Dylan bootlegs.

The Stones, Dub and Ken's other great love, were just about to tour the States for the first time in two and a half years. Aside from a collection of BBC sessions (*Beautiful Delilah*), Dub and Ken had had to resort to copying Rubber Dubber's album of a concert in Berlin for some stop-gap product (*European Tour 1970* was taped by Rubber Dubber himself, who flew to Germany to tape the show). It seemed that Dub's well might be about to dry up – fewer and fewer 'bootlegable' acts were playing the beloved Forum (Zeppelin's *Going to California*, TMQ's first pukka double, was a welcome exception).

In the nick of time, Dub and Ken were introduced to a well-dressed English gentleman with a seemingly unlimited supply of superb-quality studio outtakes and live soundboards. The gentleman in question, though, knew all about Dub and Ken's business and was uninterested in providing them with hot new product. His experience with a certain Dylan '66 bootleg had soured the medium's possibilities for him. But Dub and Ken were not about to take no for an answer.

Dub: We were always being approached with tapes ... people were always trying to sell us stuff or trade us or whatever, people just wanted to see stuff out, so there was never any shortage of supply of material to put out ... [But] this English guy, who knew someone who worked at some of the studios here in LA, had brought with him a bunch of acetates which were copies of tapes [from] this studio in London, and he had a lot of unreleased material. He had Stones, unreleased Townshend, Zeppelin, Dylan ... really good quality stuff, although it was acetate not tape. He approached us to sell us a copy of the master of *Live Cream* ... He offered us that for ten grand, and we said, 'That's too much money.' He was one of these people who loves to say, 'I've got this, you can listen to it but you can't have it ...' So my original partner, Ken, and I were saying 'We've got to get this stuff' ... I told this guy, 'You know, my roommate is a real Rolling Stones fan and he would just love to hear this stuff and I know that you don't want us to have copies but if you could just come over and play this for him, he would be just so excited ...' I knew this was stroking his ego . . . I lived in the mountains, and [Ken] blindfolded him and drove up through the backroads, so there was no way this guy was ever going to find us again . . . Meanwhile, we had a basement in the house we were renting, and I drilled holes in the floor and ran wires down from the sound system into the basement. There were all these wires and you couldn't really tell that some of the wires went down through the carpeting and through the floor. I set up two machines in the basement, we had state of the art equipment, two Revoxes, 10″ reels. So Ken brings the guy in and he puts on the acetate. Meanwhile Ken is feeding this guy grass to smoke, and the guy was getting stoned and this friend of Ken's would say 'Boy, that's really good, I wanna hear it again!' and so he played every acetate twice! This went on all day, and I was stuck in the basement, lapping it up, recording everything he had. It was really great stuff . . . After we were done [Ken] just packed him up and took him home. But about a month later all this stuff came out, *The Genius of Pete Townshend*, the Stones' *Bright Lights* etc.[18]

The release of Alan's material was actually spread out over a six-month period. Dub had managed to record the Stones' warm-up show at the Hollywood Palladium as they prepared to embark on their last great tour of the US, promoting *Exile on Main Street*. A competing album of early Stones material was unnecessary.

The Genius of Pete Townshend was another matter altogether. After much waiting, and the promise of another rock opera double-set (to be called *Lifehouse*), The Who had finally delivered their follow-up to *Tommy*, *Who's Next*, from the remnants of the abandoned *Lifehouse* project. *The Genius of Pete Townshend* comprised some very finished demos of the *Lifehouse* material, cut by Townshend (presumably with Moon and Entwistle in tow). Featuring three songs excluded from *Who's Next* – 'Pure and Easy', 'Mary' and 'Time is Passing' – and demo versions of six of the songs on *Who's Next*, the album was considerably closer to Townshend's original *Lifehouse* concept than the released album, particularly as the eight-minute hymn 'Pure and Easy' opened the bootleg and a coda from the same song was tagged on to the final track, 'The Song is Over'. *The Genius of Pete Townshend* caused quite a stir at the time, with rumours of theft from Townshend himself, from Track's vault and even from a radio station that Townshend had entrusted with an acetate.

When a further collection of Who studio outtakes came out less than three months later (*Radio London*), drawn from three separate projects – a 1968 'covers' EP, the 'Who Sell Out' sessions and an aborted 1970 EP – it was clear that the leak was not confined to one period of Who recordings. Within a year The Who would respond with their own *Radio London*-type of anthology, *Odds and Sods*, which included 'Naked Eye' from the lost 1970 EP as well as a finished version of 'Pure and Easy'.

By the time *Radio London* had been made ready for public dissemination, a serious internal disagreement had riven the Dub/ Ken duopoly of West Coast bootlegging in two. At the same time, Dub was enlisting a local artist to produce inserts with a tad more originality than the cut'n'paste style devised by Popo Productions (a small-time bootlegger responsible for *Let Me Die In My Footsteps* and *Blind Boy Grunt*, who sometimes operated as a 'consultant' on TMQ's Dylan titles). The artist in question, William Stout, had bought his first bootleg – *Great White Wonder*, of course – at a legitimate record store on Hollywood Boulevard. After things moved underground, he began buying his bootlegs 'literally on the street', before discovering Record Paradise, which quickly became the premier bootleg outlet in Los Angeles. It was here that Stout first met Dub, a meeting he recalls in a suitably dimestore-novel manner:

William Stout: I was at Shinard Institute, aka CalArts, the California Institute of the Arts, and ... an interesting policy in the illustration dept was that if we got any professional jobs we could turn them in in lieu of homework! ... Record Paradise was a draw for me because they were one of the first places in LA to carry import LPs, mostly English LPs. Then they became known for carrying bootlegs also. And the international rock & roll stars became aware of this store ... so it was a regular stop whenever they went to LA, and when they found out about the bootlegs they used to go there. The policy of the store was that if any rock & roll star came in, they could have as many bootlegs as they wanted for free.

Mick Jagger used to stop in there regularly and Holly, the lady who owned the shop, used to just load him up with all the Stones bootlegs ... I was in Record Paradise one day and a new bootleg had just come out of a concert that I had seen and I was really disappointed with the cover, because at the time covers were really simple and crude with not a lot of information. I was expressing myself out loud in the store, 'Gee, I wish someone would let me do the covers ...' and I heard a voice behind me ask if I was serious about that and I said sure. So this person slipped me a piece of paper. It had a time and an address on it, actually a two-street corner, and he said 'Be there,' and vanished. It was a Friday night and I went to these street corners, and waited a couple of minutes. This car drove up, it was an old forties car, the windows rolled down and a hand emerged with a list. I took the list and the car drove off. It was a list of Rolling Stones songs and the title of an album, 'Winter Tour', and that was the first one I did. I did it as a homage to Robert Crumb's *Cheap Thrills*. I like the idea of each song being illustrated by a cartoon. Also on the list there was a time and a place to meet again when I had finished the cover. So I finished the cover, went back to a different corner, the car came by again, I handed them the cover, they handed me fifty bucks and drove off ... Eventually, after several meetings like this there was enough trust for them to reveal themselves to me, and we began to work face to face. I would do the covers pretty quickly, fifty bucks a cover, and then they'd give me some records too when they were pressed. They were really excited about that *Winter Tour* album ... they were able to get it pressed and on the streets within two weeks of the concert.[19]

Winter Tour was certainly a logistical triumph for Dub. The concert was a benefit at the LA Forum for the victims of the Nicaraguan earthquake and a 'warm up' for a brief antipodean Stones tour. *Winter Tour* sounds as if they hadn't come down from the previous tour. The concert was on 18 January. Ten days later the bootleg was delivered to Dub, by which time he had printed up a garish purple insert comprising Stout's series of satirical takes on the members of The Stones. Stout even had the impudence to 'introduce' himself (as the devil, of course) in the bottom right-hand corner of the cover, next to the head of a cigar-chewing pig. With this 'smoking pig', Stout had also inadvertently provided TMQ's newest rival with a counterfeit logo. That rival label was run by TMQ co-founder Ken.

5 The Smokin' Pig

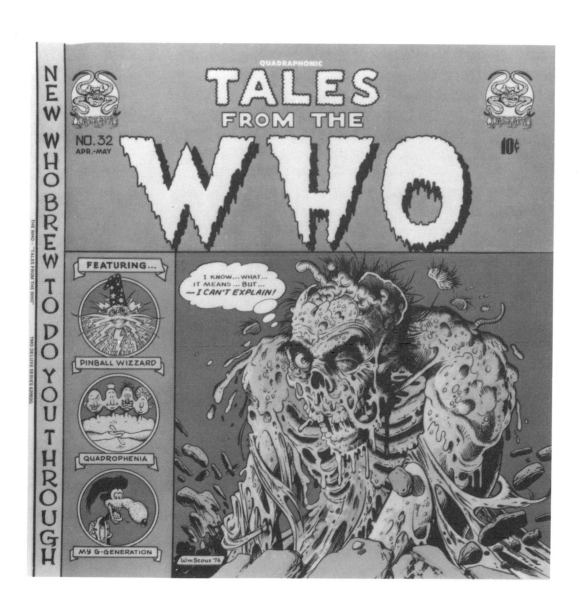

Dub: One of the reasons we started doing covers was that we wanted to differentiate ourselves from the other companies. Everybody else was still doing white covers and rubberstamps . . . so we started using coloured covers instead of white ones, then we started making the records in different colours. We were doing anything we could to keep our identity. Then we had labels made with the pig on it, and then this friend – who I did *LiveR* with – had this friend, William Stout, who did comic book art.[1]

Dub's desire to upgrade the TMQ covers, making them both original and inventive (for which Stout should take all the credit), had not been for purely aesthetic reasons. He still needed to stay one step ahead of piratical bootleggers, whose stock-in-trade was copying the original efforts of producers like Dub. By 1973 one label in particular had been copying TMQ titles wholesale for nearly two years. Contraband (aka CBM), and sister-label King Kong, were responsible for many of the worst bootlegs of the early seventies.

However, Dub's most serious rival was now his ex-partner Ken. The bust-up between Dub and Ken had occurred around the time that *Winter Tour* was put into production. Though Dub insists that the break-up was simply down to a difference of opinion about what to do and where to go with TMQ, one of Ken's later partners suggests that the dispute was more personal:

'Eric Bristow': As I was told it, Dub's dad, who was making a fairly average living as a postal worker, having realized that Dub Jr was making a hell of a lot more money than he was, said, 'Get rid of this guy. I'm your new partner.' So they just dumped Ken . . . Ken told me that they went to the pressing plant and said, 'He's nothing to do with us anymore.' Ken was young, he didn't have much money, he went to the pressing plant himself and told this sob-story of how the two Dubs were shutting him out to

the lady who owned and ran the pressing plant at the time . . . and she just said to him, 'Well, why don't I just make you your own stampers? . . . I got all his mothers here, I'll just make stampers for you!' . . . All of a sudden, there were two sets of stampers from the mothers and Ken created the Smokin' Pig. The Smokin' Pig went out and undercut the regular Pig pricewise. Every time Dub put out a title that was hot, brand new, Ken would have it out a week later . . . That was when Dub created the slightly different logo that said 'Accept No Substitutes'.[2]

Taking Stout's cigar-chewing Pig as his new logo, Ken created a doppelgänger TMQ. Given that his creative input into TMQ had been minimal, and he had as yet no access to 'original' material, he had little choice but to utilize what TMQ stampers the manager at the pressing plant had made for him and repackage earlier TMQ titles in new covers. His primary weapon – undercutting Dub's original editions – was a limited one at best, though it did succeed in confusing the punters as to the 'true' identity of TMQ. And Ken's tenacity was not to be underestimated.

Dub: We ended up in direct competition with each other. He would copy my stuff . . . We had kind of a friendly competition. There was no hostility involved [but] it became two different labels, [though] TMQ was always TMQ, that was always my label. Then everybody started copying the concept of the pig . . . Mine was always the regular pig with TMQ, the later ones say 'Genuine TMQ Disc' on them.[3]

Dub was determined to maintain the meaning of the label's name – a trademark of quality. Ken's Smokin' Pig titles rarely came on coloured vinyl, but it was really Stout's cover art that now set the TMQ titles apart. *Winter Tour*, though only a so-so recording, had sold well. With the new threat of the Smokin' Pig, Stout's continued employment was assured.

The pig logo established by Dub became a perennial motif on Stout's covers. In some of his crueller parodies it was the mainstay – witness Jerry Garcia on the cover of *The Dead at the Hollywood Palladium* or, most unseemly of all, John Lennon and Yoko Ono on The Beatles' *Get Back* 2 (a pastiche of 'Two Virgins' so

grotesque that Stout even apologized to Yoko on the cover). But Stout's finest covers were also usually tributes to the styles of comic art that had inspired him to become an artist. Thus the Deep Purple *Hard Road* cover was based on a famous twenties *Saturday Evening Post* cover by J. C. Leinedecke. The *Spicy Beatles Songs* cover, in which an extremely hog-like Ringo bemoans his resemblance to a pig, was taken from a EC horror comic, as was perhaps Stout's true masterpiece, *Tales from The Who*. Stout was also not afraid to make a point with his artwork. His cover to Hendrix's *Good Karma* incorporated Robert Christgau's review of Jimi at the Monterey Pop Festival, where he dismissed Hendrix as an 'Uncle Tom' upstart.

However, it was perhaps his Stones covers that gave him the greatest scope for satire, and are best remembered by bootleg collectors. Kicking off with *Winter Tour*, 1973 was a good year for TMQ Stones titles. The gems extracted from English 'Alan' finally came out in June. *Bright Lights, Big City* featured another of Stout's finest covers. Jagger is portrayed as a country hick in dungarees, straw in mouth, with two affectionate pigs nuzzling up to him. He is being plied with offers of killer weed, demon alcohol, cigarettes and even the pleasures of some very Rubenesque flesh.

Bright Lights, Big City, the most important Stones bootleg since *LiveR Than You'll Ever Be*, comprised two essential early Stones studio tapes and part of a recent tour rehearsal. First up were the IBC demos from March 1963 – their very own Decca audition tape. A comparison of these white r&b classics with The Beatles' own Decca audition tape, recorded the previous year, shows just why Decca turned down The Beatles but signed up The Stones. It was supplemented by five outtakes from The Stones' sessions at Chicago's fabled Chess Studios in June 1964.

William Stout: They put out a good product. I was proud that they believed in their name, 'Trade Mark of Quality'. They always used virgin vinyl. I had purchased other stuff and I had noticed that TMQ was head and shoulders above the other bootleggers . . . I kept pushing them to do higher

and higher quality production . . . Eventually I got them to print the black and white illustrations on the covers.[4]

Appropriately, the first TMQ bootleg to be graced with a printed sleeve was yet another Stones title. *Welcome to New York* was an eight-song soundboard tape from their Madison Square Gardens stint the previous summer, stolen by some enterprising kid from the mixing desk after the show. Dub had been offered a first generation copy of the tape. For *Welcome to New York*, Stout excelled himself.

William Stout: [*Welcome to New York*] was done in a Ralph Steadman style . . . I just like the way [it] came out, all the caricatures . . . The Stones had something going for them that made almost every cover I did for them one of my favourites. They had a very strong clear-cut image, they had defined themselves as the badboys of rock & roll, and that gave me a lot of material to draw from.[5]

Once again, though, Dub was having to improve the presentation of TMQ titles – and therefore the attendant costs – to keep one step ahead of Ken's Smokin' Pig. Ken was a quick learner, and after Dub 'discovered' Stout, he was determined not to be outdone. When Stout produced an atypical Townshend-as-pig cover for TMQ's *Fillmore East*, a superb 1968 soundboard featuring The 'Oo in full flight in front of a rather quizzical New York audience, Ken managed to out-Stout Stout. The cover of the Smokin' Pig *Fillmore East* was a deliberate parody of Stout's *Winter Tour* (and so in turn Crumb's *Cheap Thrills*), with each song represented as a cartoon caricature, something Stout had made a trademark (he also used this approach, with rib-tickling results, on Neil Young's *BBC Broadcast*).

By the end of 1973, Ken was also beginning to ferret out some 'original' titles to put under his Smokin' Pig banner, bringing further confusion for the punters. While he did not abandon copying Dub's titles, the winter of 1973–4 saw TMQ2 issue a handful of significant titles in their own right: Van Morrison's *A*

Spawn of the Dublin Pubs (which pre-empted Van the Man's own live double-set, *It's Too Late to Stop Now*, by a few months), The Rolling Stones' *Get Your Leeds Lungs Out* (from a 1971 BBC broadcast) and Dylan's *Bridgett's Album*, with which Ken signed off his Smokin' Pig label. A fare-thee-well on the Dylan cover announced, 'This record is the last from your friends here at trademark of quality ... we are hanging up our cigar and putting our phonograph needles out to pasture.'

Yet Ken still kept existing TMQ titles in print. He was not yet about to hang up his own rock & roll shoes. Instead he had formed an alliance with another Dub-like figure, keen to provide artistic touches, and edit and EQ 'source' material. The gentleman in question, David, was promptly christened Dr 'Telly' Phone. The record company that the 'doctor', Ken and an anonymous financier came up with was The Amazing Kornyphone Record Label (TAKRL). Their first few titles included a 'board' tape of The Beatles' famous 1966 Tokyo show and Bowie's most recent flirtation with a lad insane, *The 1980 Floor Show*. In a desperate attempt to 'do unto others', Dub now formed his own subsidiary label, the sole purpose of which was to copy Ken's bootlegs:

William Stout: [TMQ] were getting really pissed off that their records were getting copied by the other bootleggers, so they picked some of the best bootlegs put out by the other companies and copied them themselves, and put them out on the Pig's Eye label.[6]

At the same time, Dub made the ultimate concession to professional presentation: producing full-colour covers for certain new releases. With Stout's increasingly imaginative artwork and the need to once again up the stakes in his game with Ken, Dub was playing his last wild card.

William Stout: I think the first one I did in colour was The Yardbirds' *Golden Eggs*, so when I handed it to them they said, 'Oh, it's in colour ...' and I said, 'Well you can print it in black and white if you want.' I think the

first edition was in black and white, but the more they thought about it the more they felt 'Boy, this would be great if we did it in colour' ... We also did a generic cover, which was an idea I don't think worked so well. Basically it was one cover for records that they didn't want to invest printing new covers for, because there probably wouldn't be enough sales.[7]

The generic cover was actually one of Stout's best. Given over entirely to the pigs, this 'genuine collector's item' had Stout's smoking pig making a reappearance scratching his head while proclaiming, 'I jes' wanna letcha know dat dis here is a GENUINE COLLECTOR'S ITEM ... an' a pretty good record to boot.' The idea was largely lost on the punters, who preferred Ken's cut-price copies with their tacky xeroxed inserts.

Colour covers may have made TMQ's product highly prized by serious collectors, delighted as much by the form as the substance, but Ken was not unduly worried about such aesthetic concerns. Smokin' Pig stuck doggedly with paper inserts. Despite Ken's superior understanding of the economics of bootlegging, Dub and Ken maintained their amicable rivalry, even producing some titles together:

Dub: We'd master something and share the metal stampers. There was one plant here in LA that we all used and sometimes we'd use each other's metal parts and have different covers ... [but] as time went on, there were so many people [who'd] got involved and the price just kept on dropping, 'cause these people would copy our copies of things and then they would undercut us 50¢ a record and it got really crazy. After a while we weren't making that much money.[8]

The decision to 'go colour' – a last attempt to outstrip the competition and establish Trade Mark of Quality once more as king of Boot Hill – was the ultimate affront to official record companies. Here was a label producing bootlegs with full-colour covers, printed labels, track separation and professional sound quality. TMQ's first double album in their deluxe series, *Who's Zoo*, also used a format Dub had previously avoided. It collected all the various non-album b-sides and EP tracks by The Who in one definitive collection.*

For once, Stout was not simply involved in the cover design, but helped to collect and compile the various cuts. The cover was once again a Stout classic, with the Who members this time mutating into zoo inmates.

William Stout: As a big Who collector I made a list of all the stuff I would like to see on *Who's Zoo*. The stuff that was issued after '72 they wouldn't touch. They were very afraid that [that] was a definite violation. I showed that cover to a writer, record producer, label president and prominent collector and he flipped out. He thought that was just the greatest thing.[9]

TMQ continued the 'colour' experiment with two Yardbirds albums, also compilations of assorted rare and unreleased material (collected together in a form more palatable than most of The Yardbirds' official releases). By the winter of 1973–4, the importance of The Yardbirds was being belatedly recognized in collector circles. TMQ's *Golden Eggs* and *More Golden Eggs* were intended to give them their full due. If *Golden Eggs* was a fun collection, it was *More Golden Eggs* that was TMQ's great coup. Aside from another of Stout's finest satirical covers, the album came complete with an insert containing an interview with Yardbirds lead singer Keith Relf, discussing the various recordings on *More Golden Eggs* – the ultimate endorsement of a bootleg by a rock artist.

William Stout: I was really proud of The Yardbirds' *More Golden Eggs* because that was the first semi-legitimate bootleg. Keith Relf of The Yardbirds was living nearby. He was just forming Armageddon, and he needed rent money. So we paid his rent that month and in return we were able to interview him and play him the bootleg record album and he commented on each of the songs as they were being played . . . We printed the interview on the cover and as a four- or five-page insert as well, and

---

* Polydor would attempt a similar exercise in the eighties with their *Rarities Volumes 1 & 2*, though they could not secure the rights to the Fontana and Brunswick recordings.

got his signature on the cover too ... *More Golden Eggs* was done in the style of Arthur Rackham, the English children's book illustrator, a big influence on me at the time ... The idea behind the cover is that the weasel is a caricature of Mickey Most killing off the goose that laid the golden eggs. I was never happy with his production of The Yardbirds, and his decisions for them, forcing them to record certain 'pop' material, I thought were detrimental to the group [and] aided their demise.[10]

The other deluxe release that winter was even more impressive – a previously unknown radio station acetate of a 1966 Dylan acoustic performance from Melbourne, Australia. Dylan had been so stoned that eye-witnesses had expressed surprise that he didn't just bellyflop into the orchestra pit mid-gig. Stout again excelled with a cover of Dylan housed in a kangaroo's pouch and his own curious subtitle, 'The Enigmatic Story of a Boy and His Dog' (Stout often liked to give TMQ bootlegs new subtitles, much to Dub's annoyance). It seemed like TMQ was just hitting its stride. Despite the eventual passage of the McClellan Bill at the end of 1971, the FBI had not yet displayed any real interest in the activities of small-time bootleggers. But TMQ was far and away the most visible target, and their extensive catalogue and deluxe packaging implied that they were a serious threat to official record-company product.

Dub: Someone gave the FBI my real name. Up to that point everyone I knew in the business had been very discreet about who I really was. My father has my real name as his nickname, and my father was in business with me at that time. He was running the day-to-day operations, I was doing most of the producing, overseeing the manufacture and doing the studio work and all. He was actually doing all the dealing with the customers, 'cos we were basically a wholesaler ... so I decided it was time to get out at that point. It wasn't fun anymore ... We weren't making that much money. My father wasn't convinced, he said we should keep going. I knew they were going to go to the pressing plant, so the big danger was not the metal parts but the covers, that's what you've got to worry about, and the labels. So I was cleaning out the plant, taking out all of our covers and labels, and while I was there the phone rang and it was my father and he said, 'The FBI

was just here and they were asking about you.' He has the same name and they said, 'We know you're behind the whole thing. We know that you're behind all the bootlegs,' and he said, 'I'm a retired Post Office employee,' which was true ... We had a real good attorney at that time and we told him what had happened, and he told me to bring my father out to his office and he'd talk to them ... He said, 'One of my cousins works for the FBI, so I had him run your name through the computer, and nothing turned up.' So he called the agent and said, 'I hear you've been harassing my client who is so and so ...' and the agent said 'Well, we know that your client is behind all the bootlegs,' and my lawyer said, 'Well, are you prepared to charge him? ... If you're going to charge my client, we'll bring him over to your office right now, otherwise you leave my client alone,' and that was the last we heard about it. But we were always very discreet. In the beginning we did some kind of anonymous radio interviews and we did an anonymous interview for *Rolling Stone*, but we were approached by *Esquire* and *Newsweek*, and I wouldn't do it because I didn't want my ego to get involved in it. There was one bootlegger who did that and he was out of business in two weeks.[11]

Dub's understandable fear of the Big Bust had led him to destroy all the covers and labels he had found at the pressing plant, the bulk of which were for TMQ's latest release – *Tales from The Who*.

William Stout: TMQ had just put out what I thought was a real landmark bootleg, it was the first quadrophonic bootleg, which I thought was pretty amazing. I found that hilarious that bootlegs had become so sophisticated ... I immediately distributed it to all my friends 'cos I was so proud of it, and I went back to get more and there were no more. The FBI was on their trail and in a fit of paranoia they had destroyed all the albums. Only 120 of those got released. So I had to go back to Record Paradise and buy all the ones they had in the racks.[12]

Tales from The Who was a fitting end to TMQ's reign as King Hog. The cover, a pastiche of another famous EC comicbook cover, *Tales from the Crypt*, had a particularly gruesome monster stuttering lines from Who songs. It showed not only how sophisticated TMQ's records had become – *Tales* was a radio broadcast

from a Long Beach show on the 'Quadrophenia' tour, coded so it could be replayed in quadrophonic – but how Stout's covers more than matched the content. *Tales from The Who* was the formal end of TMQ. Their eighty-nine single albums, twenty-one doubles and one triple set probably contained more essential rock music than any official record label's output during the same period (1969–74). Nor did Dub entirely abandon his bootlegging ways (or the use of Stout's services). He just moved a little further away from the flame.

Dub: I have always liked film music, and [the rock bootleg business] steadily went downhill after *LiveR* on. The only way to keep it going was to come out with new stuff all the time and you'd sell a little of this and a little of that. That big surge at the beginning never came again, and there were so many people involved, supply and demand, prices kept dropping. We were wholesaling the things for a buck and a quarter towards the end.[13]

William Stout: They had another bootleg record company that put out soundtracks, The Debt Records . . . It turned out that in many ways there was a bigger market for bootleg soundtracks than there was for rock'n'roll. There are many more soundtrack collectors than there are rock'n'roll collectors, and they're much more rabid about their collecting. It's an international thing. There are guys who have to have every soundtrack ever produced.[14]

Soundtrack bootlegs were low on the record-industry 'hit' list, and Dub's move sideways was an admission that things had tightened up considerably since the early seventies. Most importantly, the record industry had finally secured the change they wanted in copyright law. The passage of the McClellan Bill in 1972 meant that the FBI, not the state police, might be knocking at the door.

Gaining Federal protection against copyright abuse had been top of the RIAA agenda since its formation in 1951 but the early seventies – with the advent of pre-recorded cassettes, whose very 'copyability' made them extremely prone to piracy and counterfeiting – required a new determination to defeat this form of modern piracy.

The record industry had been forced to rely on 'unfair competition' suits in state courts for too long. However, an injunction in one state did not bar a pirate from renewing operations in another. If the record industry had had some success in lobbying state legislators to pass penal legislation prohibiting unauthorized reproduction and sale of illicit recordings, particularly in New York, which remained a centre for counterfeiting, their priority was the passage of the McClellan Bill.

In November 1970 representatives from the National Association of Record Merchandisers and executive representatives from the major record companies had met at the Americana Hotel in New York to discuss the urgent need for Federal anti-piracy legislation. After many objections, and stalling tactics from opponents, the McClellan Bill was finally introduced into the Senate on 26 January 1971, was passed on 15 October 1971, and became law with effect from 15 February 1972. The Bill amended title 17 of the United States Code 'to provide for the creation of a limited copyright in sound recordings for the purpose of protecting against unauthorized duplication and piracy of sound recordings, and for other purposes'. The copyright was limited because, although the Bill gave both producers (i.e. manufacturers) and 'authors' the right to stop piracy of their works, it did not give them the right to collect performance royalties on unreleased recordings (this was given only to copyrighted music).

The McClellan Bill was very much an 'anti-piracy' measure. It had only a limited relevance to the bootleggers, and there were two very important exemptions:

(i) Unpublished (i.e. unsold, undistributed) sound recordings. These should not be sent to the Copyright Office, though they may be protected by the common law against unauthorized use, without any Copyright Office action.
(ii) Sound recordings fixed (i.e. first produced on a master then reproduced in copies for sale and/or public distribution) before 15 February 1972.

Nothing in Public Law 92-140 prohibited home recording from

broadcasts, tapes or records as long as the recording was used privately, with no intention of capitalizing commercially on it. Indeed 'performance piracy' and 'personal piracy' were not even specifically addressed in the Amendment. The definition of 'publication', though considerably expanded from the 1909 Act, did not include public performance, however large the audience may be.

Nevertheless, since many bootlegs were hybrid pirate/bootlegs and most bootlegs comprised published songs, the industry could now expect a degree of FBI cooperation in their efforts to stamp out bootlegging. Public Law 92-140 was also only a stepping stone to a complete revision of the copyright law, scheduled to be in place by 31 December 1974. Though the new copyright law would be subject to its own series of delays, US laws now accorded with obligations under the Geneva Convention, which was to be ratified by the US in March 1974.

New legal resources and the demise of Trade Mark of Quality may have given the record industry cause to think that it had at long last gained the upper hand in its struggle with the rock bootleg fraternity. For the bootleggers it simply meant that there was a vacuum they were only too keen to fill. TMQ1 and TMQ2 had already spawned several less obvious targets. From this point on bootleggers in general, and Ken in particular, would be considerably more coy about who was responsible for what. The Smokin' Pig had served its purpose.

6 Going Underground

'Ya know, I really would like to know what's goin' on,' I said as I put the gun away. 'What do you want to know?' asked the Beard, running his hand back and forth over one of his new albums. 'Well, for one thing, who the fuck is Linda and why does the Wiz wanna take her surfin'?' 'It's not important. All that matters is what's in the wallet,' the Beard replied. I could see this was gonna be a long night. 'And what's this shit about your covers and albums being better than his? I mean, you don't even put labels on yer records,' I fired, knowing I had him with that one. 'What are labels?' he asked. Jesus, I mean what are you gonna do with a guy like that? 'You know, they're made out of paper and . . .' 'The only thing that's made out of paper that I care about is money, so fuck labels,' he shouted as he stalked off, still running his hand all over the album. 'Yeah, but what about the people who buy your records – don't you think they'd like labels?' I screamed to him. 'Fuck them, too!' he fired back at me as the album he was fondling moaned and groaned with pleasure. What a fuckin' nightmare this is turnin' out to be, I thought. It's nuttier than a squirrel's dinner.[1]

Though Dub's output in the five years separating *Great White Wonder* from *Tales from The Who* had outstripped any of his competitors, TMQ's catalogue pales alongside what Ken and co. unleashed between 1974 and the end of 1976. A hundred-plus titles from the flagship label, The Amazing Kornyphone Record Label, were supplemented by represses of Smokin' Pig titles, thirty-two titles on TKRWM (The Kornyphone Records for the Working Man), a dozen double-albums on Singer's Original Double Disks (SODD) and sixteen releases on Highway High Fi Collector's Edition Records (HHCER) (which regularly appeared with TAKRL or Smokin' Pig labels – just to add to the confusion).

Ken had always been the hardest-working man in this particular niche of showbusiness, and Dr 'Telly' Phone was now providing him with some much-needed technical input. With the demise of

Trade Mark of Quality, Ken had little competition. TAKRL stuck to xeroxed inserts and black vinyl – the oil crisis making supplies of coloured vinyl increasingly problematic – meaning optimum profits. Yet despite their low-budget presentation, the sound quality of TAKRL product was often comparable to TMQ's. They had been greatly aided by the advent, in the summer of 1972, of the *King Biscuit Flower Hour*. *King Biscuit* was a regular, syndicated radio show that broadcast a full hour of live rock music every week. Their first broadcast featured three songs by Bruce Springsteen, making his Max's Kansas City debut.

Just when the record labels seemed to have secured a copyright law that might stamp out 'performance piracy', a new tightness in radio formats, rotating AM playlists and an inflexible AOR bias on FM stations meant that it was becoming increasingly difficult to 'break' new acts on radio. For many 'album' artists, FM live broadcasts were the only way to get sustained exposure on national airwaves. The importance of these broadcasts in 'spreading the word' cannot be underestimated. Bruce Springsteen's meteoric rise in the crucial years (1974–5) was in large measure due to evidence of his power in performance given by a series of landmark live broadcasts. Television was also now more inclined to devote airtime to rock music, *Don Kirschner's Rock Concert* attracting everyone from The New York Dolls to The Rolling Stones.

The formation of TAKRL also marked a shift in the scope of artists who could be bootlegged. Dub had kept to the 'old guard'. Though Ken's love of Dylan meant that he monopolized American Dylan bootleg product throughout the seventies, his partners were much more willing to test 'new' markets. TAKRL was responsible for some of the most unusual artists to be bootlegged in the vinyl era – everybody from Mott the Hoople, Procul Harum and The Bonzo Dog (Doo Dah) Band to Gentle Giant, Sparks and a particularly inspired compendium of quips from Marx Brothers' movies, Groucho Marx's *I Never Kissed an Ugly Woman*. Though TAKRL's 'experiments' were not always successful, aesthetically or commercially, only they were issuing something other than standard bootleg fodder, even coming up with a handful of superb

radio broadcasts of two of America's best new live acts – the Patti Smith Group and Little Feat.

In both cases, the artists' pro-bootleg stance was something of a fillip. Little Feat frontman Lowell George once told British journalist Roy Carr that he had been responsible for mixing at least two Little Feat bootlegs, arguing that, 'if anyone is going to buy a Little Feat bootleg, then at least I want to make certain the quality is good. Anyone who buys a bootleg is going to be the loyal fan who will buy every one of our official records.'[2] The two bootlegs in question – *Electric Lycanthrope* and *Aurora Backseat* – were TAKRL's first two Little Feat titles, and they are both superb examples of Little Feat's not inconsiderable achievements as a live band.

Though Patti Smith didn't go as far as mixing her early bootlegs, she certainly encouraged them, sometimes introducing 'Redondo Beach' as a song from *Teenage Perversity*, the first Patti Smith bootleg. *Teenage Perversity* was from a landmark 'Horses' show at the Roxy, LA, in January 1976, broadcast locally across the airwaves (as were shows in Washington, New York and Cleveland on the same tour).

Teenage Perversity and Ships in the Night, to give it its full title, was one of the first releases on Ze Anonym Plattenspieler [ZAP], a 1976 addition to Ken's roster of labels. By this point, TAKRL could not contain all the product Ken wanted on the streets. HHCER, TKFWM and SODD all took on some of the burden, soon followed by Flat Records (which carried the classic by-line, 'The only good record is a flat record'), but it was still not enough.

SODD (Singer's Original Double Disks) was Ken's usual medium for double-sets (still a relative rarity in the mid seventies). Though SODD only issued a dozen titles, they produced some of the Kornyphone Family's finest artifacts. Their second release – *You Can Trust Your Car to the Man With the Star* – was a radio broadcast of Bruce Springsteen and the E Street Band recorded at the Main Point, on the outskirts of Philadelphia, in February 1975, capturing in FM quality the six-month period when the E Street

Band had electric violinist Suki Lahav adding her delicate timbre to their sound. With prototype performances of 'Wings for Wheels' (soon to become 'Thunder Road') and 'She's the One' (incorporating parts of 'Backstreets'), and chestnuts like 'Incident on 57th Street' and Dylan's 'I Want You', it may well be Springsteen's greatest extant performance. But this broadcast had only been aired on local Philadelphia radio. It took the SODD set, one of a handful of Springsteen bootlegs at the time, to spread the word to all and sundry.

With such an outpouring of product, and the distrust of his fellow bootleggers, Ken was an obvious target for the powers-that-be. But while the McClellan Bill was undergoing its metamorphosis into the 1976 Copyright Act, the FBI remained largely unconcerned by Ken's activities. It was the state police who presented the greatest threat, though ignorance generally kept them looking the wrong way. However, a simple twist of fate nearly delivered him into the hands of the local Californian authorities.

'Eric Bristow': In the seventies Ken had a warehouse in Westminster, California. It was on an industrial estate, and he was going in and out with his truck full of records, with his long hair. One of his neighbours, who was a real busybody, figured 'How could this guy with long hair possibly have enough money to rent this big warehouse? He must be a criminal or a thief.' So he phoned the police and said, 'There's a guy operating a warehouse next to me who's a troublemaker and I think he's a thief. I think he's dealing in stolen goods.' The police came down and watched the place for a while, and determined that maybe there was something weird going on, got a warrant, and came back. Ken wasn't there but his wife and kids were inside, stuffing and shrinkwrapping records. The place was stuffed to the rafters with records. They knocked on the door and his wife came to the door and they said, 'We have a warrant to search this place. Is [your husband] in?' and she said 'No.' 'Well, can we come in?' 'No.' 'But we have a warrant.' 'You'll have to wait until my husband gets back,' and she closes the door on them. Fortunately they didn't do anything, they just waited. So Ken drives up and there's all these Blue and Whites parked outside. He gets out of the car and says, 'What can I do for you?' 'We've got this warrant to search this place for stolen property,' so he says, 'OK,' rolls up the big roll-up doors and in they go. They're in there not thirty seconds before one of the cops recognizes a Bob Dylan bootleg and he turns round to the old nosey bastard from next door who's walked up there, and says, 'You stupid old bastard! This isn't stolen property, these are bootlegs, for Christ's sake!' So the cop turns to Ken and says, 'I hope you understand that we're going to have to take this stuff away,' and Ken goes, 'Oh, for fuck's sake, not again. You guys, you come in here once every six months, you take all my stuff away, I end up fighting you in court for two weeks, I get it all back again. I'm sick of it!' The cop goes, 'Really?' 'This is the fifth time.' So the guy goes, 'Well, we'll take some samples and talk to the sergeant about it.' They took one of everything, and they . . . took all these photographs and off they go. The second they turn out of the street, Ken goes, 'Get the truck!' Takes the truck in the warehouse, fills the thing, and then in and out, in and out all night long, emptying the place. The next day, the police come back, they've got a warrant to seize the stuff and arrest him and everything's gone and he's not there. They go over to his house and [he has gone to] his lawyer. 'I'm in deep shit this time. The police came in and took photos of the warehouse. Help!' 'You're telling me you talked them into leaving and they didn't take the goods?' 'Yes.' 'And they didn't arrest you?' 'Yes.' He picks up the phone, and he calls the chief of police in Westminster. He says, 'I represent Ken . . . whose records you are having a problem with in your town.' 'Yeah? Where is he? We got a warrant to arrest him.' 'You don't really want to do that do you?' 'Too right we do! We've got him dead to rights this time, a bunch of photographs, a bunch of product . . .' and [his lawyer] goes, 'Let me tell you something. You had him by the balls, you had the goods, you had him dead to rights. And you let him get away. Not only did you let him get away, you let him get away with all the stuff, too. You're gonna look like the biggest bunch of idiots in America if this gets public. If you want to go to trial on this I'm going to make you and the PD look like the stupidest bunch of fools this side of the Rockies.' The next day they dropped the charges.[3]

Ken's multiple labels were not simply a ruse to confuse the authorities. Dr 'Telly' Phone was not entirely convinced about the sheer scale of product being churned out. The doctor and Ken did

BOB DYLAN
ARE YOU NOW OR HAVE YOU EVER BEEN?
(HIS GOTHAM INGRESS)

not always see eye to eye about what exactly they should be putting out. Indeed it was a disagreement over content that resulted in the formation of The Kornyphone Records for the Working Man.

'Eric Bristow': That was a direct result of Dave having no sympathy for doing things that he didn't like, so he just flat out refused to do them.[4]

David was not enamoured by Paul McCartney in any post-Beatles incarnation, nor by new American pretenders claiming hard-rock status like Aerosmith, Bachman Turner Overdrive or Lynyrd Skynyrd. If SODD was a bona-fide TAKRL spin-off, and HHCER was phased out as TAKRL went into overdrive, ZAP and Flat – both started in 1976 – were clearly intended by Ken as alternatives to TAKRL. The tension between Ken's workaholic methods (and occasional dubious quality standards) and someone like the Doctor, committed to 'approving' material for 'his' label, was bound to lead to a permanent rift. Sure enough, The Amazing Kornyphone Record Label officially ceased to function on Independence Day, 1976 (though its last 'official' release was not recorded – from the television – until September 1976). In a letter to *Hot Wacks Quarterly* in 1980, the circumstances of TAKRL's formal closure were related by 'Art Gnuvo':

It was on this day that the 'death' of Dr Terrence H. 'Telly' Phone was carefully arranged by a host of unseen persons that constantly hovered above his drawing table. As of that date, with the Doctor gone, Art Gnuvo (your humble narrator) and Deek Kibard made the conscious decision to bury The Amazing Kornyphone Record Label in proper fashion, as per the Doctor's exacting wishes. Although a few projects completed before the Doctor's death showed up after the Dark Day, all other work was regretfully, but happily, abandoned. The Doctor's wish for consistency in his absence was as important as the consistency that existed when he puffed so brave and black. However, this is not to say that all records bearing a Kornyphone imprint or logo disappeared as well ... The Amazing Kornyphone Record Label had two distinct and separate factions involved with, on one hand, the creation of the projects and, on the other hand, the dissemination of the finished materials to whatever marketplace would welcome them. More often than not, and by plan, one hand never knew what the other was doing. When Art and Deek and friends retired the creative-input side of TAKRL, the marketing/output staff continued right on, as was their choice and privilege. These marketing people, for want of a better term, kept Kornyfone going for quite a time longer, concocting all sorts of bastard children attributed to the Doctor's Vinyl Ghost. The most curious plastic beasts appeared as a result of their continuance, a few absolutely worth the effort, but most not.[5]

As a typical tip of the hat, Ken gave the final TAKRL album the same name as Smokin' Pig's farewell release, *Bridgett's Album*, and again it was a Dylan album, this time from his 1976 'Hard Rain' TV Special. In keeping with TAKRL's penchant for cryptic headings it was subtitled 'A Vinyl Headstone Almost in Place'. The farewell message this time was rather oblique:

Years ago on Fairfax it began with the blank one ... it progressed, even disguised it seems, to various plateaus in various states of dark reality around the hemisphere – years later it seemed that other pressing (no fun) matters persisted – once it was scruples, now it becomes throats – none deep enough but all hollow inside.[6]

David had had enough, not only of Ken's unrelenting demand for product, but also of the hit-and-miss nature of TAKRL's operations, the rebootlegging by other labels, and the imminent drafting of a new copyright bill destined to categorize bootlegs as pirate product. Ken was not so easily dissuaded – and there was still a distinct lack of competition from other Californian bootleg merchants. Indeed, as Art Gnuvo's letter implied, Ken continued to market TAKRL titles. However, he would never again find such a willing and resourceful partner as 'Dr Kornyphone'. Ken's post-TAKRL vinyl products were destined to largely re-tread the territory marked out by his first two cohorts.

One pretender to the bootleggers' throne was a new incarnation of Trade Mark of Quality. In 1976 some six albums, two of them doubles, were issued in the TMQ Deluxe 1976 Series. If the

quality of these releases – uniformly mediocre – belied the illustrious name, these new TMQs were indeed the genuine article. Dub had decided to dip his fingers into the mire again and, for the two final releases, even brought William Stout out of retirement to produce a lovely Kellogg's Corn Flakes pastiche for a Jeff Beck album, *Beckfast* (an idea later reused on *Michigan Nuggets*), as well as a graphic based around the HMV dog for Paul McCartney's *Great Dane*. But Dub's day was done and these releases marked a curious epilogue to his rock bootleg activities, not the flowering of a 'new', Frankenstein TMQ. Dub no longer had the access to source material that had given TMQ its edge. TMQ3 was a half-hearted endeavour at best, and the cowboys (and cowgirls) had already moved in:

Bev [a bootlegger]: Another girl and myself had seen The Stones live in '75 and [we] wanted to make a record from the tape of the show we were at . . . So we went to a recording studio and got some prices for having records made. With our tax returns coming we figured we had enough to do an EP. We went to the studio the next day with a cassette of The Stones live. We told the guy at the studio we were in a group and had a tape we wanted made into a single. He said, 'Fine, follow me.' We went into a playback booth. He asked us what the name of our group was and we said Nanker Phelge's Drag Boys. Well he thought it was funny, and the next thing I knew he put the tape into a deck and played it. We hadn't thought he'd play it. As soon as the tape started he began to smile. We both turned pale. He looked at us and said, 'Sounds like The Stones to me.' 'Well, yes,' we said and explained our plan. He took us into his office and told us he used to do Dylan bootleg albums a few years before and showed us one with a white cover and labels.[7]

The tightening of the copyright laws was clearly not dissuading nonchalant pressing-plant operatives. And bootleggers like Bev were more concerned with presentation than musical quality. Hers was a strictly small-time operation, specializing in EPs (cheaper and easier to manufacture), with covers that showed a certain flair for comic art in the Stout tradition. Bev was also part of a new breed of late-seventies bootleggers, unconcerned with sourcing the best-possible tapes.

Bev: All I do when I'm looking for a tape is go to a person selling tapes and buy the ones that are the best quality if they haven't already been made into a record by someone else. People are always selling tapes in record magazines' classified ads.[8]

The 'old guard' copycat bootleggers had pretty much fallen by the wayside by the time TAKRL closed down shop. Berkeley, founded in 1973, had shut down by 1975. Contraband had long ago run out of reasons to compete with TAKRL's increasingly impressive catalogue and distribution. Labels like Berkeley and Contraband were an anachronism. Though they were by no means the last copycat labels, mid-seventies bootleg buyers had wised up to outfits like Berkeley or Contraband.

K & S Records in Canada and, to a lesser extent, Wizardo in California continued this shoddy tradition. K & S was always destined to remain a small-time operation selling primarily to a market (Canada) where discrimination was not always an option. John Wizardo, on the other hand, might be considered Ken's first serious rival since his tussle with Dub. Though he did not adopt his moniker until 1975, John had been a fanatical collector of bootlegs from the outset.

'Eric Bristow': [John] was obsessed with cataloguing his collection, and up until [the] early or mid seventies he had made a point of getting one of every bootleg in existence. He had all of 'em, European, Japanese . . . And every single record was catalogued, categorized in this notebook of his.

After his belated entry into manufacturing, Wizardo did not waste time producing discographies. He was too busy producing the 'stuff' to fill them up with. Wizardo knew enough to mix'n'-match his sources, sprinkling his titles with a smattering of original, high-quality releases. For sheer volume of product, Wizardo was matched only by TAKRL. He was also smart enough to carve his own niche out of the ever-expanding roster of 'bootlegable'

artists, rather than competing with Ken's determined monopoly of good time English pop-rock and Californian blues-rock. The Beatles were Wizardo's great love and the one area where he could more than compete with Ken when it came to accessing material. He also selected such TAKRL no-nos as Elvis Presley, Curved Air, Harry Nilsson, Alice Cooper, Lou Reed, Captain Beefheart, Roxy Music, Jan and Dean, Kiss and Rick Derringer. Clearly the parameters of who could be bootlegged were becoming increasingly elastic.

John Wizardo, who would later breach the dam with some of the first Beatles bootleg CDs, was responsible for some forty-nine Beatle-related titles on his Wizardo label, a flood of titles unprecedented for one artist – even Dylan. Though The Beatles had long been the artists who shifted the largest numbers of a bootleg title, by the time Wizardo made his hobnailed entry into the arena they were lagging a long way behind The Stones and Dylan in sheer number of bootleg albums available. The most notable Beatles release to emerge in the early seventies had been *Sweet Apple Trax*, a one-off project by a couple of renegade Beatles nuts who had been offered some tapes from the January 1969 Twickenham sessions. The album included such long-rumoured Beatles tunes as 'The Commonwealth Song' and 'Suzy Parker'.

Dub and Ken, who had dominated the first era of rock bootlegs, did not lump The Beatles into the same category as Presley (whom they studiously avoided bootlegging). Though they occasionally snuck out Beatles fodder, they preferred the more cocksure, bam-a-lam approach of The Stones. The bulk of Beatles titles in the TAKRL family were uninspired, usually 'reissues' put out on their 'budget' label, TKRWM. These included seven hastily compiled collections of Beatles allsorts, *The Very Best of the Beatles Rarest Vols. 1–7*.

While John Wizardo expanded a segment of the market not well catered for, another new kid on the block discovered an entirely new addition to the premier league of bootlegging. Schoolteacher Lou Cohan's hero was American rock's Great White Hope – The Boss himself, Bruce Springsteen. Springsteen – with just two albums under his belt and a third one in the works for over a year – was barely known outside certain fanatical enclaves in New York, New Jersey, Philadelphia and Cleveland. But in the eighteen months that separated *The Wild, the Innocent and the E Street Shuffle* from *Born to Run* he had found convert after convert by fusing together the pazzazz of a soul revue, a dose of Celtic fire and a shot of British rhythm & blues. In particular a handful of jaded rock critics, looking more to affirm their past than embrace the future, welcomed Brooce like the brother they lost at Kaisan. It took a bootlegger to provide the audio evidence to justify the fuss.

Lou Cohan: I was a very early Bruce Springsteen fan and I would go up to these people selling these records at the swap-meet. They did not have very many titles . . . and I kept asking for Bruce Springsteen bootlegs. At that time, late '74/early '75, nobody on the West Coast had heard of Bruce unless they worked at Columbia Records, so they would say, 'Lou Stringsteen? Who is this guy?' And I kept bugging them – 'Bruce Springsteen bootlegs, Bruce Springsteen bootlegs.' So finally this girl who later turned out to be Vicki Vinyl, said, 'Why don't you make your own Bruce Springsteen bootleg?' So I said, 'OK, how?' She told me how and it seemed pretty simple to me, just get a tape, walk into a pressing plant, and nine days later walk out with about three hundred albums to sell. It would cost you about $300 for the first 300 albums and then every one after that was about 50c . . . I couldn't believe it was that simple! . . . A friend of mine in Philadelphia had taped a Bruce Springsteen show from the radio, broadcast by Ed Sciaky of WMMR, and he had part of [a radio broadcast of] 'Thunder Road' – he didn't have the complete song – so we spliced in the album version for the first twenty or thirty seconds or so, and we put out the first Bruce Springsteen bootleg, *The Jersey Devil* . . . Then I put out *There Ain't Nobody Here from Billboard Tonite*, then I guess another Springsteen bootleg came out on the East Coast, *Live at the Bottom Line*, the one in the black and white cover.[10]

The Jersey Devil was actually a very early (April 1973) Springsteen and the E Street Band show. It included the regular '73 showstopper, 'Thundercrack', and several other songs lost in the shuffle for *The Wild, the Innocent*. In the six months following the

August 1975 release of *Born to Run*, all three Springsteen bootlegs were selling. Of course, Springsteen was doing his darnedest to help the bootleggers out by airing a couple of ninety-minute radio broadcasts. The shows, from New York's Bottom Line in July 1975 and LA's Roxy in October, were intended to capitalize on the media buzz Springsteen was creating. This, though, was clearly one instance where bootlegs were helping to establish an artist, rather than riding on the back of his success.

Yet CBS, along with Springsteen, took the unprecedented step of busting a New York retailer for selling *Live at the Bottom Line*, hoping to dissuade shops from taking live Springsteen product. Of course having stopped one dealer, Columbia still had the problem of pursuing the manufacturer and distributor/s. How far they were from surmising who might actually be behind the album was illustrated by a story in *Billboard* which noted that, 'credits on the offending album identify Coral Records Ltd of Rio de Janeiro as manufacturer.' It had long been standard practice to have exotic and wildly improbable locations listed as the point of manufacture on bootleg album covers.

The demand for a live Springsteen album would continue to build as long as Springsteen resisted providing official evidence of his take on a rock & roll revivalist meeting. Lou Cohan's double-set from Springsteen's Roxy show certainly had a lot more chops to it than the relatively tame 'wall of sound' beneath which Springsteen buried *Born to Run*. He had also proved a point about the potential demand for bootlegs of a 'rookie' seventies rock star like Springsteen. Ken, to his credit, had his antennae on, responding with his own version of the Roxy broadcast followed by his own testament to Springsteen at-his-peak, *You Can Trust Your Car*.

Cohan, though, distrusted Ken's motives in jumping on the Springsteen bandwagon in the early months of 1976. He even produced an insert which he slipped inside some of his own titles that parodied the two SODD Springsteen covers with ribald little stories in the top left-hand corner of each album and plugs for a series of bizarre albums by other artists.

Dubbed SADD on the parody insert, other purported titles in the SADD series included John Denver's *I Wish I'd Been Born a Deer*, Ronald Reagan's *I Swear I Ain't No Retard*, Helen Reddy's *There Ain't No Nigras Where I Come From*, Billy Graham's *How'd I Know He Was the Devil Blues* and Kiss's *My Ass*. The 'Story So Far', instead of being the usual SF-pastiche, a battle between good and evil, was a rather pointed attack on Ken's 'motives' for his so-called labours of love (see the opening quote of this chapter). Ironically the success of his own Springsteen titles had given Cohan the impetus to expand his bootlegging activities. The bug had bitten deep.

Lou Cohan: I started seeing dollar signs and realizing how easy it was to make some money to feed my hobby of collecting ... and I started putting out bootlegs by other artists, not necessarily artists that I like.[11]

Cohan's other great loves were *de rigueur* for California's bootleggers: Dylan and The Stones. It was for Springsteen and Dylan that he reserved his best efforts. His third Springsteen release was another double – *Hot Coals from the Fiery Furnace* – compiled from two sizzling performances in December: one in Philadelphia and one at a college in upstate New York. As the first Springsteen bootleg not to be taken from one of his many radio broadcasts, the sound was not on a par with its predecessors, but performances like the twenty-minute 'E Street Shuffle', a heart-stopping 'Lost in the Flood' and a fourth side of non-stop knock-'em-dead covers – 'Wear My Ring Around Your Neck', 'It's My Life', 'Sha La La', 'Santa Claus is Coming to Town', 'It's Gonna Work Out Fine' and 'Up on the Roof' – made it perhaps the most authentic Springsteen boot yet produced.

A double-set of a May 1976 show in Fort Worth, Texas, part of the second leg of Dylan's tour with his travelling troupe, the Rolling Thunder Revue, was Cohan's most deluxe package, with a printed black and white sleeve, a dedication to the recently deceased Phil Ochs and a classic title: *Hold the Fort for What's It*

*Worth.** Though there had been a predictable flood of titles from the first Rolling Thunder tour in the autumn of 1975 – including no less than six different releases from Ken's family of labels – the 1976 leg had been wholly ignored by the bootleggers, an oversight Cohan was at pains to correct.

Lou Cohan: I always tried to put labels on the records, always tried to use coloured vinyl when it was available at the plant . . . When I made a little bit more money and wanted to get fancier and wanted to improve the quality of the product, I took the artwork to professional album-jacket companies.[12]

While the sound quality of Cohan's titles was not always top notch – and two miserable Genesis and Yes titles were produced for no reason save financial gain – his was a small-time operation run largely for the love of the form. Cohan was one of the severest critics of the Wizardos and TAKRLs of this world, because in his eyes they made it all a question of product.

Cohan did not merely reserve his bile for fellow bootleggers. 1976 had seen a new beast on the plains of America – the official bootleg. Maybe for one brief rift in time the record companies had decided: if you can't beat 'em, join 'em. In reality, the official bootleg was not intended to compete with bootleggers but to get airplay. The official bootleg was designed to replicate the sort of 'live' radio broadcasts loved by bootleggers and radio stations alike, but produced directly by the record companies. The type of 'in concert' broadcast propagated by *King Biscuit Flower Hour* was one way of gaining an artist extended air-time, but the official bootleg allowed radio programmers to choose between playing an entire one-hour performance or simply 'banding' a single cut for a conventional FM programme format. From the artist's point of view it also gave them considerably more control of the finished product than a 'live' broadcast, even if it was only one step away from a bootleg.

---

* As a further in-joke, his previous release had been a Neil Young title, *For What It's Worth*.

But collectors didn't want to hear these damn albums on the radio, they wanted to own them! The official bootleg was an ingenious concept, but the companies were reluctant to follow through and officially release the more 'in demand' of these transcription discs. In particular the Nils Lofgren official bootleg, which had created a whole new interest in Lofgren's post-Grin career, seemed an obvious candidate for legal release. Though Lofgren's record company, A&M, feared to tread this path, Cohan did not.

Lou Cohan: We were big, big fans of Nils Lofgren and [A&M] had had enormous success with the live Peter Frampton album [*Frampton Comes Alive*]. Then they put out a 'live bootleg' to radio stations only of Nils Lofgren, and it was fantastic. Everybody wanted that album, and I waited a year for A&M to release that thing, I even wrote a letter to them saying, 'Put this thing out … !' 'cos I think it would have made a difference in Nils Lofgren's career … After a year I took that album and counterfeited it as a bootleg. I probably sold about 2,500, 3,000 copies of that.[13]

A&M would eventually release a Lofgren live album, but it was not the official bootleg and it was, quite simply, inferior. A&M's experience with the counterfeit version did not dissuade other companies from issuing their own 'official bootlegs', the bulk of which were quickly transformed into the real McCoy. In the years 1976–9 there was a steady trickle of such artifacts, covering acts as diverse as Van Morrison, Talking Heads, Elvis Costello, Graham Parker, AC/DC, Nils Lofgren, Tom Petty and the Heartbreakers, Blue Oyster Cult, Jesse Winchester, Meatloaf, Kansas, Southside Johnny and the Asbury Jukes, REO Speedwagon and Derringer. In most cases the official bootlegs were intended to 'break' cult artists on the verge of becoming real contenders. The bootleggers were particularly grateful for promotional live albums of certain 'new wave' artists. Elvis Costello's *Live at the El Macambo*, a frantic show from Toronto 1978, was bootlegged in at least three different forms, most popular of which was a straight counterfeit of the CBS version, complete with white CBS 'promo' labels (CBS had considerately made their 'promo only' labels black lettering on a white background).

The most famous counterfeit-cum-bootleg that the CBS promotional department was able to devise, however, was a 12″ EP of four cuts taken from Dylan's four-hour directorial debut, *Renaldo and Clara*. Bearing the gold-stamped legend 'for promotional purposes only', the four-track EP included three live cuts from the 1975 Rolling Thunder Revue and a version of Curtis Mayfield's 'People Get Ready' from the Rolling Thunder rehearsals. All four songs, incomplete in the movie, were reproduced in all their glory on the EP, and the versions of 'Isis' and 'It Ain't Me Babe' were stunning examples of Dylan's interpretive genius. Clearly the demand for such a major addition to Dylan's work was not going to be catered for by the 'promo only' pressing. As Dominique Roques notes in his bootleg discography *Great White Answers*:

The 'promo' was pressed in 2,000 copies, and generated struggles among collectors, when all of a sudden, it was to be found very easily!! The ONLY way to recognize the 'original promo' copy is that originals have a GOLD stamp on the back (instead of black). Quality, cover design and record labels are exactly the same.[14]

There was a very good reason why this was the case. The bootleggers had not suddenly found a secret way of producing perfect copies of legitimate vinyl. The copies of the *Renaldo and Clara* EP with the 'fake' black 'promo only' stamp were indeed 'exactly the same'. Someone at Columbia's pressing plant was actually overrunning the presses at night to produce a huge surfeit of these 'promotional items'. What he did not have access to was the gold stamp with which Columbia marked their promotional items. According to one bootlegger, the 'overpress' was actually done under the auspices of the Mafia – for once aware of an exceptional opportunity for counterfeiting a promotional release. Certainly the 'overpress' gained highly efficient distribution, while Dylan lost an opportunity to recoup some of the huge losses the film inflicted on him.

Another example of an item intended for official release provided Beatles collectors with some equally welcome bootleg material. If *Renaldo and Clara* had been eagerly awaited for two and a half years, John Lennon's album of rock & roll covers had been talked about ever since The Beatles fell apart in a film studio in Twickenham, realizing that they couldn't even play old rock & roll songs particularly well together. What happened next Frederic Dannen related in his peek into the inner workings of the Biz, *The Hit Men*:

John Lennon's last album with The Beatles, *Abbey Road*, included his song 'Come Together', which sounded similar to Chuck Berry's 'You Can't Catch Me', a [Morris] Levy copyright. Morris sued, but backed off when Lennon proposed a settlement. His next solo album would be a compendium of oldies, including three songs Levy owned. Recording began in late 1973, but the project stalled. Morris interpreted the delay as a breach of settlement. He had dinner with Lennon, who promised to complete the oldies album. Morris let Lennon rehearse at Sunnyview, his farm in upstate New York ... He asked Lennon if he could borrow the unedited tape of the songs he intended for the album – just for listening. Morris then released the songs as a TV mail-order album, *Roots*. More litigation followed, but Lennon prevailed, and *Roots* was withdrawn.[15]

Roots, like *Get Back* before it, did not correspond exactly to its official equivalent, *Rock & Roll* (which Lennon finally okayed for release in 1974). In instances like this, where an album was quickly withdrawn and promptly counterfeited, the line between piracy, counterfeiting and bootlegging becomes extremely blurred. Selling a copy of the genuine *Roots* album presumably contravened as many laws as the bootleg version.

In the case of a promotional release, the legitimate version was technically 'not for sale'. Yet since the artist was (choosing not to be) making (any) money from this type of release and the record company refused to license a pukka release, the bootleggers were showing commendable public spirit by denying record companies an arbitrary right to decide what could be circulated within the Biz, be played on the radio and still not be released. 'Promotional only' releases were to come back to haunt the official companies at the dawn of the CD era.

Meanwhile, as punk appeared on the horizon, there were two new threats to the continuing prosperity of the Californian bootleggers: a new breed of rock collector, and some unprecedented interest in their activities by the Federal Bureau of Investigation.

When *Great White Wonder*, *Stealin'* and *John Birch* first emerged in 1969, few fans – even those who might consider themselves fanatics – had access to the sort of high-quality studio material that Dub and Ken first disseminated. Fewer fans still were taping concerts on state-of-the-art reel-to-reel equipment. In the late sixties and early seventies, cassette technology was still too primitive to make it a satisfactory storage medium for serious music buffs. What tape-trading went on was largely confined to reel-to-reel, an expensive, quality-conscious alternative to cassette or bootleg vinyl. However, the cassette's portability and ease of use made it inevitable that it would become the preferred carrier as and when cassette technology circumvented its many flaws in design – notably the narrow width of tape ($\frac{1}{4}''$) and its slow tape speed ($1\frac{7}{8}$ ips).

By the early seventies, more and more shows were being surreptitiously taped from the audience, generally on cassette, which was more compact and had longer running times than portable reel-to-reels, and whose recording levels tended to be set automatically, making for easier covert use. Dylan's 1974 'comeback' was surely the first major American tour to be taped in its entirety from the audience. It would not be the last.

The increasing popularity of cassettes meant that tape collecting was no longer the sole preserve of the wealthy and/or the fastidious. Material on bootlegs could now be copied at minimal expense on to cassette, either from a vinyl copy or, preferably, from a tape source closer to the master tape than the commercial bootleg version. The mid seventies marked the dawning of a new breed of rock collector – the tape-collector – collecting exclusively on tape (usually cassette) and refraining from the purchase of bootlegs. The more sanctimonious even began to frown upon bootleggers for 'extorting' money from their artist's blood, sweat and tears.

They considered bootleggers to be nothing to do with the pure, ethereal world tape-collectors were dealing in. Ironically, the new surfeit of tape-collectors meant that more and more copies of tapes were circulating and therefore likely to pass into the hands of bootleggers, not always in a 'low' generation.*

However, it was the annoying habit many bootleggers had of 'mixing' material from multiple sources – some rare and desirable, some common and uninteresting – that most infuriated tape-collectors. As Paul Cable wrote in his study of unreleased Dylan recordings in 1978:

There's so much more material on tape, it's usually of better sound quality, and in general the songs are laid out more logically from the point of view of the time period or session from which they come. There's also the point that a lot of bootleg record manufacturers exhibit a similar trait to official record companies in that they can't resist putting out albums with just a few new tracks mingled with a whole load of previously released ones.[16]

If they were to be encouraged to rediscover the delights of bootleg albums – and virtually without exception tape-collectors were (and are) first exposed to unauthorized recordings via commercial bootlegs – then bootleggers needed to present their material in a more logical, coherent manner. For more and more collectors, bootleg albums were but a stepping stone to the second degree of archiving, the labyrinth of tape-collecting, which was if anything even more Byzantine than the world of vinyl collectors. As many tape-collectors became more and more removed from the bootleggers, they became ever more distrustful, believing – whatever the evidence to the contrary – that their chosen artist had little time for these profiteers, but tacitly condoned the non-profitmaking activities of hordes of tape-traders. The Grateful Dead, in particular, encouraged this attitude. Even as virulent an anti-bootlegger as Dylan once autographed an author's copy of a Dylan tapeography with the legend, 'Keep up the good work.'

---

* Cassette generations bring considerably more degradation than reel-to-reel generations.

The bootleggers were also now taking a considerably greater risk in bringing the music to the fans. On 19 October 1976 the Sound Recording Amendment to US copyright law finally extended copyright protection to sound recordings. Covering all 'misappropriated' recordings – both counterfeit and 'pirate' – the new law made bootlegs the legal equivalent of any pirate album containing commercially released material in alternative packaging. The 1976 act also significantly extended the recording companies' own ability to bring action against bootleggers:

Prior to the 1976 Copyright Act, generally only the copyright proprietor of a work was deemed to be entitled to bring an action for infringement . . . The 1976 Act effects a major change. All rights under copyright, such as performance rights, printing rights, and mechanical reproduction rights, are clearly divisible. The owner of an exclusive right can bring an action in his own name for infringement of his right.[17]

Record companies no longer required the cooperation of the artist, particularly composer-performers, to prosecute bootleggers. Though they would still have to establish their rights to previously unpublished recordings, these recordings became protected at a federal level for the first time, provided that at least 'one complete copy or phonorecord' of said recording was lodged with the Register of Copyrights.

The bootleggers would now have to contend with the FBI on a regular basis. The RIAA were not slow to encourage the FBI to utilize their new legal powers.

Lou Cohan: Vicki Vinyl was busted, a guy who was distributing Wizardo Records was busted, a number of stores were busted, my friend back east was busted – he was sending me the King Kong and Contraband Records in trade for my records. There were [a whole] bunch of people busted in December 1976.[18]

Fortunately for the bootleggers, the FBI's new-found powers were not aligned to any kind of knowledge as to what might constitute a bootleg, nor what they should be searching for when raiding a pressing plant. The FBI had been fed some very tall tales as to the scale of bootleg manufacture in the States. Their first wave of busts was a quest for the 'Mr Big' at the heart of all this outlaw activity. They were happy to offer all sorts of 'deals' to any soul prepared to feed their fantasies. Wizardo, now working in tandem with Vicki Vinyl, managed to wriggle out of a first rap with a little kiss'n'tell. He promptly started up again, assigning new releases to the Wizardo 500 series, only to be hit a second time. This time operations were forcibly put on hold by court action. Cohan, who was also busted at the end of 1976, was lucky that the FBI did not manage to gather all the available evidence:

Lou Cohan: [When] Vicki Vinyl got busted she showed me the indictment, and some of the albums they accused her of making she didn't make ... The FBI never really got all of its information correct ... The FBI surprised me with their lack of expertise; the fact that it took them so long to find pressing plants; the fact that when they busted the place that I did business in, the pressing plant was built in an area of LA that was up a slope, and the pressing plant was on one street and the second half, where the other part of the pressing plant [was], was located in the back but actually faced another street up the hill. And the FBI busted the front building but never ever dreamed that there might be a back storage unit or a back pressing plant.[19]

When they hit Cohan, the FBI thought they had found their Mr Big. He had an extremely impressive catalogue of titles, carrying most of the bootlegs being made in the US at the time. However, as a manufacturer he was strictly small-time. The FBI file on Cohan makes great play of 'information set forth in catalog received from [Cohan] ... and investigation on other retail outlets [which] points to the fact [that] bootleg records are either being manufactured in Darby, Pennsylvania [Cohan's East Coast contact], or Darby is the location of one huge distribution center ... Buys from each of the stores reflects [the fact that] most of the product appears to be from the same manufacturer, based on labels, records and packaging.'[20]

Lou Cohan: I was a volume dealer, a lot of the other people who sold bootlegs at the Hollywood swap-meet got kinda angry with me. They would be selling bootlegs for nine, ten, twelve dollars and I would be selling them retail for three bucks, two seventy-five or five or six dollars at the most. But I would go home one Sunday a month with maybe 1,500 to 2,500 dollars in my pocket selling them at those low prices. As for my own personal bootlegs, I think the most I ever pressed was 4,000 of any one title, the average was around 2,500 ... [but] I would trade my bootlegs with other bootleggers, including a guy on the East Coast, so that by the time the FBI busted me in December of 1976 ... I carried hundreds of titles, but only about twelve to fifteen of my own. I only made, I think, twenty-two bootlegs. *Hot Wacks* says I only made about ten, because I changed label titles, I changed what was scratched in the vinyl, to try and confuse the FBI.[21]

If there *was* a Mr Big it was Ken, but busting him was always going to be problematic. He had good legal advice and was ultra-careful. Also TAKRL had ceased operations and the FBI were not sure which, if any, other labels were down to him, nor how to implicate him in their manufacture. While Wizardo's second bust resulted in a court appearance, enjoining him to cease operations, Cohan's case seemed to simply fade away.

Lou Cohan: The first thing I did was get a lawyer. I went up to this office in Beverly Hills ... This guy walks in with suede boots on and torn up, faded Levi blue jeans and a big old suede hat like you can buy in Mexico for three dollars and a big old beard and I'm waiting and waiting and finally the secretary says I can go in. That's my lawyer? This Hippie? But he turned out to be a pretty good lawyer. He took 1,000 dollars off me and said that if it ever got to trial it'd cost another 5,000 and if it ever got appealed it'd cost another 15,000. But I gave him the thousand dollars and I never heard from the FBI again ... I don't know what phone calls he made, I don't know who he talked to ... I asked him later for my records back because they confiscated about 7,000 bootleg records from me ... and he said, 'Don't rock the boat!'[22]

The bust made Cohan considerably more cautious, but it had

not entirely dissuaded him from continuing his underground activities. Like John Wizardo, he simply pensioned off his main label, Hoffman Avenue Records, and made his product more anonymous.

Lou Cohan: After the FBI bust I went to a different pressing plant – which wasn't in the Yellow Pages of the LA phone books. It was basically a lumber company and also happened to have a couple of record presses and I discovered that it was even closer to my house, like ten minutes away. I did a couple of records there.[23]

Cohan, though, was growing tired of the double-life. He had carried on teaching throughout his bootlegging days. A couple of particularly lacklustre Springsteen and Stones titles suggested that the fun had gone out of it for him and by the end of 1977 he had called it quits. However, Wizardo's association with Vicki Vinyl continued to blossom and Ken was not about to stay out of the picture for long. The FBI's first attempt to suppress California's bootleg mini-industry had not been a resounding success. They had also learnt that the RIAA was not particularly well informed on who was doing what, where.

7 Vicki's Vinyl

LIVE

ELVIS ROCKS
LITTLE ROCK

MAY 16, 1956

■ HEARTBREAK HOTEL ■ LONG TALL SALLY ■ I WAS THE ONE ■ MONEY HONEY
■ I GOT A WOMAN ■ BLUE SUEDE SHOES ■ HOUND DOG ■
■ RECORDED LIVE AT THE ROBINSON MEMORIAL AUDITORIUM, LITTLE ROCK, ARKANSAS ■

A bootlegger: [The FBI] know who I am, and they know everyone else in the business too. Fortunately, the agents are aware of what a farce this whole 'crackdown' is, they know where the real piracy is taking place, and it's only when some record company gets wind of a bootleg on one of their big artists and goes into a panic that they come around and warn us to cool it. I know the laws very well, and I have good lawyers, and like anything else they have to catch you on a technicality.[1]

Between the autumn of 1976 and the spring of 1979, California's bootleggers remained largely untouched by legal tangles. Ken's suitably anonymous multiple labels signalled the way ahead. As long as the FBI failed to join up the dots, they would leave small-timers alone. The fact that six small labels may in fact all be one bootleg producer was a concept that thankfully eluded them. The days when a label was something to be championed were over. TAKRL, Wizardo and TMQ were no more. Though Ken continued to be the king of volume, his labels outlived their usefulness every couple of years. In the years after the Sound Recording Amendment, the identities of the bootleggers became as much a mystery to the punters as the FBI.

It was into this vacuum of information that *Hot Wacks* was first flung. The very nature of bootlegs has always meant that their purchase tends to be a hit-and-miss affair, aurally and aesthetically. *Hot Wacks IV*, the first edition of the Canadian bootleg discography to receive any kind of dissemination, was published at the end of 1977. It became a vital tool for bootleg collectors, providing quality ratings, source of recording, track listings and occasional comments. It also provided a catalogue of the main labels in the form of an appendix. Published at the end of 'the first era', the 200-page tome showed just how much product had been given air in the first half of the seventies.

K & S Records

Inevitably, *Hot Wacks* was not the product of a dispassionate observer but someone who had been getting his own hands dirty. Kurt Glemser was already dipping into the mire at the time of *Hot Wacks IV*. K (as in Kurt) & S Records' first release, a collection of live Zeppelin recordings, had appeared at the beginning of 1976. In the grand tradition of copycat bootleggers, *Sin City Social* was a shoddy mix'n'match drawn exclusively from TMQ's *Bonzo's Birthday Party*, *Three Days After* and *Blueberry Hill*.

Three of the next four K & S titles, though, were original efforts – quite acceptable audience tapes from shows in Toronto by Bob Dylan, The Who and Jeff Beck – suggesting that K & S might yet establish its own identity. Sadly, Kurt quickly sank into producing small-run, multicoloured-vinyl represses of existing bootlegs.

If the Canadian authorities had applied a little intellect, the fact that many K & S bootlegs were derived from shows in Toronto might have suggested Ontario as a base for their operations. However, the Canadian authorities were as ill-informed as the FBI, and hamstrung by laxer anti-piracy laws. Indeed Canada seemed like the perfect haven for a bootlegger.

'Eric Bristow': The law was $10 per count to a maximum of $200, a count being one infringement, twenty infringements $200 fine. Beyond that it was a civil offence. Counterfeiting was different, but for bootleg records it was $10 per count to a maximum of $200, and that was only changed about two years ago.[2]

With such innocuous laws, it is perhaps surprising that so few bootlegs came from Canadian sources. In fact, Toronto had been one of the first cities in North America to sell *Great White Wonder* and its children, remaining a major outlet for bootleg titles throughout the seventies. However, there was nowhere to actually press bootlegs in Canada. Unlike California, where Kurt was obliged to get his K & S product manufactured, Canada had no blasé, Spanish-speaking pressing-plant owners.

Bob Walker: They tried to do a Springsteen one [in Canada] in 1986. It got as far as the shopfloor. It had been pressed, put in jackets and was ready to ship and one of the fellows doing the shipping looked in the crates and said, 'Hey, this isn't right . . .' and it was seized . . . There are so few pressing plants. Most of the companies which press in Canada go to [the same] three or four plants to get all their product done . . . whereas in the States you can go to Joe Blow's Small Record Company and say, 'Here's some money.'[3]

Though the FBI's autumn 1976 operation had done little to abate the flow, it did necessitate one rethink. One problem with bootlegs was that they looked like, well, bootlegs. This made it easy for even ill-informed FBI agents to recognize a bootleg at ten paces. While the legal temperature was no more than lukewarm, bootleggers resisted the sort of professional packaging that could double their production costs. From 1976 on, though, it became increasingly important for a bootleg to be stuffed in record racks alongside official goodies and be passed off as low-budget legitimate releases. Printed covers started to become the norm; xeroxed inserts began to be reserved for small, privately circulated runs.

Ken seemed willing to go with the flow. Dispensing with his two post-TAKRL labels, Flat and ZAP, he switched to black and white printed covers at the end of 1977, assuming yet another new identity, Impossible Recordworks. IRW showed that Ken was still prepared to gamble on the 'bootlegability' of new acts, embracing some of the more challenging new wave acts beginning to emerge. In the first two years of IRW such avant-garde rockers as Pere Ubu, Siouxsie and the Banshees, Talking Heads, Devo and Public Image Limited were added to the usual roster of bootlegged rock icons. Ken, though, was becoming increasingly short of good source material. The Ubu, PiL and Siouxsie titles were all copies of more obscure, one-off pressings made independently from within 'new wave' circles. Ken's new partner also seemed less suited to the business than his previous cohorts had been.

'Eric Bristow': In the late seventies he got a new partner named Mike, who worked very hard, by all accounts, but was super-paranoid. That was the time when they were doing the Phoenix releases [etc.] . . . it was like a real business. It was all being done in California and they were living in Spain. They'd get on a plane and fly here when a shipment was ready, arrive, pick it up, ship it out to everybody, and fly back to Spain, back to the beach. That's how they were living for quite a while.[4]

Impossible Recordworks and its occasional sister label, Excitable Recordworks, kept business ticking over. Along with represses of old stalwarts from the TMQ and TAKRL catalogues in deluxe, full-colour laminated covers (generally under the Phoenix logo – presumably because its releases had risen from the ashes), and a smattering of deluxe items on Saturated Records, they allowed Ken and Mike to live the life of Riley. But Ken was running out of ideas.

Ken may have been a leader when it came to volume, but on the packaging front he rarely led by example. So it was with the professional Phoenix reissues, which had been forced on him by the competition. A whole series of American bootlegs were now being released with Ruthless Rhymes labels on the records (the logo consisting of a gun pointed at the HMV dog's head). Seemingly unconnected 'companies' were attributed to each Ruthless Rhymes release. One Ruthless Rhymes label, Audiofon, was responsible for some of the most deluxe packages in bootleg history. A double-album, *Life Sentence*, came from Dylan's first Californian shows in over four years, a seven-night residency at LA's open-air Universal Amphitheater. Housed in a beautiful full-colour cover featuring photos from Dylan's 1978 tour programme, it suggested that the individual behind these releases was continuing the Rubber Dubber tradition of bootlegging on his home patch, aided by Universal's lax security.

Lou Cohan: There were certain places, like the Universal Amphitheater, which was an outdoor venue at that time, where people would take in blankets and heavy coats. I used to take in a gym bag with a false bottom, and they might look in the gym bag and see a blanket and a thermos and a few other things to keep me warm in the evening – but underneath that false bottom would be a tape recorder and a couple of microphones and a few tapes and some batteries.[5]

Audiofon's main claims to fame, though, were their Presley bootleg sets. In 1979 they were responsible for a pair of double-albums of the complete Burbank Studio sessions, which had been edited down to an hour for Presley's famous 1968 NBC TV special. Housed in glorious laminated colour covers, illustrated with stills from the actual filming sessions, and with reproductions of tickets for each show slipped inside the sleeves, these were the most deluxe packages since the final days of TMQ. The contents were also particularly magnificent, with Presley joking about his early days, running the songs together and generally enjoying the whole experience of reliving favourites like 'One Night' and 'Baby, What You Want Me to Do'.

Before 1976, Elvis Presley had been largely ignored by America's bootleg fraternity. To the hardcore 'rock' fan Presley's Las Vegas self was an embarrassment, and the bootleg producers themselves were generally children of the sixties, not the fifties. One intrepid Canadian fan back in 1970 attempted to press a record from the Vegas shows – at RCA's Canadian pressing plant. Not surprisingly he ended up losing his $1,500 deposit before sending the tapes to Holland to be pressed there. It was only rockabilly fans in Europe, particularly the Netherlands, who were willing to remind the world of the seismic effect of Presley's initial burst of records, producing classic deluxe titles like *The Hillbilly Cat* (the aforementioned Vegas album) and *Good Rockin' Tonight*.

In 1976, disappointed by the Legendary Performer series, which were RCA's idea of collector-oriented releases, the Americans came up with three deluxe Presley titles, two drawn from his mid-fifties peak – *Dorsey Shows* and *From the Waist Up*. Sales of these items suggested that further investment was in order, and when Presley considerately pulled his own plug in August 1977, he suddenly became the hottest property in bootlegging. At the same time, a flood of previously uncirculated studio recordings leaked out of RCA's sieve-like vaults. Leading from the front, Audiofon came up with the biggest scoop, courtesy of RCA's unthinking executives:

Someone at RCA decided to clean out the tape vaults containing recording sessions from Elvis's movies during the 1960s. Apparently RCA executives did not realize the historical or musical importance of these tapes. Legend has it that a janitor found the boxes of tapes and was smart enough to take them home. The tapes eventually worked their way to a Hollywood bootleg producer, and this resulted in some of the finest Elvis bootlegs. Perhaps the most impressive was *Behind Closed Doors*, a four-record boxed-set with superb production qualities. The RCA tapes contained numerous examples of Elvis's fine singing talent, and highlighted his sense of humour in the recording studio. The tapes also exhibited the methods which RCA and the movie studios used to control Elvis's more pronounced rock & roll inclinations. Many times the session engineer would request that Elvis tone down a song because it was too rock-oriented. After hours of fighting over the direction of many of his movie songs, Elvis would give in and record a pop version of the tune.[6]

After the 1976 busts, a more covert bootleg industry began to feel that as long as it maintained a low profile the FBI would be preoccupied by more serious lawbreaking. It also seemed as if the bootleggers had got some not-so-tacit support from certain artists susceptible to the bootleg virus. Bruce Springsteen, despite sharing an action against a retailer of the *Bottom Line* bootleg in 1976, was viewed as something of a champion of the form. The first Springsteen bootlegger certainly encountered no hostility when presenting a couple of titles to Bruce in 1976.

Lou Cohan: We met him a couple of times as fans after the concerts in Santa Barbara in '75–'76 and gave him copies of the bootlegs and he seemed very thrilled. It seemed to be at that time that once you were a bootlegged artist you had really made it with the fans . . . And at that time Bruce seemed like a kid receiving something at Christmas when we gave him copies of the bootlegs. Later, all that changed.[7]

Embarking on a marathon seven-month tour of the States in May 1978, Springsteen seemed to be going out of his way to 'endorse' bootlegs. Five entire shows – and his 1978 sets were invariably three hours plus – were broadcast on the radio. On two separate occasions during these broadcasts he appeared to offer moral support to the bootleggers, suggesting during a July broadcast from the LA Roxy, 'Bootleggers, roll your tapes, this is gonna be a hot one!', while at San Francisco's Winterland he prefaced 'Sandy' by dedicating it to the Jersey girls, trusting that one day they would hear it 'through the magic of bootlegging'. When questioned by a British journalist about his attitude to bootlegging, he seemed happy to condone their continued existence:

Bruce Springsteen: You find out most of the time that, number one, they're fans. I've had bootleggers write me letters saying, 'Listen, we're just fans,' that's their story. And the kids who buy the bootlegs buy the real records too, so it doesn't really bother me. I think the amount of money made on it isn't very substantial. It's more like a labour of love.[8]

But a dramatic change in attitude followed hard on the heels of the highly successful 'Darkness' tour. Live radio broadcasts would become a thing of the past (until 1988, when he needed the exposure to put 'bums on seats'). When asked about his views on bootlegging at the outset of his next US tour, in the autumn of 1980, Springsteen roundly turned on these 'fat cats':

Bruce Springsteen: When I first started out, a lot of the bootlegs were made by fans, and there was a lot more of a connection. But there came a point where there were just so many made by people who didn't care what the quality was ... The people who were doing it had warehouses full of records that sounded really bad, and were just sitting back getting fat, putting out anything and getting thirty fucking dollars for it.[9]

It hardly seems coincidental that the change came at a time when Springsteen began to be 'managed' by ex-journo Jon Landau. Landau's management style was all about control. In his mind, rock & roll was about strategy not energy. The first, and most significant, bootlegger to feel Springsteen's (and Landau's) wrath was Vicki Vinyl, John Wizardo's sometime partner, who had put out a three-album boxed-set of Springsteen's dynamic September 1978 radio broadcast from Passaic, New Jersey.

A superb, FM quality, document of the 'Darkness' tour, right at its midpoint peak, *Pièce De Résistance* could hardly be described as sounding 'real bad' or being 'made by people who didn't care what the quality was'. Springsteen had also hardly been coy about playing unreleased songs on the '78 tour, premiering songs lost in the single-album shuffle that gave the world *Darkness on the Edge of Town*, as well as new songs that were a logical continuation of the 'Darkness' material. *Pièce De Résistance* included 'Independence Day' and 'Point Blank', two of the finest new ditties to be unveiled at these shows. Nevertheless, in July 1979, CBS Inc. and Bruce Springsteen filed a civil suit in a Californian Federal District Court against 'alleged underground album manufacturer' Vicki Vinyl and her partner-in-crime Jim Washburn. Their pleading accused the defendants of 'infringement of copyrights, unfair competition, unjust enrichment, unauthorized use of name and likeness and interference with economic advantage'.

According to CBS and Springsteen, the masters were 'recorded illegally during his performances in San Francisco and Passaic, NJ'.[10] In fact, both *Pièce De Résistance* and an equally impressive triple from a November Winterland show, *Live in the Promised Land*, were dubbed directly from radio broadcasts. Thankfully, CBS and Springsteen had proved rather sedentary in filing civil suit for damages after the FBI had first tracked down Vicki (aka Andrea Waters) and busted her.

Lou Cohan: They busted her and then, months later, CBS filed the civil suit against her. By that time – between the FBI bust and CBS bringing the civil suit against her – she had given away or sold all of her property, so that there wouldn't be anything for CBS or Bruce Springsteen to get once they filed the lawsuit against her.[11]

Springsteen was at least correct on one point – his description of his early bootleggers as fans and this latter-day producer as in it for the money. Though *Pièce De Résistance* and *Live in the Promised Land* were both landmark releases, and her co-defendant was a Springsteen disciple, Vicki Vinyl had no time for Springsteen's music. Her great love was The Stones, and the release of these two triples was purely a commercial exercise. As such, she must have been mighty pleased at the ineptitude of CBS and Springsteen's management.

Vicki had apparently asked her barrister to defend her on the grounds that Springsteen had endorsed 'bootlegging' on at least one of the two boxed-sets in question. He apparently prepared a more orthodox defence, based on CBS establishing their legal right to Springsteen's live performances. Though this did not prove an appropriate line of defence either, in the end CBS and Springsteen had little to show for their efforts. The judge's verdict was eventually reported by *Hot Wacks Quarterly* in these terms:

The celebrated Andrea Waters bootleg case has finally come to an end. Ms Waters, aka Vicky Vinyl, pleaded guilty to one count of copyright infringement and received a fine of $5,000. She had been facing a maximum of nineteen years' imprisonment and a fine of $190,000. Also in December Judge Malcolm Lucas in a Federal District Court in Los Angeles awarded Bruce Springsteen $2,150,000 in damages from Waters. She was found guilty in the civil suit of infringing forty-three musical copyrights. Springsteen received a judgement of $50,000 for each infringement! He received a further $10,750 from Jim Washburn, manager of an Anaheim record store once owned by Ms Waters. CBS is to receive $1,500 of the $500,000 it had asked of the court. Waters and Washburn have also been ordered to pay court costs of $105,573. The sentences can be appealed but in order to do so the defendants would have to deposit 10 per cent of the settlement with the courts. Springsteen will probably be lucky if he ever sees one penny of the award since Waters reportedly does not have any assets to seize.[12]

The $5,000 fine imposed on Vicki Vinyl was the maximum that could be exacted under a new Californian state law, introduced in September 1978, designed to deter bootlegging in the very heartland of this mini-industry. The new law was signed by governor Jerry Brown on 29 September, at which point the sale of bootlegs became punishable by six months in jail and/or a fine of up to $5,000. At the same time, a New York statute made the manufacture of unauthorized recordings a Class E felony.

Idle Mind Productions

Vicki had wisely refrained from putting either of the Springsteen sets on her most regular outlet for product, Idle Mind Productions, which would almost certainly have involved her in further litigation. Idle Mind had produced twenty-five titles in the three years since the Wizardo bust, with The Stones providing a hefty chunk (seven) of them. An infuriating mish-mash of original and copycat releases, Idle Mind was one of the last labels to abandon its paper-insert origins. Vicki, after a lucky escape, reverted to Andrea, took the hint and shut down shop. But if Springsteen thought that his heavy-handed treatment of Vicki's vinyl had sent a message to other bootleggers, it was lost on the Europeans, whose assorted Springsteen boxed-sets kept Brooce bootleg product ticking over throughout the eighties.

Vicki Vinyl had in fact been a marked target for some months. A Canadian retailer, Michael Mess, had given FBI agents the (real) names of several key figures in 'a Long Beach bootleg ring', including Ken, Andrea and John Wizardo. He had also identified one Malcolm Moore as the man responsible for pressing K & S product. The FBI report resulting from their interview with Mess suggested that Vicki Vinyl was not the only one being singled out for action.

[According to Mess] there is one person in Toronto, Canada, who deals in large quantities of bootlegged albums. His name is Curt [*sic*] Glemser and he is responsible for publishing the bootleg record book entitled *Hot Wax*. Mess also stated Glemser frequently travels to Los Angeles to arrange for shipments of records to Canada.[13]

Mess was asked to provide a description of Glemser. It would take a year for the FBI and RCMP to organize a coordinated attack on the manufacturer-producers named by Mess, who between them were responsible for the bulk of American bootleg product. When the raids finally occurred, in February 1980, Glemser was the first target. The *Billboard* report of the raid even suggested that the RCMP were attacking the very heart of the bootleg industry by raiding Blue Flake Productions, publishers of *Hot Wacks* and *Hot Wacks Quarterly*:

A raid by federal police here on a company called Blue Flake Productions Feb. 22 could spill the beans on key bootleg concert tape suppliers in North America, and have a dramatic impact upon the availability of concert bootlegs in the open market ... While no charges have been laid against retailers who had stock seized or against Blue Flake owner Kurt Glemser, the police have seized a vast quantity of master tapes, alleged bootleg albums and videocassettes and business papers which, they feel, will eventually lead them to pull in an even larger dragnet ... The company published a catalog of purportedly illegal recordings, available by mail for $6.[14]

In fact, as Glemser's successor at *Hot Wacks* has observed, '[Kurt] was looked upon as a kingpin of some sort, but he was really a peripheral player.' The *Billboard* report was one of the most misleading items ever run in this respected industry magazine. The 'catalogue of purportedly illegal recordings' was, of course, the *Hot Wacks* discography; and the so-called 'key bootleg concert tape suppliers' were the many tape-collectors who advertised freely in *Hot Wacks Quarterly*. Unfortunately for the RCMP there was very little they could do to Glemser.

'Eric Bristow': They raided his house, took his TV. They filled a truck with everything he owned. And they laid six charges on him. You name it, they just laid it on, thick as hell, figuring some of it would stick ... they tried to plea bargain with Kurt ... In the event all charges against Glemser were stayed by the prosecutor before there was even a preliminary inquiry and *all* items seized were returned ... Of all the people they busted up in Canada during that series of raids only one guy pleaded guilty and he was a little guy who ran an independent bootleg record store out in the country and when they raided his store they found 5,000 [bootlegs]. He pleaded guilty and they loaded up the truck and he's going 'I did it, I did it,' – and it's only a $200 fine at that time – so off they go and they go to trial and they ... fine him $200. About a year later, he's in the store and a cop walks in, says 'Are you such-and-such?' and he goes 'Yeah?' 'Got some of your property outside.' 'And what would that be?' 'A bunch of records ...' and he goes 'Wait a minute ...' So he goes out to the truck and they open up the rollback of this truck and there's all these bootlegs and they're all stamped 'EVIDENCE' and they're all the same condition, and he's like 'What have you brought them here for?'

'They're yours, right?'

'Yeah . . .'

'Well, what do you want us to do with them?'

He said, 'But I pleaded guilty. It was a crime for me to have these. I pleaded guilty. You charged me and fined me . . .'

'Look, we just been given instructions to bring these back here. You want 'em or not? If you don't want 'em we're going to take 'em to the City Dump.'

'If I take these back are you going to bust me again?'

'Look, do you want 'em or not?'

'Okay!'[15]

The Blue Flake bust was part of a much wider operation designed to take out all the major bootleggers. Once again, though, the FBI failed to nail the man they most craved – Ken.

'Eric Bristow': It was a massive organizational accomplishment for the RIAA, the FBI and the RCMP in Canada. They managed to swoop down on 150 people on the same day, everywhere from Georgia to California to Ontario, Canada. The only people that they missed in this big swoop were Ken and Mike, because they were in Spain.[16]

Ken had once again eluded the FBI's grasp, but one side-effect of the bust was to make Ken's partner, Mike, even more paranoid than the supra-paranoid soul he was to begin with. It was to be Mike who put Ken (and himself) out of business – without any help from the FBI.

'Eric Bristow': Mike got really paranoid . . . His house was near Reagan's ranch . . . All these secret service types showed up outside his house and he freaked out. He phoned everybody up and he was saying, 'They're gonna get me, I gotta . . .' and he took all the stampers for the Toasted and Phoenix stuff, drove out to the ocean and threw the whole fuckin' lot into the ocean.[17]

So, for the first time, the linchpin of California's bootleg industry was no longer a player. The February 1980 raids also took out key distribution outlets. After February 1980 the FBI were determined to tackle the remaining manufacturers, the wholesalers and the mail-order merchants. The events of 1979 and 1980 had removed some of the biggest players from the second era – Idle Mind Productions, K & S (Glemser, though he eventually beat the various raps, preferred the quiet life) and, by proxy, Ken.

But the FBI had failed to sever the cord between manufacturer and punter. It was time for a new generation of American bootleggers to compete with the increasingly professional bootleg product coming from the other side of the pond. In the second half of the seventies, there had probably been as much product coming out of Europe and Japan as the traditional West Coast haven – and these bootleggers didn't have to contend with federal investigators, just private dicks.

8 White Cover Folks!

Copyright sleuths have busted England's first bootleg record producer for making a one-disc version of Dylan's *Great White Wonder* album. David Steel, the 20-year-old founder and president of F.D. Productions, the bootleg company, met with officers of the Mechanical Copyright Protective Service [*sic*], turned over the original *Great White Wonder* tape and his master tape, paid most of the $360 royalties demanded and promised not to do it again.[1]

Piracy of *Great White Wonder* was never likely to be confined to the Golden State. England, though, was not the best of choices when it came to a little illicit copying. Britain had provided protection of 'sound recordings' as early as 1911, and the 1956 Copyright Act provided additional protection for material broadcast on radio or TV. However, there was one flaw in English law that Britain's first bootlegger was able to exploit. Under the Performers' Protection Act of 1963, the most appropriate tool for prosecuting bootleggers (rather than counterfeiters), offences were required to be committed 'knowingly'. It has always been exceedingly difficult to prove intent in any legal case, let alone one involving the manufacture of illicit recordings by a third party.

Steel himself, though he had naïvely advertised his single-album *Great White Wonder* mail order, did have the chutzpah to insist that he did not know that what he was doing was illegal, even denying that he knew it was Dylan. When pressed, he insisted, 'I have never said this was a Dylan record. I always sold it as simply *The Great White Wonder*.' This might seem a tad disingenuous given that he had bought his tape of the American double-album in September 1969, when the UK music press – much like the US press – had been full of reports about this 'white label' Dylan album, *Great White Wonder*. *Rolling Stone* interviewed Steel at the time and got his account:

Steel chose the tracks he liked best, hired Regent Sound Ltd, a demo studio, to clean the tape up and make a master tape, and a record presser, British Homophone Ltd, to produce an initial run of 300 records ... At British Homophone, a spokesman said: 'We really walked into this one with our eyes shut. He told us it was some friends of his who recorded it in a hotel room' ... Regent Sound said it couldn't recall processing the *GWW* tape at all. Says the production manager: 'Anybody can bring any tape in here and we'll copy it. We don't know who it belongs to, and we're not really interested.'[2]

Steel had actually managed to sell some 1,250 copies of the atrocious-sounding single album before he was nabbed. The UK market was obviously teeming with potential purchasers of bootlegs. The demand in the UK, for Dylan product in particular, was likely to be at least as great as in the USA. A demand was already apparent for reel-to-reel copies of Dylan's 'basement tape' demos (it was, after all, in England that the likes of Manfred Mann, Julie Driscoll, Fairport Convention and McGuiness Flint gained commercial hits covering basement-tape songs). Steel, though, had not gone about the exercise in the most discreet manner. The main problem was always going to be getting records pressed.

Early English bootleggers were not easily dissuaded by the sturdy legal barriers in their way. English sixties radicalism was at its height – this was the era of *International Times*, the *Oz* trial and the Paris riots. The anti-establishment slant given to bootlegging only gave it more appeal.

Alan Henderson [a bootlegger]: We were involved in an underground youth culture/campaigning movement and part of it was, we would put on concerts and campaign for this and that on behalf of 'youth'. It was a very politicized time and we were influenced by Yippies and the White Panther party ... We used to set up 'head' stalls at various concerts and we would sell joss-sticks, candles, *The Little Red School Book* and all sorts of pamphlets, and we started buying bootlegs from Peter [Shertser] and these went well – these were the first English bootlegs ... So it started off as just one part of a lot of things that we were doing and reflected the political/community/

cultural things that we were involved with . . . I suppose we didn't have that much respect for the law. It didn't concern us. That era was a time of great optimism and change . . . and [to us] the difference between us being able to press a record and a real record company was so great that the two paths would never cross . . . [After all] everyone we knew smoked dope and that was illegal. It was more important that people got to hear the music.[3]

The rebootlegged *Great White Wonder* certainly wouldn't have won any aesthetic awards. It came in a blank sleeve with blank labels and was barely identifiable as Dylan. An English copy of *Stealin'*, which soon followed, was marginally superior, but there seemed no real future in such poor copies of American titles. The Americans had already proved that the fad could only be sustained by producing something people wanted to buy.

Now *The Royal Albert Hall Concert 1966* was something the English would definitely want to buy. From the day copies arrived from the States, *In 1966 There Was* – aka *The Royal Albert Hall Concert 1966* (minus Michael's expensive printed cover, hand-stamped with a new title, but otherwise intact) – finally gave the UK media a bootleg to get excited about and the perfect excuse to recall the heady days of 1966, and that most dramatic of rock tours. They did not stint in their praise or resist making the demand that this essential artifact be released officially.

In 1966 There Was was presumed to be a UK version of the Albert Hall tape, but it was in fact pressed by the very same Los Angeles plant that had produced *The Royal Albert Hall Concert 1966*. Rather than risk pressing his own edition in the UK, Michael's original English partner, Alan, had imported them from the US and wholesaled them to two of his counter-culture contacts.

In wholesaling the entire consignment of *In 1966 There Was* to Peter Shertser and Ian Sippen, Alan made these counter-culture figures realize just how much money could be made from the bootlegging game. These 'radicals' decided that it would be even more profitable if they made their own titles, and proceeded to copy Dub's *LiveR Than You'll Ever Be* and one of the many versions of *Get Back*. Though they had found a pressing plant prepared to do the dirty deed, they quickly realized that they were dealing with some serious delinquents:

Peter Shertser [a bootlegger]: After we started our own label, we got offered bootlegs, the first that had ever come into the UK: Dylan *Live at the Albert Hall* and The Stones' *Get Your Ya-Ya's Out* [*sic*]. They were the original tapes and the quality was very good and so artistically there was no reason not to do it. It was totally justified in terms of musical ability. We had a go [ourselves] and it was crazy: grands! We're kids and suddenly we're getting these pound notes flying in every direction. It disrupts your sense of perspective. Two or three grand at a time, when that was a lot of money. It went berserk. People were selling thousands. One day the boss of the pressing plant, who were making these bootlegs, came down to Ian's house, where we operated the company. We happened to have Snowy the Bowlegs with us, who used to do a bit of our accounts work ... It's 10 o'clock in the morning, Ian's still in his pyjamas, and there's a ring on the door. It's the owner of the pressing plant, who himself is not an unsubstantial size. And two bookends. I said to Ian, 'Oy vay, this is trouble,' and Snowy's going, 'I'm just leaving,' and I grabbed him by the collar and said, 'No you're not, you're staying here.' So he comes in with the bookends and says, 'We'd like to talk to you lads.' It's a scene out of *Performance*. He said, 'These records that you're making – that we're making – they're not strictly legal, are they?' So I said, 'Well, we do try to oversee the copyright act, utilizing certain *in vivo* situations, as it were . . .' trying anything. And he said, 'Look, we'll cut the crap, sonny. I want a grand. Now! Otherwise you're in the grinding machine.' I said to Ian, 'Make some coffee,' then I said to Snowy, 'Discuss figures with him, tell him we're not making that much . . .' I asked Ian, 'What shall we do?' 'Tell him to fuck off.' '*You* go and tell him to fuck off. We've to pay them. They'll kill us. They're about seven foot high. Are you mental? It's protection, we've got to do it. How much have we got in the case?' . . . We had about twelve hundred quid. I said, 'Give him the grand.' So they took the grand, and they were happy as sandmen.[4]

Though this experience may have dissuaded Peter from immersing himself further in the bootleg business, Ian felt he had discovered his true niche and set out to corner the early UK market. Reverting to the prudent alternative of pressing in the US from lacquers made in the UK, utilizing Alan's Stateside contact, Ian produced a steady stream of hit'n'miss titles.

Michael O: A year or so after [*Albert Hall*], they did start [regular] bootlegging . . . they couldn't get it pressed in England and they always got in touch with me to get it pressed at this little place in Inglewood. So I was always getting stuff pressed for them and then shipping it back.[5]

Ian's most successful title was a superb Hendrix collection, *Goodbye Jimi*, drawn from BBC *Top Gear* radio sessions, which apparently sold some 9,000 copies. A further collection of material, culled from The Stones' aborted *Rock & Roll Circus* TV special, and featuring Lennon's 'Yer Blues' and The Who's 'A Quick One' (though not any of the Stones' own set), gained the then unique distinction of being rebootlegged in the States (by Wizardo). However, Alan was seeing little of Ian's considerable return, even though it was largely his material and wholly his US contact that enabled these White Cover Folks to thrive.* Before the well could dry up, though, Ian disappeared in highly mysterious circumstances while holidaying in Morocco. The British connection was no more.

Peter and Ian had not been the only youthful 'radicals' to realize that here was something a little more exciting than selling joss sticks and copies of *International Times*. Another English Alan, who had begun by selling Ian and Peter's fare, decided he too could produce his own titles, also copied from US sources. Unfortunately, the only plant he and his partner could find with a no-questions-asked policy was only able to press 7″ singles. So began Bread & Circuses Records, dealing exclusively in 33⅓ rpm 7″ EPs.

Alan Henderson: We thought, 'Hey, this is good,' and then the next ones that came in [from America] were *Jimi Hendrix Live at Santa Monica* and *The*

---

* Ian's product was labelled White Cover Folks by *Hot Wacks*. His albums used thick, black vinyl in a white jacket. They all had different labels such as Hen, Steel, etc.

Beatles at Shea Stadium, and we managed to find a pressing plant that would press them in England. So we took the tapes off the records. We did them on seven-inchers 'cos we couldn't find a twelve-inch press. So we would do a pair of EPs on the Bread & Circuses label. They were white sleeves. I think the Shea Stadium had a printed sleeve for a while, and the label for Shea Stadium was a peace sign and for the Hendrix it was a clenched fist . . . The Hendrix live thing was one of the last things he'd done and at that time there weren't dozens of Jimi Hendrix records out and it was a great performance.[6]

If England's own cottage industry was smaller and more clandestine than its Californian counterpart, this was hardly surprising. They had far less access to good source material, fewer options on the manufacturing side, and were breaking far more laws. Europe in general possessed a much tighter legal net for ensnaring 'performance pirates'. From the dawn of the recording era, the Europeans had shown a much greater awareness of performance rights than the US. Britain had introduced a Dramatic and Musical Performers Protection Act as far back as 1925 and, in 1961, was instrumental in organizing the Rome Convention which, thirty years on, still provides the one solid legal restraint on bootlegging live performances.

Delegates from some forty countries had convened in Rome with a brief to draft an international convention 'for the protection of performers, manufacturers of records, and broadcasting organizations'. Though thirty-five of the countries attending voted their approval of the final draft – with just three abstentions – only eighteen countries actually signed the convention at the conference's end. The eighteen included most of the important European states – Austria, Belgium, Denmark, France, Germany, Italy, Spain, Sweden and the United Kingdom – though Belgium, France and Spain failed to subsequently ratify the convention and Germany took five years to ratify. The United States, though represented, failed to even sign the convention. Transcontinental cooperation on piracy was still some way off.

The idea behind the convention had been to ensure 'equitable remuneration by the user of a record for broadcasting or any communication to the public, to the performers, or to the producers of the record, or to both, depending on local law'.[7] Its concerns were primarily bound by Anglo-Saxon notions of 'fair dues', rather than more censorial rights. Original author-songwriters were assumed to be adequately protected by conventional copyright. What Rome signified was a considerable extension of subsidiary (or neighbouring, as they are usually referred to) rights to a wide circle of peripheral players; generally the less creative arms of the music machine:

The Rome Convention ... gives protection, not only to an additional category of artistic labourer, the performer, but also to two employers of literary and artistic labour, the record producers [meaning 'the producers of phonograms', not the studio producer] and broadcasters.[8]

Despite the UK's early ratification of the Rome Convention and revision of the 1958 Performers Protection Act to reflect new obligations, in the early seventies copyright-holders were struggling to disrupt a thriving English bootleg trade. Their best weapon – a strict monitoring of the pressing plants – could not stop the widespread importation of American titles.

In 1972 the UK's lawmakers reacted to what was a slightly tetchy flea on the backside of a medium-sized dinosaur by amending the Performers Protection Act to increase the maximum fine for 'making or selling records without the consent of the performers' from £50 to £400. This was still a drop in the English Channel. More significantly, the manufacture – and possession of plates for duplication – of unlicensed records became a criminal offence. Unfortunately, the chances of discerning who was manufacturing when all bootleg product came from overseas were less than zero. Yet in a traditional display of English optimism, a spokesman for the BPI went on record to say:

I am confident we can stop bootlegging on a regular basis. There will always be people willing to take a chance of making a quick killing on one album and then disappear, but the [new] penalties will act as a real deterrent to anybody considering trying to make a living out of bootleg records.[9]

In reality, the 'disappearance' of Ian Sippen, the central figure in early British bootlegging, and the ease with which patently superior TMQ titles could be imported into the UK, had more bearing on the demise of home-made bootleg product than any change in the law. Though genuine UK bootlegs quickly became a thing of the past (at least until punk kicked in), UK bootleggers enjoyed something of a golden age in the early seventies. Between 1971 and 1973, in most large cities, it was possible to purchase bootlegs over-the-counter from what might be termed high-street stores. One new chain in particular, Virgin Records, was extremely active in importing Trade Mark of Quality titles, the European 'editions' of which now carried the legend 'Made in Holland':

Dub: One of the things I had done to throw people off in this country was to have our plant here have labels that said 'Made in Holland' on them, because of the liberal laws in Holland. We had a distributor in Holland who received shipments from us . . . So [when] the copyright control in Britain wanted to make an example of [Virgin Records on Oxford Street] . . . and went in there, got rough, wrecked the place, confiscated the records – I heard they roughed some people up. I heard they'd smashed counters, I heard it was like a drug bust, I heard this second hand – anyway, the record companies had a big write up about this, 'Pirated records seized at major store in London,' and all of this shit. Actually it was a little hole-in-the-wall at that time . . . We would get *Melody Maker*. I'm reading about this bust . . . it said 'Scotland Yard after careful investigation has traced the operation to Holland . . .' All they had done was looked at one of the records, which was made here in LA [but] which said 'Made in Holland' on it![10]

The Virgin Records bust, and a court judgement against Richard Branson in March 1973 (which resulted in a £1,045 fine), had an immediate impact. Bootleg product disappeared from all Virgin outlets and the 'alternative' retailers began to file their bootlegs away in some dingy alcove downstairs. In a gesture of bravado, the bootlegger responsible for the 1978 Sex Pistols bootleg *Indecent Exposure* dedicated the album to Richard Branson, by then not merely the owner of a chain of retail shops but also head mogul of the Virgin record label responsible for putting out Pistols product officially. It's rear cover included a press cutting relating Branson's own prosecution for the sale of Deep Purple bootlegs.

Dub's 'Made in Holland' ruse had been designed to disguise the real origins of TMQ. In this, the Netherlands proved a smart choice. Since the early seventies, it had been the hub of mainland European bootlegging. In Amsterdam, in particular, the authorities were renowned for looking the other way, and its flea markets contained a steady flow of new titles. The Europeans were not as easily impressed by American product as the English, preferring to set their own standards.

The first Dutch effort appears to have been a Dylan bootleg (just for a change!), the double-album *Help!* Released privately by Dutch collectors 'as a protest against the very high prices that had to be paid for imported copies of the US *Great White Wonder*', *Help!* was an original compilation of miscellaneous Dylan material. Sadly, the lousy quality and traditional stamped cover did little to set it apart from its dubious American antecedents. Nevertheless, having quickly sold out of its initial 2,500 pressing, it inspired a considerably more ambitious double-set, *Daddy Rolling Stone*. This time the cover was a rather beautiful series of drawings of Dylan, metamorphosing from authentic troubador to speed king to country squire. The first edition even contained a four-page booklet with the lyrics to all the album's songs, including those Dylan didn't write. With printed labels, good-to-excellent sound quality, and three songs from a Dutch radio broadcast of Dylan at the Isle of Wight – *Daddy Rolling Stone* set new standards in Dylan bootlegs.

The third Dutch Dylan effort, released early in 1971, surpassed even *Daddy Rolling Stone*. Before Stout was a twinkle in Dub's easel, the mysterious Peter Pontiac came up with perhaps the most inspired bootleg cover of them all. Using Crumb as his inspiration, Pontiac came up with a double-sided sleeve, printed in red, black and white, with thirteen cartoons pertaining to each of the basement-tape cuts that made up *Little White Wonder*. Pontiac's sketches, though, were far darker than anything Crumb (or indeed Stout) produced. The illustration for 'This Wheel's On Fire' had a Dylanesque figure's head exploding and a note nailed to a tree, advising the listener to 'notify my next of kin'. Displaying an obvious love for, and understanding of, Dylan's work, Pontiac has a pic-eyed Dylan eyeing up a curvaceous Mrs Henry ('Please Mrs Henry'), bribing a psychotic bus driver to take him down to California ('Yea Heavy and a Bottle of Bread') and shining like a spectre above three prisoners ('I Shall Be Released'). *Little White Wonder*, on Peace Records, was credited simply to 'The Basement Singers'.

The Dutch did not confine their interest to Dylan. Sky Dog Records – which had a base in Paris but initially operated from Holland – became the first 'bootleg' label to claim quasi-legal status. It was as an underground outfit that they first released the legendary Hendrix title *Sky High*, featuring such luminaries as Jimi Hendrix, Jim Morrison and Johnny Winter, contributing to a particularly drunken jam session at a New York club. In a laminated black and white sleeve, with a skull in a bandana emblazoned on the front cover, *Sky High* was a significant seller. Sky Dog had obviously realized that it was easier to ship their albums across national borders and sell them to cautious punters if they looked like *real* records. In fact, *Sky High* was a legitimate release, at least in Holland, since the tapes had been legitimately purchased and all royalties were paid (through the Dutch copyright-house, STEMRA). In the early years of bootlegging it was relatively easy to attain 'quasi-legitimate' status in Holland:

Yellow Dog [a bootlegger]: You could have them in your shop. It was no problem. The people from STEMRA did not have their own people going after bootlegs ... [because] STEMRA were only there for the 'mechanical reproduction' rights, and as long as they were paid there was no crime. But then they got some complaints from the industry. We didn't have a law on 'neighbouring rights' that protects the performing artist and the phonograph-producers. But then the industry [began] complaining ... it was too much competition. So then [STEMRA] started telling the bootleggers, 'No, you can't do these bootlegs anymore.' They refused to take royalties . . . But since there was so much American stuff coming into the country, I don't think [a lot of] people cared whether they made them themselves or imported them. It was so easy.[11]

Sky Dog certainly were operating with a 'bootleg' mentality. Indeed, when Sky Dog's Parisian partner, Marc Zermati, met Ken in LA in the early months of 1973 he was appalled at the mercenary nature of his Smokin' Pig operation.

WITH: ELVIS PRESLEY, JERRY LEE LEWIS, BILLY LEE RILEY, WARREN SMITH / ALTERNATIVE & UNISSUED VERSIONS · · · · · · · · BOPCAT RECORDS LP-100 · · · · · · · ·

Marc Zermati: [At this point] we realized that these guys were really only in it for the money. For us it was a much more radical thing . . . [we wanted to] undermine the record industry.[12]

Sky High may have been kosher, but the other early Sky Dog title, *Evil Mothers*, was definitely not an approved release. Zermati had been given copies of the complete Brigid Polk tapes of the Velvet Underground at Max's in 1970 and had sent copies to his Dutch partner, who proceeded to release them under the Sky Dog banner, thus creating the first Velvet Underground bootleg, at a time when the Velvets' legitimate sales barely numbered in the thousands. Shortly afterwards, Zermati and his Dutch partner went their separate ways and the French-based label went 'legit' with a legendary live album of Iggy & the Stooges' final show, *Metallic K.O.*

The Dutch also discerned another significant gap in the market. In 1973 the anonymous Bopcat Records produced *Good Rocking Tonight*, a collection of outtakes from the fabled Memphis label, Sun Records. As one Presley discographer wrote, '[*Good Rocking Tonight*] looked like a product that could have come from a major record company. The cover was professional-looking, with two black and white photos surrounded by a bright red border on the front and seven more photos on the back. There were liner notes which gave generous amounts of historical data, and the song titles were annotated to show where and when they had been recorded.'[13]

While the presentation may have been impressive, it was the musical contents that provided the more dramatic reconstruction

of history in the making. Side one was devoted entirely to Presley and included four genuine outtakes from the Sun sessions. These included a bluesy stab at 'My Baby is Gone' (which later turned into 'I'm Left, You're Right, She's Gone') and an alternative version of 'Blue Moon of Kentucky', which collapses at the end as producer Sam Phillips exclaims, 'Hell, that's different! That's a pop song now, nearly 'bout.'

Indeed it was the studio chatter between takes that made *Good Rocking Tonight* such an insight into the birth of 'that rock & roll music'. The second side, devoted to Billy Lee Riley, Warren Smith and Jerry Lee Lewis, contained an even more revealing exchange between Phillips and Jerry Lee in which Jerry Lee insists that rock & roll is leading him away from the path of righteousness. Moments like these made bootlegs a very revealing form of rock archaeology, providing insights into an untold audio history. *Good Rocking Tonight* also showed that there was a substantial market for early rock & roll being overlooked by Californian bootleggers hankering for the next inaudible Beatles tape.

If *Good Rocking Tonight* was a convincing enough artifact, the Europeans were becoming ever more conscious of presentation. By 1975, there were two outfits producing bootlegs that made TMQ's recent releases look amateurish by comparison. One desired complete anonymity, swopping identities with each release, while locking into a vast market for Pink Floyd with a series of authoritative live releases (*Best of Tour '72*, *Tour '73* and *British Winter Tour '74*). *Best of Tour '72*, culled from a live BBC broadcast of *Dark Side of the Moon*, and housed in a deluxe black and white sleeve, sold exceptionally well, as did *Tour '73*, again taken from a BBC broadcast. But it was *British Winter Tour '74* that caused the biggest hoo-hah, sending the BPI into a frenzied search for the perpetrators. Recorded in Stoke – home of the biggest bootleg mail-order specialist of his day – *Winter Tour '74* consisted of just three songs, two of which clocked in at twelve minutes, the other at twenty-four. The songs in question were intended for Floyd's next album, the eagerly awaited follow-up to *Dark Side of the Moon*. The lyrics to 'Raving and Drooling', 'You Gotta be Crazy' and 'Shine On You Crazy Diamond' were printed on the back of the laminated colour sleeve. The quality of presentation and its wholly unreleased contents seemed to suggest that this might be Floyd's new album. In fact, one listen to this fair-to-middling audience tape would have convinced anyone that this was not the case. Nevertheless, over the years increasingly extravagant claims for sales of *Winter Tour '74* have appeared. Though its so-called 50,000 sales most likely devolves down to something like 10,000 copies, it was still a huge seller by European standards.

The BPI's suspicion that *Winter Tour '74* was perhaps a British production was seemingly corroborated by another UK 'special', bearing all the same trademarks, released just a couple of months later. *Earl's Court* was an equally deluxe affair, taken from one of Led Zeppelin's unremittingly tedious shows at London's cavernous exhibition hall in May 1975. As if determined to provide the most accurate snapshot of Zeppelin's three-hour-plus performance that Saturday night, the bootlegger selected for his first volume an excruciating twenty-five minute version of 'No Quarter', topped off with a side of as-acoustic-as-Zep-ever-got, prefaced by a severely stoned Mr Plant wittering on about friends who've fallen by the wayside. The poor song selection mattered not one jot, nor did the echoey, recessed sound of the actual recording: *Earl's Court* was another top-selling title.

It was the presentation rather than the content of *Winter Tour '74* and *Earl's Court* that sold these albums. Fans who were used to paper inserts and single-colour labels assumed that such lavish presentation contained contents to match. In fact, bootleggers quickly learned that the shoddier the content, the more aesthetically pleasing the packaging should be.

Thankfully, not everyone applied such logic. The Swedish label Stoned Records was a most notable exception. Though Stoned issued a mere half a dozen albums in the fifteen months they existed, all of their choices were impressively audacious. Lou Reed (*Whatever Happened to Dick and Steve*), Patti Smith (*I Never Talked to Bob Dylan*), Roxy Music (*Why'd You Think I'm a Funky Chick*) and Queen (*A Night at the Warehouse*) were some

of their 'victims'. All of their releases were from 'original' source tapes, often soundboard, generally from shows in Stockholm itself, and all Stoned albums were housed in full-colour sleeves, generally with photos from the actual show to illustrate them, and they were all marked with Stoned's four-colour label. Pressed in relatively small numbers, the Stoned catalogue was ruthlessly rebootlegged after the perpetrators were busted in the summer of 1977. Prior to the Stoned bust, Sweden had always been one of the more lucrative markets for retailing bootlegs. Clearly, though, Sweden's attitude to bootlegging was not quite as lax as Holland's. The man behind Stoned was actually sentenced to four months' imprisonment and ordered to pay compensation for the estimated 16,000 records he had sold.

The Stoned bust seemed to signal a lull in European production. Some labels switched to bootlegging the new punk bands that were creating so much interest critically, while others concentrated on one or two particular artists. A Dutch bootlegger came up with RSVP (Rolling Stones Vinyl Pressings) and a series of landmark Stones titles, including a three-album boxed-set, *The Black Box*, which came with a 'personal invitation' and a collection of Stones cuttings, all encased in a black box with a black ribbon bow. This was a pointed 'dig' at Decca for releasing the shoddy *Metamorphosis* album instead of Bill Wyman's suggested collection of Stones outtakes, to be called *The Black Box*. The RSVP *Black Box* did not actually contain anything new, comprising represses of three notable collections of Stones studio recordings – RSVP's own *Gravestones* and *Rape of the Vaults*, and a copy of TMQ's *Beautiful Delilah* – but it collected together three essential Stones releases. Using coloured vinyl for their limited edition first runs, RSVP was one of the first 'specialist' one-band labels since the MOR 'fan club only' releases of the early sixties.

The Dutch and Scandinavians knew they were operating in an ambiguous legal domain. Thankfully, authorities were rarely interested in investigating whether they were contravening the letter of the law or merely its spirit. But there was one country where it seemed possible to bypass an artist's rights altogether.

In 1973 a series of three Dylan albums appeared in Italian supermarkets. Entitled *A Rare Batch of Little White Wonder Volumes 1–3*, each of the three records, on the Joker label, had SIAE stamps on the rear cover. The SIAE stamps signified that the albums were 'copyright paid', meaning that they were legitimate releases in Italy. In fact, all three albums were composed entirely of material taken from five TMQ bootlegs, and each of the three volumes contained outtakes from Columbia recording sessions. In the case of the third volume, two of the songs had even been issued as singles in Europe – 'If You Gotta Go, Go Now' and 'Can You Please Crawl Out Your Window'.

How these albums came to be 'legal' in Italy has always been something of a mystery. They did not lie in the 'public domain' – even in Italy – as all the songs had been recorded in the past twenty years (the period of mechanical copyright protection in Italy), and they were not live performances (which are treated differently under Italian law). Exactly one song ('Dusty Old Fairgrounds' on Volume 3) was from a live performance, and that was from a show recorded by Columbia. Perhaps Columbia had simply not established their own 'a priori' claim. It seems more likely that the failure of the US to sign the Rome and Geneva conventions (they did not ratify the Geneva Convention until March 1974, by which time the joke was on them) and Italy's belated ratification of the Rome Convention in 1975 allowed Joker to temporarily exploit some copyright loophole.

Joker certainly didn't repeat the exercise with other artists, though the Dylan titles were not the only questionable releases on the label. They had also been responsible for three volumes of *Jimi Hendrix at His Best*, some truly dreadful bedroom jams recorded by a 'teenage friend', and a *Beatles vs. The Stones* collection. Whatever loophole Joker had found, when another Italian affiliate, Buhay Records, reissued the Dylan volumes, they came up with an entirely different third volume. Perhaps Columbia had finally realized that Joker's Volume 3 had two legitimately released CBS cuts (which even in Italy must have qualified as a breach of Columbia's copyright).

The biggest problem was how to stop copies of the Joker albums sprouting up in Britain, France and Germany. They were certainly illegal when exported from Italy (though no one dared test the law, save in America where a New England wholesaler was busted for selling them). If no kosher Italian label chose to follow the precedent set by Joker, assorted versions of *Rare Batch* remained in print throughout the seventies and early eighties. Italian entrepreneurs' ability to bend their laws would not be tested again until the CD age, when another little-known hole in Italian law would prove ripe for exploitation.

What these widely available quasi-bootlegs did show was the potential market for 'collectors' releases', something the larger record companies had taken little account of when considering their rock catalogues. Even in the mid seventies their solitary response to bootlegs on the same terms was official bootleg albums given to radio stations to play. *A Rare Batch* was not the last quasi-bootleg to make it to the high street.

In 1977, EMI were at last considering releasing an official Beatles live album (from the oft-bootlegged Hollywood Bowl shows). Meanwhile, a small-time entrepreneur had acquired 'King' Taylor's tapes of the pre-EMI Beatles, performing at the Star Club, Hamburg. Their imminent release was threatening to spoil EMI's party. Since Taylor's tape supposedly pre-dated the EMI contract, and The Beatles had allegedly given their permission for the show to be taped, there seemed no reason why the tapes could not be released. Indeed, with The Beatles being offered full payment of performance and songwriting royalties, it was difficult to see how a legitimate release could be stopped. EMI and The Beatles were prepared to try.

Paul Murphy, now the legal owner of the tapes, had offered the tapes to EMI but they had said they weren't interested. Considering the recording quality – a flat, unexceptional audience tape – this was hardly surprising. When an injunction to stop the album's release was issued, Murphy reminded EMI that, 'The Beatles have never said they would not give their permission for the record to be released . . . [and] I have never made a secret of my intention to put out the tapes over here.' When the judge queried why The Beatles had taken so long to make a legal issue of the tape, they had no reply. Alan Heyman, QC for Murphy and Lingasong, told the judge that they had been prepared to offer The Beatles and Apple 50p per record sold or to have profits paid into court pending a possible appeal. The Beatles' QC replied that The Beatles were not interested in these offers since they were not bringing the court action for profit. The judge dismissed the case.

Live at Star Club thus became the first 'official bootleg' freely available in all European record stores. The questionable legality of the material was to be pushed even further in the early eighties, when it appeared as part of a triple-album set in tandem with The Beatles' Decca audition tape. The Decca tapes had been bootlegged extensively in the late seventies after two East Coast bootleggers had paid an English gentleman $5,000 for the tape, before issuing it as a series of 7″ coloured-vinyl, picture-sleeve singles. The tapes were then 'legally' acquired by Audio Fidelity in the US, who attempted an official release in 1982. Once again, The Beatles took legal action to stop its release. This time they succeeded, though European imports freely flowed into the States.

The Beatles' own attitude to bootlegging had always been ambivalent. Lennon went to great pains to collect all the bootlegs he could, while McCartney, though apparently antagonistic, happily referred to 'standing with a bootleg in his hand' on the 1973 single 'Hi Hi Hi'. Ringo Starr, on the other hand, a man who is almost entirely beholden to Messrs Lennon and McCartney for his considerable personal wealth, seemed quite malevolent in his attitude to them:

Bootlegs I hate . . . because the product is usually . . . not a good representation of the artist. It's just some crumb who doesn't do anything making all the bread. I wouldn't mind a bootleg if it went to charity or somewhere, but all those [bootleggers] are very negative people. They just pick up something by luck and shove it out and make all the bread, and it's just not a good product and they're conning the kids . . . It's usually like some hip guy who's putting out the bootlegs, but he's the closest thing to The Fat Cigar I've ever heard of! He's done nothing, no talent, and he just makes all the bread ... I wish people would stop buying 'em, then the market would fall through.[14]

Starr's perception of bootleggers parasitically riding on the backs of successful acts would not be borne out by the activities of the European bootleggers in the late seventies. Following The Sex Pistols' demolition-derby of a career, 'new wave' bands the length and breadth of Britain seemed determined to plant some metaphorical gelignite beneath the towers of Manchester Square. Bootlegs were once again an in-vogue gesture of anti-establishment feelings. It was 1969 all over again.

9 Anarchy in the UK

SeX PiSTOLs

L TO RIGHT·PAUL COOK-DRUMS·JOHNNY ROTTEN· VOCALS, STEVE JONES-GUITAR· GLEN MATLOCK-BASS

inDecent

It's a dirty business

LET us all applaud the explosion of public outrage that greeted the Sex Pistols' four-letter outburst on TV.

But the day after, please note, 1,800 copies of their first record are reported to have been sold.

The Sex Pistols' filth has meant filthy lucre for E.M.I., the world's biggest gramophone company, which has them under contract.

Mr. Leslie Hills, the E.M.I. man who is responsible for the firm's records, did not condone the group's behaviour on TV. But he does not seem to mind the company profiting from the publicity.

VOICE OF THE PEOPLE

The company is said to be planning more records by the Sex Pistols and to have no intention of controlling either their songs or their behaviour in public. If that is so, there ought to be another explosion of disgust—at E.M.I.

The great majority of people, parents especially, want to protect children from the vileness of punk rock performers.

They are entitled to expect that a great and reputable record company will uphold standards of decency and not help undermine them.

EXPLOITING PUNK MAY BE GOOD FOR THE BALANCE SHEET, BUT IT IS A DIRTY BUSINESS ALL THE SAME.

EXPOSuRe

"I think EMI ought to set some sort of standard and ban records like this."

Lenny Kaye [Patti Smith Group]: It's easier to bootleg a band earlier . . . because they're much more prone to do oddball radio broadcasts, or they'll just show up someplace and it's easier to go into a club, and you get a little bit better sound and it's a little bit better [as a] moment . . . one of the reasons [the Patti Smith Group] broke up was that the larger we got the less room we had to experiment onstage.[1]

In the years before punk, the expansion of the bootleg market was partly due to a lack of new commercial rock & roll to excite the jaded palates of 'hardcore' rock fans. Only by turning back to the 'lost' recordings of their fave raves could these fans remind themselves what that spirit of rock & roll might have been. Between 1969 and 1976, rock had settled into a comfortable middle-age that belied its fiery origins. Arena rock had become the norm. Club 'scenes' were few and far between.

The notable exceptions, and perhaps the two most exciting American acts to play 'the circuit' in the mid seventies, were Patti Smith and Bruce Springsteen. Smith and Springsteen had both grown up from a groundswell of support, based on dramatic club performances. Both initially shunned the arenas that their landmark '75 releases, 'Horses' and 'Born to Run', suggested could become their resting homes. Both were also heavily bootlegged on both sides of the pond. After a heavy dose of 'Horses' bootlegs Stateside, Smith's equally ambitious European shows in 1976 were bootlegged in the UK (*Live at the Roundhouse*) and Sweden (*I Never Talked to Bob Dylan*).

One of the legendary Springsteen titles – *Fire on the Fingertips* – also originated in the UK, where a Bruce 'demo tape' had been sitting idle in a London music publishers since the early seventies. While the bulk of Springsteen bootlegs to date had documented his exhaustive live performances, *Fire on the Fingertips* centred on studio material, with its six unreleased early cuts, including regular rabble-rouser 'Thundercrack', that prototype for all the stories of lost souls refined on *Born to Run*: 'Zero & Blind Terry', and a good-time stab at sixties schlock: 'Seaside Bar Song'. It was the first Springsteen bootleg to really hint at the sheer wealth of songs he discarded in his most creative years. Reviewed enthusiastically in the *New Musical Express*, *Fire on the Fingertips* was the bridge between *Greetings from Asbury* and *The Wild, the Innocent and the E Street Shuffle*. Despite the fact that Springsteen had barely charted with *Born to Run* in the UK, and was very much a 'cult' act still suffering from early comparisons with Dylan, *Fire on the Fingertips* sold extremely well.

Clearly the cult appeal of acts like Smith and Springsteen did not hamper their 'bootlegability'. They also managed to retain their original fans while transcending the club scenes that had spawned them. In this sense they were precursors of the next generation of bootlegged bands – the English punks.

The history of punk, particularly the English brand of punk, is bound up with the bootlegs that document the early days of the movement. Unlike any commensurate explosion in rock history, it would be impossible to consider either the social or musical impact of English punk without considering The Sex Pistols' *Spunk* and *Indecent Exposure*, The Buzzcocks' *Time's Up*, Siouxsie and the Banshees' *Love in a Void* or Joy Division's *Warsaw* – albums as central to the movement as *The Clash*, *Never Mind the Bollocks* or *Pink Flag*. For a brief moment, the lines were down.

Part of the demand – the need – for these artifacts resulted from the fact that, though punk in England ignited very quickly, the flash of inspiration that led bands to form, reformulate and disintegrate, all within such a combustible environment, often meant that a band's 'peak' was over and gone before any save the hip, London- or (to a lesser extent) Manchester-based youths were even aware of it. It could be argued that the influence and impact of the original punk bands lingered on only because their music was bootlegged. By January 1978, The Sex Pistols were no more and the demand for recordings of their live performances had never been higher. In this case, fans had no choice but to accept substitutes. Likewise, the original Devoto/Shelley incarnation of The Buzzcocks played just a dozen gigs, and recorded some demos and one EP, before they broke in two; Magazine being what Devoto had wanted The Buzzcocks to be, while The Buzzcocks were now cast solely in Shelley's image.

It is a curious phenomenon of punk that the incarnations of bands responsible for the original hoo-hah were almost never the ones to make the vinyl statements that made their mark in the marketplace. Even in New York, the founders of the CBGBs scene, Television, released no hard evidence before Richard Hell quit. Nor did the originators of Cleveland's contemporary punk scene, Rocket from the Tombs, before they mutated into the Dead Boys and Pere Ubu. In London, the pukka Pistols, with main songwriter Glen Matlock on bass, released just one single, 'Anarchy in the UK', before personalities got in the way of a musical future and Matlock was nudged out. The Clash, founded around the twin-guitar thrust of Keith Levene and Mick Jones, dispensed with the services of a narcotic-lovin' Levene before 'White Riot'. Siouxsie and the Banshees' original guitarist, Pete Fenton, and co-author of early Banshees favourites like 'Love in a Void' and 'Make Up to Break Up', was also ousted before their first release. Laura Logic, X-Ray Spex's most visual focal point and instigator of the sax sound that set them apart, contributed to just 'Oh Bondage Up Yours' before devising some Essential Logic of her own. As such, punk has a secret history all its own and the bootlegs were a necessary medium for punk excavations.

The UK had not been a central point of bootleg manufacture for some time, largely because of the inherent risks involved. Now, though, just as English punk was putting UK rock back on the map, the demand for punk bootlegs was both substantial and largely based in the UK. Given the obscurity of the punk acts, it seemed a risk worth taking for some shrewd soul to make alternative artifacts exclusively for the home market. Sure enough, in July 1977 an article in the NME, 'Now the Boot's on the Other Leg', announced:

And welcome to the inevitable. Any week now, your friendly neighbourhood bootleg cellar will be adding two new delicacies to its rock and roll smorgasbord: *No Fun* by The Sex Pistols and *White Riot* by The Clash . . . The Pistols bootleg is particularly rough: it's grade Z mono, makes *The Beatles at the Star Club Hamburg 1962* sound like a Yes album by comparison.[2]

Appropriately, the first two 'punk' titles both came from shows in Manchester, home of The Buzzcocks and second home of English punk. The Sex Pistols' *No Fun* was from a June 1976 show at the Lesser Free Trade Hall and, as the *NME* was quick to point out, was truly lo-fi. However, it was also probably *the* single most important gig in punk's brief epoch. Attended by barely seventy superhip souls, the gig was The Pistols' first real sortie beyond the home counties. Among the chosen few were Steven Morrisscy, later of the Smiths, who snapped a couple of shots of the show and penned a series of letters to the music press extolling the virtues of The Pistols' brand of punk. Also inspired by the performance were four young men from Macclesfield soon rehearsing under the name Warsaw, before choosing Joy Division as a more appropriate moniker. More immediately inspired were Pete Shelley and Howard Devoto, two local lads who had already travelled south to witness The Pistols at home county shows in February. Six weeks later they would make their band debut as The Buzzcocks, supporting The Sex Pistols on their return to the Lesser Free Trade Hall at the end of July (where the Cockney rabble premiered 'Anarchy in the UK').

As an exercise in spreading the word there can surely be no other gig which has inspired so much from so few. Even through the murky gloom of *No Fun*, collectors could see why. Here was a band at its belligerent best, no niceties, no platitudes, just the sound of youthful anger and arrogance in one resounding roar. The Pistols were just two singles old when *No Fun* hit the streets, but already that sound, driven by some shameless off-key harmonies and the ballsy basslines of Glen Matlock, was no more.

White Riot, the other document of Mancunian punk hospitality, captured The Clash on their first headlining tour of the UK roaring through their first album set. Several rungs up from the well that The Pistols gig had been recorded in, *White Riot* was an equally exuberant document of young punks in flight.

However, it was the next Pistols bootleg which caused the biggest furore of any bootleg originating in the UK. *Spunk* in its many forms probably ranks third to Prince's *Black Album* and Dylan's *Great White Wonder* in bootleg vinyl sales and is probably the seventies' most legendary bootleg.

Spunk was entirely composed of top-notch studio material, recorded by the original Pistols, with producer Dave Goodman, between July 1976 and January 1977. Part demos, part first EMI session, part attempt to cut songs for their debut album, *Spunk* was the essential Pistols album. It was also in the shops (at least the right ones) a couple of weeks before The Sex Pistols' long-awaited official debut, *Never Mind the Bollocks*. In an extensive two-page story on this artifact from the void in October 1977, *Sounds* journalist Chas de Whalley attempted to answer the primal question: How come an album of pristine quality early Pistols studio recordings should come to be released at this particular moment in time? When *Sounds* asked Nick Mobbs – the A&R guy responsible for signing The Sex Pistols to EMI – about EMI's own tapes, Mobbs had no problem recalling where they had gone:

Nick Mobbs: Obviously we have a cassette or two of the stuff The Pistols did for us, just as keepsakes. But Malcolm McLaren retained the full rights to everything the band ever did and he took the master tapes with him when he left the label.[3]

The Pistols and their management company, Glitterbest, had indeed 'retained the full rights to everything the band ever did'. What they intended to do with the tapes had never been entirely clear. In March 1977, Goodman had played *Spunk* to Tony Parsons, an *NME* journalist, who promptly wrote it up as if it was The Pistols' forthcoming album. The headline of Parsons' piece was 'Blank Nuggets in the UK'.

When the bootleg version appeared, the label was indeed Blank, not as in 'blank' but as in 'Blank Records', with a gun thrusting out from its pink backdrop. The album was simply credited to *Spunk* and the song titles were all apocryphal. Thus, 'Anarchy in the UK' became 'Nookie', 'Pretty Vacant' – 'Lots of Fun', etc. The quality of both the pressing and the mastering was exemplary. This was hardly surprising as the album had been pressed at a famous independent pressing plant and bore the instantly identifiable matrix-number prefix LYN. Though the copy bought by *Sounds* journalist Chas de Whalley at Rough Trade's Ladbroke Grove grotto had the matrix number scratched out by the shop assistant, the bootlegger himself was not unduly concerned by the album's traceability:

Alan Henderson: *Spunk* had this LYN matrix number which sort of advertised Lintone in huge letters. Which [my partner] and I thought was so amazingly uncool and made us really worried about dealing with the guy because we just thought he was not living in the real world. We thought, 'Who is this guy who says, "Yeah, went down to Lintone, told them to press up this record, gave 'em a load of cash. Yeah, so it's got LYN on there. Who's gonna notice?"' We were rather shocked that anyone would have the effrontery to do this, but of course anyone could do that: take one risk, do it, maybe Lintone knew what it was and didn't care. By that time 'Anarchy in the UK' had been released . . . And the first few thousand we took out into my back garden and spray painted a stencil with *Spunk*. [The bootlegger] had no past record of doing bootlegs and, of course, as soon as it came out the Europeans copied it and put it in a green sleeve.[4]

Despite Parsons' assertion in his March 1977 review, there had surely never been any question of The Pistols issuing *Spunk* as their debut album. Most of the songs sound like the demos they are – gut-wrenching, taut performances captured in all their rough'n'ready earthiness, but demos none the less – and as an exercise in assaulting the mainstream of rock, destined to fail. The whole thing was just too edgy, too stripped-down, too cacophonous. This 'Anarchy in the UK', in particular, said everything that needed to be said about how The Pistols really could sound. The version on *Spunk* was in fact the one they had cut with Goodman as their debut single. It is announced over pounding drums and bass, Rotten bellowing, 'Vinyl quotation number WOOON!!' The roaring feedback and Rotten's sick-to-death vocals make this The Pistols' ultimate studio *tour de force*. As a first vinyl statement – particularly if packaged with a seven-minute take of The Stooges' 'No Fun' on the flipside (as originally intended) – it would have been the most radical gesture imaginable. EMI were not happy with the results:

Dave Goodman [record producer]: EMI were a bit put out that we hadn't done what they wanted and they said the production wasn't good enough. So they brought in Chris Thomas, who really only copied my demos note for note but made them into pop records. In fact, he told the *NME* recently that he hadn't really been needed for 'Anarchy in the UK' and they could have released my version with no trouble.[5]

No way could *Spunk* be The Pistols' legacy to the pop world. But as an alternative 'debut' it was brilliantly conceived. *Never Mind the Bollocks* might have sounded like a good hard-rock album for the seventies, but *Spunk* was just four teenagers locked upstairs in a room on Denmark Street, cutting loose and blowing away the cobwebs of the seventies. As Chas de Whalley noted at the end of his *Sounds* piece that introduced *Spunk* to the world:

All in all, and despite the fact that it's a bootleg and illegal and everything, *Spunk* is an album that no self-respecting rock fan would turn his nose up at. I've been playing it constantly for a week, and I'm not bored yet.[6]

De Whalley had also attempted to ask the person many fans suspected of being the source for *Spunk* what he thought of it:

Seasoned Pistols observers suggested that Malcolm McLaren might have been behind the Blank Label (in the interests of Anarchy and Complete Control – dig) but this was firmly denied (in his absence) by his secretary.[7]

Despite Virgin's understandable chagrin and some belligerent threats from Rotten on BBC radio, suggesting that he knew exactly who was behind the album and fully intended to deal with

him, and even the incautious behaviour of 'the bootlegger' himself – pressing at a famous plant in the UK, leaving the matrix number on the album etc. – no one was ever prosecuted for *Spunk*. Indeed, over the years the songs have all been released officially in dribs and drabs – on Virgin's *The Great Rock & Roll Swindle* and two independent releases, *The Mini Album* and *Early Daze*. When Jon Savage published his huge tome on The Pistols and early punk, *England's Dreaming*, in 1991, he strongly implied that *Spunk* was a McLaren project all along:

McLaren preferred [*Spunk*] to the finished album, although Cook and Jones were embarrassed by the quality. In fact, Glitterbest owned the tapes – as they had paid for both recordings outside any contract – but the release was in breach of the Virgin deal.[8]

Whatever the identity of the mysterious gentlemen who delivered *Spunk* to Alan, it was one of Rotten's drinking buddies who was responsible for another collection of early studio recordings by one of punk's first wave, Siouxsie and the Banshees. Like *Spunk*, many fans considered *Love in a Void* superior to Siouxsie and the Banshees' debut album, *The Scream*. Issued at the beginning of 1979, shortly after *The Scream*, *Love in a Void* comprised two John Peel sessions, recorded after original guitarist Fenton had left the Banshees but before they signed to Polydor, and three demos recorded for Track Records (with Fenton in tow) – including 'Make Up to Break Up' and the title-track, both omitted from their Polydor debut. Issued on Sioux records, the Banshees bootleg caused severe ructions in the Banshees camp, who were not at all happy to be reminded of their roots, in particular the anti-semitic reference to 'too many Jews for my liking' in 'Love in a Void'.

Most punk bands liked the kudos of being bootlegged and did not necessarily want their outlaw, edge-of-the-industry stance to be called into question. The Banshees, though, had always set themselves apart from the scene, and when manager Nils Stevenson was asked what objections he had to the artifact in question, he insisted that it was all about control:

Nils Stevenson: If you're making records you should have the right to decide what records go out and what quality they have. If these bastards start putting out stuff you don't want to put out, then they're taking away your control ... The bootleggers wouldn't have bothered to produce it unless the market was already there for it. They didn't create the market by putting it out, they cashed in on a market that was already there.[9]

Love in a Void may not have created a market, but the truth is that many Banshees fans were disappointed by the takes of songs like 'Carcass' and 'Helter Skelter' on *The Scream*, preferring the versions they had heard originally on John Peel's radio show. After all, it was the two Peel sessions, recorded in November 1977 and February 1978, that had first brought the Banshees to national attention. Banshees co-founder Steve Severin, questioned on the matter by bootleg fanzine *Hot Wax Quarterly*, insisted that he only objected to its vinyl form:

Steve Severin: We object to bootlegs, but not because we want the material heard in one way, it's nothing to do with that. It's just that people who have no interest in the band are making a lot of money off people who are. The thing that annoyed us about [*Love in a Void*] was the fact that it mainly consisted of two John Peel radio shows that were repeated five or six times over the year. Anybody could have taped them for their own enjoyment at home, but the fact that somebody had put them together on an album and made it a desirable item and were charging up to £9 for them, we thought it was ridiculous![10]

The Banshees felt *Love in a Void* to be so ridiculous that they took legal action against the bootlegger, suing him for damages and winning. 'Meet the new boss, same as the old boss!'

In fact *Love in a Void*, though it sold well enough, was not the 'bestseller' that *Spunk* had been. It was not simply that the Banshees were less commercial than the now defunct Pistols. Many fans had indeed taped the Peel sessions and were quite happy with their cassette copies, and the bulk of *Love in a Void* was still very much the same band (and sound) as *The Scream*.

On the other hand, The Buzzcocks of *Spiral Scratch*, their

privately pressed debut EP, was most certainly not the band now signed to United Artists and in the process of putting out a series of singles that defined English powerpop. The demand for *Time's Up*, a collection of four-track demos recorded in preparation for *Spiral Scratch* one afternoon in October 1976, was perhaps second only to *Spunk*.

The Buzzcocks had, after all, been one of English punk's original foursomes. Along with The Clash, The Pistols and The Damned, the Devoto/Shelley line-up shared legendary bills at London's 100 Club and Screen on the Green and Manchester's Lesser Free Trade Hall and Electric Circus. However, it was not until their fourth single, 'Ever Fallen in Love', that they would achieve the commercial success Shelley's powerpop demanded. Howard Devoto had left to form Magazine (who beat the Buzzcocks to the charts with their magnificent debut 45, 'Shot by Both Sides') even before The Buzzcocks' first United Artists single, a Devoto original on the joys of self-abuse, 'Orgasm Addict'. *Time's Up* presented the *Spiral Scratch* sound at a time when even The Buzzcocks' solitary EP was long deleted. For many it was their first opportunity to hear punk's finest provincials.

Time's Up was housed in an attractive red sleeve with a murky photo of the Buzzcocks Mk 1. It came out just as The Sex Pistols were imploding. Along with the seemingly simultaneous release of a genuine document of the Pistols *circa* 1976 (*Indecent Exposure*), *Time's Up* became a crucial document of an era that was already over. Punk was now New Wave. The Pistols and Buzzcocks Mk 1 were no more. Once again, the pressing plant responsible for this British punk 'boot' was Lintone, with that instantly identifiable LYN matrix number again etched in the vinyl. In fairness, only the hippest of plant operatives would have known who that drawling northern monotone belonged to, and since the songs were cut at a time when The Buzzcocks had no contract (at a cost of £45), it seemed to be a matter between the band and the bootlegger. Yet Buzzcocks manager Richard Boone was still approached by the BPI.

Richard Boone: The BPI asked if we were aware [copies of *Time's Up*] were on the streets. We said we were, and they said they were looking into it ... We didn't object to its existence *per se*, just to the fact that someone is making something out of it at the expense of not only the group and their reputation, but at the expense of fans of the group ... We liked the material, and I'm sure it's got fantastic historical merit ... and it does mean you've got a certain amount of status and a certain market, which is quite nice. In fact, it's very flattering.[11]

Unlike *Time's Up*, the live Pistols document *Indecent Exposure* was pressed in Italy, though it was in every sense a UK production. After years as a distributor, the figure behind Bread & Circuses had re-entered the fray. He had had the tape for some time but had held off releasing it for fear of stealing the thunder from *Never Mind the Bollocks*. He need not have worried!

Alan Henderson: I [had] met up with an Italian guy who had offered the facility of being able to manufacture some records, so we did some rather awful Stones live at Earls Court, *Have You Seen Keef Standing in the Shadow*, one I recorded myself, *Patti Smith at the Roundhouse*, and following Patti Smith, who I was really into, came the punk thing, and I was given various tapes of the Sex Pistols from '76 and at the same time I was suddenly excited by music ... Because basically the music that we'd been doing on the bootlegs was full of loads of boring stuff like Yes and people beyond their peak. And suddenly I was off down to all these [punk clubs] ... I saw The Sex Pistols just prior to the Bill Grundy [show] and stood at the back wondering what the hell was going on ... And then for the first time I felt really bad about doing a Sex Pistols bootleg before they'd actually had their own record out because when you went to the Vortex or the Speakeasy you'd bump shoulders with them and you'd go and see The Slits headlining with Adam and the Ants second on the bill and Siouxsie and the Banshees opening. It was all a totally different attitude ... So I was very slow in getting the live Sex Pistols bootleg together, which was *Indecent Exposure*, sort of deliberately because it would have been so big at the time and therefore would have been very hot![12]

How many people the 'Matlock' Pistols played to may be a

matter of conjecture, but it certainly numbered in the hundreds rather than the thousands. Given that throughout 1976 theirs was essentially a local notoriety, restricted to the cloistered confines of a London punk scene driven by the music press, and that this was before audience-taping was the norm rather than the exception, it is perhaps surprising that there are even a couple of dozen audience tapes from The Pistols' first year of gigging. However, with the exception of the September 1976 Burton-on-Trent tape used for *Indecent Exposure*, none was of more than adequate sound quality. The Burton tape, though a tad 'thin', and despite The Pistols not being as locked in as at Manchester in June or at the 100 Club Punk Festival four days earlier, remains a surprisingly fine document of the 1976 Pistols, lurching through their customary mixture of sixties covers like '(Don't You Give Me) No Lip', 'Substitute' and '(I'm Not Your) Steppin' Stone' and anthems for a blank generation like 'Anarchy in the UK' and 'Problems' (initially drowned out by feedback).

Indecent Exposure was also a perfect antidote to the lacklustre bootlegs of The Pistols' final show at San Francisco's Winterland now rolling in from across the pond (Ruthless Rhymes' *Gun Control* had a shot of Rotten and Matlock trading dirty looks on the cover!). *Indecent Exposure*'s fold-out sleeve took the form of a cut-up of some of the extreme national press coverage that The Pistols had generated and was an integral part of a 45-minute insight into a revolution in gestation.

Punk bootlegs seemed to hype the bands better than any marketing department. This promotional facet hit overdrive with Devo, a band from Akron, Ohio, who had barely managed two independent single releases in the US – imported into the UK by Stiff Records – when two full-colour bootleg albums and an EP were to be easily found in the racks of Britain's forest of independent record stores, now catering almost exclusively to the galvanized punk consumer.

Workforce to the World, in particular, gave a far more concrete idea of what Devo was about than their first two singles, the quirky 'Jocko Homo' and their metronome cover of The Stones' 'Satisfaction'. An excellent soundboard of a 1977 show at San

Francisco's Mabuhay Gardens, this European bootleg sold surprisingly well on the back of a much hyped first trip to the UK for shows in Manchester and London. The *Mechanical Man* EP, four demos from 1974–5, was a more traditional bootleg presentation, with its stamped cover and no notes as to the source of the songs.

It seemed that bootlegs were now a 'legitimate' way of affirming a hype surrounding a particular flavour of the month. The notion that only mainstream bestsellers could be bootlegged was definitively put out to pasture by punk. At the end of 1979, The Specials achieved a similar buzz to Devo with their *Live at Aston University*, another pristine soundboard that suggested an insider had been determined to provide the evidence to back up some serious word of mouth. The Slits went one step further a year later, issuing their own official bootleg of a particularly cacophonous show from 'the days of punk', while Throbbing Gristle made the ultimate gesture to their collector-fans when, upon disbanding, they issued a limited edition boxed-set of individually annotated cassettes of every live Throbbing Gristle tape they could locate.

The end of that moment when bootlegs were alternative signposts came at the beginning of the eighties. The commercial world felt it had digested the more palatable parts of the New Wave. The deaths of Sid Vicious and Ian Curtis had marked the end of a period of innocence, and official companies took over marketing fans' death-fixations. An aborted first Joy Division album, recorded between the Warsaw EP *Ideal for Living* and the first Factory album, *Unknown Pleasures*, was the only essential punk bootleg release of 1980. The first edition of *Warsaw* – an odd title given that Joy Division had already made the name-change when the sessions took place – even included a 'free' EP of the first Joy Division John Peel session. *Warsaw* was more rock than soundtrack-to-the-apocalypse and placed the passage from Warsaw to Herzog in a stark new perspective. Despite Factory issuing their own double 'official' bootleg of lost Joy Division recordings, *Still* (as in a 'bootleg still', geddit!), the surviving members have chosen not to issue *Warsaw* officially, preferring its illicit status. But the lessons of punk were such that bootleg evangelists soon realized that there was no need to live outside the law, just at its outer reaches.

In France, where they had caught the punk bug early on, assorted quasi-legit labels sprang up, inspired by the example of Sky Dog. Sky Dog had convinced the Flamin' Groovies to sign a piece of paper allowing them to issue two vintage Groovies EPs, *Grease* and *More Grease*. They followed up with a re-release, no questions asked, of the long-deleted, third and last, independent MC5 single, the explosive 'Looking at You b/w Borderline', and at the end of 1976 came up with their greatest coup – a single album of (part of) Iggy and the Stooges' final show from February 1974. *Metallic K.O.* was the album that defined Iggy's onstage persona and 'attitude' as a punk originator just in time to influence the punk generation. Sky Dog had managed the ultimate switch from bootlegger to legitimate record company – same name, same individuals. They were the exception. Most had to disguise their more questionable origins:

Alan Henderson: Prior to [punk] there'd been no real opportunity for someone to make a real record label from scratch. In [1979] I began realizing that there was an opportunity so I started my own official label and found a punk band and gradually concentrated my time more on trying to do that.[13]

While the American 'old guard' in the late seventies were required to consider new vocations by FBI action, in the case of Britain's 'old guard' the inspiration of punk had simply highlighted more legitimate ways to resist the undertow of conformity.

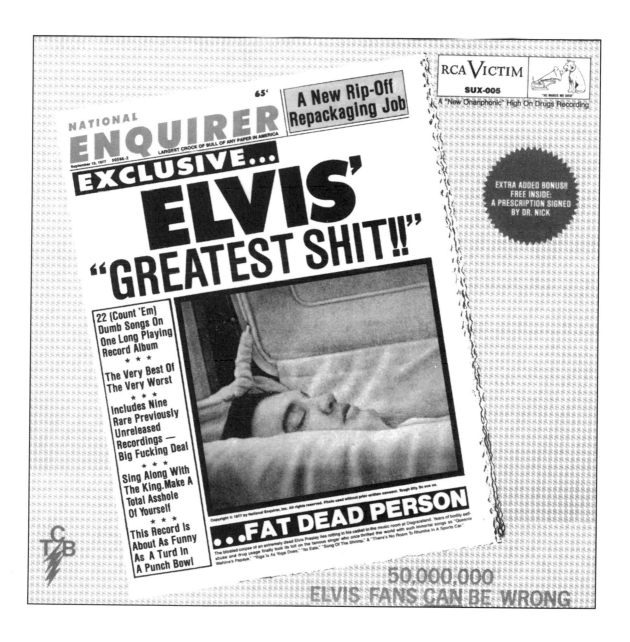

On Thursday, August 14 [1980] . . . shortly after 1 p.m., a group of fifteen to twenty armed FBI agents wearing business suits and carrying walkie-talkies entered the [Memphis] Convention Center. Each agent had a separate search warrant issued for a specific dealer's area. Dealers were instructed to stay inside their booth, not to try to leave, and not to sell any more Elvis merchandise. Many of the fans believed that it was a drug bust. But the FBI was after another type of contraband on this warm afternoon. Virtually every album sold by the dealers was confiscated. Only obvious RCA product was not seized. According to a number of eyewitnesses, records were tossed into a pile, stepped on, and generally abused. One dealer became so enraged that he allegedly assaulted an agent and was arrested.[1]

The August 1980 raid on a 'fan' convention in Memphis was the first time the FBI had ever busted this type of 'private', admission-by-ticket gathering, though there were an increasing number of such conventions taking place in America, primarily for The Beatles and Presley. The raid sent shock waves through all collecting circles. Yet the FBI continued to be crudely misinformed as to the actual contents of their booty. An FBI agent actually informed the press that the bootleggers had been remixing existing Presley recordings, and altering studio cuts by hiring musicians to play over existing Presley tracks (something which would have required access to multi-track studio masters!). 'Gullible collectors' were apparently paying 'hundreds of dollars' for these 'fake' albums.

In fact, the Memphis convention bust was just the appetizer in a concerted assault on the underground Elvis industry. The following day, in a coordinated raid, FBI agents entered the home of one John Greco, of RTO Records in Staten Island, New York, and seized 50,000 bootleg LPs, EPs and singles. More importantly, they confiscated Greco's business records showing the exact nature of his operation.

It was almost certainly information gleaned from Greco's records that led the FBI to the men behind the flood of recent Presley bootleg product. In November 1982, a federal grand jury indicted four men for 'manufacturing and marketing bootleg Elvis Presley recordings'. William Samuel Theaker (aka Vic Colonna), Paul Dowling, Aca Anderson and Richard Minor were all charged with conspiracy, interstate transportation of stolen property, copyright infringement and mail fraud. Although convicted on all counts, Dowling challenged the felony charge of interstate transportation of stolen goods all the way up to the Supreme Court, where his conviction was overturned. The Supreme Court stated that, 'copyright infringement does not easily equate with theft, conversion or fraud.' The court also stated that the misdemeanour charge of copyright infringement could not be the basis of a felony charge.

Minor, and his father, had already had 100,000 albums and 'a number of master tapes' seized in a March 1982 raid on their Miami homes. The haul was valued by the RIAA, in typically extravagant fashion, at $7 million. Though Minor had only recently hooked up with Theaker, Dowling and Anderson, he was already manufacturing his own Presley bootlegs (from tapes supplied by the trio). It was Theaker who had been manufacturing the majority of the bootlegs. From a plant near his Glendale home he had apparently been responsible for such renowned Presley titles as *Rockin' Rebel*, *Behind Closed Doors* and the two volumes of *Burbank Sessions*.

Even more ominously, on 24 May 1982 President Reagan signed into law a new bill that dramatically increased the criminal penalties for 'record piracy and counterfeiting'. From now on, virtually every case of 'piracy' was to be considered a felony, even for first offenders. The new law provided maximum penalties of five years in prison and/or $250,000 in fines, making no distinction between piracy and/or bootlegging.

To complete a year when the FBI and RIAA seemed to have at last made a major dint in the bootleggers' operations, on 4 December 1982 'vice' officers of the LA Police Department, broke another taboo and busted a regular monthly swap-meet at the Roosevelt Hotel in Hollywood. Throughout the late seventies, the Hollywood swap-meets had been a veritable hive of hot wax. Several of the key manufacturers were regular attendees, though not usually retailing. Twelve dealers were arrested in the December raid, all on misdemeanour charges of 'selling unauthorized recordings'. Most of the 1,134 albums seized were apparently 'concerts made with surreptitious tape recorders'. Though the bust itself was inconsequential enough, it alerted dealers that swap-meets, like 'fan conventions', were no longer immune from attack. But such sorties against retailers were dealing with the symptoms, not the virus. It was the manufacturers that needed to be rooted out and, despite the enforced 'retirements' of figures like Vicki Vinyl, Kurt Glemser and Vic Colonna, there would always be some intrepid soul prepared to fill the void.

In March 1983 the RIAA announced the tally for unauthorized sound recordings seized in 1982. FBI, state and local law enforcement agencies had impounded some 135,554 bootleg records, but just 46,155 pirate and counterfeit albums, singles, eight-tracks and cassettes. Given the hundreds of thousands of counterfeit cassettes that were being sold in America, the statistics showed the RIAA applying a very odd system of priorities.

Yet the RIAA was no closer to ending bootlegging than piracy in the USA. Their main problem remained the same one that had plagued the private investigators of *Great White Wonder* twelve years earlier – the surfeit of independent pressing plants in Los Angeles. With the gradual decline of vinyl in volume and market share, the plants were running increasingly short of capacity. They were also rarely manned by the brightest sparks since Edison.

'Eric Bristow': The first time anybody tried to make a bootleg at [the] pressing plant [we used] they phoned the police. The very first time. It was like a hundred copies of *Get Back* they were making. The second they recognized them they phoned the cops. So the FBI and the RIAA drive over there, and they walk in and they say, 'Well, where are they?' and they say, 'They're over there . . .' and they show them this little stack of records.

'You called us all the way out here for *that*? I mean, Jesus Christ! We thought you had like 50,000 records in here! Give me a break!' The RIAA guy looks at these two brothers and goes 'Don't ever call me again unless you've got something serious going on here!' And these two dopes interpreted that as 'Oh, that means it's OK. We can make these here now.'[2]

With a large, Spanish-speaking contingent of unskilled labour, Los Angeles had some of the most unquestioning employees on God's earth.

Lou Cohan: The pressing plant [I used] was manned by many people who did not speak English, run by a very old lady, [and] the owner was never there. It's my understanding that they would not have known who these artists were ... Most of the people who worked in the pressing plant either didn't know, or if they did know, they would not have cared. To them it was just another customer, more business for them. I often wonder what took the FBI so long to find these pressing plants because all you had to do was look in the Yellow Pages of the LA phone book and it says 'Pressing Plants' in the back of the book.[3]

The more prudent bootleggers still tried to ensure that they could not be traced, paying cash at the plants, giving false names, and making it as difficult as possible to trace their records. Most plants had their own identifying 'house numbers'. These were known to the legitimate record companies, since they too used the services of the independent pressing plants.

Richard [a bootlegger]: The only place you could do a record was a place that does legitimate records. There was no bootleg pressing plant that only pressed bootlegs ... [but] you can request that there's no house number on it. And I requested that ... Since I knew that Capitol only put so many serial numbers on their records I didn't want any extra numbers, and it turned out that it was a good idea. Later [on] I made a point of making sure there were never any house numbers on because that is a way of tracing things.[4]

Richard was concerned about the number of digits used by Capitol for their serial numbers because he was attempting to pass his first effort off as a Capitol Beatles product – something which nearly backfired on him. Capitol took umbrage at the gall of this apprentice bootlegger, the first of many controversies Richard's titles were to cause. Nevertheless, 1979's *Collector's Item*, Richard's introduction to hot wax, was the beginning of an auspicious decade of product from Richard Records. Richard was to be responsible for some 105 releases in the years before CD, all with miscellaneous labels and 'identities' (save for *The Lost Lennon Tapes*, the first fourteen of which were on Bag Records).

It was no longer a good idea to make the FBI suspect a connection between one product and another. Far better that they never realized just how few bootleggers were active at any given time, and just how many titles each was responsible for. So it was that Richard's first two releases – *Collector's Item* and *Casualties* – came with purple Capitol labels, a dig at Capitol for not releasing the same material as well as a ruse to avoid detection. Richard saw himself as directly following on from the TMQ of Dub and Stout, sharing the technical quality of their presentations, the wit of Stout's artwork and Dub's love of anthologizing. Stout, in particular, was a key inspiration.

Richard: The first bootleg I bought was *Great White Wonder* . . . It was $14 in 1970 money. It was a lot of money, and it was like, 'I got this underground thing, it's gonna be great!' and I took the thing home and I think it sucks! I think it's a terrible record, it's unlistenable. I enjoyed the 'forbidden fruit' of you getting to hear this stuff that's not out, but except for a few tracks on there it's unlistenable garbage! . . . The next one I bought was called *Kum Back*, which was a variant on *Get Back/Let It Be* . . . I liked that a little better because it was better quality soundwise, but it had a blank jacket with a stamp that said *Kum Back* on it. At the time I thought that was kinda cool, but after seeing about a hundred records with a rubber stamp on the front, I thought it sucked . . . and then I started seeing the ones with the William Stout drawings that were mainly shrinkwrapped on an 8½ × 11 sheet . . . and then once in a blue moon, something like *Who's Zoo* [and I thought,] 'Now this is what a bootleg ought to look like!'[5]

Richard wanted to produce the sort of records that record

companies *should* be releasing, not simply put out the latest evidence of some rock extravaganza – something like *Who's Zoo*, which compiled all those impossible-to-find Who b-sides and odds-'n'sods, not the TMQ of *Burning at the Hollywood Palladium*. Many of his most memorable releases crossed the line between pirate and bootleg.

Richard: I figured that rather than do bootlegs in the style of bootlegs I'd rather do real records that you can't really [get], something closer to what you'd consider a real record in the way it looks [and] in the way it sounds.[6]

Collector's Item, Richard Production No. 1, was certainly an attempt to make a Beatles album that could be put alongside Capitol releases. Save for the stereo 'Penny Lane', with trumpet ending, and the take of 'I Am the Walrus' – which had both long introduction and the complete middle-section – everything on *Collector's Item* had already been commercially released. But trying to find these bits'n'bobs Stateside in 1979 would have been an extremely expensive, not to say time-consuming, exercise.

Richard: I was a big Beatles fan, and . . . there were a number of Beatles songs that were never on an album in America, which always irritated me. So I decided to cure that and make a Beatles album [with] all the b-sides and weird mixes that were never on album. So I put the tape together . . . and then I had to come up with a cover. I had a whole load of memorabilia, but I got in touch with a memorabilia dealer and borrowed a bunch of stuff from her and put together a display in my living room, shot a picture of it and that became the cover of the album called *Collector's Item*. I didn't like bootlegs because they had a slipsheet in them. They didn't have a real cover . . . I got carried away and I put it on Capitol Records and I put 'PROMO' on it and it fooled virtually everybody. It's indistinguishable from a legitimate Capitol Records [issue] – to the point where it made big news . . . What was even weirder was that there are two Beatles tracks on there where I re-edited [the] songs to make more complete versions. These were official versions, not outtakes, and I got together all the versions and reconstituted them into the most complete versions. I put 'Penny Lane' into stereo but I put on the trumpet ending which was only available on a rare promo, and I reconstructed 'I Am the Walrus' so it has all the missing bits that were edited out of different versions, so that it was the most complete version of the legitimate track … Months later Capitol put out an album here that was called *Rarities* – there's one in England too, but it's a different record – and they did the exact same thing that I did on those two tracks and tried to claim that it was a coincidence … And the record was amazingly good quality because I did get tape sources, I don't want to say how. Only one track on the album is off a record, the rest are off a much better generational source. So the record was, in all ways, equal to a real Capitol album … I used the current label. It had to be photographed with a special filter, to separate the difficult combination of colours, but it got done. It was kinda expensive. On the back cover I put all the other Capitol albums, which is what Capitol did, but I had the whole catalogue on the back … 'If you enjoyed this album, you might …' I made a thousand of the first version, and then I did a second that was slightly modified … but it was close to the original, and I did 2,000 of those. It was incredibly expensive and I got ripped off every step of the way with colour separations and the printer. Everybody charged me a premium, which I didn't know because I had never done anything like this before. I made about $1,000 out of the whole shebang.[7]

Richard took another leaf from the TMQ step-by-step guide to bootlegging, taking care to tweak the tapes a little in the studio to gain optimum sound. Like Dub, Richard soon came into contact with the sort of people he needed to know.

Richard: Luckily, through connections I [was able to] work at the second-best studio in South California, a real place that had real quality control standards with real mastering engineers. At first I did it in conjunction with an engineer, I would say how I wanted it to be and he would twiddle the knobs and do it. But after a couple of albums he would take a nap or leave. After I knew how to run the board I would clean everything up myself.[8]

After *Collector's Item* came *Casualties*. Again, it was essentially a collection of alternative mixes from obscure, legitimate sources. There was just one exception: a 'basic track' version of 'I Am the

Walrus'. Though the quality of the album was not on a par with *Collector's Item*, the cover was a genuine coup.

Richard: I had gotten hold of an original transparency for the 'Butcher' cover* through a friend, a pretty valuable thing to have . . . so the LP was basically an excuse for the cover. I'm not that crazy about the record. The fans seem to like it and there was a picture disc version of it (there was only 1,000 of that) and a vinyl edition of 2,000 and that's also on 'Capitol records'. More people figured out that that one probably wasn't a Capitol record![9]

After *Collector's Item* and *Casualties*, Richard came up with a 12″ single. This time it was 'on Parlophone', though the cut 'What a Shame, Mary Jane' dates from 1968, i.e. after The Beatles' tenure with that label. According to legend, the song, a typically 'experimental' Lennon effort, was given by Lennon to a bootlegger in exchange for some bootlegs he wanted for his own collection. The cover, though, began a tradition of controversial artwork from Richard Records.

Richard: That's when I found out that Beatles fans, as a whole, don't have much of a sense of humour. I used a bubblegum card we had over here of [The Beatles] with bald heads surrounded by a bunch of naked girls taken by a photographer named Earl Leif . . . The front [cover] was the Beatles with these naked girls wearing monster masks and on the back was this chick, who was supposed to be Mary Jane, and there was all kinds of flak about the cover. People wouldn't buy it or they'd buy it and go 'Euhhhh!'[10]

As the eighties beckoned there seemed to be a renewed interest in Beatles product. Certainly Richard was not the only Californian to be concentrating on Fab Four releases. Mr Wizardo had found a new partner, an Englishman named Peter, and between them they generated a whole slew of new Beatles artifacts, the most grandiose of which was an eleven-album set from the *Get Back* sessions, housed

---

* The original cover for *Yesterday and Today* had The Beatles as butchers, with dismembered baby dolls to hand.

in a film can. Disc eleven was a 'best ever' version of *Get Back*. The other ten volumes were all taken from the Nagra reference tapes. The set even came with liner notes explaining the history of the tapes:

During the recording of the *Get Back* sessions, a pair of portable Nagra two-track recorders were utilized for recording a running journal of that day's events ... The recordings were taken from the two boom mikes, were called 'synch-tracks' and were used mainly by the film crew in making work prints and in cataloguing the different songs that were recorded each day and at approximately what time.[11]

Unfortunately, Wizardo's new partner was, if anything, even more fastidious than Richard in ensuring that the form matched the substance. He was also fiercely jealous of his 'rivals', and not the sort of 'volume' producer that Wizardo was used to working with.

'Eric Bristow': Peter's favourite motto was 'When the Beatles left Capitol, they signed with me'. And he believed it! The guy was wacko, and he firmly believed that nobody had the right to make Beatles bootlegs except him and that if they did they couldn't possibly do as good a job ... He despised [Richard] because he made Beatles bootlegs – no other reason! He'd see him in the same room, at a Beatlefest, and he'd start muttering under his breath ... He did this jacket with the [famous] shot of the Beatles where they're leaning over the balcony [of Manchester Square], he took that and used a Scitex computer to put the young ones on the balcony above, looking down on the ones below. And it was seamless ... Just amazing stuff. He did *Get Back* with the Apple label 'cos it had to be just perfect.[12]

What Peter most required was a sense of humour. Though his packaging was second to none, it lacked the sly humour of Richard's releases. One of Richard's particularly close-to-the-knuckle items was *The Beatles vs. the Third Reich*, a parody of the famous *Beatles vs. Four Seasons* album. A complete set from one of the 1962 Star Club tapes, Richard pitted The Beatles against 'a bunch of drunken Krauts ... yelling and belching'. Alan Williams,

who had been The Beatles' original manager, is quoted, apocryphally, on the front cover:

Hey, I'm not as stupid as I look, mates – Of course I've held on to some unreleased Star Club tapes. Besides, I enjoy sticking it to those bloody buggers at EMI. By the time of these recordings I had already given the lads away, so all's I did was change the dates on the tapes and blimey if the judge didn't believe my wild lies! Cor! I don't recall exactly which complete performance this is because I was pissed out of me gourd as usual when it was recorded. As for EMI, sod 'em – they've made enough money off these boys, now it's my turn.[13]

Richard was incorporating the sort of artwork that no legitimate company could get away with. For gloriously bad taste, his most savage 'dig' at 'fan worship' was the magnificently executed *Elvis Presley's Greatest Shit*. After two years of virtually no Presley bootlegs – thanks to the events of August 1980 – the July 1982 release of *Greatest Shit* seemed like the ultimate slap in the face for Presley devotees.

Richard: [*Presley's Greatest Shit*] was designed to offend some people and make some people chuckle. It was inspired in part by the Goldman book, but what really inspired it was this woman on Melrose Avenue in LA who has a shrine to Elvis on her front lawn and a cadillac that I guess Elvis had given her. So that was the centrepiece, this, I think it was a pink cadillac, surrounded by all these little statues and plaques as though Elvis was Jesus or something . . . and I used to drive by this place all the time. And it got me thinking about all these Elvis nuts and how he is deified. I wanted to put it into perspective. I'm a big Elvis fan. Some people caught on . . . It wasn't a total attack. I just thought I put it into perspective and that's a case in point of someone ignoring the record inside. I think the record is great. I like the record more than the cover. I think it's a real entertaining record. All the songs are bad, but they're funny bad . . . It was great to be at a swap-meet and be standing by Elvis fans who were totally pissed off. Then some Elvis fan would go, 'He's right about this here, actually. This guy must be an Elvis fan, he knows too much . . .'[14]

Full of subtle in-jokes, the attention to detail on *Greatest Shit* was something to behold. The record label was not RCA-Victor but RCA-Victim, the logo was of a dog puking into a phonogram. The subtitle was '50,000,000 Elvis Fans Can be Wrong', and on the rear sleeve were four other supposed Presley albums (SUX 001–004), with titles like *The Shower Sessions*, *If My Aunt Had Nuts, She'd Be My Uncle* and, tackiest of all, *Dead On Stage in Las Vegas August 20th, 1977*, the blurb for which ran:

Recorded just days after Elvis' death due to polypharmacy (a big word meaning he zonked out on about twelve different drugs), the release of this album vividly illustrates the depths a money-hungry, greed-crazed manager and record company will go in order to churn out more and more pointless posthumous product to milk Elvis' legion of not-too-bright fans out of their hard-earned money.[15]

Greatest Shit even came with a fake prescription from Dr Nichopolous, Presley's physician. The track listing was designed to collect together all the most embarrassing Presley cuts in one motley collection. 'There's No Room to Rhumba in a Sports Car', 'He's Your Uncle, Not Your Dad', 'Dominic the Impotent Bull', 'Do The Clam Bake' – they're all here. The ultimate joke was on the bootleg collectors. Their drive for a complete collection generally meant that whatever distaste they may have felt for the artifact, they still had to purchase the profane relic. And, as Lee Cotten wrote in *Jailhouse Rock*, 'Elvis would [probably] have approved of the song selection. It is truly Elvis's "Greatest Shit".'

Controversy over *Greatest Shit* was largely confined to the collectors Richard's digs were aimed at. But Richard's most famous collection generated the sort of controversy that nearly put him in the clink. CBS had been planning a five-album boxed-set of Dylan's work since 1983 but had twice shelved the project when, in the spring of 1985, Richard decided to do his own boxed-set. Richard preferred his Dylan vintage, which meant 1961–6, and he devised a ten-album set that incorporated all the circulating studio outtakes from Mr D's pre-accident years plus complete versions of the three other primary pre-accident bootleg sources – the Minneapolis Hotel tape, the second Gaslight tape and *Albert Hall '66* –

all in one lavish boxed-set. Taking his liner notes from Paul Cable's book on Dylan's unreleased recordings, Richard put out the set, dubbed *Ten of Swords*, at the end of the summer, on Tarantula Records. The reaction to what was – save for the exemplary quality of his source tapes and the conceptual integrity of the set – really a rather humdrum release, particularly when compared with some of the Dylan releases then coming out of Europe, was nothing short of astonishing.

Richard: I never really liked Dylan bootlegs, and I hardly owned any. I always thought they were a hodgepodge, I didn't like the way they mixed up eras ... I wanted to do it chronologically. I stole that stuff from Paul Cable's book ... I re-edited his stuff. I tried to put in bits of humour here and there, 'cos I thought that he was incredibly dry, but basically said what he said ... I knew about [CBS's] *Biograph* [set] and I thought it was never gonna come out. That's what the word was. [But] there is virtually nothing on *Biograph* that's on *Ten of Swords* and in the few cases where it is, Columbia edited their tapes ... they edited it unnecessarily for that album, so the real company botched it up ... When *Ten of Swords* was done I had six done in one place and four done in another, to split the work and try to get it all done at once. Otherwise it would've taken longer to get made.[16]

It was fortunate for Richard that the problems of putting together the set required the services of two plants. When *Biograph* was finally released in the autumn of 1985, several journalists seized upon *Ten of Swords* as the more important release. When Cameron Crowe, who had actually been responsible for the booklet that accompanied the *Biograph* set, gave *Ten of Swords* a rave write-up, along with *Rolling Stone* and an entire clan of sixties-relic rock journalists, Columbia reacted with ill-considered venom.

Temporarily withdrawing its advertising from *Rolling Stone*, Columbia claimed that the magazine was endorsing an illegal product. The *LA Times* proceeded to remind Columbia of a 1969 press release from the time of the appearance of *Great White Wonder*. According to Columbia, *Great White Wonder* was 'an abuse of the integrity of a great artist ... crassly depriving [Bob

Dylan] of the opportunity to perfect his performances to the point where he believes in their integrity and validity.' Six years later, Columbia released *The Basement Tapes* officially, presumably no longer of the opinion that it was 'an abuse of the integrity of a great artist'. *Ten of Swords* also served to highlight that the seventeen unreleased cuts on CBS's $50 boxed-set were another form of extortion from an official record company. CBS decided they were going to nail the bastard bootlegger who had sent such yolk in their direction.

Richard: [*Ten of Swords*] was scary, because Walter Yentnikoff seemed so sure that Columbia would track down the perpetrator/s and they nearly pulled all their advertising from *Rolling Stone* and they had that battle going on. That was funny, 'cos I hate *Rolling Stone* and I was glad that they were being hassled by something I had done ... but I was scared because the heat was on ... friends of mine sent really huge newspaper articles from all over the country, half-page articles and stuff. That thing got really famous and I goes, 'This is good and this is bad,' and it sold out really fast for a ten-record set that was really expensive ... [But] there was no way I was ever going to make it again, even though there was a huge demand.[17]

Thankfully, it never occurred to the FBI that the set might have been pressed at two or more plants, or that its impressive packaging might provide them with their best lead. When they did the rounds of usual suspects, they predictably came up blank.

'Eric Bristow': I went into my pressing plant right after *Ten of Swords*, and the guy who owned the pressing plant called me into his office, which was unusual. I was a bit worried, 'cos I used to just deal with the foreman ... and he says, 'Have we got any Bob Dylan here?' and I looked at him and I went 'Yeahhh ...?' and he goes, 'It's not a ten-record set, is it?' 'No ...' and he goes, 'Oh ...' So I say, 'Why?' and he says, 'Because we had some FBI guys in here asking about a thing called *Ten of Swords* ...' I said, 'It wasn't me ...' He says, 'Do you know who did it?' I said, 'Yeah.' 'Did he do it here?' 'He might have!'[18]

Deke [a collector]: The really funny thing about that whole affair is the

box itself. It can only be made by one company in the whole United States –
a place that manufactures boxes for kid's toys.[19]

Ten of Swords had once again raised the profile of bootlegs
after a couple of years out of the news. Richard's experience with
his boxed-set, though, did not entirely sour him towards Dylan
bootlegs. The following year he came up with two far more
significant Dylan releases. As a supreme irony, the emergence of
these tapes was a direct result of all the media hoo-hah generated
by *Ten of Swords*:

Stanley Washington [a collector]: I was working in a record store in
the North West in 1985. Through my various connections with collecting,
it turned out a friend of mine knew a person who knew the man who made
Ten of Swords, and he had been shuttling the various Beatles albums up
to us. My [LA] friend had been involved in the creation of the *Ten of Swords*
package, and when the box was finally done he had promised us that we
could buy some at wholesale. I believe the price was $55. So I decided to
get one, my father wanted one and the order [soon] got up somewhere
around nine or ten. On this funny day just before we were about to [place
our] order [for] *Ten of Swords* one of our regular customers had come in
and said that he had been told by another employee of the store that I
might be one that would know where Dylan bootlegs might be purchased. I
asked him what he was looking for. He said he was trying to pick up a
ten-album box called *Ten of Swords*. To which I replied, 'Well, funnily
enough I am just about to place an order for same and we are gathering the
money together right now. It's going to be sent down to California post-
haste.' And he said, 'Well, I would very much like to get one of those. I will
give you the money but [also] in return for making that happen I have a few
tapes you might be interested in.' I asked what they were. And he said that
he had been a roadie for Dylan in '74 and somehow by being in that
position he had been given some reels of basement-tape material that had
never been released. I immediately thought that this is probably the
basement-tape outtake material that has been around since the dawn of
bootlegs, though I was intrigued by the fact he said there were three reels
of it. He said that the tapes had been sitting in a trunk and had been
unplayed for years. So the next day he came into the store and handed me

over three [3¾ ips] seven-inch reels with song-titles written across all three boxes. A quick summary of the count was somewhere well over sixty or seventy tracks, with a lot of titles that I did not recognize. At that point I thought that we may have stumbled on to something. I called up my friend who was a Dylan collector of some renown for years and years and years, and he came over and we threaded the tape up on the Revox. Right off the bat, when the tape started playing, we knew this was basement-tape material we had not heard before, and very quickly we realized that upwards of twenty-five new songs were included on the tapes along with what we identified as the Tiny Tim session with The Band. While we had the tapes in our possession it was decided that three sets of tapes would be made, one for me, one for my friend [the Dylan collector] and one for my [collector] friend in LA, knowing full well that it was going to end up in the hands of the man who made *Ten of Swords*. The tapes were in LA about a week later, although the basement-tapes albums really took a while. Part of the reason is that we told [Richard] that we felt we might be able to get something very substantial [tape-wise] for the tapes and we wanted that time to pass.[20]

Previous basement-tape material, because it had come from Dylan's music publishers, had centred entirely on original Dylan songs. The 'new' basement material was almost entirely composed of old country and folk standards that Dylan and The Band were conjuring up from their common musical heritage. As such, it added a whole new dimension of Americana to these most American of sessions. And yet, as if to highlight the sheer perversity of the collector's market, Richard's two double-albums of basement tapes, the first 'new' Big Pink recordings in over fifteen years – a major find aesthetically and historically – never generated anything like the same reputation as *Ten of Swords*. Sales proved to be extremely disappointing.

Richard: [*The Basement Tapes*] is an album I art-directed over the phone because the guy who owned the tapes lived in another state and wanted to contribute in some other way and I was doing five other albums at the same time, and I told him to get a box with a tape on it and put a cat on one, take the cat off the other, put a boot in the background (to see if

anybody got the joke) . . . Only 2,000 'Basement's' were made and it took forever for them to sell. I was really pissed off.[21]

Richard had had understandably high hopes for his basement-tape doubles. He had done a remarkable job in the studio cleaning up the tapes (arguably superior to the one Fraboni and Robertson had managed for the official release). And like the Albert Hall bootleg back in 1970, the two sets generated some very favourable press in the UK – where copies were difficult to track down – but were barely mentioned Stateside. They remain essential companions to Columbia's double-album.

Richard had not, however, lost his ability to generate controversy. Next to The Beatles, his great love was the cantankerous Frank Zappa. Despite having only a minimal commercial profile, Zappa had always had a substantial 'cult' audience, and there had never been any shortage of Zappa bootlegs. Richard in his time was to be responsible for one ten-album set, one four-album set and ten single albums, including the legendary *'Tis the Season to be Jelly* (one of Richard's classic covers). Once again it was the ten-album set that sent the artist in question into a frenzy. Zappa had always been a control freak and hated the idea of bootleggers offering an alternative to his own, sometimes questionable, decisions about what should and should not be made available.

Richard: I'm a big Zappa fan. In fact my *Mystery Box* got Zappa as upset as Columbia got over *Ten of Swords*. Zappa in America has a hotline for his fans to call and he went so far as to have the woman who does the hotline ask for help in tracking down the perpetrators of this heinous boxed-set, and Zappa called the FBI and the FBI didn't want to be bothered . . . I guess the problem was that Zappa was doing his [own] *You Can't Do That On Stage Anymore*, his ongoing series which has just ended, and *Mystery Box* was like a giant *You Can't Do That On Stage Anymore*. A lot of reviews were saying that *Mystery Box* was better because it was chronological and didn't jump all over the place and didn't have all these stupid edits in it. That kind of thing can annoy you if you're an artist putting out your own thing . . . Zappa's reasoning behind that was that he was losing tons of money and in fact he wasn't losing any money. Most people who do Zappa bootlegs do so because they like Zappa. They don't do it for the money. I can imagine people making money off a lot of other bootlegs but not Zappa.[22]

Though Richard seemed to have a penchant for controversy (particularly with his lesser-selling items), there was one release that was always intended to be a labour of love. *Michigan Nuggets* was an album that could never have been released officially simply because of the logistical difficulties in clearing permissions from so many tadpole labels. A double album of singles, drawn entirely from Detroit bands of the mid-to-late sixties, it was centred around the early 45s of The MC5 and Bob Seger.

Richard: Probably my very favourite thing I ever did was *Michigan Nuggets*. That was like my homage to my roots, all these fantastic, rare singles. Actually I compiled the album exactly as it is in 1974 or something. I had some of the singles and a friend of mine had virtually every single by every Michigan group, and he worked at a radio station and had professional equipment and I had a professional deck. I've always been an audio nut . . . So I had him make me a 15 ips full-track mono of all these singles and then I put them in order and I spliced in all these little things, like a religious nut who hates rock & roll . . . I had this tape in 1974 and I would use it to make cassettes, and I [told myself] 'I would love this to be a record. I'm gonna do it [even if] no one's gonna buy it.'[23]

As per usual Richard excelled himself in his attention to detail. The front cover consisted of a breakfast cereal packet on which an emaciated Iggy Pop (who is not actually featured on the album) struts his stuff. The promise of some 'Michigan Nuggets' lay within. There were extensive sleeve-notes on each of the thirty cuts, and the release, on Belvedere Records, was once again so convincing that it was assumed by many to be a legitimate release.

Richard: I did 1,000 and they were all numbered the first time around . . . I did a gatefold too, I can't think of any other gatefold boots, a double gatefold, fully annotated inside, [and] it sounds as good as any 45. I thought,

Dark Side of the Moo

'This is only going to appeal to me and people from Detroit.' In fact everybody thought it was made back there, which is how I wanted it. Bob Seger's manager went through the roof. He was running all over everywhere in Detroit ... But it sold out in a month. I was flabbergasted ... I realized that what sells something is the packaging, so that's what I concentrated on.[24]

Repressings of *Michigan Nuggets* continued to sell, though it never came close to Richard's own benchmark for a 'platinum' bootleg – 10,000 copies. Prince's *Black Album* was (predictably) Richard's bestseller, with over 20,000 copies of his edition alone (a very exotic production, with purple lettering on a jet black cover). A couple of The Beatles titles also nudged close to the 20,000 mark, notably *Not for Sale* which, like *Collector's Item*, concentrated on excellent-quality studio material, combining songs from the aborted EMI *Sessions* album with some of those alternative stereo mixes that give Beatles fans a reason for carrying on.

Richard's other great commercial success was, like *Casualties*, only really intended as an excuse for an album cover. *Dark Side of the Moo* collected all the Pink Floyd b-sides and miscellaneous official tracks that had steadfastly failed to appear on US albums.

Richard: It sold 15,000 – I was amazed! I was flabbergasted! *Dark Side of the Moo* was just a pun and a picture of a cow I took 'cos I thought it would be a great cover and title. It sold more than everything and it's still in print ... People still ask for it now, and I don't get it. There's no writing on the cover, just a picture of a cow on the front and two cows on the back. I had to slap a sticker on the front to say what it is.[25]

Though the primary appeal of Floyd product was financial, they inspired some of Richard's finest artifacts. By the mid-eighties it was becoming increasingly difficult to source new and exciting tapes. Many bootlegs were simply upgraded versions of oft-bootlegged items. However, the packaging of labels like Brigand and Archive, and Canada's Rock Solid, made them increasingly difficult to distinguish from official product – save that the bootlegs tended to be a shade more inventive.

Richard's triple-set from the Floyd's 'Wish You Were Here' tour was called *A Great Set*, an on-the-button parody of the Floyd's *A Nice Pair*. As with the original, the pictures were meant to replicate certain well-known sayings (a fork in the road, a bird in the hand is worth two in the bush, etc.). As a three-album set, the central shot was of a naked lady's breasts (as in 'a nice pair'), but this time she had a 50 per cent bonus. Richard also excelled himself with a double set of early Floyd BBC sessions, *Rhapsody In Pink*, which was presented in the style of a classic movie soundtrack.

Richard shared Dub's love of movies and movie soundtracks and, much like Dub, he collected bootleg soundtracks while still running his rock & roll operation. By the late eighties, Richard had grown tired of the bootleg industry. He was no millionaire. The attention he put into his products and his unwillingness to wholesale to 'unknown quantities' ensured this. The switch to bootleg CDs gave him the perfect excuse to move into a more legitimate domain of the Biz. $5'' \times 5''$ CD jewel boxes gave him little opportunity to produce the kind of artwork that had always given him the most pleasure. He also found, like many before him, that all the attention to detail did not make wholesalers willing to pay a premium for his product in preference to some hokey pirated version.

Richard: The dealers got into this mode of wanting to carry everybody's product, so they could appear to have a good variety. This idiot company Starlight springs to mind, who did the very worst crap. I found people paying the same money for Starlight garbage and they wouldn't pay more for my stuff even though it was costing more and more to do. I saw my orders being cut by a third ... people were buying these really awful records ... That was the whole point, I was in it for the art. It sounds fruity but it's the truth. I was just making enough to live on, and then I started doing the 'Lost Lennon Tapes' and so [it was] a combination of that being really redundant, sick of it for having done it for so long, and where do I go from here? And I was doing legitimate records. I'm not going to name any of those. That was my foothold into the real world. I don't know if you know this but a bunch of people with TMQ started their own record

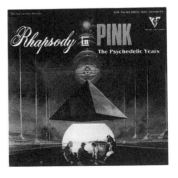

company and are multi-millionaires now. The people that had more ambition than to toot coke all day, which is what half of them did, got into the real record world.[26]

For consistent quality of product and for innovation in artwork, Richard must rank second only to the Father of the Rock Bootleg. Unfortunately, like Dub, he had found that rock fans were not prepared to pay for a quality-looking artifact in quantities sufficient to make the exercise worthwhile on a purely financial basis.

His only real Stateside competition in the quality department came from the Byrdman, the East Coast producer of the Archive label (and, later, Brigand). He too was suffering from the collectors' myopia when CDs threw down their lifeline. Though the bulk of product had continued to flow out of the West Coast in the eighties, it was the East Coast that was generating much of the material.

The Byrdman: East Coast titles were farmed out to LA and to a couple of heartland plants. [At least] they were farmed out if the items were too hot, like the Misfits . . . Like the 10″ series I did, the 10″ dies I had wouldn't work in the factory I used to use so . . . all coloured vinyl 10″s were farmed out. I love the format, the last gasp of exotic vinyl . . . If you look at most of the ordinary-quality titles from the late eighties they're mostly East Coast but they were pressed by the West Coast. All the tapes were funnelled through a contact and then farmed out to the main pressing plants . . . So much product came out. I would handle in a given year 150 to 250 on an exclusive to semi-exclusive basis.[27]

The East Coast market, though, was radically different from the nostalgia-oriented Californian nexus. A hipper, more 'street' product was required in the one American city to have fully embraced the punk ethic. The Brigand division of the Byrdman's enterprise reflected his divided loyalties, concentrating on cultish pre-punk exponents – The Velvet Underground, The MC5, The Modern Lovers, The New York Dolls, The 13th Floor Elevators, Captain Beefheart, etc. – and the post-punk wave of American rockers, whose huge underground audience also warranted some archival documenting.

The Byrdman: At the same time as the Brigands were being done there were other titles that were being done . . . [like] the Funkadelic singles collections . . . Brigand was for sixties and seventies groups, 1,000 each for the most part; New York Dolls, Mott the Hoople . . . Then there were custom productions that I would commission other people to do and I would take the entire run. So I'd do two or three Sonic Youth 10″s, a Dinosaur Jnr album.[28]

Though relatively late to enter the vinyl fray, not starting in earnest until 1986, the Byrdman was responsible for seventy-plus titles in the three years before bootleg vinyl dropped off the map. And what an unorthodox collection of artists he catered for. If the odd Prince, Zeppelin or Floyd title kept production on the economic straight and narrow, the release of bootleg titles by some important, but seriously obscure, punk outfits might seem like a most curious financial operation. Titles by Sydney's Radio Birdman, London's Only Ones and Cambridge's Soft Boys were all packaged in deluxe, laminated sleeves, in limited runs of 500 copies only. 'The authorities', on the lookout for Beatles albums *not* on Capitol records, or non-Columbia Dylan titles, hardly knew where to begin ascertaining whether a live performance of the Sonic Rendezvous Band was legitimate or not. West Coast bootleggers had sometimes been as reluctant as their portly legitimate twins to recognize the potential of 'new' bands. Yet the sales of some new wave bootlegs were quite startling.

The Byrdman: In keeping with general trends in the business, the worst release in regards of artistic merit, [at least] one of the two or three worst . . . was my absolute biggest seller. The Misfits' *If You Don't Know The Name of the Song What the Fuck Are You Doing Here?* – I didn't know the names of the songs, that's why I called the album that – was the only one that ever got over 5,000 copies, though under 10,000, maybe 7,000 or 8,000 . . . It just exactly meshed with the demand in the marketplace . . . The [demand for the] Misfits was mad. The level of intensity was approaching that of Springsteen '84 . . . or Prince '87. A band just has a huge buzz on them and

anything will sell. There were probably a hundred Misfits titles came out in the space of eighteen months.[29]

Like Richard, the Byrdman was not averse to blurring the lines between piracy and bootlegging. As a long-standing fan and collector of seventies punk, sixties garagebands and obscure fifties rock & roll, he had actually begun his vinyl activities by making his own anthologies of difficult-to-find singles and rare cuts from these eras. These were obscure enough to slip through an East Coast pressing plant. Two volumes of fifties hard urban r&b, five volumes of ultra-obscure seventies punk singles and even a single volume of rare sixties Euro-beat represented the beginnings of the Byrdman's roster. Once again, a bootlegger was mining a vein wholly overlooked by the official record companies, for whom the logistical difficulties of clearing permissions made such releases impractical. These 'pirate' compilations also put the Byrdman in contact with the studio world.

The Byrdman: From the start I would always go to the studio to get these things set up on $7\frac{1}{2}$ or 15 ips reel-to-reels, from whatever the source was. [Cleaning up the tapes] absolutely worked. The Flying Burritos' *Avalon '69* tapes I brought into a studio and brought up to 15 ips [and] farmed that out to someone else 'cos I didn't want to do that myself. I never got the tapes back. I go back to my original cassette and I can't get the sound as good as the record ... I went to five different studios ... We were doing comps of fifties, sixties and seventies rare singles. That was how we got our initial entrée into presenting [bootleg material] to anyone ... They'd see you playing the singles and you'd say now we have unreleased tapes, and if it's Hüsker Dü, or Dinosaur Jnr, nobody knows.[30]

The 'risk-free' nature of such low-key bootlegging had certain attractions, though it left little margin for miscalculating demand. Occasionally a Bruce Springsteen title might have to be put through the system to finance a particularly disastrous alternative release.

The Byrdman: [Manufacturing costs at the time were] $3. That would be about 1,000 copies. You'd pay $1 to $1.25 for the cover, full-colour laminate, $1.25 for your first 1,000 discs, 80c after that, buying your labels for a nickel per release, just pennies . . . and then if you figure in that you're buying the tape, doing the film work, and the artwork, on 1,000 copies you've certainly got $2.50 materials and 50c in startup, so it's a question of $3. If you're selling for $5, it's not an enormous mark-up.[31]

One such financing exercise was required after the release of a particularly ambitious Captain Beefheart double-set, *Another Chapter in the Life and Times*, a lavish creation indeed. Collecting together early Beefheart studio outtakes, rare A&M singles and BBC sessions, the set was lovingly wrapped in a gatefold sleeve with notes lifted from an early feature in *Rolling Stone*. Unfortunately the full-colour gatefold sleeve could only be printed in a minimum run of 3,000, though the album itself only sold in the hundreds. The Byrdman was suffering the same problem as Richard – having to compete with the volume merchants.

Richard: The bootleggers that did the work I don't like, the cheap, cheesier covers with no attention to detail, no effort put into the mastering or getting good tapes, were making a fortune. My stuff was costing me a fortune, because the people that were doing the printing and the mechanical crap that it takes to make a record knew what the deal was and were charging me a premium price to make up for the fact that they were doing something that I couldn't get done anywhere [else].[32]

Aside from the Beefheart package, perhaps the most perfectly executed of the Byrdman's vinyl efforts were two titles dear to the heart of this true New Yorker: a Velvet Underground double-set, *Sweet Sister Ray*, and a Television single album, *Double Exposure*. *Double Exposure* was the better package, housed in a gorgeous purple sleeve with a shot of the Richard Hell incarnation of Television on stage in double vision. The rear sleeve had the original Television poised to pose, Hell and Tom Verlaine clutching a television. Even the typeface was taken directly from one of Television's 1975 posters. Within lay a superb-quality version of the so-called 'Eno' demos recorded in New York in March 1975, just before Hell called it quits. With prototypes of songs like 'Marquee

Moon', 'Prove It', 'Venus de Milo' and 'Blank Generation', *Double Exposure* sold extremely well, notching up 4,000 sales.

Sweet Sister Ray was an equally remarkable collection, perhaps the most avant-garde statement ever from the Velvets. The first album comprised a forty-minute prelude to 'Sister Ray' recorded in April 1968 at one of John Cale's final shows at Cleveland's La Cave. Two versions of 'Sister Ray' itself, both from the Doug Yule era – the so-called 'guitar-amp' version from Boston in March 1969 and a slightly more sedate performance from a show in Philly the following year – made up the second disc. If the packaging did not quite match *Double Exposure*, the release of the long-rumoured, improvisational title track made *Sweet Sister Ray* another white-hot platter, particularly in Europe. As the Byrdman is quick to point out, here was a release no record company would have countenanced. A forty-minute improvisation made from a so-so audience tape back in 1968? Unthinkable.

So 'targeted' was the Byrdman's distribution that there was very little point in rebootlegging his items. The volume dealers were uninterested in experimenting with cult acts. There was a whole other market for bootlegs and it was one that the volume dealers were keen to exploit. 'Heavy metal', part prog-rock, part hard-rock, part-punk, part-thrash, was the new beast of burden. Even those granddaddies of them all – Led Zep – were back in vogue, and the man behind Canadian-based Rock Solid was a long-term Zep fan.

So it was that the mid-eighties brought the sort of explosion in Zeppelin bootleg titles previously exemplified by Presley in the late seventies and Dylan in the late sixties. Though Rock Solid was operating out of Canada, it was once again the LA pressing plants that were working overtime to keep their volume up. Between 1984 and 1987 Rock Solid churned out nearly a hundred titles, of which the most extravagant was the ultimate in boxed-sets. After Dylan's ten-album and twenty-album boxed-sets (the latter, *History*, coming from Europe), The Beatles' eleven-album set and Zappa's trio of ten-plus platters (*The Mystery Box*, *The History and Collected Improvisations of Frank Zappa* and *Twenty Years of Frank*

Zappa), Rock Solid produced a seventy-album acrylic case of Led Zeppelin live recordings. It was a project that went beyond collecting (and reason), simply to prove a point (or two) – that it could be done *and* that it would sell. Not surprisingly, *The Final Option*, as it was appropriately named, was a logistical nightmare.

'Eric Bristow': [We did] 150 of 'em. We made 150 boxes, and about forty or fifty arrived smashed, so we had to remake the boxes ... and it was a fuckin' marathon putting them together. [Ken] used to have a record store, so he had all these record bins from his shop that were eight feet tall, eight feet wide and stood against the wall. So what we did was we put 150 of each record in each pigeon hole – there's seventy pigeon holes with a different record in each – and [it was] the only way you could put it together and make sure you hadn't duplicated a record ... And of course the first time we did it the box was too bloody small! ... The records were made at two different places, [and] some were thicker than others ... we ended up having to dump two of the records, the double-album *Wrench in the Works*.[33]

Rock Solid stuck to mainstream acts. Their most radical release was a recording of Texan slide-guitarist Stevie Ray Vaughan! Their extensive catalogue was largely a prog-rock/HM mesh – bands like Rush, ZZ Top, Twisted Sister, Motley Crue, Kiss, Van Halen, Iron Maiden, and Metallica. With crunchy live tapes of these bands 'Eric Bristow' tapped into a market largely overlooked by earlier bootleggers, laying the foundations for the vast HM repertoire that has saturated the CD market.

Meanwhile the new king of volume was forming an important new partnership – with that original potentate of numbers, Ken. According to legend, Ken was diagnosed as having a fatal heart condition shortly after (and probably because) his partner in 'Phoenix' tossed their stampers into the ocean. Ken decided to see the world in his few remaining months. After two years of living off the fat of assorted lands, he obtained a second, more optimistic opinion. Broke, Ken attempted to get back into the business he had been instrumental in generating. But he had very little to offer the newcomers. They knew the pressing plants and could locate their own source tapes, and Ken's strong point had never been packaging. Nevertheless, at the 1984 Beatlefest, Ken came out of the woodwork, hooking up with his old rival, John Wizardo.

'Eric Bristow': I'm sitting around and [someone] goes 'Oh, look, Uncle Ken's here . . .' Ken was sitting very quietly off to one side, taking it all in, listening to everybody. He was broke and he wanted back in and he needed to know who was running the show. He ended up teaming up with John [Wizardo] and Peter, because somehow Peter had 'inherited' the TMQ plates. He'd gone to the pressing plant and the woman at the plant was going to throw them in the trash so he said, 'I'll keep them!'[34]

Ken, though, did not share John and Peter's undying enthusiasm for The Beatles, and their endeavours were a little too painstaking for him. When he realized how geared up the relocated Englishman behind Solid Rock was, he suggested a union. Though he had very little to bring into the alliance save his reputation for hard work and his contacts, 'Eric' felt the need for some fresh impetus.

'Eric Bristow': I was making ten titles a week and [John and Ken] had to beat Peter over the head with a stick to get one a month out of him! . . . In the end [Ken] decided he wanted out of his relationship with Peter and wanted into a relationship with me. All he had to offer when he got into a partnership with me was the TMQ stampers and a jacket manufacturer. I had the pressing plant and all the customers.[35]

It was still a marriage made in bootleg heaven. One of their first titles together was one of the great logistical coups of eighties bootlegging. Pink Floyd's *World Tour '87* proved that no major rock tour was safe from the hot wax merchants.

'Eric Bristow': Pink Floyd, when they came back in '87, the first show of the world tour was in Ottawa, and a friend of mine drove up there, taped it, bought a concert programme, Fed Ex'd the tape and the programme from Ottawa the next morning to me [in California]. I handed it all in. It was mastered that afternoon. I had plates by the day after on the other side of the continent! We had records, in a double gatefold, on pink vinyl, with four-colour labels, out on the streets in eight days . . . And we sold 7,000 of those . . . One of the guys who worked for the Floyd went into It's Only Rock and Roll in the Village [in New York] and he saw this bootleg and they hadn't even played there yet! 'Jesus Christ! I work for these guys, let me see that!' He looked at it and was absolutely stunned. He took it back to the hotel and showed it to the band. They were so freaked out they sent him back to buy three more for them. This is a week and a half after the show.[36]

In what was to be his last spurt of vinyl, Ken celebrated his return to the business by reviving the most famous of bootleg labels. The new TMQ titles, in two-colour covers that parodied the original hand-stamped TMQ 'look' – using Dub's logo, not Ken's Smokin' Pig – were particularly shoddy items, mostly inferior copies of the deluxe European bootlegs then assailing the North American continent. Toasted Records, the most famous of Ken and Eric's assorted 'inventions', at least drew on the Phoenix tradition of deluxe copies of famous Ken 'originals' – and all came from the original plates. Albums from the repertoires of Smokin' Pig, TAKRL and Impossible Recordworks all appeared in new guises.

'Eric Bristow': We were doing Toasted, TMQ, Kornyphone, Pharting Pharaohs, Suma, Shogun, Screaming Wazzo, Wiggle, Widget . . . there was all kinds of 'em . . . Rock Solid, BoxTop . . . I had all my plates. I had done about ninety titles on Rock Solid on my own before I teamed up with him. He had all the TMQ plates . . . I pretty much stuck to what I liked.[37]

Ken and Eric were certainly cranking them out, even if their sales were largely confined to the US. In fact they were exploiting their very own protectionist niche. It was becoming increasingly difficult and expensive to import fancy Euro-product, which was rarely pressed in large numbers and was usually sold to an established client-base removed from the American swap-meet/independent store circuit. The new 'TMQ' titles, stripped of any production expenses save stampers and vinyl, savagely undercut this Euro-product. Ken and Eric could afford to retail their albums for $8 (as opposed to anywhere between $15 and $25 for imported items). Quality was no longer a concern.

As one English bootleg dealer observed, in an article at the time, 'the only things around are crate-loads of American gear . . . but the American stuff is what gives bootlegs a bad name.'[38] For the first time, Californian origins were not considered an endorsement. The trademark of quality had been irretrievably tainted.

II Real Cuts at Last

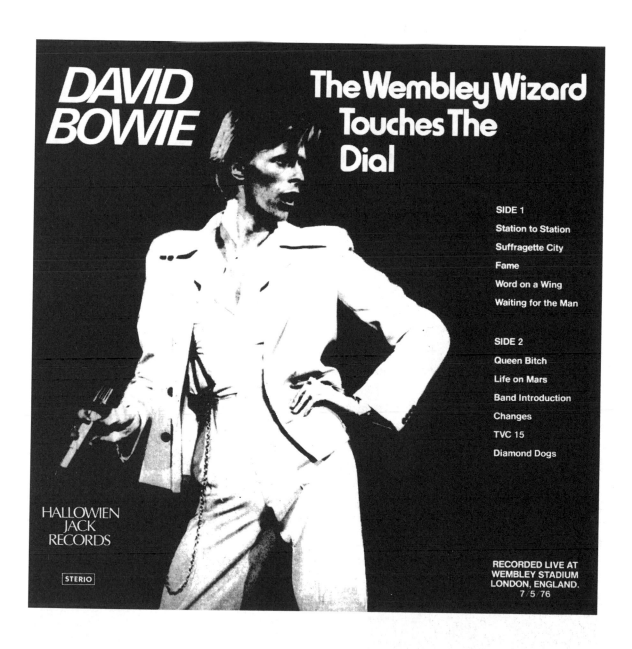

Allen Ginsberg [to Bob Dylan]: Can you ever envisage a time when you'll be hung as a thief?[1]

While the emergence of punk was creating Britain's first home-grown bootleg mini-industry in the late seventies, the BPI had 'woken up' to a far more insidious form of piracy, home-taping. As copies of *Spunk*, *Time's Up* and *Indecent Exposure* sold the sort of numbers that would have put them in the lower reaches of the pop album charts, the BPI were busy prosecuting a nineteen-year-old Manchester lad who had been selling bootleg cassettes of shows by old-wave gladhanders like Be Bop Deluxe and Roxy Music. With a list of some two hundred 'illicitly taped rock concerts', Mr Neil Corkindale hardly qualified as a big player, even in the bootleg tape trade.

By 1978, because a large number of collectors were simply trading tapes, without any money changing hands, small-time collectors looking to expand their collection beyond the now standard fare of bootleg albums were looking to purchase bootleg cassettes. Though there was invariably far more material circulating on tape than on record, most tape-traders were uninterested in selling tapes or dealing with anyone who did. Their tape-lists often contained dire warnings as to what might happen should they ever discover their precious booty being sold as a cheap commodity.

Purchasing tapes had become another degree in the art of collecting unreleased recordings. Hopefully a tape-collection would eventually accumulate to the point where it was possible to trade rather than purchase tapes. This was infinitely preferable, since most bootleg tape-sellers were dealing with collectors a long way removed from source, and they rarely took care to use the best tapes or recording equipment. In this sense, at least, Corkindale was the exception. He had been taping shows himself.

The BPI was not content to be seen to punish those indulging in 'pocket money' exercises like selling bootleg tapes. Shortly after the judgement against Corkindale, the *NME* ran a feature on home-taping in which they asked the BPI's press officer, Richard Hobson, how they hoped to stop people taping music in the privacy of their home. The reply was, to quote the *NME*, 'both smug and foreboding':

The idea has been kicked around that maybe we should bring a prosecution against a private individual as an example. There are ways of getting access to people's premises provided one has reasonable grounds for suspecting they are breaking the law.[2]

The BPI had already singled out their chosen victim for a test case on the rights of ordinary citizens to tape radio shows and trade such recordings with like-minded souls. Terence Piggott-Sims of Holt, Norfolk, was sued by the BPI 'on behalf of record companies and artists' indeterminate in name and number. BPI investigators had visited Mr Piggott-Sims' home in December 1977, seizing 447 cassettes and thirty-two records. According to his QC, Mr Vivian Price:

Mr Piggott-Sims was a hi-fi enthusiast who made tapes of 'live' broadcasts for his own private use. He began swapping tapes with other collectors for his own private use to improve his collection, but [with] no commercial gain involved.[3]

Displaying a profound ignorance of bootlegging (not to say UK law), Mr Robin Jacob, representing the BPI, informed the media that Mr Piggott-Sims' 'collection was of immense value to a bootlegger. He really had no way of knowing what sort of people he was swapping his tapes with.' In the eyes of the law, any illegal activity that might result from a tape traded by Mr Piggott-Sims in good faith was irrelevant. In fact, since Mr Piggott-Sims did not tape shows himself, and a large part of his collection was derived from FM radio broadcasts, it was rather unlikely that any part of his collection would interest a commercial bootlegger, the bulk of whom operated outside the UK and had their own well-established network of collectors.

When the case finally came to court at the beginning of 1980, the judge agreed that there had been a technical breach of copyright but refused to order up the delivery of Mr Piggott-Sims' 447 tapes. The tapes, retained by solicitors while the BPI decided whether to appeal, were eventually returned without being erased. The BPI also failed to get costs awarded. Their motives in taking such action against the most innocuous form of bootlegging – tape-trading – has to be questioned. Quite clearly it seems to have been part of a general campaign to pressure the government into introducing a levy on all blank tapes, a means of extorting money from all blank-tape users to pay for alleged copyright infringements by a minority of tape-owners. This was just an opening volley in a campaign of lies, damn lies and statistics. (Which continues to this day. When submitting a memo to a parliamentary committee on CD prices in May 1993, the BPI insisted that it was 'essential to take full account of the losses incurred by the industry in respect of home copying'.)

If cases against bootleg tape-dealers and tape-traders were designed to heighten the profile of the BPI's anti-piracy unit, they certainly succeeded. However, it was 'Operation Moonbeam' that generated the greatest media coverage for the BPI. Unfortunately for them, most of the coverage (outside pats on the back from industry magazines) was severely critical of both the organization and its methods.

Part of the BPI's problem had always been its ambiguous role in the scheme of things. The BPI is not the FBI. It has no legal powers save those available to any private company trying to ensure its interests are not infringed. Like the RIAA, it was set up to act in the interests of itself and its members, not necessarily coincident with what might be termed 'the public interest'. In the recent parliamentary committee hearing on UK CD prices, the BPI presented itself in very benign terms:

The BPI has a pivotal role in safeguarding the interests of the industry at large. For example, the BPI's Anti-Piracy Unit, which is entirely funded by record companies, undertakes extensive work in conjunction with the police and trading standard officers in investigating and preventing sound recording infringement . . . The BPI also endeavours to foster wider knowledge and understanding of the music industry throughout British society and to assist both music related and non-music related good causes.[4]

The key phrase here is 'entirely funded by record companies'. The BPI must constantly present evidence that it is succeeding in its battle with piracy simply to keep the coffers full. The other telling phrase is 'in conjunction with the police and trading standard officers', showing just how powerless the BPI is without a legal hand to hold. In a recent case, where they had attempted to ensure that certain 'live CDs' were impounded by customs officers, the importer took the matter up with Customs and Excise:

I had this argument with the customs last year, because about five or six people all had stuff stopped at customs coming in from Europe via UPS . . . I got on to the customs and asked why they prevented the stuff being released. And they said, 'Because it's illegal.' I said, 'Who says it's illegal.' And they said, 'The BPI.' I said, 'Why are you allowing a private limited company to inspect my goods, because they have no legal powers. They are not the law. If they were importing stuff into this country you wouldn't allow me to inspect their goods, so what right have you got allowing them to inspect my goods?' . . . I [then] talked to the [Customs and Excise] lawyer at great length and he virtually admitted to me that they were in the wrong. I said to him . . . if my name and address is on those goods and subsequent civil action is taken by that third party because you have given them information, then we [can] take action against you for divulging confidential information. He was stumped and . . . they released the goods. But in the meantime it had been inspected by the BPI and when we got it back it had BPI stickers all over it.[5]

'Operation Moonbeam', launched in the summer of 1979, remains the most extreme example of the BPI bending the law in the interests of 'stamping out piracy'. A report in *Billboard* in August 1979 suggested that 'Operation Moonbeam' had been a highly successful PR exercise:

The BPI believes it has smashed this country's biggest bootleg operation as a result of simultaneous raids conducted in four cities recently ... The investigations started following a tip about a Manchester-based bootleg operation importing US bootleg product into Holland ... One investigator, posing as an illegal disc-maker, actually pressed up 2,000 copies of a Bowie album in order to maintain his cover ... Says the [BPI]: 'This "Moonbeam" operation was the most costly ever mounted, and its success will drastically cut the flow of bootleg records and tapes into and around this country.'[6]

'Operation Moonbeam' was a classic 'sting' operation, with one minor variation – it required the BPI, 'an organization pledged to eliminat[ing] the manufacture and trade of bootlegs', to press up their own bootleg and follow it through the retail chain. How a bootleg pressed by the BPI, with the apparent collusion of RCA – the label with whom David Bowie (the artist in question) had an exclusive contract – was still a bootleg, was an issue that the BPI can be grateful never got tested in the courts. When the question of entrapment was raised by the music press, the BPI's press officer, Richard Robson, insisted that, 'All we did was re-press and mark an album that had already been in circulation.' When the *NME* ran a three-page feature on 'Operation Moonbeam' in August 1980, Mr Robson was even more unequivocal, insisting that the BPI 'repress' was a minor legal issue in a straightforward case of bootlegging:

Richard Robson [BPI]: [The *Wembley Wizards*] weren't pressed to implicate. They were pressed purely so the guy could maintain his cover ... All the investigator did was to act as a middle man. He was approached by the gang and the gang said to him, 'Look, you say you can manufacture records, we would like you to go and get 2,000 [copies] manufactured for us.' The guy had to say yes because of his cover. But there is no question of those records being used to implicate anybody. There were already literally tens of thousands of them around at the time. It's in the press releases. They were being pressed in America and coming over via Holland.[7]

Either Mr Robson was very good at the bare-faced lie or astonishingly ignorant about the operations of the organization he represented. The album pressed up by the BPI was called *The Wembley Wizard Touches the Dial*, for which the BPI was responsible for *all* 2,000 copies. The record in question was a copy of another bootleg, *Don't Touch That Dial*. Recorded at one of the London shows on the 1976 'Station to Station' tour, *Don't Touch That Dial* was (and is) one of the rarest Bowie bootlegs ever manufactured. Pressed by Japanese bootleg label Marc – previously responsible for rather esoteric titles by the likes of Suzi Quatro, Rory Gallagher and Camel – *Don't Touch That Dial* was virtually impossible to track down outside of Japan. In common with most Japanese titles, Marc's product was primarily targeted at the home market. Such product, provided it was recorded before 1978 by a non-Japanese artist, was perfectly legitimate in Japan. So much for the 'literally tens of thousands ... around at the time ... [all] pressed in America'.

At least the BPI were right in one of their claims. The Marc albums were coming over via Holland. A mail-order company by the name of Unique Records had managed to secure a small number of copies of *Don't Touch That Dial*. However, they had nothing like the number of copies required to meet the demand in the UK, where the 1976 Wembley shows had particular resonance. The sales of two double-album bootlegs of Bowie's 1976 Nassau FM broadcast, *Resurrection on 84th Street* and *Thin White Duke*, had been spectacular. *The Wembley Wizard Touches the Dial* was therefore a copy of a bootleg, and a particularly godawful one at that. It was entirely created by the BPI.

The BPI's main investigator at this time was one Bill Hood. He had hooked up with a motley crew of Manchester bootleg retailers and was convinced that they could help him unravel the entire chain of bootleg shops in the UK. The Mancunians were operating from Bookchain, a shop on Peter Street inhabited by staff familiar to anyone who had ever frequented Manchester's original bootleg store, Orbit Books. According to the *NME*:

[Bill] Hood successfully infiltrated the gang and actually visited the home of a supplier. And yet, mysteriously, he was still 'unable to gain concrete evidence against the major suppliers' . . . By his own admission, stocks came largely from Holland via pressing plants in the US [*sic*]. The Northern 'ring' was merely part of the chain of distribution. Hood chose not to follow the tortuous path back to origins but to 'involve myself in the manufacturing process. It was decided by me and my superiors that I pose as a presser of bootleg records . . . I had been told that one of the members had some metal casts and that he wanted some pressings done urgently. After a very short time I was given these metal casts and asked to press 2,500 records from them. I took the casts back to London where a member of the BPI did the necessary pressing for me' . . . [Gardner, the key figure implicated in the bust, insists that he] had only ever seen one *Wizard*, the asking price for which was upwards of £25. And not only did Hood's pressing amount to practically the grand total, but the whole Moonbeam bust, he claims, hinged on this one pressing . . . There were no *Wizards* to speak of until Hood did his pressing . . . The BPI even got it wrong on the subject of who took possession of the illegal 250 [copies]. Investigator Lackie swears in an affidavit that Gardner was at the wheel of the van and that his partner was the owner of an antiques shop. But Gardner can't drive and the shop owner, he claims, was in Newcastle, not Manchester, on the day in question. And the charge itself was served under the wrong name.[8]

Clearly the BPI Anti-Piracy Unit were not employing the most competent of investigators. Yet Operation Moonbeam did have one significant result, implicating Rough Trade Records of Ladbroke Grove in the retailing of bootlegs. Rough Trade was the leading independent retail outlet in the land. Like Virgin Records a generation earlier, and Rhino Records in Los Angeles at the same time, Rough Trade was a well-known retail outfit on the verge of becoming an independent record label. All three had also been found guilty of dipping their hands into the bootleg mire. Rough Trade had in fact been the major retail outlet for a flurry of UK punk bootlegs that began to dry up shortly after the Moonbeam bust. It was time that Rough Trade concentrated on one of Belfast's more legitimate exports, Stiff Little Fingers (though not before being fined ten grand for their part in the bootleg business).

The BPI were struggling to maintain a strong public image.

Before Moonbeam, their self-portrait was 'fetching in the extreme. A picture of staunch and fair-minded vigilance in the face of ever-mounting odds.' After Moonbeam, and the failed prosecution of Cheapo Cheapo, a Soho retailer whose stock was almost entirely promotional material (the BPI claimed that since promos were stamped 'Not for Sale', they could not be sold), Bill Hood resigned from the BPI (the judge in the Cheapo Cheapo case had severely criticized Hood's conduct). The following year the Law Lords judged that 'pirates' caught via an Anton Pillar 'search and seize' order, a crude but common method of gaining access to the premises of those suspected of copyright infringement, were 'perfectly entitled to stay silent about their customers and suppliers . . . alleged offenders [being] protected from self-incrimination by long-standing legal privilege.'[9]

At a time when the BPI needed a boost in credibility, they attempted to paint bootleggers as part of 'fairly big-time crime syndicates', a charge that must have tickled the solitary entrepreneurs responsible for all UK bootlegging. Perhaps what the BPI needed most was a change in the law. The RIAA had certainly benefited from the FBI's involvement since 1976. In Britain, if a bootlegger was prosecuted under criminal law, the BPI could not also sue for civil damages. A criminal deterrent could not therefore be reconciled with the 'substantial damages' the BPI was looking for to keep their precarious finances afloat. John Deacon, director-general of the BPI, admitted as much to an industry conference in 1980:

John Deacon: In practice . . . the criminal provisions of the Copyright Act 1956 and the Performers' Protection Acts 1958–72, are of no practical assistance to the legitimate record companies, and are not used by them or by the police.[10]

All the while the scale of bootlegging, at least commercial bootlegging, continued to be exaggerated by both music biz and media. Frankly it had always been a strictly small-time operation in the UK (with the possible exception of the years 1977–9). Throughout the eighties, sales of most bootlegs had declined from 'in their thousands' to 'in their hundreds'. This was not really the result of the BPI's higher profile, though certain retailers were always happy to use the time-worn excuse of 'legal risks' to excuse another price hike. The switch to increasingly deluxe packaging and limited runs from mainland European producers was pushing up bootleg prices, which in the heyday of punk had been somewhere between £4.50 and £6. A series of price increases in the early eighties made 'a tenner' the norm for any new title by 1985.

The switch to tape had also continued to eat into the bootleg vinyl market. Cassette technology had come on in leaps and bounds in the late seventies. In particular, the advent of Sony's brand of portable Walkman cassette-recorders had made more and more people experiment with taping their own shows and then trading them, a practice certain rock artists found considerably more palatable than the dreaded vinyl artifacts:

Stephen Morris [New Order]: The thing in England, I don't know if it's caught on in America, is the kids have got Walkmans that record and they go to the gig and record the gig on that. There's a sort of network of these people that swap cassettes but don't sell. They actually swap them, which is great. It's just like collecting bubblegum cards really.[11]

Before the eighties, bootleg tape vendors had tended to operate strictly by mail-order from PO boxes or accommodation addresses, working a small client base and advertising discreetly in the music press, offering 'rare recordings' by favourite acts. In the eighties, tape-sellers became ever more common figures at the circuit of record fairs popping up in market town after market town. The record fairs, which originated in the States as adjuncts to monthly swap-meets, were where collectors unloaded unwanted goodies and hopefully stumbled on more desirable 'rarities'. They had come to the centre of London in the late seventies before spreading like a rash across Britain and Europe in the early eighties.

Bootleg tape vendors were initially slow to respond to the demands of this new market, offering common material (sometimes from bootleg vinyl sources) on cheap tapes, with poorly xeroxed inserts and no track listings. Soon enough, though, consumers began to demand at least one of the better tape-brands (TDK or Maxell), 'real-time' copies and accurate track details. The more astute sellers also began to realize that there was a considerable demand for 'souvenirs' of recent shows and began to record shows themselves (or arrange for them to be taped) in order to have them on their stalls for the following weekend's fair. The language of tape-trading circles − 'It's an ECM-909 with a D-6 on SA X, no Dolby' (which means that it was recorded with a Sony ECM hand-held microphone using a Sony Walkman Professional cassette-recorder, dubbed on to TDK SA-X tape without any noise reduction) − began to become part of the parlance of this new commercial form of bootlegging.

The UK centre for this new trade, initially West London's Portobello Road, quickly relocated to London's Camden Lock, fast becoming Britain's fourth-largest tourist attraction and a perfect opportunity for anonymous street vending. On Saturdays and Sundays the tape-dealers would line both sides of Camden High Street, straddling the two sections of Camden Lock market, selling to visiting rock stars, curious tourists and well-heeled regulars who preferred the certitude of hearing the tape before purchase to the vagaries of tape-trading.

It was inevitable that such an overt display of 'black market' economics would soon come to the attention of the BPI and, sure enough, at the outset of another tourist season, in the summer of 1987, they finally took action. The lead story in the trade organ *Music Week* the week after the raid detailed another triumph for the forces of good:

The music industry struck at the heart of the bootlegging trade . . . with a carefully coordinated series of raids which stripped Camden Lock market − the most notorious centre for live bootlegs − of all its illicit tapes . . . 4,605 tapes with an estimated street value of more than £20,000 were seized . . . A member of the BPI's Anti-Piracy Unit explained that their surprise swoop was designed to send a message reverberating through markets and record fairs up and down the country that bootlegging is no longer an untouchable activity. 'It is well known that Camden market is the centre for bootleg tapes in the country and it's often been said by bootleggers that they get their masters from Camden,' said the unit leader . . . 'The profit on each tape is amazing. The fans are being ripped off really.'[12]

Unfortunately the raid was not quite as 'carefully coordinated' as they might have hoped. The BPI's main target in the raid – a notorious tape-trader known simply (and appropriately) as 'Big Al' – was not in Camden on the day of the raid but in Rotterdam, taping the opening show of David Bowie's first European tour in four years. And the police were allowing tape-dealers to keep video tapes of rock concerts on the grounds that their instructions had simply been 'audio tapes'. Whatever message the BPI hoped was 'reverberating through markets and record fairs', busting tape-vendors was considerably less effective than raiding bootleg manufacturers. Most of the vendors at Camden Lock were 'assistants', paid to sell the wares of more covert entrepreneurs, and were under instructions to give false names to the cops as they helped load the tapes into their vans. For the tape-vendors, their only real loss was a day's takings and the cost of a few hundred blank tapes wholesale, a dubious return to the BPI for such a difficult and expensive operation. Nevertheless, they chose to repeat the exercise at the end of 1988, and this time *Music Week*'s fairy-tale department excelled themselves:

The market is the recognized centre of the traffic in unlawful cassettes in this country and is a main distribution point for illegal master tapes . . . The BPI/MCPS team has no intention of taking legal action against any of the sellers whose wares were confiscated at Camden. The view is taken that the people working with trays of tapes are merely low-level employees of substantial organizations and that there would be little advantage in taking them to court . . . At the stall I saw raided, the young man refused to give his name and address, [but] he signed a letter acknowledging that his stock had been seized . . . Among the happiest people of the afternoon were the police. Their enthusiasm had been apparent all day . . . at the thought of depriving villains of £20,000 of income – money they believe could have gone into anything from drug trafficking to pornography.[13]

As one wag responded, when told his profits might be going into drugs and pornography, 'Chance would be a fine thing.' *Music Week* once again repeated the BPI's unfounded claim that tapes on sale at Camden were being utilized to manufacture bootleg albums. In fact the live bootleg album was already on its last legs (in part because 'souvenir' cassettes were cheaper and more readily available) – not that any self-respecting bootlegger would use the lo-fi fare on sale at Camden. What few bootleg albums were in the racks were invariably collections of studio recordings like Prince's *Black Album* or European multi-album sets of three-hour Bruce Springsteen or Led Zeppelin shows.

The BPI had also just received a bit of a drubbing in what was destined to be their last major action against a 'bootleg manufacturer' under existing copyright legislation. 1988 was to see the advent of a new UK Copyright Act as well as the first wave of bootleg CDs from Europe.

The high-profile bust of one Tim Smith for manufacturing vinyl versions of two bestselling bootlegs, Prince's *Black Album* and Paul McCartney's *Russian Album*, seemed as clear-cut a case as the BPI could ever hope for. Tim Smith, though, was not about to plead guilty:

Tim Smith: You can't assume that something is illegal. When the BPI seize stuff or inspect stuff [and declare it] illicit, it's not necessarily so for numerous reasons. It has to be applied to the individual product and they have to closely investigate each individual product to find out if it was illegal – dubious or immoral [maybe], but not necessarily illegal.[14]

The BPI had not learnt their lesson from Operation Moonbeam. Once again they displayed a penchant for extravagant, unsupportable allegations. In Smith's case, this meant accusing him of fraud and conspiracy, serious criminal offences, and convincing the police that here was the British end of an international multi-million-pound operation:

Tim Smith: The only reason the police were interested in the first place was that they reported to the police that we were, in their words, part of a multi-million-pound international fraud ring, which is ... the only reason that detectives of that [high] rank worked on our case, and they quickly began to get egg on their face, after spending a huge amount of public money. The report in *Music Week*, which was supplied solely by the BPI, said that a lot of papers referring to foreign dealings and names and addresses had been 'found' at our address, but the papers referred to legitimate Italian, German and Dutch companies who pay tax and run totally upfront businesses, supply goods on receipt, import stuff into this country, duty paid [and so on] ... [So] these detectives flew to Germany and Holland investigating this so-called multi-million fraud ring and found legitimate companies at the other end.[15]

While the police conducted their investigations at the tax-payers' expense, Mr Smith was remanded in custody. The BPI had assured the police that an international cartel of bootleggers would now begin to unravel. When it became patently obvious that Mr Smith was part of no cartel and that the sums involved were some way removed from the BPI's grandiose projections, Mr Smith and his partner were finally granted bail.

The two titles that Smith was alleged to have made were certainly shrewd choices for a bootlegger. Prince's *Black Album* was to have been the follow-up to *Sign of the Times* when, at the last minute, the diminutive Minnesotan decided to nix the release. Prince's reasons for this decision have never been explained. *The Black Album* was a typically funky fusion of black rock à la Sly Stone and Funkadelic, containing the usual hard-edged tales of erotica, sonically spruced up for mass consumption. Warners had actually got as far as pressing CDs and review tapes had already been sent out to the reps when the album was recalled. The chances of suppressing all copies of the album were nil. Given that by 1987 Prince was the hottest bootleg property going, *The Black Album* was bound to be the eighties' biggest bootleg bonanza. Richard's American vinyl edition sold an estimated 20,000 copies, and Tim Smith reckons the UK version sold in excess of 30,000, while other pressings – of which there were many – probably account for total vinyl sales in excess of 100,000 (and

probably an equal number of CDs), a figure that may even exceed the true sales of *Great White Wonder*. Prince's apparent ambivalence towards bootlegs – suggested by the amount of studio material that has leaked out and his often strained relations with Warners – and the veil of secrecy that surrounds his business dealings, bound to make his cooperation in any legal action against Smith unlikely.

Paul McCartney's attitude to bootlegs was less problematic, but then the case of *The Russian Album* seemed like a straight act of piracy. McCartney had long threatened to replicate Lennon's idea of an album of rock & roll covers, and in 1988 he released thirteen rock & roll standards, recorded over just two days in July 1987 (a marked contrast to the two years Lennon spent on *Rock & Roll*). However, McCartney's album was only released in Russia, supposedly as a gesture 'of peace and friendship to the people of the USSR'. Again, the demand for a worldwide release was not one that the bootleggers were slow to respond to. What, surely, did Mr McCartney expect?

Tim Smith: On the morning we went to court, our lawyers suggested to the judge that the McCartney *Russian Album* couldn't be illegal because it was put out on Melodiya and [no reciprocal agreement on trade existed] between the two countries. At the time the Iron Curtain still existed. [Because they were not bound] under the Berne Convention, if the Russians wanted to copy Levis and Chanel there's nothing that we could do about it. Equally it works in reverse. In general, no one would want to copy a Russian product. It's always been the other way around. So what our lawyers argued was that we had copied a Russian product and there's nothing to stop you doing it. The BPI then argued that they owned the copyright and the artist, blah blah blah, and we've got the rights to put it out in this country. What the judge said was [that] both arguments carried legal substance but where one law contradicts another it can't be justice to see a man punished, and he wouldn't hear the eleven charges [relating to that album] . . . We thought, 'Things are looking up!'[16]

The part of the case relating to the Prince *Black Album* was not so straightforward. The onus still remained on the BPI to prove that the album was illegal, not on Smith to prove it legitimate. Their first problem was proving that the album had been manufactured in Britain – it had not (it had been produced in Europe and shipped to the UK – the usual arrangement with UK bootleg productions).

Tim Smith: The BPI insisted that the picture-disc vinyl version of *The Black Album* was pressed in a place called Adrenalin in Slough, and their evidence to show this was based on ID markings in the matrix . . . They obviously weren't aware that Adrenalin don't make picture discs! And [it was] easily proven by the machinery they've got. When we got to the pre-hearing, this chapter was removed and along with it the [whole question of the] picture discs.[17]

The BPI had also failed to get any paperwork from Prince or his management confirming that *The Black Album* was produced under contract for Warners. Since any legal breach in this, as with most bootleg cases, related to certain rights in the 'exclusive' contract between an artist and his official record company, this was a crucial part of the BPI's case.

Tim Smith: All our lawyers did was ask them to prove why it was illegal as it had never been released. Our lawyers wanted proof that it was illegal. They furnished all sorts of papers to say that no licence had been issued, but then again did a licence have to be issued? . . . On the day we went into court we pleaded not guilty to everything because over [and above the] twenty-one charges [of copyright infringement] we were charged with fraud and conspiracy. We [had] prepared over the course of a year a lot of legal arguments . . . I can't remember if [Warners] had paid [the recording costs] . . . because a top artist can be signed to a label for all of his recordings or for the next album or for five albums . . . Anything outside of those five albums isn't theirs – that's what our lawyers were picking at . . . 90 per cent of the paperwork was the BPI acting on behalf of WEA. It wasn't even directly from WEA, it was 'we are the representatives of . . .' [meaning] the BPI . . . By twelve [o'clock on the first day] the judge had removed *The Russian Album* part of the case, which left *The Black Album* and the two criminal charges of fraud and conspiracy. They then started bargaining among themselves and they came to us and said if you plead guilty to five charges they'll remove the others. I believe the first five [included] fraud and conspiracy . . . the ones we weren't going to plead guilty to. Anyway we refused point blank and they went away again. Another two hours, we were well into the afternoon and still hadn't entered court, they came back and said plead guilty to three charges . . . and we'll remove the rest, and the three charges were the one track [issued officially], fraud and conspiracy. Bollocks! We said no, we'll just fight the trial . . . We were on full legal aid, it never cost us a penny . . . [It's] four o'clock in the afternoon . . . It's not in the BPI's hands, it's in their lawyer's hands, and I think they knew by then they weren't going to win these parts of the case . . . And what they must have decided in the end was that any conviction will do because then you can talk about it as a conviction. And what they did [afterwards] was give a statement that said the two men were convicted, but they never said of what! At four in the afternoon, they came back to us and said if you plead guilty to knowingly contravening the copyright of the one track ['When 2 R in Love'], they would remove all the other charges. I said what about the fraud and conspiracy, and they said they'd remove that.[18]

So, after a hugely expensive investigation, a year of legal bills, and some twenty-six charges, Smith and his partner pleaded guilty to contravening the copyright on the one song from *The Black Album* to be issued officially. The irony of this was that 'When 2 R in Love' hadn't actually been released at the time that the bootleg came out; it had only been issued on 1988's *Lovesexy* album. The vast waste of resources on this 'multi-million-pound international fraud' did not sit well with the police, souring their relationship with the BPI for some time to come.

Tim Smith: One of the [detectives], who I think was the higher rank, was taken off the case long ago by his superiors who realized that it didn't warrant what was happening. The one copper who was left on it . . . felt that he'd been made a fool of and didn't like the fact that we were obviously guilty of something.[19]

Yet the BPI had overlooked the most blatant case of bootlegging in the final vinyl years, one that would provide a very ominous precedent for the future. In Europe, the Germans and Italians had really hit overdrive between 1984 and 1987, churning out hundreds of bootleg titles. The German labels, particularly those run by one Dieter Schubert, had developed a reputation for deluxe, coloured-vinyl releases from quality source tapes. Best of the bunch were the Royal Sound double-albums and a handful of titles on a label that revived the logo, if not the name, of TMQ – The Swingin' Pig. As a vinyl label, The Swingin' Pig issued a mere fifteen titles. But Mr Schubert was just gearing up for the next bootleg revolution.

The Italians were acting even more brazenly. In 1985 a Dylan boxed-set recalled the controversy surrounding Joker's 1973 Dylan albums. The three-album *Gaslight Tapes* set was an excellent collection of early Dylan acoustic performances, housed in an attractive box with a bleary-eyed Dylan (*circa* 1974) peering out from the cover. It was not only being sold in Italy but was being exported across the whole of Europe, where it retailed for considerably less than a legitimate triple-album set. The album was a perfectly legal release in Italy. It lay outside the period of copyright protection for live performances in Italy (another double-album of Dylan acoustic recordings had been issued in 1982 as *Historical Archives*, utilizing the same hole in Italian copyright law). Yet it was certainly not legitimate in countries like Britain, France and Holland, where 'mechanical' protection ran for considerably longer than the twenty years applied in Italy.

Despite such technicalities, the set was freely available in all the major record stores in Britain only a matter of weeks before CBS's five-album boxed-set, *Biograph*, was due to reach the shops. When *Biograph* was delayed a couple of weeks and fans wandered into stores asking for 'the Dylan box' it was usually *The Gaslight Tapes* that they walked out with. Though *Ten of Swords* had caused a furore in the States without ever selling more than a thousand copies, *The Gaslight Tapes* created the most minimal media hubbub.

Because of the Italians' belated awareness of the ever-expanding market for CDs, it would be a couple of years yet before the producers of *The Gaslight Tapes* repeated the exercise on CD, thus opening up a whole new jewel box of worms. However, the free availability of the *Gaslight* set showed the huge sales potential if bootleggers could ever find a large enough gap in European copyright protection to enable them to come out of the recesses of record fairs and flea markets and on to the high streets. In the bright, shiny world of the silver CD they could even sell collectors the same recordings all over again – just like the real record companies.

But then CD manufacture seemed like a closed book. It was high-tech, largely confined to the western world and Japan, and even by 1987 there were a decidedly finite number of plants worldwide able to do the deed. Yet ever since the advent of the medium four years earlier, collectors had mused upon the idea of bootleg CDs, making generational loss a thing of the past. An ostrich-like music industry refused to address the unthinkable, more concerned with ensuring that all blank-tape users paid a tape levy, whatever their reasons for purchasing cassettes, and killing at birth that most dangerous of beasts – a recordable digital medium, superior even to CD: DAT, the Digital Audio Tape. In both the US and Europe, commercial bootlegging had dropped down the totem pole of priorities, giving way to a whole new bugbear – home-taping. When the unthinkable happened, the Biz was looking the other way.

12 Complete Control

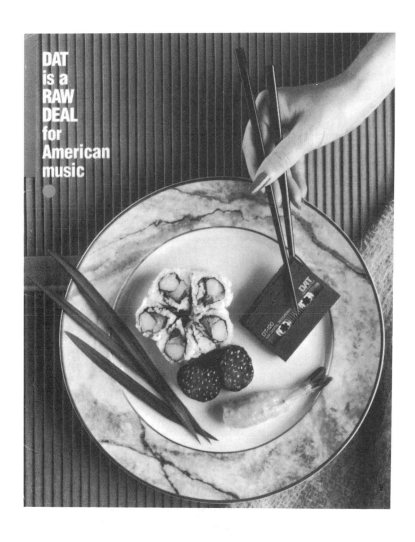

Enobarbus [*Guardian Gazette*]: Historically the most successful purveyors of copyright material have sold it in a form and at a price that made infringement unattractive. Gramophone records that cost little more than blank tapes will not be pirated; legal forms that cost no more than the price of a Xerox copy will not be pirated.[1]

Arguments over the impact of bootlegging may have raged across the great divide for a quarter of a century – and rock bootlegs may have grabbed far more headlines than more orthodox forms of piracy – but for much of the eighties they were pushed out of the press by the issue of home-taping, in particular the disturbing ramifications of a digital audio medium (DAT) that could perfectly replicate any recording – no quality loss, no hiss. It was these issues which fuelled the International Federation of Phonogram Industries' demands for a levy on blank tapes and recording hardware. This was bound to have long-term consequences for those music buffs hoping to extend their listening beyond the (increasingly antiseptic) commercial fodder pumped out by legitimate labels.

Inevitably, the industry's determination to exert total control over all forms of recorded music would eventually work against them. By 1988 they had helped to create the ideal climate for the advent of bootleg CDs, the ultimate 'performance piracy' medium. Throughout the previous decade, the primary 'check' on commercial bootlegs had been the expansion of the blank-tape market. The switch to tape-collecting was largely born of frustration at the poor quality of many bootlegs (and, indeed, legitimate cassettes).

While the ever-expanding 'home entertainment' industries continued to reinvent technology, the record industry's concerns remained stolidly the same: to ensure that however, whenever and whatever music was available, it was enjoyed only at their discretion. The record industry refused to see themselves as simply the manufacturers of the bulk of pre-recorded audio software. They did not want a slice of the pie, but rather the entire dessert trolley. They wanted consumers to consume, and to refrain from making their own (non-commercial) music or establishing any alternative tape-trading circuit.

Obdurately uninterested in competing with bootlegs, the post-punk record industry had yet to fathom out a way of deriving revenue from something as patently unofficial as a commercial bootleg. Instead they sought a 'compensatory' levy on all cassette tapes – based on the premise that they were invariably being used to record copyrighted material. This campaign grew in reverse proportion to the steady decline in record sales in the early eighties. Perhaps the music industry was entering a period of permanent decline. After all, if people were uninterested in new music, and the companies could not extend their rights beyond a once-and-for-all sale, then the future looked less than rosy.

Tony Martin [record retailer]: People are losing interest in records. There are now four television channels, countless commercial radio stations, the daunting prospect of cable and satellite TV. Videos, home computers and video games are all time stealers and all represent money and time not being spent on records. There is no concerted national conspiracy to tape records. The record has had a good run, but it's no longer the ultimate in home entertainment.[2]

In fact Phillips, the parent company of Polygram, by 1983 had created the record industry's lifesaver, 'the ultimate in home entertainment': the compact disc (though they were – and are – some years away from convincing the bulk of consumers to junk their record collections). The 'majors', Polygram excepted, were not convinced that the 5″ silver disc was here to stay. The price was prohibitive and the sort of punters who might be interested in the new medium – serious music buffs – were also likely to have substantial record collections. It was to be some time before the compact disc was fully embraced by all record companies.

By the time CDs were on the launching pad, retail sales of the pre-recorded cassette were fast approaching those of vinyl. The switch from artifact to disposable music carrier seemed to be nigh. The problem was that the ephemeral nature of pre-recorded cassettes, their poor sound quality and cheap feel, and the ease with which cassettes could be duplicated, meant that fans were as likely to copy a friend's vinyl album on to a blank cassette as buy the pre-recorded tape version.

Indeed if they copied said album on to a high-bias, chrome cassette, in 'real time', the results would be some way superior to a pre-recorded cassette, which retailed in most cases for more than the vinyl equivalent.*

As cassette production increased, costs fell well below those of commensurate vinyl versions. Yet cassette prices remained the same. The record companies further benefited from a standard clause in recording contracts. When pre-recorded cassettes were first introduced in the early seventies, their distribution was usually effected through licensees rather than directly by the labels. In order to offset the costs involved, the companies offered a reduced royalty rate for cassettes (generally half of the royalty due on vinyl sales). However, long after the companies had integrated cassette distribution into their own network, the reduced royalty rate remained a standard clause in recording contracts. Heads they win, tails you lose!

Rather than considering a cost-cutting exercise (to reflect the leap in cassette production in the early eighties) or a significant increase in production quality, the industry preferred to mount a sustained assault on home-taping, which they began to refer to by a new, emotive moniker, 'home piracy'.

One voice resisted the set of blinkers that seemed to come with industry mogul status: Chris Blackwell at Island Records. In February 1981, Blackwell launched the 'One Plus One' series, pre-recorded cassettes dubbed on high-bias, chrome tapes with

---

* Official cassettes continue to be recorded on normal bias, ferric cassettes – the lowest of the low – using high-speed duplicating equipment, that copy in three minutes or less. Poor sound quality and audible hiss are the inevitable result.

a complete album on side one and a blank side two for 'home use'.

Chris Blackwell: For too long the record industry has ignored the fact that the cassette has a very major role to play. Currently, cassettes account for around 15 to 20 per cent of the market. In five years' time, the situation will be reversed ... Record companies are over-pricing them. The cassette, in the majority of cases, is priced the same as the album, yet is clearly not of the same value, quality or feel. The industry is encouraging home-taping by over-pricing cassettes. Quality control just does not go into pre-recorded cassettes ... Albums should be like hardbacks, first editions, something to collect, while cassettes, like paperbacks, should be a cheap attractively packaged practical alternative, but with quality content ... All tape machines [and] music centres have record buttons. Thus to a large extent the battle has been lost. Twenty years after the invention of the cassette is not the time to start complaining [about home-taping].[3]

At the same time, Island cut its list price for cassettes from £5.29 to £3.99, reflecting the production-cost differential between vinyl and cassette. Howls of indignation from other members of the BPI greeted Blackwell's innovation. Though the 'One Plus One' experiment was abandoned before the year was out, Blackwell's bold predictions came to pass. Cassettes continued to close on vinyl sales, all the while shadowed by a commensurate increase in blank-tape sales. If the 'majors' were not prepared to compete with 'home piracy' by producing well-packaged, competitively priced pre-recorded cassettes, their only alternative was to try to make the price of blank tapes prohibitive. The companies didn't like the idea that home-taping might be killing music – they felt they were making a good enough job of that themselves!

The big players in the blank-tape market in the early eighties were all Japanese companies – TDK, Maxell and Sony. None of these outfits were affiliated to record labels in America or Europe. If blank-tape manufacturers were on the other side of the fence, the main hardware manufacturers – with the notable exceptions of Phillips (owners of Polygram) and JVC (part-owned by RCA) – shared their lack of concern for any copyright ramifications from mass-marketing 'double-decks' (two cassette decks in one unit), a requisite part of the rack systems now entering the lo-fi end of the retail chain.

As early as 1974, the BPI had threatened legal action against 'hardware manufacturers whose advertising of tape equipment emphasizes its potential for home-copying of copyrighted material such as recorded music'. For the remainder of the decade, though, the BPI failed to discern a single transgression flagrant enough to warrant action in the courts, despite a self-evident explosion in the cassette market as fans began to discover the delights of re-recordable blank tape.

However, the BPI had the shining example set by two American corporate bullies who had ganged up on Japanese giant Sony in what the media dubbed The Home-Video War. Their feud in the American courts gave the BPI hope that legal threats would dissuade hardware manufacturers from producing the sort of technology that might aid a breach of copyright. It was 1976 when MCA/Universal, in tandem with Disney, instigated an unprecedented attack upon technological innovation. Their case against Sony was brought on the grounds that the simple act of manufacturing and distributing Betamax video machines contributed to copyright infringement. The use of Betamax VCRs to record TV programmes allegedly violated their copyrights, and Sony were guilty of contributory copyright infringement by marketing this 'copying tool'.

The intent behind this action was to tie Sony up in the American judicial system. Certainly MCA and Disney had little prospect of reversing the home-video revolution. The Sony case was not finally resolved until January 1984, when the Supreme Court overruled a 1981 judgement by a lower court, adjudicating that Sony was not contributing to copyright infringement. By then Sony had lost the battle for the home-video market. The technologically inferior VHS system had triumphed over Sony's Betamax format. The cost to Sony, and the element of uncertainty that had reigned in the home-video market throughout the dispute, inevitably made hardware manufacturers wary of any future copyright disputes – whatever the actual legal arguments or eventual outcome.

While home videos were still a new toy in the late seventies, cassette decks had long been an essential part of any music system. Any serious music buff was likely to have two decks wired up to record cassette to cassette, vinyl to cassette (and maybe even reel-to-reel to cassette). When some of the more forward thinking manufacturers decided to actively market double-decks that worked as a single unit, the BPI followed Disney's lead (though they lacked Disney's immense resources).

In 1984 they made formal complaints to both the Advertising Standards Authority and the Independent Broadcasting Authority about Amstrad's advertising for their music centres, which highlighted the ease with which its two-in-one cassette deck could duplicate tapes. Their complaints were dismissed. The ASA pointed out that it was not unlawful 'to advertise [the] features and capabilities of lawfully constructed appliances'. Amstrad were not about to play dead when the BPI then brandished threats of legal action.

The odds were stacked against the BPI from the outset. As Lord Justice Lawton commented, during preliminary legal skirmishes, 'Mere knowledge on the part of the supplier that equipment would probably be used to infringe someone's copyright does not make the supply unlawful.' The BPI could also ill afford such expensive litigation.

Yet, in an initial victory for the BPI, Lord Justice Nicholls decided that Amstrad may well be 'inciting others to infringe copyright in circumstances where the copyright owners have no practical remedy against the actual infringers'. Amstrad, like Sony before them, successfully took the case to appeal. The Law Lords finally decided that Amstrad could continue to market their machines. In his summary of the case, Lord Templeman suggested that a law like the one relating to home-copying, 'which is treated with such contempt, should be amended or repealed'. He also clearly implied that it was the greed of the record companies that was primarily responsible for music lovers choosing to make their own cassettes:

Some home-copiers may break the law because they estimate that the chances of detection are non-existent. Some home-copiers may consider that the entertainment and recording industries already exhibit all the characteristics of [an] undesirable monopoly – lavish expenses, extravagant earnings and exorbitant profits – and that the blank tape is the only restraint on further increases in the prices of records. Whatever the reason for home-copying, the beat of *Sergeant Pepper* and the soaring sounds of the Miserere from unlawful copies are more powerful than law-abiding instincts or twinges of conscience.[4]

The music industry was not content with its attempts to bully hardware manufacturers. In 1982, before the Amstrad case had yet become an issue, WEA's UK managing director Charles Levison threatened to withdraw advertising from periodicals that 'support or encourage either piracy or home-taping'. This was clearly an attempt to censor the music press, which had run features – painting the record companies in less than glowing terms – on attempts to institute a blank-tape levy. The BPI's action against Amstrad and WEA's thinly veiled threats against the likes of the *NME* and *Melody Maker* were intended to highlight the industry's case for a levy on both blank tapes and hardware.

As early as 1977, the BPI were sponsoring a market-research exercise intended 'to determine the current level of home-copying'. The brief given the market research company was simple:

It is hoped that the report will provide ammunition for the [BPI] to impress upon the DTI [Department of Trade and Industry] the need for the implementation of the Whitford Committee's recommendation in favour of a compensatory levy on [tape] hardware.[5]

When the survey did not provide sufficiently damning evidence of 'home piracy', the BPI commissioned a second survey, in which the original estimate of £75 million worth of lost sales annually jumped to £100 million. The surveys were destined to continue. By 1980 the £100 million 'lost sales' had shot up to £200 million. The following year the BPI had come up with an even more extravagant £304.9 million – amounting to a 400 per cent increase in home-taping (or statistic-bending) between 1977 and 1981.

AIM, who conducted the BPI's March 1979 survey, admitted to *Billboard* magazine that they had been hired to produce 'once-and-for-all evidence which would be used to get the copyright law changed'. The AIM survey also provided ammunition in America, where pressure was also mounting for a tape-levy:

New information that Britain's record industry loses about 20 per cent of its turnover to home-taping has set off alarm signals here [in the US] ... It is expected to galvanize industry lobbying of the government to amend current copyright laws, or to introduce a compensatory tax on blank tape.[6]

Though the record industry was busy accumulating cooperative statisticians, when it came to the issue of home-taping there were plenty of other voices crying to be heard. When the BPI came up with its original figure of £75 million in losses to home-taping back in 1977, Henry Pattison, chairman of the European Tape Industry Association, dismissed the figures as 'absolutely hypothetical ... money that was never spent and there is no way of knowing if it ever would have been'. As Pattison was quick to point out, 'the total value of the blank-tape market in the UK is less than half the BPI figure for [their] losses.'[7]

BASF had conducted their own survey of blank and pre-recorded cassette sales in the same year. Their figures certainly belied the BPI statistics. Worldwide pre-recorded cassette sales had leapt 66 per cent in 1977, while so-called 'premium ferrite' blank tapes had only grown by 34 per cent and low-grade 'promotional ferrite' tapes (most likely to be used by someone taping a friend's album) had actually fallen by 7 per cent. Another survey by Maxell showed that 'premium' cassette users bought twice as many records as non-tape users – yet these were the very same dudes who were apparently killing music with their home-taping. The chairman of the European Tape Industry Association summed up the home-truths on home-taping best when he told one industry magazine:

Bob Hine: Surely the answer to the problem and an increase in record company profitability is the proper promotion of pre-recorded cassettes and a willingness to move with the times ... Production costs of cassettes have remained static for eight years while disc costs have soared 150 per cent. Yet pre-recorded cassettes are more expensive than discs, which are coming in for increased criticism over sound quality. The public is disenchanted with the product released by the record industry.[8]

What did the record industries stand to gain from a tape-levy and where would this money go? The BPI's suggestion for a levy of 1p per minute on blank tape would have amounted to a 100 per cent increase in the cost of the average normal-bias C90 tape. This would raise approximately £70–80 million in revenue in the UK alone. The beauty of a tape-levy was that it did not operate like a normal mechanical royalty, where the lion's share (minus deductibles) went to the artist:

The great advantage to the record industry of the levy solution was that it normally entitled record producers, who are not protected by the Berne Convention, and who are not protected by the Rome Convention in some member states, to a share of the levy.[9]

Indeed it was intended that a whopping two fifths of the levy would go directly into record-company coffers. The major record companies, by their own figures, would have been dividing up an annual £30 million windfall in the UK, five times that in the US. And this was despite a mountain of independent statistical evidence that the majority of tape-consumers used blank tapes to give themselves a listening format unavailable on conventional pre-recorded tapes or records (i.e. compilations of current favourites, radio programmes, tapes of live performances, etc.). Thankfully, such a punitive levy was never a realistic objective.

The moral arguments put forward by a newly galvanized BPI shared the same sieve-like quality as their financial 'evidence'. The BPI's most whimsical suggestion was that this £30 million windfall would be pumped into the parts of the industry that were 'least profitable':

Chris Wright [BPI]: In reality we would stay in business [without a tape-levy] and we would still make records by groups like Culture Club and The Police, but the areas that would suffer would be the least profitable, the classical recordings, ethnic music, music for minority tastes – those areas that need support.[10]

In reality the 'majors' had long abandoned 'ethnic music' to the clutches of those independents hoping to maintain a balance between aesthetic and financial considerations. The industry was not about to emphasize what it stood to gain from a tape-levy: money, lots of it. Far better to portray the 'tape pirate' as stealing from struggling artists.

Charles Ferris [Audio Recording Rights Coalition]: Although that argument plays on emotional attachments to the artistic community, it is completely unsupported by the facts – which demonstrate that the scheme by which the music business compensates virtually all singers, instrumentalists and songwriters makes it improbable that anything but essentially insignificant monies would ever be seen by creators . . . little in the history of the industry's dealings with artists or in its traditional compensation structure suggests that it will be generous.[11]

The American music industry's home-taping literature – which came under the 'Save American Music' banner – was no more original. According to the SAM literature, 'the huge losses to the record industry have already reduced the diversity of music available to consumers. In the past three years (1979–82), new releases have declined by a third.' Peter Titus, in his feature in *New York Rocker*, 'The Man Can't Scotch Our Taping', punched holes in SAM's apocalyptic picture of a beleaguered industry with the best of motives and the worst of problems:

The trend towards fewer new titles stretches back twenty years, not just the past home-taping period. Between 1963 and 1978, new releases declined by almost 50 per cent, while the record industry grew sixfold in terms of units shipped. The logic of this process is simple: because of the economics of mass production and distribution, fewer numbers of larger-selling titles are many times more profitable than large numbers of smaller-selling releases . . . The idea that less-commercial music somehow depends on hits for subsidization has never held water. Record companies don't release losers on purpose. In fact, their executives work night and day trying to eliminate losers altogether. This practice won't be reversed by transferring revenue from foreign tape manufacturers to American record firms.[12]

The juxtaposition of 'foreign manufacturers' with 'American firms' said it all. SAM's literature was designed to appeal to the worst kind of protectionist thinking. Thankfully, US consumer organizations could be relied on to mount a concerted campaign to defeat the American music industry. In particular, the Audio Recording Rights Coalition prepared its own statistics, determined to discredit a Warner Communications survey that had claimed the record industry was losing $1bn annually through home-taping. Three basic conclusions emerged from the figures provided for the ARRC:

(i) A majority of home-tapers say they have bought a record or pre-recorded tape after taping all or part of it;
(ii) 65 per cent of home-tapers do so for the advantage of program-ming their own selections;
(iii) 51 per cent of all music tapes made at home were made from records or tapes owned by the taper.

The lack of popular support or sound statistical evidence in their favour eventually counted against the 'levyists'. When the home-taping bill reached the Senate in 1985, one of its supposed co-sponsors made it clear that he had serious reservations about the industry's data and motives:

Senator Metzenbaum made it known that he is far from signing on as a co-sponsor of the Mathias [home-taping] bill. He sent signals to the recording industry that he has growing doubts about how the money would be distributed – and to whom – and further, that conflicting financial data concerning the health of the industry makes it unclear whether it has suffered from the $1.5 billion in lost sales it alleges are due to home-taping ... [Senators] say record companies have been partly to blame for the situation because they have not kept up with technological changes and, especially, the need for consumers to have high-quality cassettes.[13]

The bill never made it as far as President Reagan. Some good ol' Anglo-Saxon pragmatism was enough to halt the home-taping bill in the Senate. In Britain a government green paper did recommend a tape-levy, but only one that would generate around £5 million per annum, and when it came to the crunch in 1987, the Cabinet decided that the levy still qualified as a new tax and dropped the plan to incorporate a levy into a new copyright bill:

Kenneth Clarke [Trade and Industry Secretary]: The levy proposals went beyond the principle of the Government providing legal protection to the intellectual property of a creative artist. They involved the Government in the collection of a new tax.[14]

In Australia, the courts decided that a tape-levy, which had been made law in 1989, was unconstitutional on the grounds that it was clearly a tax, not a levy, and the Government was forced to redraft legislation. The levy was dry.

Yet the tape-levy lobbyists were not about to abandon their hopes of forcing this tax on English-speaking countries by more roundabout methods. In Britain's case, it was hoped that a European Council directive on an EC-wide levy, set at the highest existing levy ($0.60 per C90 in the Netherlands), would force Britain into line with the rest of the EC.

Mainland Europe had proved considerably less resistant to the blank-tape tax plans of the IFPI. By the end of the eighties, levies on blank tapes and/or hardware were in place in France, Germany, the Netherlands, Portugal and Spain, with legislation pending in all other EC countries save Britain, Luxembourg and Ireland. Attempts were also being made to extend the levies to cover video tapes and machines in those countries where the levy only applied to audioware. With video, the arguments for a Europe-wide levy were even more porous. An EC Green Paper had previously concluded that, 'for audio-visual recordings only a small proportion of the recordings made on blank tape were intended to be permanently retained.'[15]

Of course, video tapes could be used solely for audio purposes. (The economics actually favoured video-tape. Despite its bulk, it often retailed for less than blank audios of a corresponding length and fidelity.) For much of the eighties, video also offered the only practical digital recording medium.

In the early eighties Sony had launched a new video medium that it hoped would become the domestic standard. Video-8, like Betamax, was patently superior to VHS in all departments, and was considerably more compact. One of its major innovations was that it had the capability to record audio signals digitally. (Using a PCM – pulse-code modulated – converter, the Video-8 encoded analogue audio signals into a PCM digital signal.) What Sony had actually devised was the basis for a whole new audio medium, DAT (Digital Audio Tape), and a whole new set of controversies.

For a while, DAT threatened to become the standard recordable music carrier, matching CD's digital sheen and surpassing its portability and playing time. This, though, was something that the record industry was determined to ensure did not happen.

With DAT, Sony and its partners in design had created the perfect bootlegging tool. Digital recordings could be made and 'cloned' with no quality loss. For those who collected unauthorized recordings on tape, DAT was a godsend. Generational flaws would become a thing of the past and tape-collectors could now enjoy all their unofficial tapes in the best quality possible. What it also meant was that commercial bootleggers were far more likely to be able to 'source' tapes in a quality that corresponded closely with the 'master' tape. However, the record industry was largely unconcerned with the implications of DAT as a bootlegging tool. They were far more concerned with the ease with which DAT could replicate their own digital medium, the compact disc. The home-taping war had just entered a new phase, and clearly the Luddites were alive and living in America.

The artists themselves welcomed DAT with something approximating to open arms. The possibilities for making their own demos and board tapes digitally, with minimum fuss, was bound to appeal to most musicians. But DAT was also an extremely compact, user-friendly way of disseminating the best possible 'clones' of a recording. When the industry tried to rally support behind attempts to suppress the new medium, there were some very notable voices of dissent.

Michael Jackson: The record company argument – which is that it's like giving away the master tape, and we have to stop it – is obviously a logical argument. But personally, I really don't care ... the thought of people borrowing my records from their friends and taping them has never bothered me. My concern is that as many people as possible hear the music. In fact, since they're going to do it anyway, I think I'd prefer that they do it with digital quality. I'm still going to make enough money to live on one way or another, whether it's through publishing royalties, live performance or whatever ... Personally, I think it might in some ways even be a good thing. Because if the profits get smaller, then maybe the lawyers and the accountants will start to fade away, and the music business can again be run by people who love music.[16]

This was not the kind of attitude that industry moguls expected of their biggest earner. Yet their initial response to DAT was not to use it to reinforce their arguments for a tape-levy. Rather, they returned to an idea that had been waiting for its time since the days of the Apple Corporation, when The Beatles were happily financing hare-brained schemes galore. What the industry wanted was a spoiler 'encoded' in all commercial music, designed to stop all acts of piracy. The type of spoiler that Apple had been sponsoring was actually a supposedly inaudible tone that would 'mix' with the high-pitched bias signal generated by all tape-recorders, creating an audible whine. The problem, as one critic pointed out, was that 'this kind of spoiler system can be made to work in the laboratory, but not in real life'.

The industry's attempts at a DAT 'spoiler' were only marginally more practical. The CBS Copycode system, which was enthusiastically adopted by the RIAA, relied on circuitry in the hardware itself, which would detect an 'inaudible' trigger signal in an 'encoded' source recording and would then shut the machine down. The RIAA intended to back up their support for CBS's spoiler by lobbying for legislation that would force manufacturers to incorporate such a system into all DAT machines as a matter of course. One problem: Copycode didn't work.

CBS claimed that the Copycode system could be incorporated via a single IC chip at a cost of about $1 per machine. CBS insisted that the effects would be inaudible. The reality is that no filter can cut-off instantaneously. There is always a gradual cut-off slope. It is also impossible for a filter to cut out one frequency without also affecting neighbouring frequencies. The filter in the CBS system was centred on 3,838 Hz (roughly the next-to-highest note on a piano). Music in virtually all audible frequencies would be affected by such a filter. Yet CBS insisted that their system would not have any noticeable effect on the sound quality of a protected recording. The RIAA actually lobbied Congress to enact a law requiring that the CBS anticopy chip be included in all DAT recorders sold in the US, even though the system had yet to be proved to work.

It was not just in America that the record industry was attempting to force through Copycode. In West Germany, the third largest music-buying market in the world, the IFPI put a deposition to the Ministry of Justice asking for Copycode to be made compulsory in DAT hardware and software *and* asking for a substantial hike in the tape-levy already in place in Germany (from 3 per cent to 10 per cent).

But it was in America that the record industry was at its most belligerent. The RIAA made it clear that any manufacturer who imported DAT machines, available in the Far East in the early months of 1987, into the US would be the subject of a lawsuit on the grounds of 'copyright infringement'. The industry seemed on the verge of outright victory when, on 25 March 1987, the Energy and Commerce Committee of the House of Representatives approved a measure banning the sale of DATs for one year unless they contained a copycode chip – something opposed by the Consumers' Union, the HRRC and the Consumer Federation of America. The rights of the consumer to listen to music in the best possible fidelity was simply not an issue.

Why was DAT such a threat? Could it be that it introduced a competitive element into the digital audio market, something that cut to the very core of the music industry's increased profitability at a time when they were selling an all-time low number of units worldwide? If DAT was able to establish itself as a mass-market music carrier, any marked disparity in price between CDs and blank DAT tape – what with DAT's potential to record up to two hours of music (compared with an average playing time on CD of fifty minutes) – would result in a considerable incidence of home DATing.

Charles Ferris [ARRC]: We suspect that the most determined push against DAT comes from those in the recording industry who are enjoying the high, stable prices they are getting for compact discs and don't want new competition from within their own ranks.[17]

This is exactly what had happened in the cassette market, where the price of such an unimpressive and flimsy artifact as a pre-recorded cassette remained out of all proportion to its manufacturing costs.

A compromise was required. DAT could not be uninvented, and the history of innovation suggested that the industry's attempts to turn back technology were doomed to failure. The first bridge between the hardware manufacturers and the record companies was built by Sony, who purchased Columbia Records, hoping to neuter perhaps the most virulent opponent of DAT. But the American record industry was still determined to find a means of limiting digital cloning with DAT.

The Serial Copyright Management System was a lovely euphemism for the system that was devised to supersede Copycode. This allowed a single digital copy to be made from a digital source, but when a second-generation digital copy was attempted, a binary code inserted in the information-storage section of the tape made the machine inoperable. The system was cheap to install and, unlike Copycode, appeared to work ninety-nine times out of a hundred. The problem with SCMS was the same one as all processes designed to defeat mass copying:

If one technician can figure out a way to put an anti-copying chip into the recorder's circuitry, another technician can definitely figure out a way of taking it out, even if it means redesigning some of the circuitry.[18]

This was indeed the case. In Europe, a German company freely advertises a little box which for $150 will override SCMS codes, making multiple-generation digital copying a breeze. The distinction between domestic and professional DAT machines has also hardly been absolute. A non-SCMS machine in the US costs around $1,200, an SCMS-encoded machine is likely to retail for $800 – the difference is the cost of forty blank DAT tapes. Clearly a dedicated music buff is likely to make the jump to a non-SCMS machine (particularly as only one of the two decks needed to dub digitally has to be non-SCMS).

Of course, whatever the hysterical pronouncements coming from the RIAA, no one was about to start marketing pirated DATs commercially. The whole beauty of counterfeiting and/or pirating commercial cassettes – which accounts for over 90 per cent of genuine losses to the record industries – is the minimal investment required, the low cost that such items can be marketed for, and the high profit/cost ratio. No one was ever likely to start buying up $10 DAT tapes, copying them digitally in real time, and then selling them for $12 (to undercut a $13.99 CD).

DAT only really comes into its own as a medium – given the sheer outlay involved in buying good hardware and blank tapes – if one is attempting to preserve the sound quality of material not currently available on CD, i.e. studio outtakes, soundboard tapes etc. The compactness of DAT also made it the perfect medium for audience taping, a fact not lost on the huge tape networks that surround bands like The Grateful Dead. As early as 1987, PCM recordings were being made of Grateful Dead shows. There was no turning back now. The commercial bootleggers were not far behind in acquiring DAT technology, looking to preserve as much sound quality as possible in the transfer to vinyl or, preferably, to compact disc.

Audiophiles

13 Eraserhead Can Rub You Out

"... Just one moment, madam!"

A performance exists at a particular moment in time. It is always, from the artist's point of view, 'live'. It is shared at the same moment that it is created. There may have been all sorts of preparations, including the writing of a script or song or score, rehearsals and so forth; but the actual performance occurs in a moment and necessarily expresses that moment . . . The performing artist retains no control over his or her performance; as soon as it is brought into existence, it is given away.[1]

What often seems remarkable is the sheer scale of recorded material that exists on magnetic tape, constantly emerging from some decomposing tape vault or private hoard, and which bootleggers have taken upon themselves to disseminate. It is this sheer volume of music, and the demand for 'unauthorized' material, however scrappy, half-formed, out-of-tune or unimpressive it may be, which the Biz has struggled to come to terms with. It is their own inability to market cutting-floor highlights that has fed the bootleg beast. In this DAT-Walkman era, when DATs and CD-R (recordable CD) players are able to make perfect digital copies of any tape, it is difficult to conceive of a future without commercial bootlegs, in myriad disguises.

All bootlegs begin life on tape (cassette, reel-to-reel or DAT), often passed hand to hand (or Jiffy bag to Jiffy bag) from collector to collector, before reaching an enterprising entrepreneur, who transcribes them on to vinyl or CD. In certain cases the bootlegger 'originates' a tape – i.e. tapes a show himself, produces a bootleg from a master audience tape, or even 'sources' a tape that is not currently in collecting (meaning tape-collecting) circles. The vast majority of studio and soundboard tapes originate from some amenable soul within the industry – an A&R guy, an engineer, a musician – who passes it to someone inside collecting circles (either directly or indirectly). If few bootleggers these days go to the trouble to 'source' tapes, collectors invariably know which bootleg labels have had a good track record on this score. The reputation enjoyed over the years by labels like Trade Mark of Quality, Rubber Dubber, The Amazing Kornyphone Record Label, Scorpio and Swingin' Pig has largely been based on their ability to access recordings 'close to source'.

The idea that, in today's DAT world, a bootlegger would waste good money obtaining by felonious means a 'board' tape of a particular concert is patently absurd. Yet in an August 1992 *Billboard* feature, Martin Schaefer of the International Federation of Phonographic Industries unequivocally stated that, 'recordings of high quality are obtained by bribing the sound engineer to plug a line into the mixing board.' I am not aware of a single bootleg manufactured from such a tape. The truth is, since the early eighties the divide between 'in-line' (or 'board') recordings and audience tapes has been diminishing with every nanosecond, to the point where the bulk of soundboards from Dylan's Never Ending Tour (1988 to the present) that have passed into collecting circles are inferior to the best audience tape of that particular show.

So what is a 'line' recording, and what distinguishes it from an audience tape? Erik Flanagan, editor of the 'Going Underground' column in *ICE* magazine, defines it so:

Soundboard indicates a recording made from the mixing board or other source in-line with the PA system used at the concert. These can be the best possible recordings, as they are largely free from audience sound . . . Master soundboard recordings are usually excellent, but the soundboard tapes used on most [bootleg] CDs are many generations removed from the master and may or may not be of excellent quality . . . When a show is being broadcast, it is mixed separately from the in-house mix, since it will be heard in a very different environment in someone's home . . . [Though] most fans feel audience recordings are inferior to soundboard recordings, a high-quality audience tape can sound just as good as a board tape.[2]

'Board' tape has become a generic term, referring to any tape self-evidently not from an audience source. In fact the various types of 'line' recordings all give perspectives different from the actual experience of seeing the show itself.

Joel Bernstein [musician/archivist]: 'Soundboard' is a very much abused term in tape-trading circles. The only tape that would truly be a soundboard tape is a tape made directly from the output for recording line-level, which is not at all like the speaker output. You couldn't [just] take any output of the board and get a board tape. In fact, when I worked for Prince the sound company actually had Velcro-backed boards with acoustic cloth on them and before the show – once they had checked every connection – they would put these things on [the board] and there would be no exposed Canon inputs or outputs on the whole board . . . Almost every soundboard tape is made either by the mixing engineer or his assistant, either for the artist or for their own amusement. They used to be made from cassette-decks that would often be in the rack itself. The problem [with a soundboard tape] is [that] it's not an accurate representation of what it sounds like at that point in the room. I remember on the Jackson Browne 'Running on Empty' tour in '77 that the engineer started recording binaural recordings with the dummy head at the soundboard [to get a more 'authentic' sound] . . . When you're playing in a 15,000-seat arena you have to boost the level of every instrument, but if you get into a situation like a small club and Neil Young is playing onstage with a huge loud guitar amp, you're going to put very little of it into the PA mix. So if you then take the tape from that [PA mix] and listen to it the guitar will hardly be there. It will be much lower than the voice and you will go, 'Why is it so unbalanced?' Well, it's because the guitar was so loud live, why would you want it into the PA mix? Most PA engineers – their job is not to make a tape – it's totally incidental to their job. Their job is to do a great mix. If somebody [else] was really into making tapes every night you would do what's called a 'fold back' mix to two-track, in which you do a separate mix of the same inputs – which it is possible to do on today's consoles – and feed that to a separate line that doesn't have anything to do with the PA system but is going to a tape-deck. Nowadays what people would do instead would be to take a system like [eight-track] DAT. [But] Unless you're listening carefully and are familiar with mixing, you might confuse a truck monitor mix with a soundboard mix. If the show is being recorded by a remote truck then typically you get the levels during soundcheck, and during the show the main goal is not to record a two-track mix tape at all. The main goal is to do a good multi-track tape on which every source is going on to its appropriate track. That's your job. But in order to do that you're listening to a mix of the whole show, and there are always tapes running of that mix, usually for the artist or manager to hear right after the show – but this is a live mix. That is what we could call a truck-monitor mix.[3]

Of course, the most readily accessible (and fully mixed) sources for 'line' recordings are the airwaves. Radio and, to a lesser extent, TV broadcasts have probably generated more bootlegs than either 'studio' tapes or audience recordings. The various types of radio sources would make a book in itself, but basic bootleg sources for bootlegs have tended to be three fold:

(i) *Transcription discs*   Transcription discs (in the form of acetates) were the sources for the first bootleg recordings back in the forties and fifties. Most radio programmes at this time were broadcast live, but radio stations would make an acetate of a broadcast they might wish to preserve, or intend to re-broadcast. These acetates would have a very limited life because the grooves would start to wear down very quickly, perhaps surviving a dozen plays before becoming too noisy for broadcast purposes. Acetates were eventually replaced by transcription discs – cut at a later date from reel-to-reel dubs of the shows – which could then be distributed for syndication to local stations scattered around the US. These transcription discs would sometimes be pressed in quite substantial numbers. Oscar Brand's *World of Folk Music* was broadcast from transcription discs by over 3,000 stations in 1963, when Dylan appeared on the show (making one such transcription disc extremely valuable). *Westwood One* and *King Biscuit Flower Hour*, both reliant on a large network of stations to broadcast their nationwide 'in concert' programmes throughout the seventies and eighties, also used transcription discs before switching to CDs in the late eighties. Because radio reception can sometimes be poor and, even when reception is on the button, is limited by the 15 kHz sonic range of FM broadcasts, collectors have often preferred broadcasts direct from transcription discs rather than off-air copies.

The largest source of transcription discs has undoubtedly been the BBC World Service, simply because even to this day they cannot guarantee that every tinpot station relying on World Service programmes has the facilities for more sophisticated software (reels or CD). Cost, as always with the Beeb, has also played a part in their dissemination in this form. The importance of BBC World Service transcription discs, not merely to bootleggers but to archivists in general, lies in the fact that only in the mid seventies did the BBC begin to keep copies of most live sessions and 'in concert' programmes. Many of The Beatles' BBC sessions exist only because transcription discs were filed away years ago and have been belatedly located at (say) some Indian public-service radio station by dedicated collectors.

(ii) *Live sessions*   Again it has largely been the BBC who have been responsible for the vast archive of live sessions extant in collecting circles – and again it is often thanks to the collectors who taped these shows off-air on reel-to-reel recorders in the late sixties and early seventies that many historic recordings are preserved today.*

These BBC sessions provided such a fertile feeding ground for bootleggers that in 1987 Clive Selwood formed Strange Fruit Records, in conjunction with BBC Enterprises, with a view to releasing officially the best of twenty years of John Peel sessions. Subsequently, Windsong also began a steady trickle of BBC In Concert releases. However, because the BBC has always sought the permission of all the performers *and* their record labels (Virgin are one label who have always apparently refused permission),

---

* As an example, Fairport Convention conducted over twenty sessions at the BBC between 1967 and 1974, many of which featured songs never recorded officially by them, of which the BBC has archived exactly three sessions, two from 1969 and their final session in 1974.

many of the most desirable Peel sessions have simply failed to appear. Thankfully, the bootleggers have never been unduly concerned with the niceties of clearing permissions, so at least bootleg punters can hear all of Led Zeppelin's early BBC appearances or Pink Floyd's post-Syd sessions, though there is little likelihood of either band's internal politics ever allowing a sanctioned release.

The BBC's 'live' sessions are perhaps the most prized of all radio broadcasts. This is due primarily to the limits of time and technology imposed by the BBC. The one-afternoon, four-songs session that has always been the norm (for John Peel's sessions anyway) allows just enough time for getting good finished takes without allowing the opportunity for multiple overdubs, or making sure the drum sound has suitable oomph, or even setting up click tracks. Thus the four songs are generally cut live in the studio, with no (or minimal) overdubs, reflecting the feel of a live performance but with the sound quality a studio set-up can afford. As one member of British new wavers The Only Ones once observed:

> When somebody who'd never heard The Only Ones wanted to know what we sounded like I'd always play them the Peel Sessions in preference to the studio albums. They're rougher but there's more feel 'cos the songs were more or less recorded live. You'd do four songs in an eight-hour session, then mix the same evening on an eight-track desk that looked like it had been there since Reith; the faders worked back to front so if you leaned on one by mistake the surge didn't blow up the transmitter. There were no effects beyond reverb and some compression, but you could do whatever you wanted ... The great thing about recording under those conditions and at that speed is that it shows whether the songs stand up by themselves.[4]

(iii) *'Live' FM broadcasts* These have often been the preserve of local radio stations in the US, simply because of the logistical difficulties involved in setting up a national 'live' hook-up. So in 1978, when Bruce Springsteen still believed his shows needed a little 'on air' promotion, there were five full-length, three-hour FM broadcasts of shows on his mammoth 110-date 'Darkness' tour. Only in this way could he ensure that all the major bases of fandom received at least one show over the airwaves. Likewise, live broadcasts in Europe have generally been confined to one country, save for the *Rockpalast* simulcasts in the late seventies and early eighties. With a substantial base of hardcore fans around the world unable to hear (or record) these live broadcasts, it has been the bootleggers who have taken it upon themselves to disperse this material far and wide.

Of course, without the artist's cooperation and his or her record label's tacit acceptance, there would be no radio broadcasts. They must presumably feel that the exposure received outweighs the 'damage' that bootlegs will inflict. Bands like U2 have continued to broadcast live concerts long after they required the exposure, in one particular instance inciting the BPI's ire by distributing cassette inlay cards for a New Year's Eve radio broadcast before the show, an open endorsement for home-taping off the air.

Nevertheless, it is usually only while rock bands are climbing the ladder to the stars, or perhaps when a would-be star is trying to get back up the ladder after a fall from grace, that radio broadcasts appear on a regular basis. Thus Springsteen, after regular radio appearances between 1973 and 1978, deemed them unnecessary in the glory days of the eighties, until the ill-attended 'Tunnel of Love Express' tour in 1988, when suddenly the need for bums-on-seats outweighed 'bootleg' considerations. By 1992, when his stock had sunk even further, he required a pre-tour worldwide 'pep' broadcast and, later on, a two-hour *Unplugged* TV special to rouse his ex-fans from their torpor. Inevitably, despite Sony's Europe-only CD release of *Unplugged*, some fans insisted on acquiring not only the full uncut performance from which *Unplugged* was compiled but also the rehearsals for the show (both available from 'line' sources).

Of course, 'line' recordings from the pre-Walkman era (i.e. the sixties and seventies) are considerably more prized by collectors than modern 'board' tapes. Artists are now acutely aware of the 'desirability' of board tapes in this era of 'protection gap' CDs (see Chapter 14). Accordingly they are more fastidious about who might have access to these tapes (many artists record crude 'board' tapes for reference purposes). Though modern 'board' tapes – at least the non-FM variety – are actually far more common than in former times, they tend to be a rarer commodity in trading circles.

There are inevitably exceptions. There are no Richard Thompson soundboard tapes from the sixties or seventies, save for a few FM broadcasts, but in the last decade the number of board tapes has probably exceeded audience recordings. This is largely because of the sheer number of American shows Thompson has undertaken, generally in clubs with in-house PAs. But then taping live shows has always been more prevalent (and acceptable) in 'folk' circles, where traditions are maintained by such practices – which is presumably why Dylan's early sixties folk appearances are so well documented, and contemporary shows of The Stones and The Beatles are hardly documented at all.

The sound quality of 'rock'-oriented audience recordings in the late sixties and early seventies was at best primitive, at worst primeval. (The folkies were also far better set up for recording at this point. Many owned reel-to-reel machines and it was not considered incongruous for someone to be sitting at the front of Gerdes Folk City or Club 47 taping the show.) The sixties was also a period when a lot of the most collectable bands might be considered to have been at the peak of their performing powers. Zeppelin's early shows, Dylan's 1966 tour and The Stones' 1969 tour all generated their fair share of audience tapes (though none, save perhaps for Dub's remarkable tape of The Stones' November 1969 Oakland shows, could be considered a high-fidelity experience). Yet the process of rock archaeology demands that each lead is pursued, each whiff of uncirculated audience tapes savoured.

The tape-collecting beast feeds on itself. If you have a tape I want, then I have to find a tape that you want. Money doesn't usually work, only 'trades'. Most tape-collectors have disclaimers on their list, stating unequivocally that their tapes are for trade only – a tape for a tape. And all the while the ease with which a 'newly sourced' tape can be copied – making the contents worthless as a commodity, but perchance priceless as a listening experience – makes it inevitable that some, if not most, such tapes will eventually pass into the hands of a bootlegger, who may or may not be a collector himself. In the early seventies, the bulk of bootlegs were coming from sources close to the master. That process began to taper off as the albums became artifacts first, audio experiences second.

What is perhaps surprising is how much audience taping was actually being done in the late sixties and early seventies, before cassette technology and the modern rock PA systems afforded the likelihood of an acceptable recording. Without a tapers' network, still very much in its formative stages, many of the tapes done in this period were made by isolated archivists seeking a simple audio document of shows they attended. Only by the odd innocuous comment made to a member of one of the modern tape-cabals, and some foraging through long-forgotten boxes, do such tapes come to light – and come to light they still do.

As to how much concert-taping was being done at this point, the most accurate information Stateside comes from a survey conducted in 1974 by the Gilbert Youth Research firm. The survey was intended to provide evidence that home-taping was rife in the heartlands. Amidst the misleading and ambiguous statistics lay one important revelation: that out of their sample of 2,500 tape-machine owners, 'a surprising number – 15.4 per cent – are smuggling tape recorders into concerts to get their own live performances on tape'. By 1979, when a similar survey was conducted and published in *Billboard*, the incidence of tape-owners recording shows had increased to '21 per cent of those who tape music . . . A majority of those who have done so, [having] taped three or more performances'.

There has been a marked increase in audience taping in the last decade – thanks mostly to the increased portability of equipment* and the Neanderthal nature of security at arena shows.

But it is only thanks to the anonymous figures who throughout the seventies 'targeted' specific venues (hence all those good tapes from the LA Forum, Seattle or New York) that tape-collectors can still enjoy performances from an age when technology had not made the process so straightforward.

The essential point is that the connection between the audience taper and the bootlegger – the translator into vinyl or CD – is generally tenuous at best. It is usually members of what I once dubbed the Secret Sennheiser Society (after the most popular high-tech, covert microphone) who do the actual sourcing. Thus, when *Rolling Stone*, in a story about the advent of the bootleg CD, refers to, 'mixing-board cassettes of six 1980 Springsteen shows [being] stolen from the glove compartment of his soundman's car while it was in the shop' or 'much of the Dylan material bootlegged over the years – including an infamous ten-LP collection, *Ten of Swords* – [leaving] the vaults under the arm of a trusted Columbia Records executive', they are imagining the bootleggers' trade to be far more clandestine than it actually is.

If the truth be told, the one (no, not six) Springsteen soundboard tape *Rolling Stone* is referring to was indeed 'borrowed' while the soundman's car was in the shop, and was dubbed and returned to its rightful place prior to the car being picked up. It was a tape-trader, with no more reprehensible a motive than to have a soundboard copy of a show he already had as an audience tape, who did the dirty deed. Its eventual transmission on to bootleg vinyl was unconnected to the 'sourcing'. Likewise, the 'infamous ten-LP collection', *Ten of Swords*, contained nothing that had not been in Dylan tape circles for a good few years.

Inevitably, accessing non-audience tapes involves its fair share of

---

* How portable? Well, Sony's new DAT machine, the D-7, allows a would-be bootlegger to record a concert with record levels pre-set, and without even needing to turn the tape over. And yet this digital audience recording, which could be up to four hours long, would be superior to 95 per cent of audience tapes made prior to 1985.

broken promises, backhand deals and novel shenanigans, but the fact of the matter is that most 'studio' (and soundboard) tapes leak because too many people have copies of the tape within the artist/ record company circuit. Demos reach A&R people who give them to their friends, who have friends, who know someone . . . But then that's why they are called demonstration recordings! Studio tapes are dubbed by engineers, musicians or girlfriends as mementoes, played to impress friends and influence uncles. The process of recording and re-recording tapes is now so sophisticated that tapes are often copied without the 'original owner' even being aware that it has taken place. And all along the moral ambiguities of such activities are relieved by that one thought: what makes Geek A&R Person, who does not even like this band, but because of his job gets a copy of the tape, any more entitled to hear or own said tape than I, Hardcore Fan?

It is the 'buffer' that the tape-collector provides between boot-legger and 'source' that makes it so difficult to stop the flow of material – that and the sheer amount of material available to the serious collector. In the case of the Big Five, The Beatles excepted, a 'completist' tape-collector would own well in excess of two thousand hours of unreleased tapes. And it is extremely question-able, particularly in the light of new tape-levy legislation in America and Europe, whether the free trading of bootleg tapes can be termed an illegal activity.* Certainly the only reported instance of a prosecution against a tape-trader ended with the BPI wiping metaphoric yolk from its public face. It is difficult to believe that the bootleggers will ever be starved of material.

But then the relationship between major tape-traders and bootleg-gers in the eighties had largely been a 'hands off' affair, with all but the most specialized bootleg labels some way removed from the core of collecting circles.

---

* Concomitant with the collecting of a levy on blank tapes is an explicit acceptance that such tapes may be used for copyrighted recordings as long as they are for 'private' or 'non-commercial' purposes. In America, with the 1992 Audio Home Recording Act, the ownership of material on DAT or any digital tape is legal, because a small (2 per cent) levy now exists on such tape, while on analogue cassettes it does not. Huh?

However, the advent of bootleg CDs in 1987 threatened to change all of that. While the low cost and ease of storage of cassettes enabled fans to file away all those excruciating audience tapes from the early seventies, recordings that they might actually want to listen to were best accessed on CD, particularly as the medium allowed you to skip a particularly tedious 'Dazed and Confused' in the process. A CD bootleg also dispensed with all the sound loss involved in the mastering of vinyl from tape, an analogue process that always involved some deterioration. With DAT now an affordable digital tape-medium (certainly for a commercial bootlegger), and with fans increasingly disillusioned with the official companies' repackaging of rock's first era, the stage was being set for a new bootleg medium.

Certainly the record industry's contemptuous attitude towards its consumers – evidenced by the artificially high price of CDs throughout the world, their concerted efforts to institute a tape-levy without any moral foundation or legal precedent, and their determination to ensure a patently inferior digital medium, Digital Compact Cassette (DCC), succeeds in the marketplace simply because it can never provide the sort of serious competition to CD that DAT could – has meant that there is little love lost between the record companies and the music collector. It is he or she, after all, who has to bear the brunt of price increases and shoddily compiled boxed-sets with a smattering of enticing 'rarities'. As one industry insider observed:

One of the major problems is the widespread public perception of the bootleggers as Robin Hoods outwitting the filthy-rich record companies to bring eager fans special low-price recordings of their favourite artists which they cannot get from the big labels.[5]

But then, rhetoric aside, the music industry has always placed a capital 'I' at the front of Industry and a soft, lower-case 'mmmm' in most of its music. With the exception of those tape-collectors who considered commercial bootlegging immoral but tape-collecting somehow 'fair game', most tapers were delighted by the emergence of the first bootleg CDs.

14 It Was More Than Twenty Years Ago . . .

The Live Dylan
with the Band

ROYAL ALBERT HALL
LONDON
MAY 26, 1966

Steven D'Onofrio [RIAA]: In bootlegging, we've moved from vinyl to CD, and the numbers have increased exponentially.[1]

In the days of vinyl, the question of what defined a bootleg had rarely arisen (though as a portent of things to come, the two most blurred of 'boots' – Dylan's *A Rare Batch of LWW* and *Gaslight Tapes* – originated in Italy). The very illegality of manufacturing and selling these artifacts was considered an intrinsic part of their appeal – the idea that fans were acquiring something they were not meant to have. Though some early bootleggers, notably Rubber Dubber, had argued that live performances could not be protected in the same way as studio recordings, there had never been a sustained legal assault on the citadel of legitimacy – copyright.

The bootleggers assumed that rock artists were tied to the record company with cast-iron small-print. This edifice first began to crumble in the mid-eighties as the trade barriers that had been erected around European nation states were dismantled in preparation for 1992 and a European community that operated as an economic whole. Mainland European bootleg operations thus began to enjoy a remarkable Indian summer of quasi-legality.

As far back as 1983 German lawyer Harold Weinig had informed an industry gathering that national copyright laws may well be in conflict with EC law. In 1986 came the first test of the industry's mettle in the face of this new threat. A Danish company, Card Exclusive, had begun to export some of their titles to the UK. The Card Exclusive releases comprised fifties rock & rollers like Elvis Presley, Fats Domino, Buddy Holly, Cliff Richard and Nat King Cole. All were legitimate releases in Denmark, where copyright on sound recordings only ran for twenty-five years. However in the UK, where mechanical protection lasts a full fifty years, the albums in question clearly breached British copyright law.

How do such anomalies come to exist?

In considering a recording of a performance (live or in the studio), there exist three main areas of copyright:

(i) the copyright in the sound recording;
(ii) the copyright in the song composition;
(iii) the copyright of the producer-manufacturer.

The copyright in the sound recording takes the form of exclusive rights to reproduce the work, to distribute copies of the work, to perform the work publicly and to make a derivative work. These exclusive rights are usually bound up with an exclusive recording contract that the artist has with a producer-manufacturer, who will in all likelihood have their own copyright on these recordings, which they most likely arranged to happen and which they paid for upfront. The producer-manufacturer's rights, though, are usually referred to as 'neighbouring (or subsidiary) rights' and are not recognized by every state.

The copyright in the song itself is, effectively, a non-exclusive right since most countries operate some kind of compulsory mechanical licensing scheme. What a compulsory mechanical licence means is that once a work has been recorded, the publisher is legally obliged to license it to anyone who wants to use it on a phonorecord as long as they pay the statutory rate of royalty fixed by that country. Whereas the copyright in a sound recording (i) and any attendant neighbouring rights (iii) are usually restricted to a finite number of years – generally somewhere between twenty and fifty years – the copyright in a song composition usually runs for at least fifty years after the author's death. However, this *primary* copyright only entitles authors to a reasonable remuneration, a royalty on their song; it does not confer any of the monopolistic rights given to copyrights (i) and (iii). It is these latter rights which were threatened by the free-trade rules of the European Community.

Exclusive reproduction rights were originally intended to ensure that those who had financed an original recording had a reasonable timespan to recoup their costs (and make a profit on their investment) before such rights passed into the 'public domain'. In the UK, EMI had fifty years to recoup the two days in the studio it took to make the first Beatles album. Denmark, on the other hand, felt that twenty-five years was a perfectly adequate time to provide such rights of exclusivity. The Rome Convention only obliged signatories to a period of protection of twenty years. After all, copyright law was originally intended to provide a balance between the interests of the public and the artist-producer. Clearly an exclusive right amounted to a monopoly and in the wrong hands could be subject to considerable abuse.

Of course, the Danish exports were a threat because they were undercutting 'legitimate' English companies, who had been generating profits for over twenty-five years from these recordings (and paying the most desultory of royalties to the artists in question, negotiated back in the dark ages of rock & roll exploitation). The record companies had always jealously guarded its profit margins against 'market forces'. After all, if you wanted the Beatles albums, you could buy them on EMI, EMI or EMI.

In theory, EC rules on free trade were designed to override national laws. Certainly the Danish distributor of Card Exclusive, All Round Trading, believed that once a record had been marketed in one EC country, they could circulate the records legitimately in any other community country. The consequences, if such an interpretation was upheld in the European court, terrified the record industry, which was facing the prospect of genuine competition for the first time in its hundred-year history. If Beatles albums could be manufactured by *any* label, then EMI were only going to be able to maintain their 'edge' in the market by pricing their versions attractively, packaging them professionally and mastering them from the very best tapes (which they owned – an advantage they would always retain – even if plenty of EMI back-catalogue CDs had been taken from tapes generations removed from the studio masters).

Denmark was not alone in considering twenty-five years (or less) an adequate period for exclusive sound recording rights. Indeed Denmark was strictly a small-time player when it came to such matters. Two EC countries with even less stringent protection were Germany and Italy, who between them accounted for $3,000 million worth of sound-carrier sales by 1988. Germany and Italy had been responsible for almost all of the bootleg vinyl manufactured in Europe in the eighties (the only other major player being Belgium). There were at least a dozen bootleggers in these countries following the legal battles involving the Danes with a personal interest.

By 1987 the need to clarify EC copyright law had become a maximum priority for the IFPI. Even a country like the Netherlands, which had stringent copyright protection for authors and songwriters, had no 'neighbouring rights' protection for producers and performers and was thus heavily exposed to parallel imports. When Dutch exporter Boogaard Trading attempted to import some Danish 'public domain' titles, BMG, the German media corporation, took them to court, alleging unfair competition. Though BMG won an initial victory, it was overturned on appeal. Peter Crockford, legal adviser for IFPI, commenting at the time, noted that there was a very real danger that 'if the principle of free movement prevails, copyright protection in the EC will be reduced to the lowest level provided by any member state.'

EMI-Electrola v. Patricia Records was the test case that would establish the sovereignty of national copyright over free-trade regulations. Patricia had been exporting Cliff Richard recordings made more than twenty-five years earlier for EMI-UK. These recordings, EMI argued, while they may have fallen out of copyright in Denmark, were pirate releases when sold in the UK.

The judgement in the EMI-Electrola v. Patricia Records case came at the end of 1988, and gave the record companies the protection they craved. The European court decided that the original producer-manufacturer was allowed 'to prevent the sale of records which incorporated the same music, but which had been legally imported from another member state where the period of protection had expired'. This was just the beginning of an ongoing struggle to rationalize Europe's haphazard copyright laws.

By the time of judgement in the EMI–Patricia case, other legal

gaps within the EC had begun to open up, gaps exploited not just by the likes of Patricia Records, issuing hackneyed compilations of old rock & rollers. At the end of 1987, Dylan's *Gaslight Tapes*, which as a triple-album had caused nary a ripple in the winter of 1985 (despite impressive Europe-wide sales), was transformed into a CD (minus its 1961 volume). The legitimacy of the item in its country of origin, Italy, was not under dispute – though the reason for its legitimacy was not commented on in the media for fear of sparking a series of copycat releases. Its widespread export on CD – it was freely available in all HMV and Virgin megastores – also passed uncontested. The EMI–Patricia judgement was still some way off, and it seemed better to ignore this 1962 live recording than to contest its legality.

The Gaslight Tapes, though, was only the first of a new brand of bootleg – the 'protection gap' CD. *Gaslight Tapes* was a CD which, because of discrepancies in national copyright law, could be legitimately manufactured in Italy but which in countries with tighter copyright protection – meaning most countries in the EC – would qualify as a bootleg, pure and simple. *The Gaslight Tapes* inspired a couple of small-time Italian entrepreneurs, who had been viewing the situation from the sidelines for some time, to take the plunge:

Rinaldo Tagliabue [managing director, Great Dane]: [In 1987] I met this Springsteen collector who we'll call the Lawyer, who was actually in discussion with some people about the possibility of doing 'public domain' concerts on CD. At that time there was just one CD pressing plant in Italy. It was very hard to find plants in other countries, and it was expensive. The Lawyer was a connoisseur of rock music and he specialized in copyright. The 'twenty years' [protection periods] story is well-known amongst any-one working in the record business in Italy. It was simply never used for rock music. It was very common to use the twenty-year rule for classical music, for jazz music, for lyrics, but not for rock, simply because there were no recordings. As soon as we got to the [late] eighties . . . the Lawyer put up the [money for the] first CD company, called Bulldog Records. The very first CD was pressed by MPO in France. CDs were very unusual and [we weren't sure] they had a real market. I [had taken] part in discussions but I didn't want to get involved, mainly because I wasn't very convinced by the [validity] of this [twenty-year] rule. There was considerable excitement after the release. They were pressing interesting quantities – five or ten thousand.[2]

With Bulldog Records the Italians had founded the first legitimate bootleg label. There had been some famous bootlegs which had already made the transition to official vinyl,* but here was a label systematically releasing some of the most famous bootleg albums on CD under the banner 'It Was More Than Twenty Years Ago Today...', a witty poke at The Beatles' prophecy on *Sgt Pepper* and an open admission that they were exploiting an actual 'protection gap'. It turned out that Italian copyright protection was most peculiar, in that it offered a different term of protection for live performances from that given to studio recordings. Studio recordings would have been protected for a full fifty years in Italy. However, any live performances were only covered by the minimal requirements of the Rome Convention (which Italy had ratified in 1975) – that is, twenty years' protection. Hence 'it was more than twenty years ago...'

Bulldog's first release came as no surprise – Dylan at the Albert Hall 1966, lifted direct from a clean *In 1966 There Was* (even the CD version came complete with pops and clicks). However, this was a mass-market exercise. Bulldog were no underground outfit, and their titles could be produced very, very cheaply. They were all copied from existing vinyl, without any 'de-clicking' (a process designed to remove most vinyl noise), they were paying no royalties to the performers, and their covers were not even graced with a photo of the artist in question (Bulldog preferred artistic impressions). Bulldog were selling them into Italian supermarkets at substantially less than conventional CDs. This made it very difficult for the record companies to pressure the retailers to avoid Bulldog product. Of course, their pressing-runs were still far smaller than

---

* When Dylan's *Basement Tapes* was released in 1975, Dylan stated that he thought all his fans already had it!

legitimate chart releases, but the proliferation of Bulldog titles only served to highlight just how much profit the legitimate companies had been taking from CDs for the past five years. Bootlegs had never been so cheap.

So why had it taken so long for someone to exploit this gap in Italian copyright? Since Italian law only gave 'public domain' status to live performances of more than twenty years' pedigree, it was only in the late eighties that the requisite rock performances began to fall out of copyright. And there was a whole body of fans who were uninterested in nineties rock, preferring the sounds of yesteryear.

From the Biz point of view, worse was to come. The Bulldog CDs and albums were, like *The Gaslight Tapes*, extensively exported. Despite the EMI–Patricia case, the illegality of the Bulldog titles outside Italy was not so assured. The EMI–Patricia case had been decided in EMI's favour because Article 36 of the Treaty of Rome, which established the EC as an entity and affirmed the principle of free trade between member-states, had a proviso that free movement 'shall not preclude . . . the protection of industrial and commercial property', such as early recordings of Cliff Richard owned by EMI.

Such restrictions, though, must not 'constitute a means of . . . disguised restriction on trade between member States'. Who was to say that EMI owned the rights to Beatles live performances, just because they released Beatles studio albums? EMI? The Bulldog releases were recordings not previously released by legitimate record labels, and Italy did not recognize a record company's 'right' to prohibit the release of live performances.

The country most flooded by Bulldog exports was Germany. It was the largest European market, and exporting from Italy to Germany was an easy enough exercise. The IFPI's attempts to restrict the distribution of Bulldog titles led to a legal battle in the German courts that only served to highlight a Teutonic equivalent of Italy's protection gap:

The Magna Carta for the [German] bootleggers . . . is a test-case decision by the Federal Supreme Court in Karlsruhe. The case involved a bootleg recording of a concert by Bob Dylan, issued on an Italian label. The court ruled that, under German law, a foreign artist cannot claim protection in Germany against the sale of unauthorized recordings if the performances took place in countries that are not signatories to the Rome Convention . . . German nationals, on the other hand, are protected in Germany for all their performances, irrespective of location. And if performances of foreign artists in Germany are recorded without their consent, they benefit from the same protection as German nationals.[3]

Italian and German bootleggers were unlikely to be cursing their misfortune at being unable to market titles by Can and Kraftwerk. The Supreme Court's interpretation of Germany's obligations under the Rome Convention was a virtual carte blanche for live performances from the rock era. While the twenty-year rule had yet to be tested in Italy, it did not apply in Germany. If the artist was a non-German national and the concert took place in a country that was not a signatory to the Rome Convention, then any willing entrepreneur had the court's blessing. And Italy did not sign until 1975, France did not sign until 1987, Japan until 1989 – while there were plenty of European countries yet to sign: Spain, the Netherlands, Belgium. And there was one very significant absentee from the list of Rome signatories – the US of A. Even those who were signatories to the Rome Convention afforded no protection to performances made before their ratification. The only really adequate protection was in the UK, which had ratified as early as May 1964. As the second home of rock music, and with the BBC's generous roster of live broadcasts, Britain had always been a primary source for bootlegged performances.

But then there were always ways of getting around the minor inconvenience of a recording made in a signatory country, the most expedient of which was to lie about the source. There were several classic examples, like *Copycats Ripped off My Soul*, a CD of a 1986 performance of Van Morrison that claimed to be recorded live in Belgium, on which Morrison's first spoken words are, 'Good evening, Frankfurt', a flagrant breach of German copyright. But GEMA, the German organization responsible for copyright-clearance, were not checking the details of the CDs submitted to them.*

For a while it seemed that all CDs coming out of Germany were helpfully annotated with the legend 'Live in Europe' or 'Live in the USA'. In one supremely ironic example, Italian label KTS issued another rather fine audience recording of a Van Morrison concert – from Utrecht, Holland, in 1991 – credited simply as 'Live in Europe'. When Mr Morrison decided to bootleg the bootleg himself to provide bonus cuts for two CD singles, he was unable to ascertain the source and these official cuts just carried the legend 'Live in Europe'. Of course, many bootleggers from the vinyl era had been unhelpful in attributing sources to the items they peddled, but now there was actually a sound legal reason for the bootleggers' coyness.

Italy and Germany had been the hub of European bootlegging throughout the eighties, which meant that a small, well-informed group of collector-entrepreneurs was already in place to exploit these new-found flaws in European copyright. The Italian Bulldog releases were soon in competition with two more 'vinyl copying' labels, both based in Germany, Early Years and the more adventurous Living Legend. All of these labels relied almost entirely on existing bootleg sources. But in 1989 the European market – save for the premium-priced product of German label Swingin' Pig – was pretty much theirs alone. American titles rarely made it to Europe and, even when they did, they lacked the SIAE or GEMA stamp required to 'legitimize' their distribution in Italy and Germany.

SIAE is the Italian house responsible for collecting royalties due on any release, the German equivalent being GEMA. Each legitimate CD is required, under Italian law, to carry its own individual SIAE stamp. For the first time in the history of bootlegging, producers were paying royalties on their product in order to get

* In many instances this actually benefited the bootlegged artist, because if the bootlegger couldn't establish the author of a song on the CD he would simply attribute it to the performer, who would then receive a royalty for a song he never wrote.

that SIAE stamp and so be able to expand into conventional retail outlets. (They were also far less likely to be turned down by a manufacturing plant if their company had an SIAE number assigned to them. Even plants in the Far East liked to give the pretence that 'legitimacy' was an issue.) The SIAE stamp also made it difficult (though by no means impossible) to 'run on' CD pressings, paying royalties on a smaller number of copies than were actually manufactured, a long-standing practice in the so-called legitimate record industry.

Because GEMA releases carried no such stamp (they usually just had 'GEMA' embossed on the CD itself), 'run ons', indeed unlicensed CDs in general, proved far more difficult to monitor in Germany. The GEMA logo began to appear on virtually all bootleg CDs, whether originating in the Far East or Europe, and whether they were 'copyright paid' or not. The authorities were so ill-informed as to who was paying royalties that they didn't even clamp down on the most obvious abusers of this new 'protection gap'. Even SIAE, who were more fastidious about the accredited source of Italian releases, made one concession to Italian business practices by having two offices assigning copyright, one in Milan, one in Rome, neither of which knew what the other was doing.

With the gradual removal of trade barriers within the EC, it was inevitable that these protection-gap CDs, manufactured and distributed legitimately in Portugal, Italy, Germany and Luxemburg, would freely circulate in other EC countries, even those with firmer laws and a tradition of copyright vigilance, in particular England and France. Since all these CDs carried full-colour covers and the same jewel boxes as legitimate releases, it was almost impossible to distinguish 'bootlegs' without some prior knowledge. Even the sound quality, particularly on Swingin' Pig releases, would not give the game away. The imaginary threat that bootlegs had previously represented had become a genuine threat, something the IFPI was now belatedly forced to admit:

Martin Schaefer [IFPI]: The majority of buyers of illegal bootlegs are usually hardcore fans who tend to acquire everything – legitimate and illicit –

available by their favourite artists. But the protection-gap repertoire is being professionally marketed by well-organized companies and handled by major distributors. This repertoire can definitely undermine sales of the artists' official recordings.[4]

In fact, the traditional bootleg punters were shying away from these European CDs. The switch to CD was a slow process among those with humungous vinyl collections anyway – meaning most bootleg collectors – and the 'vinyl copying' labels were quickly deemed to be a waste of time. Bootleg buyers, always among the best informed of music fans, were dismissive of Early Years, Bulldog and their ilk.

CD bootlegs, if they could realize the potential for digital perfection, could yet reunite the worlds of tape-collector and bootleg buyer, returning commercial bootlegs to the glory days – qualitatively and commercially – of the early seventies. What was needed was a new *Great White Wonder*, with that degree of impact, to truly kick in the CD era.

15 Some Ultra Rare Sweet Apple Trax

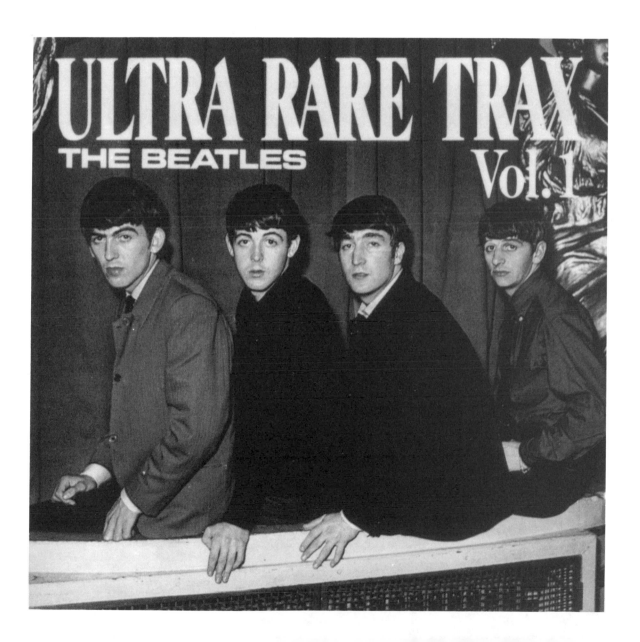

Dieter Schubert [managing director, Swingin' Pig]: The basic philosophy of Swingin' Pig is to make available historically important, previously unreleased recordings which would otherwise never see the light of day. Take, for example, *Ultra Rare Trax* by The Beatles . . . The Beatles themselves say they don't want them out because they feel the outtakes are not up to normal standards. The public obviously has a totally different opinion . . . The tapes are over twenty years old now, some nearly thirty. Twenty more years in the archives would possibly destroy the tapes, like many outtakes from the fifties, and they'll be lost forever. So even if the quality is sometimes not up to today's digital standard, this is not the point. 'Casual listeners' should, by all means, avoid buying Swingin' Pig releases; they will only be disappointed.[1]

G*reat White Wonder* may have been the first rock bootleg album, but it was perhaps the two Dylan studio collections *Stealin'* and *John Birch Society Blues*, plus The Beatles' *Kum Back*, that first truly showed the potential of the medium. Though the bulk of post-*LiveR* bootlegs have explored the live performances that have punctuated the rock years, it has been bootlegs of studio outtakes that have been most eagerly sought by collectors. Partly this is because of the rarity of such material – at least with non-CBS artists – and attendant studio quality; partly it is because of the likelihood of hearing something in its formative stages – something worked on, then abandoned, consigned to the scrapheap of vaultdom.

That said, it has been as live artists that the kings of bootlegging – Dylan, Springsteen, The Stones, Zeppelin – have been in their element. The exception to this dictum has always been The Beatles, whose live career was brief, uninspiring as any kind of performance art, and invariably set to a soundtrack of caterwauling pre-pubescents. The considerable market for bootleg Beatles material is largely derives from 'variants' – often merely in the mix, rather than actual alternative takes – from studio recordings and/or BBC sessions.

Ironically, The Beatles were a band who rarely extemporized or radically rearranged their material once they were cutting a song in the studio. This, and the fact that before the CD era there were very few actual outtakes from their studio sessions in general circulation, would seem to make theirs an extremely unrewarding occupation for a collector. Yet they have remained the most bootlegged – and most 'bootlegable' – of all acts.

Of course, the very dearth of new Beatles material necessarily inspired an awful lot of repackaging. It also meant that each genuinely new Beatles source was pursued until tapes were believed to be forthcoming. Unfortunately, at this point these tapes were usually perceived by the owner to be far more valuable than they really were.

Perhaps the most prevalent of all bootleg myths relates to the actual commercial value of 'source' tapes. Invariably the media, in pursuit of a good story, and the industry itself, likes to propagate the idea that huge sums are paid for bootleg source material. After all, if a bootlegger has paid several thousand dollars for a tape he must be selling an awful lot of copies to get a return on that kind of investment.

As these stories grow with each retelling, the fortunate few who have tapes that collectors crave, and who are more interested in mercenary value than aesthetic worth, come to believe that their tape of the Flying Mandingos at the Hole in the Wall in the Summer of Love, recorded with the very best kind of tin can and string, will become their very own personal pension fund.

This type of myth has even been propagated by those who should know better. *Hot Wacks*, the standard reference source for most bootleg albums since the late seventies, claimed that the 1971 studio tapes of The Who used on Scorpio's *From Lifehouse to Leeds* CD cost the bootlegger $10,000. In reality, the figure was something like $1,000. And the notional value of such a tape is diminishing as I write, since the ability to copy without deterioration on CD denies the original bootlegger an edge on his competitors. In the case of *From Lifehouse to Leeds*, the original release only managed to sell 1,500 copies, though it has been re-bootlegged extensively.

The Byrdman: It's at the point now, thirty years on from The Beatles, or whoever, that if you have the material, I'll put it out. [But] the people that are interested in it are dying off, so people will sit on stuff they think is worth a million dollars and it's just not the case.[2]

Which is not to say that money does not change hands as part of the process of acquiring studio and soundboard recordings – just that it is often small change, the sort of sum that might just about cover the average executive's business-lunch bill for a week. Most bootleggers feel that there is so much material out there that can be had for free, why pay for a tape – whatever its pedigree. Thankfully, the more historically inclined bootleg labels (like Scorpio and Yellow Dog) have been prepared to be a little more flexible in their financial dealings.

In fact the mid to late eighties saw a whole new source of studio tapes become publicly available that required only a relatively small infusion of cash. They were the increasingly popular 'pop memorabilia' auctions. In London and New York, Sotheby's and Christie's began to auction off the obscure and the arcane to the wealthy baby-boomers with a yen for one of John Lennon's infantile scribblings.

Though Beatles recordings were not a regular feature at these auctions, and those that did go under the gavel were usually of secondary importance, there were various other sixties icons whose studio reels were 'fair game'. These reels, many of which presumably came from the legendary (and recently refurbished) Olympic Studios, were invariably sold 'without copyright', meaning that nothing official could be done with the material. The bootleggers were happy to snap up reels of The Stones and The Who for a few hundred pounds – 'without copyright' meant diddley to them. The Olympic hoard soon dried up and, as people became more aware of the potential booty at these auctions, less and less of interest was filtering through.

Obviously, if the artists in question were unduly concerned about this material being auctioned off into unknown hands they could always buy it themselves. Indeed one particular Who recording (a live show at the Young Vic, recorded for the 'Lifehouse' project) was apparently purchased on behalf of the band themselves, who could no longer locate the master (which didn't stop a bootleg CD later appearing). Real Beatles rarities, though, all seemed to be purchased anonymously, often for astronomical prices.* Here was one outfit where the steady dissemination of cutting-floor outtakes was not strictly *verboten*.

But then only Beatles studio material – because of its rarity and the inordinate demand – would warrant substantial financial investment by a bootlegger. Indeed each successive lifting of the Abbey Road veil has tended to involve the passage of funds.

After *Kum Back*, the first notable collection of Beatles studio tapes was a double album of Twickenham jams, *Sweet Apple Trax*, purchased for a few hundred dollars by two fledgling bootleggers back in 1972. Though Twickenham material began to periodically slip out through the film connection, the Beatles' EMI studio efforts remained beyond the reach of a vast army of Beatles collectors. In 1978, though, two New Yorkers acquired one of the legendary Beatles items, the Decca audition tape. Recorded in 1962, before EMI decided to sign the foursome up, the audition tape made The Beatles sound at times like a Scouse novelty act, with excruciating covers like 'Sheik of Araby' and 'Besame Mucho'. There was certainly precious little evidence of a hard-hitting English r&b sound in the perfunctory renditions of 'Memphis Tennessee' and 'Money'. No matter. It was a truly historical recording. As part of a $5,000 deal, the New Yorkers flew the owner of the tape to New York. In order to recoup such a substantial outlay,

---

* The exception was The Peter Sellers Tape, which, because it was not auctioned at one of these 'pop memorabilia' affairs, was purchased by a Japanese gentleman who promptly made the necessary CD transfer.

the session was initially released as a series of two-track 45 rpm singles, on coloured vinyl in picture sleeves (on the Deccagone label).

The Abbey Road vaults, though, remained resolutely closed, the inevitable bootlegs of *Sessions* excepted. *Sessions*, an album of Beatles outtakes originally scheduled for release in 1984, was in fact the result of a thorough review of Beatles material in the EMI vaults, initially undertaken by an EMI studio engineer, the late John Barrett. When it became apparent that at least one copy of some of the more interesting material found during this exercise had been made, approaches were made by a couple of European bootleggers hoping to purchase the goodies. One Dutch Beatles collector/bootlegger ended up acquiring some eight hours of Beatles studio recordings in 1986 for the outlandish sum of $20,000. He was requested to keep the tapes to himself.

While he was as good as his word, a middleman operating between the Abbey Road 'source' and Europe's wealthier 'collectors' arranged to offload a considerably more edited version of studio 'highlights' to a German collector. This time it was understood that the material was not going to stay under wraps. The price, for a single album's worth of stunning-quality Beatles outtakes, was $10,000. The purchaser of these recordings had been an extremely productive vinyl bootlegger until the German authorities had temporarily stopped him in his tracks in 1987. However, he was not looking to put this material out on vinyl.

Even before Bulldog products had begun appearing in German stores, Dieter Schubert had come to realize that previously unreleased recordings, provided that they were made abroad before Germany's ratification of the Rome Convention (in 1966), were deemed 'public domain' in the eyes of Germany's courts. Schubert decided to test the limits of German law by making this new Beatles tape the first releases of an underground CD label. Taking William Stout's famous Smokin' Pig, Schubert made his own pig into a finger-snapping, fedora-wearing dude: the Swingin' Pig.

However, Schubert, like his Deccagone predecessors, needed to recoup the money he had paid for the tapes before his efforts could be copied (as they undoubtedly would be in the Far East). Schubert took the basic dozen cuts purchased from the English middleman and added half a dozen cuts from acetates he had already acquired, and another two or three cuts from a pristine copy of the *Sessions* tape. Intercutting the stunning-quality recordings acquired from EMI masters with his own acetate material, cleaned up in the studio but audibly inferior, Schubert now had two thirty-minute CDs, *Ultra Rare Trax* Volumes 1 and 2.

The effect of the release of these CDs late in 1988 was nothing short of cataclysmic. In an October 1988 lead story, CD newsletter *ICE* speculated, on behalf of the entire collecting world, what exactly *Ultra Rare Trax* might portend:

The concept of bootleg CDs graduating from mere copies of noisy bootleg records to professional-sounding entities within themselves has exploded into reality with the arrival of [these] two new Beatles bootleg CDs of session outtakes. Sounding every bit as good – and in some cases, better – than EMI/Capitol's official Beatles CDs, *Ultra Rare Trax* Vols. 1 and 2 contain never-heard alternate takes of such classics as 'I Saw Her Standing There' and 'Strawberry Fields Forever', as well as several unreleased songs ... but the real story here is the sound quality, which leaves mouths gaping everywhere ... A question that begs to be addressed is whether or not this is just the tip of the iceberg, a sort of 'greatest hits' harbinger of things to come ... [After all], the discs ... cover a large time span of The Beatles career, not just one session or album.[3]

Hearing the second cut on Volume 1 of *Ultra Rare Trax* – the original *Please Please Me* outtake of 'One After 909' – in perfect stereo was enough to convince even the most jaundiced of Beatles fans that bootlegs had entered a new era. The sheer clarity of that one cut gave the game away. This was an inside job and EMI was understandably mortified. Unfortunately they were trying to close the studio doors after this particular horse had bolted. Mike Heatley of EMI admitted to *ICE* that they had as yet failed to figure out just how Swingin' Pig had secured tapes that *good*. But then, with the advent of DAT, it was at last possible to run a perfect copy of a studio tape on to a highly portable sound-carrier.

Mike Heatley [EMI]: What we don't know yet is if [the tapes] escaped recently, or if they're something that someone managed to get years ago and just sat on. I've had several people say to me, 'There must still be a leak from Abbey Road because this stuff keeps on appearing.' Well, if it was only material from Abbey Road that was appearing, then I would say that's probably right. But recently, a lot of material that was recorded well before Abbey Road has, after many years, started turning up . . . What amazes me is that there are lots of other peculiarities [that exist in the vault]. Those that have surfaced are interesting, but not devastatingly so. There are other things that have not surfaced that I find even more interesting.[4]

Heatley's final words were to prove provident. Like all remarkable successes, *Ultra Rare Trax* demanded a sequel (or four). While Schubert prepared to continue the series, the other European collector/bootlegger who had acquired his own batch of EMI tapes decided to prepare his versions for the marketplace. After all, the embargo on these tapes was obviously off. It was time to recoup some of the $20,000 ante.

Ultra Rare Trax was certainly not the first bootleg CD. It was not even the first Beatles bootleg CD, nor the first release to exploit new-found flaws in European copyright law. But it was *Ultra Rare Trax* that showed bootleggers and punters alike the way ahead.

Bob Walker: The first time I got excited was [when] I got hold of *Ultra Rare Trax* . . . it turned the tide in that they were saying 'This could be really good. We've got the technology, we've finally got the product. We're going to do it well and you're going to want these CDs.' And the Swingin' Pig held up on that promise all the way through, and junk labels [began to] die out.[5]

The Byrdman: Everyone's minds were blown when the Beatles' *Ultra Rare Trax* came out. That was probably the single most important release in the history of CDs, because it showed the potential of the medium to maximum effect . . . it didn't matter that the covers were indifferent, the quality just blew people's minds. That's when people knew that CDs were here to stay and the biggest breakthrough in people hearing unofficially released music ever . . . You never get that great a pressing on a bootleg [record] it seems, [with] certain exceptions. [It was] the little extra difference between going down to vinyl and CD, [where] you can boost it a little bit, clean it up a little bit, make it sound more spectacular, more clear.[6]

Sadly, Schubert followed up his two outstanding debuts with four more *Ultra Rare Trax* volumes, each progressively more disappointing than its predecessor. The allure of the *Ultra Rare* series was tarnished by every successive volume. Inevitably, *Ultra Rare Trax* also made Swingin' Pig a prime target for IFPI lawyers. The sheer quality of the CDs and their presentation (though the initial versions came with garish orange and green inserts, subsequent pressings had full-colour covers), and the wide distribution that their quasi-legit status in Germany afforded them, made *Ultra Rare Trax* the first serious threat to the music industry's monopoly since the advent of CDs. Like most pioneers, Mr Schubert was a marked man and he was sailing in some very dubious legal waters, issuing collections clearly derived from studio sessions financed and organized by EMI themselves. Sure enough, in January 1990 the warehouse in Westphalia owned by Perfect Beat, Swingin' Pig's Luxemburg parent company, was raided, and some 14,000 copies of Volumes 5 and 6 of the *Ultra Rare Trax* series were confiscated by the authorities.

According to Ian Haffey, the legal advisor for the IFPI, this raid was possible because, 'non-German recordings are protected in Germany only from the date that Germany joined the Rome Convention, in October 1966. In terms of The Beatles, the problem with earlier Swingin' Pig titles is that all or most of the recordings were from before October 1966. But Vols. 5 and 6 are mostly from after that date.' The bizarre aspect of this belated assault on Swingin' Pig was that every volume of *Ultra Rare Trax*, including Volumes 1 and 2, featured recordings dating from after Germany ratified the Rome Convention. Indeed Volume 4, perhaps the most ordinary volume of them all, had seven of its ten cuts recorded after that date. Since the exclusive rights to reproduce these recordings in Germany still resided with EMI, how come EMI had not acted sooner?

Schubert insisted that Perfect Beat would fight EMI all the way. He also suggested that he was just gearing up to export the Swingin' Pig titles to the four corners of the world – a typical act of bravado.

Dieter Schubert: Perfect Beat will go to court against EMI to be able to carry on distributing *Ultra Rare Trax* Vols. 5 and 6 in West Germany. There is a really strong chance we'll win the case. Things are not as easy as they might look for them; there are some important parts in German copyright laws which are on our side ... [And] regardless of what the RIAA says, Swingin' Pig will do a detailed investigation [to determine] if their product can be legally imported into the US. Talks with experienced lawyers will start soon. All is not bootleg that the record industry calls 'bootleg'![7]

In the eighteen months that separate *Ultra Rare Trax* Volume 1 from *Ultra Rare Trax* Volume 6, Swingin' Pig had certainly not stinted on product, though the running times of their CDs remained notoriously short (the most extreme example being a Byrds radio broadcast from Stockholm 1967 which lasted barely twenty minutes). As Schubert's own passion was really The Rolling Stones, he issued some six Stones titles in the interim, reviving the reputation accorded early TMQ titles like *Bright Lights, Big City*, *Get Your Leeds Lungs Out*, *Welcome to New York* (for which he simply purloined Stout's original TMQ cover) and *LiveR Than You'll Ever Be*, preparing what purported to be best-ever versions of each of these releases. In the case of *Get Your Leeds Lungs Out* he certainly did the band proud, producing the definitive live Stones recording. With the others he was less successful. Swingin' Pig had quickly swung into product mode, pumping out primarily sixties recordings by the likes of The Doors, Hendrix, Cream, Led Zeppelin and Pink Floyd. Schubert was exploiting what he felt to be a temporary breach of the record industry's hold on Europe.

Swingin' Pig were also beginning to attempt a transition to legiti-

macy, hoping to assume some of the vestiges of respectability. With their high profile and their legal difficulties, it was inevitable that they would have to phase out the studio-based CDs that had established their reputation. The acquisition of these tapes was fraught with difficulties and the record company's ownership of the masters was in all likelihood irrefutable. A new concentration on live CDs, marked by the wholesale deletion of titles that might infringe the Rome Convention (like *Ultra Rare Trax*, the Stones' *Get Your Leeds Lungs Out* and Pink Floyd's *The Embryo*), indicated a desire (or perhaps a need) to be seen to operate wholly above board, at least within Germany. Swingin' Pig's bootleg origins – even the existence of Swinging (with a 'g') Pig as a bootleg vinyl label in the early to mid eighties – was quietly masked over.

Schubert's also became the first protection-gap label to begin to use new technology to clean up its source tapes. Unfortunately, his attempts to produce superior versions of famous tapes met with howls of protest from the collecting fraternity. Shortly after his first legal problems with *Ultra Rare Trax*, Schubert began to use the NoNoise process to remove hiss from tapes and pops and crackles from vinyl sources (such as acetates, test pressings and transcription discs), hoping to produce a professional-sounding CD that could sit comfortably alongside an EMI live album in the racks of German record shops. The NoNoise process, though, was very difficult to use successfully. As 'Going Underground' editor Erik Flanagan has observed:

Along with the hiss, studio processors (such as the NoNoise system used by Swingin' Pig) also tend to cut some of the high end. But the most undesirable effect is a sort of breathing in and out quality to the sound. The sound rises and falls in level and noise, and occasionally the vocals will clip, so they seem to start with a short burst. The reason for this is that most of the processors cut out more noise when the recording level is relatively quiet (and hiss would be more noticeable), and cut less noise when the recording level is high (and covers up most of the noise). Because the machine is constantly adjusting to the level, the sound acquires this breathing quality. When used properly, the effect isn't very noticeable, but when overused, the sound becomes unnatural.[8]

In certain instances, notably *Manchester Prayer*, a superb de-clicked version of the acoustic set from Dylan's fabled Manchester 1966 gig, taken direct from Columbia acetates, Swingin' Pig's use of NoNoise enhanced the recordings beautifully. Unfortunately, in most cases the effect was like throwing a blanket over one's speakers. The two Stones titles, *Welcome to New York* and *LiveR Than You'll Ever Be* came in for particular criticism, being compared unfavourably with their famous vinyl predecessors.

Dieter Schubert: People are starting to compare Swingin' Pig to normal record companies, and that's pretty tough because we're only able to work a little bit on the sound, instead of remixing for months and months.[9]

Swingin' Pig, though, proved considerably more resilient than other first-generation protection-gap labels, which simply faded from view as soon as bootleggers with access to genuine source material began to compete with their dubious efforts. Indeed Schubert was determined to push the legal interpretation of Germany's Rome Convention obligations to the limit. In 1990 he issued an audience recording of The Rolling Stones in Basel, Switzerland, recorded just a couple of months earlier. Switzerland was not a signatory to Rome at the time, but nobody had had the sheer nerve to issue something so contemporary, so obviously threatening to the record-company monopoly. The actual recording was unexceptional, but *Basel '90* was simply intended to prove that it could be done (and thus allow an expansion of Swingin' Pig's activities in Germany). When Sony's inevitable injunction against *Basel '90* failed to establish an *a priori* right to The Stones' live performances, the way was paved for Swingin' Pig's greatest coup, *Atlantic City '89*.

Atlantic City '89, a triple-CD encased in a black and silver 12″ × 12″ box, was taken direct from a 2½ hour American pay-per-view cable broadcast, part of the first leg of The Stones' decidedly lifeless 'Urban Jungle' tour. Though Sony intended to release their own live set from the tour, they had only a single-CD cut-up in mind. Swingin' Pig's pre-emptive release was a superb-quality recording, gaining the full benefit of a cable stereo signal. Though recording engineer Bob Clearmountain failed to fully mask the tedium of a 1989 Stones stadium show, the demand for the set was vast and Swingin' Pig's distribution by 1990 highly efficient.

Sony once again attempted to tie Swingin' Pig up in legal loops. Unfortunately, America's failure to sign the Rome Convention meant that there were very few legal options available to them. Ingeniously, Sony hit on the thirty-second taped section used by The Stones at the beginning of '2,000 Light Years from Home' – which came from the copyrighted studio recording – as a clear breach of copyright. This was a stalling tactic at best. Schubert simply re-edited the set to exclude the offending tape-loop (the first edition has '2,000 Light Years' intact), and *Atlantic City '89* was soon back out on the streets. Sony next sought to claim copyright on the cowbells used on 'Honky Tonk Women'. This time the German court dismissed their claims.

With total sales apparently topping 70,000 for a premium-priced three-CD boxed-set, Swingin' Pig's legal bill for fighting Sony was a drop in this particular ocean of profit. Dieter Schubert had proved that the law did not always side with the big boys, turning the protection gap into a protection chasm. Small-time CD labels could now issue 1990 recordings made in America (as well as Belgium, the Netherlands, Switzerland, etc.).

Most underground producers quickly forgot their previous historical bent. 1990 tapes, even 1990 audience tapes, were streets ahead of late sixties 'live' recordings (and were so much easier to access). There were also a whole slew of rock fans who wanted a memento of a show they had just seen, to go with their souvenir programme and $35 T-shirt. The sales of *Atlantic City '89* had gone well beyond the traditional bootleg constituency.

No Swingin' Pig release would ever again have such an impact. Though Swingin' Pig had broken the dam, Schubert lacked the vision, the source material and the collector mentality to follow through on his promise of a high-fidelity future in bootleg heaven. It was left to others to realize the potential hinted at when Swingin' Pig first rode the One After 909.

*Bruce Springsteen
Born in The Studio*

Charles Ferris [ARRC]: The CD is one of the best examples of the recording industry crying all the way to the bank. Unable to manufacture them half as fast as they can sell them, [they are] making elevated margins on every sale ... [but] like the devices that made a recording industry possible, the CD was not invented by an entertainment company – rather, it was invented and developed by the same industry that created the market for records and pre-recorded tape.[1]

Before *Ultra Rare Trax*, the issue of commercial bootlegging had faded from the news – and the 'old guard' bootleggers had liked it that way. In fact, the eighties had seen an enormous expansion in the number of titles being manufactured. The pressing plants of Europe, Japan and America were devoting an increasing number of man-hours to this part of the black economy. Part of the reason for this was the marked decline in official vinyl sales. Finally overtaken by cassettes, and with CDs closing fast, vinyl was in danger of becoming almost entirely a collectors' medium. For the bootleggers, though, the market remained steadfastly vinyl. Certain West Coast, Italian and German pressing plants were now almost exclusively given over to such 'grey' artifacts. Official orders could no longer sustain these plants. Bootlegs became not just an easy earner but these plants' primary produce. Until 1987, CD bootlegs had seemed like little more than a pipedream given the sophisticated technology required to produce a glass 'master'.

Though collectors seemed content to collect unreleased recordings on outmoded analogue mediums – vinyl and cassette – some old-guard bootleggers remained open to the possibilities of this expanding new media. The video bootleg market had expanded at a rate of knots in the eighties, with many shows now targeted by collectors with video equipment. The race to do the first bootleg CD was also on. Aside from the potential for larger profits, the kudos of a bootleg CD was something worth acquiring. And CDs had certain intrinsic advantages over vinyl:

Stephen Locke: CDs have a remarkably high value-to-weight ratio. They do not break in the post. They are indeed indestructible. If there was ever a commodity that could be easily transported around the globe and profitably, CDs are probably it.[2]

The Gaslight Tapes may have been the first of a new generation of piratical product, a protection-gap CD rather than a bona-fide bootleg, but it was inevitable that someone would produce a CD which was wholly illegal in manufacture and distribution, i.e. a bootleg along more traditional lines. Indeed around the same time as *The Gaslight Tapes*, a particularly shoddy Springsteen bootleg CD arrived in Europe. *Son You May Kiss the Bride* was a copy of a vinyl bootleg, complete with serious sound faults, manufactured to see if a particular conduit worked.

It was in America, though, that the greatest rewards lay for someone prepared to risk all. Perhaps the 'first bootleg CD' award should really go to the anonymous young soul on the East Coast who, before the 1987 Beatlefest, decided to take a (huge) gamble. He went to a legitimate CD pressing plant in Pennsylvania and, thanks to a fine line in bullshit, convinced them to make him some 'promotional' CDs.

'Eric Bristow': That kid with the three EMI CDs, he went to Technotronics in Philadelphia and lied to them, 'I work for EMI, I need 500 of each of these as promos,' and they just pressed 'em! And then he showed up at Beatlefest in LA with a rucksack with 1,500 CDs in it and sold 'em for $100 apiece. Walked out with a sackful of money. I mean, how hard could it be to sell 500 bootleg CDs of The Beatles at a Beatlefest? To this day, I don't know who that kid was. He just walked in and walked out with $150,000.[3]

The three CDs in question were all standard fare – the *Get Back* acetate, some BBC sessions and *Sessions* – all carrying the kid's mock EMI labels. The sheer novelty of bootleg CDs ensured that the kid with no name made a killing at Beatlefest (though 'Eric' is incorrect in suggesting that he managed to retail all 1,500 CDs at the convention). However, such 'take the money and run' exercises were unlikely to become a regular feature of bootlegging. Something a little more formalized was required to make CD bootlegs a major headache to an industry that had convinced itself the requisite technology could remain under their direct supervision. It was one of the West Coast's true old guard, John Wizardo, who made the first important connection. He had managed to get a Beatles CD (*Off White*) pressed on the quiet at a plant in Troy, Michigan, but again it had been a one-off and the plant in question was not likely to be caught out again.

Wizardo, though, was determined to make more Beatles bootleg CDs. At a record-industry gathering in Louisiana, he ran across a representative from a small Korean CD plant being singularly ignored by the Biz honchos who were there for some mutual backslapping. He decided to enquire if they could perhaps produce some CDs for him, no questions asked. In this most incongruous setting, beneath the very noses of expense-account executives, Wizardo had found someone who spoke the same language. When the new *Off White* and two volumes of Beatles *Backtracks* (Volume 1 of which 'knocked off' *Ultra Rare Trax* Volumes 1 and 2 on a single CD) proved that the connection worked, Wizardo admitted to 'Eric' and Ken that he had found a CD manufacturer in Korea.

It had always seemed that the most likely conduit for bootleg CDs would come from the Far East, where they asked fewer questions, had looser copyright laws all round, and were yet likely to be on the cutting edge of new technologies like DAT and CD. Countries like Taiwan, Singapore and Korea had previously contributed little to the history of bootlegging, but this was largely because most pressing plants had devoted themselves to purer forms of piracy. Throughout the eighties, the IFPI had been applying pressure on the governments of these countries to amend their copyright laws and police their pressing plants more thoroughly. Though this achieved some results, piracy remained a way of life in these countries.

In Korea, pirates were estimated to supply 90 per cent of the cassette market and 10 per cent of the album market, and their copyright act of 1957 afforded no protection to foreign works. Indonesia also offered no provision for the protection of foreign works (despite revising their copyright laws as late as 1982). When in 1987 the US threatened to initiate a '301' action – a provision allowing the US trade representative to impose trade sanctions against countries identified as denying adequate protection of American intellectual property or market access – Korea promised to formulate a new copyright law. Yet Korea in 1988 – for all its technological advances – continued to have the business attitudes of a third-world country. Thus it came as no surprise when the Korean connection took bootlegs into the digital age big time:

'Eric Bristow': Ken and I discussed [doing bootleg CDs]. He just let me know that John had found a place in Korea. I thought that if John could find a place in Korea, how many places in Korea could there be? So we went out, got the *Billboard Buyers' Guide*, looked it up and there were two. We knew right away which one it was . . . Ken was really reluctant to do CDs . . . 'They're not gonna sell, there's no market for them.' He was very perceptive in some ways but not in others. So I said, 'Look, why don't we just send them a letter or fax them and see what happens. See if they give us a response' . . . So they faxed us back this absurdly low price, 79c a disc, landed, duty paid in California, including mastering! All we had to do was send them an analogue tape and a cheque. [Minimum order] 2,000. We needed a way of doing business with them so we wouldn't get caught. I had a friend in the telecommunications business who had just set up a thing which was brand new at the time, a fax service. You could call his 800 number which meant there was no registering on your phone bill, and you could collect your faxes from his computer. His computer was also on an 800 number so you could fax to it without it leaving a trace. And because he was a friend he let me rent the service without leaving my real name. If anyone came looking he would show them the file with this fake name on it. It was a watertight system of communicating with the pressing plant, which ended up saving our ass at the end. So I sent off a tape of Led Zeppelin from the BBC, called *Classics Off the Air*, and a Pink Floyd one called *Bytes of the Talisman* . . . The Floyd tape was the first one I sent, and it started with the track 'Embryo' which was incredibly rare . . . I [thought I] would test the waters by putting this totally unknown Pink Floyd track at the start of this tape. They would never recognize it for what it was . . . No sooner had they received the tape than we get this fax back from them in perfect English – the guy who was in charge of the plant was a Harvard graduate – the fax said, 'Dear whoever I was, we were amazed to learn that you have the rights to Pink Floyd. We would like to know if our company could sub-license this record for all of the Asian market.' Oh, fuck. What do we do? Do we say no, we don't have the rights – which is obviously not the right answer – or yes, we do have the rights and no, you can't rent it, which is also not a good answer. So finally Ken said, 'Tell 'em we run the fan club and it's a fan-club-only promo . . .' They bought that, or at least we thought they did.[4]

For Ken and his partner, the economics of importing CDs from Korea needed to outweigh the risks involved. They were paying, landed, with jewel box and duty paid, something like $1.22 per CD. They were wholesaling them for ten bucks each. And there was no shortage of demand – despite the lack of originality they displayed in their titles. Initially their CDs – straddling at least two labels, Toasted and Neutral Zone – were largely repackaged versions of 'classic' vinyl releases. Much like the legitimate companies, Toasted relied heavily on 'Eric' and Ken's back catalogue. It did not really matter. Bootleg collectors in the US and Japan snapped up the CDs, and first pressings (generally 2,000, save for certain Zeppelin titles) were rarely around for long. In barely a year they managed to put out some fifty-plus bootleg CDs.

As 'Eric' noted, 'We made more money out of the CDs in ten months than we had in the previous four or five years out of records.' But it was also inevitable that the US authorities would be very keen to nip this particular strain of the bootleg virus in the bud.

There were also considerably fewer independent CD plants in the world than rinky-dink vinyl plants. It hadn't taken Wizardo or

'Eric' long to figure out the logical place to manufacture bootleg CDs. The IFPI were pretty sure that the Toasted CDs must be coming out of the Far East (despite Ken's whimsical insistence on the CD tray cards that they were being made in Australia, a country with even fewer independent CD pressing plants than Korea). When the IFPI/RIAA figured out the connection, 'Eric' and Ken's fax service produced its final, most apocalyptic message.

'Eric Bristow': It turned out [the plant in Korea] knew all along what they were but they didn't give a shit. They were taking the money, until the RIAA got wise and sent a couple of investigators over there and threatened the pressing plant, because the pressing plant was the major supplier of product to WEA . . . They said if you don't stop doing this stuff we're going to pull Warners' contract . . . [The plant] fired the Harvard guy, but to his endless credit, when they fired him, he phoned us and said, 'Look out, they've got your tapes, they've got your money, they got all your glass masters, and they've got your phone number' . . . [There] was about $18,000 dollars [involved] . . . It didn't seem like a lot at the time. We were using a very tough individual to clear [our CDs] at customs when they arrived. He was getting paid a very good chunk of change to do it. Very tough man, not to be fucked with, and they tried to sting us. We knew, though, and we told him that when the next shipment arrives don't accept it . . . they can't touch you. So the shipment shows up. Normally they would bring it to him, he'd sign for it and that'd be it. This time they phone him and the broker says, 'Can you come down and get this?' and he goes, 'I didn't order anything.' 'Oh, but it's here and it's for you, you got to come down and get it . . .' 'I'm not coming down. I didn't order anything.' So without his release approval they then brought it to him. This sweaty little Korean truck driver, the guy was really nervous, wheels in this carton of CDs and says sign here and [he] says, 'Fuck off out of here! I didn't order anything! I'm not signing anything. If you don't get out of here I'm going to call the police.' The little Korean guy wheels them back out again. A few seconds later in come the FBI, 'We know you ordered these, we know you've been clearing them, we're gonna get you.' He says, 'You got a warrant?' 'Yeah.' 'Well, go ahead then . . .' 'Well, we know there's nothing here' . . . And that was pretty much that. At about that point I'd had enough, I turned around to [Ken] and said, 'You can have the business, I'm going home,' and I quit.[5]

Ken had never been entirely comfortable with the new medium and thought about returning to vinyl. He too, though, was tiring of the business and the money 'Eric' and he had made in ten months meant that he had little need to take further risks. After all, this titan of American bootlegging had escaped scot-free for twenty years. It was fast reaching the point where he was not playing the odds. Though he lingered on for a while, producing a few items on his own, when vinyl finally fell off the map at the beginning of 1990, Ken pulled out for good.

The RIAA's attempt to 'hit' Toasted was not a complete flop. By the time they had closed down Toasted's Korean connection, European bootleggers were already battering down the floodgates on the other side of the world. A deal had been struck between the Europeans and the Americans to trade 5,000 Toasted CDs for 5,000 European CDs, manufactured in Germany on the Early Years label. The Early Years CDs were particularly excruciating, being derived entirely from vinyl bootlegs, with appalling artwork and zero attention to detail. This transferring of analogue sources, complete with pops and crackles, to CD reflected the paucity of material available to early European CD bootleggers. No matter. A deal was struck.

According to the younger Bristow, when the Early Years CDs arrived at Chicago's O'Hare Airport in March 1989 they were impounded by customs. Eventually they were released, but when the bootlegger drove down to the airport to pick up his stuff, the FBI and RIAA grabbed him. However, there was no big media hoo-hah about what would have been a substantial coup for the RIAA, and the Europeans were disinclined to believe that such a 'sting' had ever occurred. Whatever the truth, the Europeans never got their 5,000 CDs. A period of mutual distrust between new world and old world bootleggers, which was to last a couple of years, set in.

The US authorities had lost the battle with bootleg vinyl because they could not find out who was making the records. With CDs, the chances of manufacturing in the US lay somewhere between slim and non-existent. That meant that American bootleggers had to import their product, adding a whole new rung of risk to the procedure (though this also made it especially difficult for the RIAA/FBI to prove that an 'importer' was also the manufacturer, unless they could get back to the plant and join up the dots).

The RIAA had considerable powers when it came to restricting imports because of a previous judgement against parallel imports. This meant that it was just as illegal to import a legitimate CD on which an American record label held the copyright as a bootleg CD. For instance, if there was a UK Bruce Springsteen CD single with a cut unavailable in the US, Sony still owned the copyright on the recording and could stop the importation of the UK Sony CD. In the months following the Chicago bust it certainly seemed like customs were seizing all import CDs, whether intended for commercial sale or simply purchased by a private individual. The vice-president of the RIAA's piracy division was called on to defend the scale of seizures:

Steven D'Onofrio: It's like any other contraband. You can bring in one gram, or a whole kilo, and it's still violating the law – so where do you draw the line? Who's going to be the judge of how many copies [are necessary] before we seize it? . . . The importation itself is an act – even if you don't physically import it, but cause it to be imported . . . Obviously, if customs opens a package and sees goods that they're sure are illegal, they're not going to let it go through, regardless of the quantity. That would almost be sanctifying the goods.[6]

Clearly, the authorities were worried that the bootleg market in the US might explode again if the importation of CDs continued unchecked. It was not just 'Eric' and Ken who took the sudden demise of vinyl as an excuse to get out of the business.

Richard: I never did CD bootlegs. Everyone who was doing them was getting busted, that was one thing. Another is I didn't want to design a CD package because a 5″ square thing doesn't appeal to me . . . I couldn't see myself designing CD packaging. It just bored me. When CDs started getting done they thought they were bootleg-proof. They were proven wrong fast and they were very pissed off . . . I knew they were going to go after those people, and people were getting hit left and right.[7]

In the vinyl era, the post office and customs had always seemed to turn a blind eye to individuals importing bootlegs for their own collections. Though the law had never been tested, it was assumed that importing an item 'legally manufactured' in another country for one's own private use could not be a criminal act. In England the legal right to import a single copy of a bootleg for private purposes had now been enshrined in the 1988 Copyright Act. However, in at least one instance – again involving Chicago customs officers – a private collector who had ordered twenty-five different bootleg CDs from a company in Frankfurt was followed home by RIAA and US Customs officials and told to either sign a certificate of abandonment and surrender the CDs, or be charged with illegal importation. This was the sort of zeal that was only bound to antagonize music collectors.

A bootleg dealer: They're treating them like shipments of 'crack' or something . . . Now there's guys telling me they're turning away stuff just because it's been put on hold in customs; when it finally comes to them, they just refuse the packages. There's another guy I know who deals in imports – regular stuff, not bootlegs – and he's not getting anything through either. They're stopping anything with 'compact disc' on it.[8]

The irony of such injudicious scare tactics was that it played into the hands of the commercial bootleggers. If there was a risk involved in importing directly from Europe, a collector breached no laws when he purchased a bootleg CD from an American retailer. Needless to say, the risk-takers were charging a premium for their endeavours, forcing the price of bootleg CDs, at least temporarily, to around $40.

At the end of 1989, it seemed that the RIAA might finally be winning the CD war. 9,000 CDs were sitting at Los Angeles

International Airport waiting to be collected. 'The guy who owns those paid for them up front, and he's goin' crazy,' admitted one dealer. Meanwhile a substantial number of copies of the Beatles *Unsurpassed Masters* CD remained tied up at a New York port; while in Houston one unlucky dealer had $100,000 worth of bootleg CDs and LPs seized by authorities, along with a briefcase full of names, addresses and phone numbers. For the first time, the RIAA confiscated more CDs than bootleg vinyl in 1989 (38,766 CDs compared with 29,615 albums), a marginal increase on the fifteen bootleg CDs confiscated in 1988.

They had also seen off an attempt by Bill Cole Enterprises to legitimize the importation of legally produced European protection-gap CDs. It was inevitable that someone would want to test US copyright law given the legal situation in Europe. Bill Cole Enterprises had been importing a handful of titles by the Flashback label, including a Presley CD, *The Hollywood Sessions*, which included outtakes from his movie soundtracks in sound quality comparable to Swingin' Pig's *Ultra Rare Trax*. *The Hollywood Sessions* was freely advertised by BCE, who insisted that this was no bootleg. However, by March 1989 BCE had issued a terse statement confirming that it was discontinuing the sale of the Presley item, and all other European quasi-legit CDs. The legal threats of RCA and the RIAA had proved to have somewhat more substance than BCE might have originally supposed. American copyright law had held firm.

Yet the US market was far too large a market for the bootleggers not to attempt more clandestine ways of breaching its borders. The largest American bootleg importer, with some notable under-world connections, had long been able to get his product into the country unobserved. The relative ease with which bootleg CDs could be purchased in New York's Village was in marked contrast to the West Coast, where prices held at $35–$40 (compared with a $25 norm in New York).

West Coast retailers were reluctant to buy direct from Europe and the Far East and disliked buying the sort of bulk the major importers were wont to insist on. Having been spoilt by the ease with which they had previously obtained vinyl bootlegs, West Coast dealers now found themselves having to buy their product through at least two grades of middlemen. They were also exposed to a far more enthusiastic state police. Bootlegs were never a high priority for the over-stretched NYPD. But in October 1990 Los Angeles' biggest monthly record swap, in Buena Park, was busted by local police (with 'help from the RIAA'). Once again, though, the authorities had problems distinguishing 'bootlegs' from the real thing (the police were told to look for specific labels like Swingin' Pig). A police spokesman told the *LA Times* that, 'the RIAA wanted a high-profile bust [to] send a message' to dealers everywhere that such shows are being policed.

Despite the RIAA's best endeavours, though, many of the best bootleg CDs in the years 1989–90 were coming out of America – generally from one label, Scorpio. The man behind Archive and Brigand Records had graduated to silver discs. By 1990 the scope of the Byrdman's CD titles was as impressive as his vinyl – and a lot more mainstream. He had not abandoned vinyl entirely, often pre-empting subsequent CD releases with small-run vinyl editions (his version of Patti Smith's magnificent May 1975 WBAI broadcast, *Free Music Store*, was one such album that later became a CD). Initially, he refrained from giving his CDs a singular identity.

The Byrdman: The very first CD bootleg I did? Probably Zeppelin, Paris Theatre '69, a version of that, from a high-quality tape ... the BBC has always been of great service to people who want to hear music, with all those radio shows and transcription discs around. It's a fine thing. That was taken right off the records, a fabulous source. That's a killer, [as was] *Bowie at the Beeb*.[9]

How Many More Times, the Byrdman's first Zeppelin CD, was credited to Quality Compact Productions. But it was through the CD incarnation of Archive and then Scorpio that he would really develop a reputation for exemplary Zeppelin product. And in many ways it was Led Zeppelin who fuelled the initial CD explosion. Many collectors consider *Live in Zurich 1980* to be the first pukka bootleg CD. Made exclusively for an American outlet

by a European bootlegger, via the Korean connection, *Live in Zurich*, when it emerged at the beginning of 1988, sent the same sort of tremors through Zeppelin circles as Swingin' Pig's *Ultra Rare Trax* was to do for Beatles fans. A previously uncirculated soundboard from Zep's final tour, *Live in Zurich* was an exemplary product – and entirely illegal in manufacture and distribution. It represented only the trickle before the flood. Toasted/Neutral Zone's junior partner, 'Eric', was also a serious Zeppelin buff – he was the lunatic responsible for the seventy-album boxed-set – and Ken had observed first-hand the sales of Rock Solid's vast Zep catalogue. Not surprisingly, they rattled off a dozen Zeppelin CD sets in the ten months that they operated as a CD outfit.

The Zeppelin bootleg CD phenomenon is hard to explain. Though Zeppelin had always been extensively bootlegged on vinyl, they were rarely referred to in the same terms as Dylan or The Beatles, where the amount of vinyl seemed quite simply out of control. They had also passed out of vogue when the punk revolution had kicked in – Zeppelin's studied playing, extended (sometimes to absurd proportions) solos and emphasis on a derivative r&b sound was the very antithesis of punk's inflammable material. As the eighties progressed, though, America's large contingent of metalheads began to see Zeppelin (as opposed to genuine forefathers like Cream, Fleetwood Mac or the Jeff Beck Group) as the founding father of hard rock, and, in a curious osmosis, The New Yardbirds slipped back into vogue just as the CD revolution hit.

Of course, CD was the perfect medium for latter-day Zeppelin performances given the sheer length of their shows (and the ease with which a thirty-minute 'No Quarter' could be skipped over in mid-CD). Now even the most extravagant Zep show could be contained on three CDs. Zeppelin were also a band whose reputation was founded on their live shows, yet they had repeatedly refused to release a representative live performance officially (*The Song Remains the Same* – the soundtrack of the 1973 'in concert' film – they quickly disowned). Thus the bootleggers were filling a very considerable void.

In the first eighteen months of the bootleg CD explosion, the Zep mania was also fuelled by a steady flow of previously uncirculated Zeppelin soundboards, of which some were genuinely exciting (Fillmore West in April 1969, Texas International Pop Festival in August 1969), most of which were from the same tedious 1973 tour as *The Song Remains the Same*. They all sold.

As so many times before, the mania was largely Japanese-fed. Since any Zeppelin title sold in Japan, the Japs soon went into production for themselves. The Japanese produced or acted as main distributors for a bewildering number of Zeppelin CDs (certainly over a hundred) in the crucial CD years (1988–91). Scorpio itself was selling the bulk of its Zeppelin product not in its home territory – where it was barely distributed outside the East Coast – but in Nippon. It was also supplying the source material for a whole series of Japanese CDs it preferred not to put on the 'prestigious' Scorpio label.*

But it was the Scorpio titles, concentrating on the early years of Zeppelin, that sold and sold. *Studio Daze* (a collection of early studio outtakes), *Jennings Farm Blues* and the double-CD *Destroyer*, which put on CD for the first time a Cleveland 1977 soundboard that had previously made up a legendary four-album vinyl bootleg of the same name, all became perennials, helping to finance Scorpio's descent into the CD maelstrom.

Given that Scorpio was operating out of the US, and given the heat being directed at the retailers in America, it became necessary to exercise a little discretion when routing the CDs into the US. Though Scorpio was using a similar manufacturer to Toasted, the Byrdman was going through a European conduit, hoping to disguise the CDs' true origins.

By the beginning of 1990, Scorpio had overtaken Germany's Swingin' Pig as the premier CD label in terms of presentation, sound quality and the sheer desirability of its releases. With outstanding studio material like Zeppelin's *Studio Daze*, Springsteen's

---

* JSC [Japan-Scorpio] CDs include *Knebworth 4/8/79*, *Best of Tour '73*, *Another Magic*, *V 1/2*, *One More Daze* and *Lucifer Rising*.

Born in the Studio (which collected together best-ever versions of outtakes from *The Wild, the Innocent* and *Born to Run*, previously scattered over half a dozen vinyl bootlegs) and The Who's *From Lifehouse to Leeds* (which included half a dozen killer cuts from what sounds like a rehearsal session for the 'Lifehouse' project, in superb quality, direct off reel-to-reel tapes purchased at a 'rock memorabilia' auction in London), Scorpio was at last exploring the full possibilities of a digital, 72-minute musical medium.

In keeping with his previous vinyl excursions, the Byrdman used some of the revenue such 'bestsellers' generated to fund more obscure, but equally worthwhile, Scorpio releases. His last pre-Scorpio CD, on Archive (like the Zeppelin *Destroyer* set), was a 1972 Lou Reed radio broadcast and – like its Zeppelin predecessor – it was swiftly copied by Swingin' Pig. If anything showed the shift in prestige, it was such acts of piracy by the previously esteemed German label. The Reed CD, *Despite All the Amputations* (renamed *Hero and Heroine* by Swingin' Pig and packaged in a patently inferior way), was the debut representation of Reed's first post-Velvet touring combo, a bunch of Long Island teengenerates, The Tots. Recorded at Ultrasonic Studios in Hempstead, *Despite All the Amputations* caught the effortless groove of Reed's early solo work with a crystal clarity. It was perhaps Scorpio's finest hour.

Almost as impressive was *Killer Highlights*, Scorpio's collection of BBC performances from The Faces, a band little bootlegged but much celebrated, particularly in Japan. Ironically, Scorpio were releasing The Faces on CD four years before their official American label (Warners) deemed them worthy of back-cataloguing on CD. If some of Scorpio's more obscure releases found less favour (The Kinks' *Good Luck Charm* was a mish-mash of good and bad and was probably the worst selling of Scorpio's titles), the label could never be accused of lacking ambition.

At a time when other labels were shying away from any recording longer than a single CD – save perhaps for Zeppelin and Springsteen, where fans demanded complete performances – Scorpio produced the ambitious *Into the Mystic*, a double-CD of

the complete 1971 Pacific High radio broadcast of Van Morrison, previously utilized on the justifiably famous *Van the Man* and *Belfast Cowboy* bootleg albums. With such unorthodox 'covers' as 'Friday's Child', 'Hound Dog', 'Just Like a Woman' (on which Van makes explicit the implied transvestism of the lyric with the line 'there's a queer in here, ain't it clear') and 'Buena Sera Senorita', plus the bonus of 'Caledonia Soul Music', a sixteen-minute outtake from *Street Choir*, *Into the Mystic* was a remarkable insight into Van's music at a time when it was always too late to stop now.

Perhaps inevitably, though, Scorpio began to explore the possibility of manufacturing CDs in America on the sly. This was a wildly dangerous exercise, whatever the potential economic rewards. It would be an out-and-out felony, and US CD plants were still carefully scrutinized. Scorpio also failed to test the procedure with a band obscure enough to pass most plant employees by starting with the Stray Cats, a band irksome to the Byrdman but hot property in Japan. Scorpio's usual CD production route, which involved two European middlemen before reaching its Far East haven, meant that he was having to pay a premium on his CDs, even though he was not paying any 'mechanicals' (unlike most of the Europeans). This made it difficult to gamble on small runs of weird, cult acts.

The Byrdman: [The Stray Cats CD] was done for a guy in Japan who wanted 2,000 copies, just for his Japanese Stray Cats mail letter. To do it in Europe would've cost about eight bucks and I figured I could give it to this guy in America, who said, 'Cool, we'll do it all underground. It's all being shipped overseas, we'll just do it in-house,' for like a buck and a half. So this would have been an instance when I would have made some real money, which would have all gone into putting out some unheralded bands like Can and The Move and The Bonzo Dog (Doo Dah) Band. The Stray Cats have co-opted enough influences into their style from people who haven't seen much by way of return from them . . . The place that manufactured it sent it out to be mastered instead of doing it in-house and someone at the mastering place figured out that it wasn't the group the Runaway Boys.[10]

At the end of 1990, the Byrdman's bootleg empire came crashing down around him. Tracing the Stray Cats CD back to him was

easy enough, and when the FBI raided his West Village record store they found wonders to behold – a hefty hoard of tray cards, CDs and sleeves waiting to be boxed up in the back of the store, most bearing the emblem Scorpio. If they couldn't definitively prove that here was more than the East Coast distributor of Scorpio, the Stray Cats CD was another matter. It was this bust that accounted for much of the huge jump in CDs confiscated by the RIAA in 1990 (152,466 items, a fourfold increase on 1989). However, the FBI were reluctant to test the exact laws relating to CD manufacture for export to another country with less stringent laws. They preferred the old 'Capone' technique, prosecuting the Byrdman for tax-related indiscretions.

The Byrdman: At the end of the story . . . they didn't want to get into a real 'locked horns' dilemma about [the] proprietary [rights to] this material . . . It could probably have been shown to [a court's] reasonable satisfaction that the entire production was to be sold in a territory where this material would present no legal problem. So, if it was done in Europe and sent to Japan – no problem, but if it was done in the States and sent to Japan – problem. The morality of that's a little bit weird . . . so they structured their complaint [in a way] that gave me a more palatable alternative to plead to. Which I did.[11]

Several post-Scorpio US productions have been attributed to the label (primarily because of their SC matrix numbers), though the connection remains ill-defined at best – even if *Live! Music Review* recently ran a story on a whole new batch of US bootleg CDs under the banner 'Scorpio: The Legend Continues'. But with the demise of Scorpio proper, East Coast bootleggers concentrated on distributing European CDs, being manufactured with such ease on the other side of the pond. After all, the largest margins on bootleg CDs had always been at the wholesale and retail ends, and it must have seemed like the RIAA was keeping the lid on Stateside. Bootleg CD seizures plummeted in 1991 (to 36,857) and again in 1992 (to 16,213), suggesting that the problem was fading from view. Or maybe the RIAA anti-piracy unit was just not doing its job very well.

17 It Was Less Than Twenty Years Ago . . .

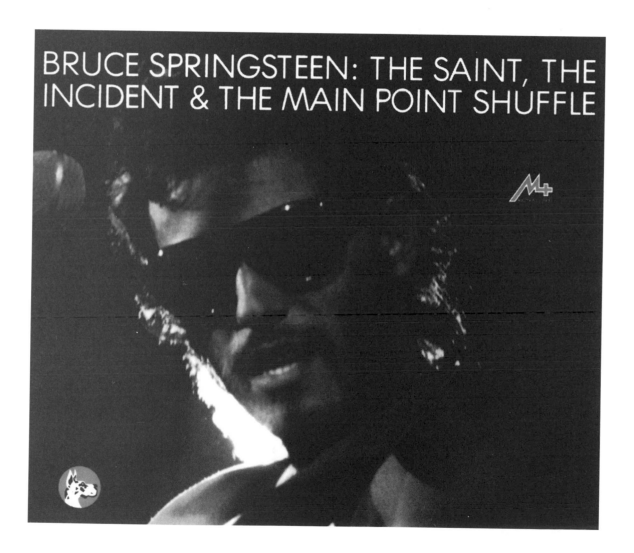

Rinaldo Tagliabue: Great Dane consists of a group of collectors. We select artists using our 'heart', [and] we select our production considering three things: popularity of the artist, quality of available tapes and the sales potential. There's nothing original in this, except for the fact that we consider Europe as our market.[1]

Swingin' Pig's *Atlantic City* may have opened up Germany to a whole new wave of contemporary 'protection-gap' CDs, but in Italy the twenty-year rule had already been breached by a new CD label with a distinct Springsteen bent. Great Dane's first title, released in the spring of 1989, was a superb ninety-minute soundboard of Springsteen and the E Street Band, provisionally attributed to a January 1974 show at Kent University. It was an explosive performance, kicking in with an exuberant 'Does This Bus Stop on 82nd Street?' and maintaining the unrelenting tempo until the obligatory 'Rosalita' finale. Great Dane's packaging also matched the contents. Issued as a full-length CD with bonus CD-single, *You Mean So Much to Me* transgressed the twenty-year rule by a good five years. Rinaldo Tagliabue, a long-time collector of Springsteen, had recently hooked up with one of the terriers who had so tenaciously dug into the maze of Italian law.

Rinaldo Tagliabue: After a couple of years [of Bulldog] the partners had [come to have] a different point of view. At that time I was contacted by them again. That was the time that my partner expressed the opinion that it would be quite reasonable to do concerts that were less than twenty years ago. 'Cos in Italian law it is written that a fair compensation should be given to the performer if the performance is less than twenty years old, but there is no mention of the authorization of the artist and it does not even mention what this fair compensation is. At that point we had a reference – the artist's royalties that they took from SIAE. So we were pretty sure that

the cost of such compensation wasn't huge and only referred to [payment on] the number of copies you were going to sell. We decided to put some money in a bank account for each release and we mentioned that on [each] CD. We were ready to give [it] if anyone asked but no one did. The very first CDs that were under twenty years were done by Why Not? – an Eagles [title] and another one – [which was] Bulldog under a different label.[2]

Springsteen had been largely overlooked by bootleg CD merchants before Great Dane's emergence. The Japanese bootleggers who so ruthlessly pillaged Zeppelin's live catalogue were uninterested in Springsteen, and the Europeans were too busy exploiting the sixties to start on another decade. With Great Dane, though, the dedication of Tagliabue, access to the very best tapes, and the legal efforts of the Lawyer, created one of the most impressive catalogues of a single artist in the history of bootlegging.

In the first eighteen months of Great Dane's operations, they were responsible for one five-CD set, one four-CD set, two triple-CD sets, some five double-CD collections and a solitary single CD all devoted to the first eight years of Springsteen and the E Street Band in concert. Springsteen's marathon performances – running anywhere from two to four hours – were ideally suited to the generous seventy-five-minute playing times CDs could afford. Thus a classic three-hour show like the September 1978 Passaic broadcast could be snugly fit on a triple-CD version of the legendary *Pièce De Résistance*. Great Dane even managed to remaster (and upgrade) the famous ten-album Springsteen bootleg set *All Those Years*, jamming it all into a five-CD box. The original vinyl version, which had also originated in Italy, had excited considerable comment in the wake of Springsteen's own disappointing three-CD collection *Live 1978–85* (*sic*). Now Great Dane's five-CD version, with its concentration on the peak years of 1973–8 and a healthy dose of rare covers and lost originals like 'The Promise', 'Frankie', 'Rendezvous' and 'Don't Look Back', highlighted how far removed the perceptions of Springsteen and his manager, Jon Landau, were from those who bought their records.

Tagliabue initially concentrated on putting out the classic Springsteen radio broadcasts of the seventies, like those from the Main Point in 1973 and 1975, and from Winterland and Passaic in 1978. Tagliabue even adopted a record-industry practice of upgrading releases if substantially superior source tapes turned up. This proved to be the case with both Main Point releases, *Thundercrack* and *The Saint, the Incident and the Main Point Shuffle*, reissued in Great Dane's 'Master Plus' series. Inevitably, though, Great Dane was far too lucrative an exercise for Tagliabue to stick with Springsteen. The remainder of the Great Dane catalogue also expanded exponentially. By the end of 1990 it included nearly forty non-Springsteen titles, spanning everybody from Joy Division (*Shadowplay* – a particularly superb soundboard from one of their final shows in April 1980) to mainstays of the bootleg industry like Zeppelin, Pink Floyd, The Stones and The Who.

Having established the most benevolent of protection gaps, and with SIAE stamps on all its releases, Great Dane helped establish Italy as the second home of Europe's new underground. Unlike Swingin' Pig, though, they stuck with live recordings, arguing persuasively that these were fair game for any label who wished to give a performance more permanent expression. Of course, CDs of studio recordings were also considerably more problematic in legal terms.

Rinaldo Tagliabue: We don't think the artist should have the right to control what already belongs to the public. Live performances and radio broadcasts are played to the public and – from our point of view – the performance doesn't belong to the artist anymore. On the other hand, studio material is the author's property and must be under his control ... To huge companies like CBS, 'taking the risk to sign an artist' means nothing in terms of pure cost; it's a drop in the ocean. Of course Great Dane takes a 'free ride' publishing records from artists like Springsteen, The Rolling Stones and Led Zeppelin, but the record companies have the ability to publish those things and put Great Dane out of [business] at once. They

simply don't do it because this will generate a pure loss for the companies and no real extra profit for the artists. So Great Dane has good reason to exist because we publish things that otherwise will never be available.[3]

The other originator of this European CD revolution had no such qualms about using studio material. Indeed it was with several collections of outtakes that Yellow Dog established its reputation. Operating out of Luxemburg, like Swingin' Pig's parent company Perfect Beat, Yellow Dog were casting their net wider than Swingin' Pig or Great Dane. In the early days of CD, Ken in LA took care of Yellow Dog's US distribution, while Yellow Dog's Beatles bias made them massively popular in Japan. Though Yellow Dog was nowhere near as prolific as Swingin' Pig or Great Dane in the crucial years of 1989 and 1990, their product continued to sell and sell.

Yellow Dog's origins were in fact more ancient than either Swingin' Pig or Great Dane. It was in the more anonymous guise of Disques du Monde that Yellow Dog had been responsible for the first CD versions of *Get Back* and *Sessions* (the Beatlefest 'fake EMI' versions excepted) in the early months of 1988. At the same time, Yellow Dog had brokered the Zeppelin *Live in Zurich* CD for an American duo. Through at least one middleman, Disques du Monde had been using the same Korean connection that Ken and 'Eric' were about to discover.

Meanwhile, Yellow Dog set about preparing his own set of Beatles studio rarities, hoping to shame the Swingin' Pig *Ultra Rare Trax* by offering full-length CDs and displaying a chronological coherence that the *Ultra Rare Trax* volumes plainly lacked. With eight hours of studio material to perm from, and a genuine love of The Beatle, Yellow Dog's releases should have been the definitive Beatles underground CDs. But when *Unsurpassed Masters* Vols. 1–3 arrived from the Korean plant, they sounded more like *Sweet Apple Trax* than *Ultra Rare Trax*. The CDs had been mastered incorrectly. Only one of the two stereo channels was present, making them two-track mono.

Corrected stereo versions would have to be made in Europe, where quality controls were likely to be a tad more rigorous.

Yellow Dog was obliged to turn to a manufacturer he had met at the record industry's annual MIDEM shindig for the stereo represses. Unfortunately, the gentleman in question was also a dab hand at bootlegging:

Mrs Toad [a bootlegger]: Andy and he got on okay but Andy always wants to have a percentage of the production to wholesale himself, and he had better distribution than Yellow Dog. What finally did it for Yellow Dog was when he arranged a deal with [one of the Japanese wholesalers], and Yellow Dog had sold 'em to [the Jap gentleman] at 15 marks, nothing unreasonable, and Andy had sold 500 of each to [another Japanese wholesaler] at 13![4]

While EMI swung into action against The Swingin' Pig, Yellow Dog decided to look beyond the EC for a possible manufacturing plant, hoping to produce *Unsurpassed Masters* on a quasi-legitimate basis similar to that temporarily enjoyed by Swingin' Pig. While other bootleggers squabbled with plants in Germany and Italy – who were being pressured to refuse their product by the legitimate record companies – Yellow Dog was quick to recognize the possibilities of Eastern Europe.

Yellow Dog: After we found out that [some wholesalers] got stuff before we got it, we decided to find our own way [to manufacture]. So I went to Hungary to a pressing plant and said, 'I have a CD here that I want to make – a guitar CD.' We wanted to try [first] with that. But they didn't want to do it without authorization from the Hungarian copyright society, so I had to go to them. I talked to a lady and she said, 'You can't do it here. You can make the CD in Hungary if you want to but you can't pay copyrights here. You have to go through STEMRA.' 'I don't want to go through STEMRA,' I said. 'What if I have a Hungarian company here?' 'Well, of course, then you can pay [royalties] here.' I said, 'Well, I have a Hungarian company here.' And she didn't believe me but the partner in my record shop was part-owner of a company in Hungary and they had a shop in Budapest. So I went to the manager of the shop and [told him] to go to [the Hungarian copyright society] and say that you're going to pay the copyright. And that's how we made the 'guitar' CD. Neighbouring rights are only protected in Hungary for twenty years. So that's why we could [also] do The Beatles stuff.[5]

It seemed that the whole of Europe was slowly opening up and there was little that the authorities could do. Yellow Dog, like Perfect Beat, had registered their company in Luxemburg, the EC country with the most liberal copyright laws, and once Yellow Dog overcame its initial difficulties, the *Unsurpassed Masters* series became *the* document of The Beatles' EMI years. With each volume dedicated to a particular era and with generous running times, *Unsurpassed Masters* lived up to its name, eventually surpassing *Ultra Rare Trax* in repute.

If Yellow Dog's reputation was founded on his Beatles releases, he was soon obliged to expand beyond his own primary interest. Reluctantly the Dog also expanded his bevy of labels. Black Cat was reserved for audience recordings of historical interest. Yellow Dog remained reserved for pedigree stock, such as a previously undocumented one-hour 1962 broadcast of Dylan on Cynthia Gooding's WNYC show. A series of Springsteen titles, named after The Beatles' *Unsurpassed Masters*, managed to mix best-ever sources of early circulating tapes with a smattering of genuinely new goodies. Yellow Dog's record for turning up uncirculated items was perhaps second only to Scorpio.

And for the first time in many years, it was often bootleggers rather than tape-collectors who were sourcing 'new' studio recordings. An American five-CD set of Dylan basement tapes collected all that was circulating and supplemented it with a good 50 per cent that was not. Two European Hendrix titles, *Studio Haze* and *Demos from 1967* (actually from 1966), gave Hendrix collectors the most interesting studio material to emerge in years – officially or unofficially.

Unfortunately for Yellow Dog, in 1991 their Hungarian connection was severed when the record shop in which they had a part interest went broke, while Yellow Dog's Dutch arm became embroiled in legal difficulties in the Low Countries. As such, for much of 1992 and 1993 Yellow Dog's catalogue expanded only fitfully, at a time when its competitors' catalogues were spiralling out of control.

Yellow Dog was not alone with its legal headaches. By 1992,

all three functioning first-generation European CD bootleg labels were having their fair share of problems. Swingin' Pig was finding it increasingly difficult to get their product into record stores. The German division of the IFPI was seizing on the slightest breach of the country's hazy boundaries of copyright. In one instance, Schubert apparently escaped a lengthy legal battle with EMI by providing evidence that their retail chain HMV was stocking his titles, a clear case of double standards. A case resulting from a Doors live in Stockholm CD, one of Swingin' Pig's first releases, also hung over Schubert's head throughout the early nineties, pending a decision from the Supreme Court (the set was unquestionably recorded after Sweden's ratification of the Rome Convention). A double-set of Dire Straits recorded in Basel, Switzerland, in 1992 also resulted in an interim judgement against Swingin' Pig, on the grounds that Dire Straits were citizens of the EC and were entitled to the same protection as German nationals.

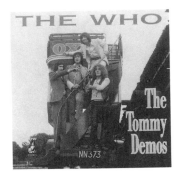

In reality, Swingin' Pig's credibility as anything other than a money-making machine had long taken a nosedive in collectors' eyes. The beginning of the end came when they began 'knocking off' other labels' better releases, like Scorpio's *Destroyer*, *Despite All the Amputations* (into *Hero and Heroine*), *Bowie at the Beeb* (into *White Light/White Heat*), and *Everybody Knows* (into *Neil Young in Concert*). When, after their victory in the courts over *Atlantic City '89*, Swingin' Pig releases came out by the likes of Midnight Oil, Depeche Mode and the Eurythmics – none of whom would have been standard bootleg fare before Schubert uncovered the legal loophole – the Pig's transition into a 'legal underground label', to use Schubert's own words, was complete.

Swingin' Pig's consistently high wholesale prices, even when the prices of bootleg CDs were plummeting elsewhere, their notorious stinginess with playing times, and the NoNoise controversy, all worked against them. By 1992, few bootleg dealers outside Germany were interested in stocking Swingin' Pig titles, and Perfect Beat were desperately trying to dump the huge surfeit of Swingin' Pig vinyl they had been lumbered with when the bootleg vinyl market collapsed in 1990.

Great Dane's problems were similar, if less terminal: a lack of exciting new material, a high wholesale price, the avaricious intentions of newcomers, and the label's high profile. By the end of 1992 they also had a problem shared by all Italian labels, the weakness of the Italian lira.

Pressure was also being brought to bear to make sure that SIAE 'delayed' licences for certain releases, in particular live performances by Bruce Springsteen (which was bound to hit Great Dane hardest) and U2, who had both spent much of 1992 on the road after a long break from touring.

Simone [a bootlegger]: GEMA is allowing everything which is legal under [German] law, and they learned exactly what was legal . . . In Italy, the SIAE is just cashing in. It's a weird situation. They are just there for the money. They don't check anything. They don't take care of anything . . . In 1991 they had pressure from the majors. So they said, 'Let's stop those ten artists.' They are giving us pressure on behalf of Madonna, so Madonna is forbidden. Which is totally against the law . . . It's nonsense. Right now, for over a year, we cannot produce any CDs from Bob Dylan. The only reason is somebody stole the tapes of Dylan's forthcoming album in 1993.[6]

Though SIAE was ultimately obliged to grant a licence, this was one more headache for Great Dane who, unlike Swingin' Pig, had continued to market what might be termed traditional bootleg fare: Dylan, The Stones, Bowie, King Crimson, Pink Floyd, etc. Though they lacked the contacts required to make all these releases the equal of their Springsteen items, the occasional gem snuck through. Their first Van Morrison title, *Can You Feel the Silence*, was a superlative-quality broadcast from 1983. Their Dylan 'Rolling Thunder' 1975 double came in for much praise, though *Get Ready! Tonight Bob's Staying Here with You* had its share of sound problems and GDR accidentally omitted the title-track. By 1991 Great Dane badly needed new impetus in order to continue as one of the premier underground labels.

In the first two protection-gap years (1989–90), Great Dane, Swingin' Pig and Yellow Dog had only one serious competitor at the premium end of the market. Oh Boy!, who operated out of

Luxemburg, maintained their own niche: the prog-rock of the early seventies. Though they occasionally strayed into more glam aspects of that era, with titles by the likes of Slade (a corking 1972 soundboard), Mott the Hoople and Lou Reed (a disappointing copy of the 1976 *Stoned* album), their roster included a number of bands few others would consider bootlegging: Canned Heat, Ten Years After, Man, Soft Machine, the Edgar Broughton Band, Humble Pie, West, Bruce and Laing, and Baker Gurvitz, to name a few. Though Oh Boy! rarely put out anything with less than exemplary sound, their artwork was usually unoriginal and the market they were aiming at curiously ill-defined (though the Japanese loved these outlandish prog-rock releases). Oh Boy! pumped out an impressive amount of product before production ground to a halt in the early months of 1992.

The emergence of companies like Great Dane and Oh Boy! did not entirely signal the end of the vinyl-copying labels, though they clearly could not continue to market 'records on CD'. In fact for much of 1989 and 1990, the three main producers of 'copycat' CDs continued to pour their product over the face of Europe with little thought as to the consequences. It was these labels that represented the most serious threat to legitimate companies.

18 The Third Generation

VAN MORRISON

PAGAN STREAMS

Simone: There are now a couple of big distributors who have jumped into the business. They take all the CDs they can find and they copy them with ugly covers and they sell them with a retail price to the public of 10,000 lire, which is about $6. Of course we can't do anything about it because the whole thing is built on this legal loophole. So there is no protection. If I make a Pearl Jam CD, I cannot say it's mine, copyrighted by me. I pay the copyright, but I cannot protect my own title, because they can just change the cover and title and that's it. The music is not protected at all.

A German gentleman by the name of Wolfgang was the most mercenary, and undiscriminating, of this new breed of underground merchant. In the worst traditions of bootlegging, Wolfgang's first CD label was wholly designed to ride on the back of Swingin' Pig's success. The Genuine Pig had its own series of *Ultra Rare Trax*, this time devoted to The Stones. Unfortunately, none of the tracks were remotely rare and they were all scratchily reproduced from records. Genuine Pig soon got known for wallowing in the mud, but Wolfgang was the master of inventing new labels for the same old fodder.

Live & Alive was the most shameful Wolfgang incarnation. By 1990 there was no need to copy vinyl bootlegs. There were so many CD bootlegs that could be cut-up and edited, in short disguised. The quality of the items he appropriated was usually excellent. Wolfgang, though, was not interested in competing with his fellow labels. Live & Alive was strictly designed for supermarket shelves, in huge numbers by bootleg standards. He was even prepared to indemnify Britain's largest independent wholesalers from legal action in an attempt to get his CDs into the second largest (and most inaccessible) of EC markets. All of Wolfgang's items were manufactured and shipped out at low, low prices. Wolfgang's understanding of economies of scale and his complete

lack of principles made his product the most widely distributed of the protection-gap rackjobbers. Of course, he might as well have been selling baked beans or fake Levis to the Russians.

Mr Toad [a bootlegger]: [Live & Alive] is crap, real bottom of the foodchain stuff . . . [Wolfgang's] stuff's available now for 5½ marks [and] he's got 200,000 CDs he wants to sell . . . There seemed to be this magic time when you could get anything and sell it. Then it all changed.[7]

The creator of Early Years had also come up with a successor label. Chapter One, though, was not much better than its predecessor. With few exceptions, Chapter One artwork was appalling, with many releases excruciatingly copied from the noisiest vinyl they could find. When they came up with a non-vinyl source it was usually a copy of a Japanese CD that had eluded other European labels. Whenever they accidentally issued something genuinely new, from a tape source, and there were a couple of nice original John Lennon comps on Chapter One, many fans – once bitten, twice shy – ignored their release.

The most erratic of the vinyl copyists, though, was Torsten Hartmann, whose Living Legend was by 1989 providing belated cut-price competition for Bulldog and Early Years. Hartmann lacked the necessary source material to put good product out most of the time, but when the right tapes came his way the results could be impressive. Living Legend's Velvet Underground release *The Wild Side of the Street* was a revelation to all Velvets fans. This copy of the oft-bootlegged August 1969 Hillside Festival was audibly superior to any circulating version and provided the definitive audio document of the Velvets. Likewise, their two double-CD sets of the Monterey Pop Festival, compiled from Westwood One's nine-CD syndicated radio broadcast, was the most intelligently constructed, best-sounding version available prior to its official release on Rhino. But Hartmann was having to fight his own legal battles.

Torsten Hartmann: [The MCM] tried to put pressure on dealers to stop them selling our repertoire. But we have good lawyers and we offered legal advice to the dealers who were threatened by the major companies.[8]

The problem with these cheap, vinyl-copying labels was that not only were their releases undermining quality-conscious bootleggers like Great Dane and Yellow Dog, they were seriously undercutting – and thus competing with – the official record companies. And the big boys weren't used to having their monopoly challenged.

The IFPI may have seemed helpless against the onslaught of new titles, new labels and new legal setbacks, but the protection-gap kings were still bound by the glue of capitalist economics, 'market forces'. By the end of 1991, Europe's retailers were fast approaching saturation point with the flood of new titles. The fact is, whatever the scaremongering statistics of the IFPI seemingly implied, bootlegging – pure, under-the-counter, no-copyright-paid bootlegging – has been, and always will be, a specialist market. The fans who seriously collect unreleased recordings worldwide number in the tens, not the hundreds, of thousands.

The increased accessibility of live-performance CDs may have convinced a few new punters as to the delights of hearing a show, warts'n'all, and in turn tracking down the full panoply of live bootlegs by the artist, but the bulk of regular consumers want their hits in chintzy, high-end stereo – lifeless reflections of their own deathless existences. They might have dipped into the mire once or twice to experience the whooping realism of an audience tape at an arena show, but after the second or third CD in which assorted drunks holler into the poor unfortunate taper's mike at some crucial point of the performance, they probably decided that this was a little too much like the real thing, and retreated back to the greatest hits section of Our Price.

Like bands of third-world revolutionaries, most bootleggers were too busy fighting with each other, copying each other's titles, to actually mount a sustained campaign to convince the punter of the delights of live performance CDs.

Mr Toad: Most of the guys now, without exception in Germany, it's nothing to do with music, they just want to make money . . . This is why you've got so many Madonnas and U2 and Guns'n'Roses and Metallica . . . I gave [Red Phantom] a four-CD set of Clapton, which would be a class thing to do, and he wants a fucking radio broadcast of Metallica, yet again! It puts it in a nutshell.[2]

The copying of outstanding bootlegs, often originally pressed in limited editions, had always been a feature of the mini-industry. However, with CDs it was fast reaching the point where piratical bootleggers were killing off the originators. The bootleg beast had stopped feeding on the industry's cast-offs, and was now feeding on itself. This made it particularly difficult to ascertain what a 'classic' title was selling. Because the world market was rapidly being partitioned into its primary sectors – Europe, the Far East, the US – with none of the labels able to dominate all three markets, an American-based outfit might copy a European CD and sell it to Japan or vice versa. Of course, the record industry was still in the game of exaggerating the bootleg phenomenon, imagining tens of thousands of copies of a single CD. The reality was a little different, even when it came to the Big Five:

The record companies want you to believe that the bootleggers are highly organized companies bringing in millions ... Sure, there is a profit to be made, but the largest profit percentage is made on the retail level. And when you compare something like 5,000 copies sold of *Live in the Promised Land* or *Born in the Studio*, to over 10 million copies of *Born in the USA*, you realize that bootlegs may annoy record companies, but relatively speaking, they are a tiny, tiny problem.[3]

The bootleggers – at least in the peak years of 1990–92 – were probably producing a couple of thousand titles per annum, but they were still reliant on the same 100,000 people worldwide for the bulk of their sales. Even if every serious bootleg punter was buying fifty titles a year – and many of these fans only buy new titles by one or two specific artists – this still suggested average sales of less than three thousand copies per title, well below the margin necessary for a legitimate label to sanction release.

One of the major reasons that bootleggers thrived in this period had been the record industry's insistence on maintaining an artificially high price for CDs in all the major economies, even though production costs had plummeted by 70 per cent since CDs were first launched in 1983. This huge drop in production costs had actually resulted in something like a 20 per cent increase in the price of CDs. This had been possible because, unlike computer hardware, where market forces operated – at least in the PC market – CDs contained copyrighted material. As such, the price could be dictated by the copyright holders, in this instance the record companies.

Tony Bates [EMI]: As an organization [EMI] do not price from cost up. We price from the market back and along with many other businesses we take a price decision in . . . the offer we make to the consumer, setting the price we feel is appropriate for that product.[4]

The companies were quite prepared to test the limits of what consumers could withstand, even though their myopic view of the marketplace was stunting the expansion of the CD market and allowing the bootleggers to offer their wares at a price not only comparable to legitimate CDs but in many instances cheaper. Unlike the legitimate companies, they were subject to free-market forces (i.e. anyone with money, a tape and distribution could make a live bootleg).

Bootlegs historically, at least since the early seventies, have always been expensive items. Indeed when they first appeared in CD form, prices were often as high as £20 (or $40) per CD. With the small runs and attendant legal risks while the bootleggers remained wholly underground, such a pricing system was inevitable. The 'legitimization' of underground CDs was bound to push prices down.

This wasn't the only competitive problem that first-generation CD labels had to contend with. The marketplace was changing before their eyes. If the Big Five remained reliable staples of most bootleg repertoires, only the Led Zeppelin market had expanded in the late eighties. It was the grunge of Nirvana, Soundgarden, Red Hot Chili Peppers and Pearl Jam and the monster-metal of Guns'n'-

Roses and Metallica that maintained a level of interest in new product among fledgling bootleg punters. There was a whole new generation of fans who were barely aware of the icons of the sixties and seventies. To them 'All Along the Watchtower' was a U2 song, 'Baba O'Reilly' a Pearl Jam ditty, 'Live and Let Die' a Guns'n'Roses tune. And there was a whole new group of labels (Why Not?, Backstage, Red Phantom, etc.) prepared to push the legal interpretations of Italian law to the limit:

Simone: We were the first ones, in 1990, to start with up-to-date concerts. The [Italian] people were previously working low profile, and in 1990 they were only doing concerts up until 1982–3, close to the ten-year mark. But me and my friends looked at the law and tried to see all the details of the law. And we found out we could also do 1990. So we started with U2.

Particularly in Europe, there were now entire labels specializing in the likes of The Spin Doctors, Soul Asylum and Soundgarden. Some of the established protection-gap labels made a half-hearted effort to cater to this new rock audience but merely displayed a lack of awareness of what might interest this new generation of rock fan.

Unable to move with the times, previously exemplary labels like Swingin' Pig, as much as bootleg rackjobbers like Live & Alive, were fast becoming anachronisms. Required to fight perpetual legal battles to stay in business, and unwilling to go back underground, companies like Living Legend and Live & Alive's parent company, Imtrat (who between them were responsible for the bulk of cut-price crap polluting the European market in 1991–2), were now merely biding their time before a chink in copyright law was closed, and they were forced to burrow back from whence they came.

Germany was no longer seen as the safe European home of bootlegging. Italy, whatever its currency problems, was the country with the fewest legal anomalies for the IFPI to actually exploit. Simply put, the Italian labels were not required to get an artist to authorize the release of his or her live performances. Nor did the Italians consider live performances to be bound by exclusive recording contracts. The options available to the legitimate record companies to apply some brakes to the train of live performance CDs steaming off the presses of Italy were few and far between. Applying pressure on SIAE to refuse to stamp certain labels' releases seemed like a suitably Italian solution, and they did succeed in holding up some titles in the summer of 1992, but ultimately the SIAE was obliged to grant a mechanical licence to anyone who wished to pay the statutory royalties:

Rinaldo Tagliabue: Record companies had to prove that these things are illegal. In order to get the authorization you have to pay copyrights first, and you are obliged to pay copyright in Italy through SIAE. At a certain point, record companies somehow persuaded SIAE not to give authorization for some artists, for reasons I do not know. At that point we were in a situation where some artists were impossible to release. We told SIAE [through our lawyers that] they had been established with the purpose of collecting copyrights for the artists, [and] record companies were not actually entitled to act for the artists themselves as individuals. That was the basic position of GEMA and all the other companies. We now have no problem with SIAE. The fact that we have the authorization from SIAE does not entitle us to say that our products are legal, but we are put in a situation where we are not robbing anyone.[5]

There was also another issue, which was that the Italian protection-gap labels were helping to keep Italian jobs in CD manufacturing – and the large multinationals were not:

Simone: The record industry doesn't press CDs in Italy. They have to roll their machines in Germany. Warner Bros. has a pressing plant in Germany, and Sony as well. Even CDs by Italian artists are manufactured abroad. So the state of Italy doesn't see one penny. The SIAE doesn't see any money, because the copyright is paid abroad. And the [Italian] pressing plants don't get any money. We don't have many pressing plants over here. We have six or seven. The live CDs gave life to these pressing plants. They were going to close because there weren't enough CDs to manufacture in this country. Everything is done abroad.

Van Morrison

The Church of our
Lady St. Mary

Most of Germany's protection-gap merchants were old-guard bootleggers who had adopted a quasi-legitimate façade, with only the more obscure 'part-time' labels like Real Live being operated by new kids on the block.

In Italy, though, two new gladiators entered the arena at the end of 1991. KTS and Red Phantom had no roots in the vinyl era. They were run by young and energetic interlopers who had realized what an opportunity Italy's laws now presented.

Their youth and inexperience meant that they lacked the initial repertoire of tapes most bootleggers accumulate before setting up shop, but they were prepared to compensate by whatever means necessary: offering bootleg tape and/or CD dealers a small percentage of a first pressing (generally fifty copies) in exchange for tapes; purchasing tapes from the stalls of tape-dealers; or simply taping shows themselves (or arranging for certain shows to be taped). Unlike the conventional model of a 'bootleg label', in which the quality of its product rapidly deteriorates as the bootlegger exhausts his initial contacts and expands his roster of releases, KTS and Red Phantom's product improved as they learnt from early errors.

One of KTS's first efforts was a Van Morrison tape supplied by a notorious English tape-dealer. Though it was a unique performance, an unpublicized show held in a church in Devon, the quality of *The Church of Our Lady St Mary* was excruciating. The difference between this release and their subsequent Van title, *Pagan Streams*, showed how far KTS were able to come in its first year of trading. Morrison himself copied six of the cuts on *Pagan Streams* for two live CD singles, though the source was only ever an audience DAT tape. But *Pagan Streams* was a superb recording of a wild show – it includes the longest-ever 'Summertime in England', a *tour de force* that any Van fan should hear; Van gets back to his roots with half a dozen r&b romps; and even throws in 'Send in the Clowns' as a coda – and the KTS packaging was at least the equal of any pukka eighties Van title. If, by the end of 1992, most KTS titles came with picture CDs, *Pagan Streams* was perhaps their finest.

Red Phantom lacked KTS's organization, and its owner was less willing to gamble on which new rock bands might appeal to the bootleg/protection-gap fraternity, but their packaging was often spectacular. A double-CD set, *The Start*, from Lou Reed's first 'Magic and Loss' performance in Milan in January 1993, was not only on the streets in less than six weeks but came with an exotic poster-size insert. A Pink Floyd triple-CD of *The Wall* was no great document, but the 12″ × 6″ box and lavishly illustrated book suggested that certain underground CD labels were looking to replicate the success of boxed-sets with booklets, such a thriving part of the legitimate CD market in the last five years.

Great Dane's dearth of new material was not matched by a lack of ideas on the packaging front. Boxed-sets of The Doors and Led Zeppelin, though they recycled a vast amount of existing material, did so in a form most punters found attractive. KTS responded with a similar Rolling Stones set (*The First Decade*), before Great Dane outdid all-comers with one of the ultimate bootleg sets, a nine-CD collection of every extant Beatles BBC session in 'best-ever' sound quality. A four-CD Dylan set, *You Don't Know Me*, though a frustrating mixture of the quintessential and the humdrum, came in a hardcover 10″ × 5″ format that shamed the official Dylan *Bootleg Series*. Clearly, Great Dane was not prepared to be counted out just yet.

Perhaps most indicative of the new climate, though, were the labels of an Anglo-German duo, Silver Rarities and Wanted Man. Mr Toad, the British end of Silver Rarities, was one of a small number of collector-bootleggers who were interested in overseeing the creation of genuine bootlegs in these new, legally favourable conditions. As with early US producers like Toasted and Scorpio, the initial Silver Rarities releases were made with traditional bootleg markets in mind.

In countries like the UK, US and France, the legal barriers in the way of protection-gap fodder meant that these smaller, more specialized markets had been slower to reach saturation point. In the summer of 1991 the realization dawned on the more astute European manufacturers that their Indian summer, when everyone made money – the good, the bad *and* the ugly – was over.

What was needed was an alliance between those with access to

the requisite manufacturing technology and collector-bootleggers with good material, aesthetic awareness and serious collecting contacts. It was time to get back to some real bootlegging.

In the case of Silver Rarities, though the partners set up the label to operate from Germany, it was not with the high-street market in mind. The British half of Silver Rarities had already dabbled in manufacturing his own items, producing a couple of Dylan vinyl items, including an exemplary single-album, *Deadpan Twist*, from Dylan's landmark Hammersmith residency in 1990. When he attempted his first CD bootleg, though, he found that manufacturing a bootleg CD was not so easy.

Mr Toad: The first CD was torturous, absolutely and utterly torturous. *They Don't Deserve It* was a shambles when it arrived. We sent them seventy-five minutes and it came back as seventy-two, bits had been chopped here and there . . . the volume level is all to cock and it wasn't like that on the tape that went off, nothing like it. It went to Israel, Korea, you name it . . . And when it came back, the back cover was exactly as [Mrs Toad] had typed it out to give them the information. They'd just taken the white sheet.[6]

Mr Toad had naïvely attributed all his source recordings correctly. Instead of using suitably vague 'Live in Europe' credit, *They Don't Deserve It* was quite clearly identified as a recording of Dylan at the Hammersmith Odeon, London, in February 1991. Recordings from England breached the Rome Convention. A further problem was that it was sent off in the same batch of titles as a CD version of the U2 'Salome Demos', which had caused such a furore when it had come out on vinyl in 1990. The vinyl edition contained three hours of U2 rehearsing material for their next album, *Achtung Baby*, which was not even scheduled for release when the bootleg appeared. Even a belated CD version was a sensitive item.

Mr Toad: About August '91 I [went] to Germany . . . and that's when Silver Rarities was conceived . . . We didn't really decide we were going to do a label. [My German contact] wanted me to give him more tapes. He knew I could get more tapes . . . and I was trying to work out how much money I'd got and what I could afford to pay to make titles and could I distribute them.[7]

What they ended up agreeing on was Mr Toad receiving a certain quantity of free CDs and a 'special price' on any additional copies. In return he would supply sequenced DATs to be mastered to CD and the necessary artwork for each Silver Rarities release. Mr Toad was thus exempt from any financial risk, while Silver Rarities' German manufacturer at last had some worthwhile material to release. Mr Toad's German contact was one of those mysterious individuals who had been churning out appalling 'vinyl copying' items since the outset of protection-gap CDs. He knew he lacked the necessary conduits to obtain good tapes and the ability to put them together sensibly, and the two of them shared a not entirely healthy love of the green stuff and a desire to do something different.

Mr Toad: We had no idea what was going to happen. We had no preconceived ideas about a label, quality, artists, nothing, we just got together some tapes. I was determined to do a Led Zeppelin. I did *Melancholy Danish Pageboys* [first], which sold 2,000 copies![8]

Though Zeppelin was Mr Toad's first love, Silver Rarities' best titles were not destined to be Zep CDs. The well had pretty much run dry on Zeppelin at this point. All that remained was an endless stream of increasingly lo-fi audience tapes. On the Dylan front, though, Silver Rarities came up with two remarkable releases, a double-CD set of a Houston 1981 show from a superb soundboard tape (*You Can't Kill an Idea*) and the first complete 'Godsquad' show on CD, *Contract with the Lord*. Before the advent of Silver Rarities, the Europeans, when they had considered Dylan releases, had generally stuck to sixties material. The sales of the first two Dylan sets surprised Mr Toad's German partner:

Mr Toad: *You Can't Kill an Idea*, when that came out you could count the amount of good Dylan CDs on one hand. There weren't these huge sections that everyone's got now. People just weren't doing Dylan. The Italians were scared to death.[9]

The success of the handful of Dylan titles on Silver Rarities inspired the pair to form a Dylan-only label, Wanted Man. The initial flurry of titles augured well for such a specialist label. A three-CD collection from Dylan's much-misunderstood 1987 'Temples in Flames' tour had consistently impressive quality and gave fans a welcome opportunity for re-evaluation. Another collection (*Golden Vanity*), this time from Dylan's on-going Never Ending Tour, pulled together virtually all the traditional acoustic performances that had punctuated these shows. Wanted Man's first release, *Long Distance Operator*, though, was perhaps their biggest coup: a previously uncirculated recording of Dylan and the Hawks from December 1965. Though only a so-so audience tape, its historical import as the first known Dylan/Hawks 1965 tape outweighed any sonic reservations.

Sadly, the Anglo-German duo couldn't resist saturating even this previously solid market. When a truly turgid collection of mid-eighties rehearsals, a four-CD set of Dylan's ropey rehearsal for the 1990 tour, a double-CD of a lop-sided 1991 soundboard, a triple-CD set of Dylan's Blackbushe 1978 performance and a goodish 1988 audience tape all appeared within weeks of each other on the Wanted Man label, it seemed that the lessons of the protection-gap era had eluded even these arch-exponents of live-performance CDs.

By this point, in the early summer of 1993, Silver Rarities had sunk into a similar rut, displaying the same lack of consistent quality control as recent Wanted Man releases. But the occasional gem still cut through. A staggeringly good soundboard of a Neil Young and the MGs festival show that summer was on the streets within eight weeks of the tour. *Separate Ways* was certainly quite a coup given the paucity of Neil Young board tapes and the stringent security that usually surrounds Young's shows. Equally impressive was a collection of Bowie's BBC sessions from a non-radio source, *Starman in Session*. What let down even these exemplary releases was some fairly grim packaging, the one tradition retained from Chapter One and Early Years.

Unfortunately, while KTS found increasingly inventive ways to

[re]package just about every FM broadcast going, and Red Phantom wrung every possible permutation from seventies Genesis and Floyd tapes, Mr Toad became more and more concerned with petty acts of revenge against anyone who might dare threaten his own little monopoly of Dylan and Zeppelin product. Thus most of the titles he was responsible for in 1993–4 were attempts to run some interference with other manufacturers (his 1993 Springsteen titles were all inferior copies of Crystal Cat items) or 'knock offs' of someone else's originals. An independent English bootlegger, who had had the temerity to import some Silver Rarities titles himself, found a Mr Toad copy of his *Queen at Earl's Court* CD on the streets just two weeks after his original. Though Mr Toad likes to cast himself in the mould of a modern day 'Dub' (even paying Stout to produce his first bootleg cover in eighteen years, for a 1972 Zeppelin triple, *Burn Like a Candle*), his recent actions daub him in the same colour as Ken – the colour of money.

So much for one second-generation CD producer and his original high ideals. The allure of operating like a jobsworth promoted to chairman of the board has long replaced any concern with producing a refreshing alternative to the Live & Alives and Living Legends of this world.

19 The First Rays of the New Rising Sun

The Byrdman: [Japan] is always a brilliant market once you can get into it. Those people are really into music . . . they've got a great network, people follow the music there forever . . . they've got all the equipment to play it on! They have all the hardware and they need something to listen to.[1]

The Americans (and Europeans to a lesser extent) may have only begun to manufacture their bootlegs in the Far East with the advent of CDs, but Japanese bootleggers had always preferred to press their bootlegs 'locally'. Before the CD explosion, Japanese bootleggers had been remarkably isolated. The major American labels had never really managed to organize anything more than fitful distribution in Japan. This was very much a lost opportunity. Japan remains the second largest market for recorded music in the world. Also, until 1971 Japanese copyright law only gave protection to Japanese-originated recordings. Period. Even after 1971 it was still possible to produce an unauthorized release legitimately as long as 'the record used as the master' was pressed outside of Japan.

Japan's belated ratification of the Geneva Convention in 1978 did not commit them to retrospective protection, so any master recordings made before October 1978 remained unprotected. The bulk of rock recordings that Japanese collectors might be interested in were fair game. The Japanese bootleggers duly carried on copying European and American bootlegs, rarely originating titles of their own. Those Japanese bootleggers who flourished in the late seventies and early eighties relied heavily on the lack of access that Japanese punters had to American and European titles. Virtually all Japanese bootleg vinyl was pressed in small numbers in the Far East and distributed almost exclusively in the home market.

In 1987 the American media, going through one of its occasional bouts of anti-Jap feelings, was prompted to highlight Japan's lack of copyright protection:

While Japanese copyright law leaves entire catalogues of superstar recordings exposed to legal piracy, the law is quite protective of the rights of songwriters and music publishers. The copyright in a musical composition has a privileged place in Japanese law and is protected for fifty years ... [but] a recording has at most twenty years of copyright protection and in many cases no copyright protection at all. Thus, though the Japanese music publishing society, JASRAC, is able to collect full mechanical royalties on the compositions embodied in unauthorized releases by many of the superstar performers of the fifties, sixties and seventies, neither these performers nor their record companies receive anything.[2]

Not surprisingly, the Japanese were among the first to realize the commercial potential of bootleg CDs. In such a technology-driven society the Japanese were bound to want all their favourite 'rock' moments, legal and illegal, preserved digitally. However, the Japanese bootleggers of the late eighties suffered the same problem that had always plagued their earlier efforts – access to good bootleg tapes.

In a desperate attempt to solicit some of the vast repertoire of recordings in tape-collecting circles, one Japanese manufacturer even advertised in America's main collectors' magazine, *Goldmine*, asking collectors to send their tapes, in exchange for which they would receive fifty copies of a CD version. Of course, ignoring the questionable legality of such a suggestion, no major collector was likely to send their prize goodies on such a wing and a prayer. Nevertheless, the Japanese did manage to surprise the Americans and Europeans on a few occasions with CDs that matched, and even surpassed, the best that the West had to offer.

One early example was a beautiful version of the Beach Boys' *Smile* album, the aborted sequel to Brian Wilson's ground-breaking *Pet Sounds*. The Japanese *Smile* CD, which shamed a particularly unimpressive release by Early Years, came with the original *Smile* cover (front and rear, with the front cover superimposed on to the

CD itself), was in sterling quality and included a seven-minute 'Heroes and Villains', a fifteen-minute cut-up of assorted 'Good Vibrations' sections, a finished take of 'Surf's Up' and a total playing time of over an hour.

This time it was the Europeans' turn to copy the Japanese. Given that Capitol had yet to release anything from the vaults that related to the *Smile* sessions, the 1989 Japanese *Smile* CD was a most welcome release. (Though, as CD newsletter *ICE* was quick to point out, it was difficult to maintain that *Smile* was a great lost masterpiece strictly on the basis of these outtakes: 'Those hearing *Smile* here for the first time will be left wondering what all the fuss was about, since it sounds exactly like what it is: a collection of scraps from an unfinished project which – if properly completed – could've been a masterpiece, but doesn't even come close in this form.'[3])

Despite their technological wizardry, the Japanese were given little opportunity to bootleg visiting rock artists, and when they did the results were usually unimpressive – possibly because the economics of touring Japan required bands to play cavernous acoustical graveyards like Tokyo's Budokan Hall. The usual trading fare of American and European collectors eluded them. There were few serious tape-traders in Japan, and many Americans and Europeans were distrustful of Japanese collectors. Yet the market for commercial bootlegs in Japan was out of all proportion to the number of worthwhile titles its own producers could provide.

Mrs Toad: The [Japanese] market we never even knew existed until we met the Byrdman [and] he got this coffee table and said, 'If that is the world, everything is Japan except for this little tiny corner and that's the rest of the world' . . . The Byrdman could make 1,000 and sell 900 to [the Japanese] . . . they [also] took an awful lot of the Toasted-Condor stuff.[4]

While the Europeans were too busy exploiting a buoyant home-market, the Americans found the Japanese to be generous payers and the Japanese bootleg business neatly divided between just a handful of wholesalers. So it was that Japan quickly became *the* major market, not just for small, limited pressings of famous bootlegs but for the full gamut of American CDs. And after Toasted's demise, the void was quickly filled by that most notable of American CD manufacturers, Scorpio.

What the Japanese were able to do, and the Europeans shied away from, was produce subtly pirated alternative versions of legitimate CDs. If ABKCO didn't want to put out the correct UK versions of the early Stones albums, Japanese pirates would oblige. Not only could these be sold legitimately in Japan, they were also hard to identify as illegal product and so tended to pass through customs with relative ease – that is until some overly ambitious Japanese producer came up with a version of *Sergeant Pepper* (to celebrate its 25th anniversary) that featured not just a mono version of the album but an entire bonus CD of outtakes (largely multiple versions of 'Strawberry Fields Forever'). Even the Japanese authorities realized that this was not a legitimate export, and the bulk of copies leaving the country were confiscated.

That the Japanese bootleg market was kept buoyant in the early years of CDs – despite some very questionable product – was largely due to the regular publication of *Gold Wax*, a Japanese magazine that included complete track listings, some sort of quality rating (generally inaccurate) and some brief reviews in Japanese. This magazine, which unlike *Hot Wacks* doubled as a catalogue, illustrated the fact that by 1990 the manufacture of bootlegs had shifted almost entirely to Europe. The American manufacturers were dicing with some very strict copyright laws and extra-vigilant customs officers, and the Japanese were obliged to begin buying the bulk of their supplies from European labels.

And yet it was still from America that most of the pressure was coming for copyright reform, not just in Japan but in the entire Far East. Of course, the traditional hotbed of piracy in the American media's eye had always been the Far East. The popular perception of Taiwan, Korea, Singapore and Japan as magpies of technology was founded on a long tradition of non-existent copyright protection for foreign innovations or products. Even in Japan,

the second largest music-carrier market in the world and home of
Sony, TDK, Maxell and JVC, copyright protection for foreign
works was a long time coming.

This allowed not only a considerable amount of 'legitimate piracy'
to continue well into the eighties, but also its inevitable bootleg
tentacles. With the increasing intervention of foreign companies in
Japan – the result of a relaxation of government rules on foreign
ownership – pressure mounted for a more satisfactory demarcation
date for protection of foreign works, though it took until 1991 for
the laws to change, by which time Japan had one of the most
thriving bootleg CD markets in the world. Under the revised
legislation, which took effect on 1 January 1992, the period of
protection for foreign recordings, previously only thirty years, was
extended to the same period afforded Japanese artists – fifty years.
More importantly, the law now offered protection to all non-
Japanese recordings made after 1968. For the first time, a major
new copyright revision was made retroactively. This ten-year
'backtracking' covered the bulk of rock music that a Japanese
consumer might wish to buy.

At the same time as the copyright law was amended, foreign
rights-owners were granted 'protection' against CD rental in Japan.
CD rental, before this change, had been a thriving business in
Japan. The number of stores renting CDs had expanded from
1,910 to 6,213 between 1984 and 1989. Despite the fact that these
stores paid an annual rental royalty of $2 per CD, the international
companies felt that this open invitation to home copying was
dramatically eroding sales.

The absurdity of the 'home taping is killing music' argument
was beautifully illustrated by the figures for the first half of 1993,
the first figures available after the removal of foreign repertoire
from CD rental stores, which showed a 1 per cent decline in CD
production on the same period in 1992 and sales of international
repertoire growing by a mere 5 per cent. So much for the illusion
that all these would-be renters would now spend their hard-earned
yen buying CDs!

The 1968 demarcation date for foreign works was absolute (at least until another piece of retroactive legislation pushes it back again). A window of opportunity for sixties rock remained. Mono versions of The Beatles' *Help, Rubber Soul, Revolver, Sergeant Pepper* and *The White Album*, all taken from commercial reel-to-reel tapes sold at the time, are freely available in Japan, as are stereo/mono CD copies of original American-only Beatles albums like *Yesterday and Today, VI* and *Meet The Beatles*.

Meanwhile, the genuine bootleg market continues to thrive in Japan. Clearly the customs authorities are not unduly determined to scrutinize foreign titles arriving from Far Eastern plants. Indeed Japan itself, with its surfeit of CD plants but a stagnant CD market, is susceptible to CD bootlegging (though most Japanese bootleggers prefer to deal with the more *laissez-faire* Taiwanese or Korean manufacturers). In one remarkable coup, a Japanese bootlegger managed to have a show given by Coverdale/Page in Tokyo on 12 December 1993 on the streets of Tokyo by 28 December.

Elsewhere in the Far East, purer forms of piracy have been the real target of IFPI's increasingly economic threats. The IFPI are now able to give their local anti-piracy units some legal teeth, thanks to the far more worrying expansion of computer software piracy. Because of this, both the EC and the American government have been ready to apply a little judicious economic pressure on the notoriously piratical countries of the Pacific Rim. America's primary weapon has been a form of trade sanction, the 'Special 301', which it recently threatened to use against Taiwan and Korea unless both countries showed a revised attitude when it came to protecting foreign works and copyrights. Such economic muscle is hard to resist. In 1992 Taiwan signed a Memorandum of Understanding with the United States agreeing to enforce its copyright laws and take action to eliminate the production and export of pirate CDs, just one month after the Special 301 had been imposed.

Yet the Taiwanese have proved most obstinate privateers, not because of a lack of will on the part of the government but because of the sheer surfeit of CD plants. The entrepreneurial spirit of the owners of these plants has remained at odds with the IFPI's increasingly wide definition of piracy. By 1990 Taiwan had some eight independent CD factories with a total annual capacity of 80 million units. By the end of 1992 domestic sales had only just nudged above 10 million units a year. The remaining seven eighths of capacity can only be taken up by exporting, legally or illegally. By 1992 four of the eight plants were in the process of obtaining export-licence approval from the IFPI, a trade organization that had seemingly taken on the authority of a government agency. Three of the four recalcitrant Taiwanese plants were apparently 'successfully raided and individuals have been, or will soon be, charged'.

The Yih Chang Laser Inc. company bore the main brunt of the raids, being hit first in 1991, when four of its employees were arrested. Seemingly unperturbed by custodial sentences for all four, the Yih Chang Laser plant was again raided in February 1993, and on this occasion 3,900 units of a compilation called *American Old-Style Love Songs* were seized, together with seven CD master stamps. At the same time, the authorities raided the Vic Tech factory and the Tu Tun distribution company, which specialized in pirating 'popular Chinese-language artists'. The proprietor of Tu Tun, like several other Taiwanese pirates, decided to move his operation to mainland China.

For the Taiwanese, bootleg CDs will always represent a small part of their business, though they are easy enough to lose in the shuffle of pirate and counterfeit items shipped to the Middle East and South East Asia. Despite the fact that under a 1992 copyright amendment foreign repertoire is at last granted protection under local law, Taiwan has yet to ratify any of the four major international copyright conventions: Berne, Rome, UCC or Geneva.

In the early years of the protection-gap, Korea was far more prone than Taiwan to exporting CDs of dubious legality to Europe and America, though according to the IFPI's figures only 292,000 units of pirated sound-carriers were exported from Korea in 1992, compared with 9.5 million units of legitimate product (though some protection-gap titles may well be part of the legitimate figures). The International Intellectual Property Alliance of the US (!) had previously accused Korea of registering licences to manufacture 'foreign repertoire' without checking on the legality of the licences. The Korean authorities, threatened with preliminary action under 'Special 301', agreed to examine the process by which production licences were issued and to consult with the IFPI office before issuing licences.

This was a remarkable situation, since the IFPI had a very obvious motive for refusing licences to live-performance CDs being exported to, say, Italy. As a trade organization, it is hardly likely to exercise its new-found powers with a due sense of responsibility – even if it can establish what is and what is not an illegal product in Italy (or Hungary or Australia or Japan).

The new licensing agreement in Korea, which gave the IFPI's local body, the Korean Phonographic Association, the responsibility for checking the legality of all licensing agreements for international repertoire, has had one immediate effect on bootleg product. Any Korean-manufactured 'bootlegs' were now required to be shipped 'copyright paid' (meaning that 'mechanicals' were charged by the plant at source and passed on directly to the respective collection agencies). On the other hand, when items were shipped to a local holding company then no such clearance was required. Though new copyright legislation is pending in Korea, there is still no retroactive protection for foreign 'works' created before October 1987. The possibilities for abuse of copyright remain.

While the US has been applying a little clout in Taiwan and Korea, the EC has taken parallel action against Indonesia and Thailand. Like the US, Europe has a system of preferences in its foreign trade and has been able to threaten to downgrade these countries should they not show a willingness to offer improved copyright protection. In fact, Indonesia had radically improved copyright protection as far back as 1988, a situation that the local IFPI considered one of its greatest triumphs.

Giouw Jui Chian [IFPI]: We have never seen a campaign to eradicate piracy as swift as that witnessed in Indonesia, where music pirates virtually monopolized Western repertoire. That situation was overturned literally in less than a week after Indonesia extended copyright protection to foreign works in mid 1988.[5]

Ultimately the GATT treaty, signed by all these countries, may yet prove the most effective form of bullying. It has, after all, committed all these Far Eastern economies to a very western form of copyright protection. Whether the locals will now display any greater respect for property rights is something legislation alone is unlikely to reveal.

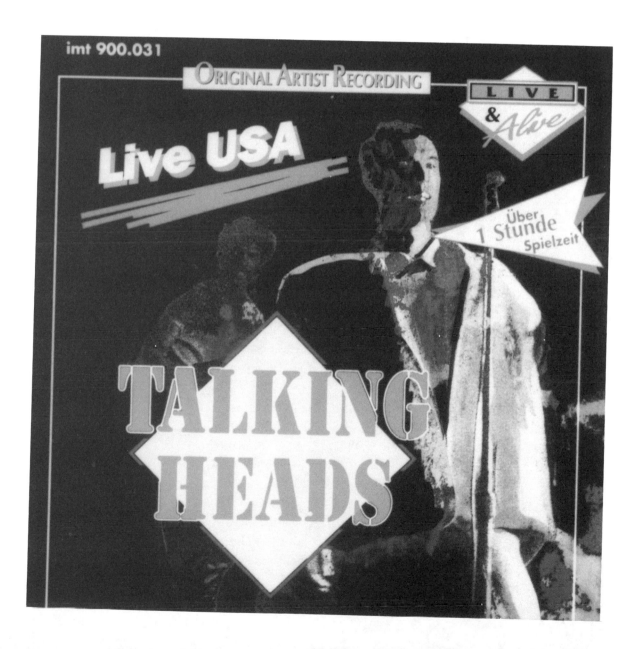

imt 900.031

ORIGINAL ARTIST RECORDING

LIVE & Alive

Live USA

Über 1 Stunde Spielzeit

TALKING HEADS

The Byrdman: The number of plants was still under control in the early days, but now I think those machines are in the third-world countries and so the cat is out of the bag, and [bootleg] CDs will always be made from this point on ... There'll always be some weird country that doesn't have copyright laws that you could get a machine into or something ... It's probably one of the lesser problems facing the world at this point.[1]

Europe's protection gap was creating a new type of consumer for live-performance CDs. Bootleg consumers had always tended to be highly informed about the music they were interested in. Regular buyers knew which bootleg labels were likely to put out something worthwhile. They could also tell who was producing a CD by the artwork and label design, even if there was no giveaway moniker to identify the release. The quality of the artwork and the coherence of a collection were often as important to these punters as the sound quality of the CD.

The new consumers of protection-gap CDs were of a different disposition altogether. They were often looking for a souvenir of a tour attended recently – hence the spate of titles by bands like Simply Red, Dire Straits and Depeche Mode, outfits who would not fit easily into the rock aesthetic that had driven most vinyl bootleg production. They were looking for live, but hopefully identikit, versions of songs they knew well. The arcane science of hunting down that one unique performance of some off-the-wall cover was lost on them.

Few underground CDs crossed the border separating the bootleg-in-spirit from these excuses for product. A new live title by REM (like KTS's *The Trouble With Michael*, a DAT audience tape of a secret gig performing the *Automatic for the People* songs in Atlanta, Georgia) or a particularly sterling U2 source-tape, might appeal to both types of underground consumer, but generally it was 'never the twain'. Labels became known to punters by their aesthetic, or lack thereof. Protection-gap CDs remained largely confined to Europe, where they could still find a market. Genuine bootlegs were usually distributed to the UK, the US and Japan, where the underground circuits were still intact and operational, as well as some of the larger European record fairs. If these items were selling fewer numbers, they were also still commanding a premium price.

A major problem for the IFPI was that there was so much protection-gap material passing around the world that it was difficult to recognize something that was a pure bootleg – wherever manufactured, whatever its source. After all, the EC was not alone in having its protection gaps. They were springing up all over the world, in Eastern Europe, in the Far East (particularly Japan), even in Australia.

Martin Schaefer [IFPI]: Now that the so-called legal bootlegs have found their way into regular outlets, it becomes increasingly difficult to prevent illegal bootlegs entering with them. The protection-gap bootlegs have indirectly extended the retail base for illegal bootlegs.[2]

The record industry was used to getting things its own way. In the past, most legal authorities had taken their word that what they said was illegal really was so. Several unsuccessful prosecutions of protection-gap labels and a certain hostility to what were seen to be entirely money-motivated organizations were now tainting their efforts in the European courts. In at least two instances, 'bootleggers' were able to secure injunctions restraining major labels and the IFPI from designating their product as 'pirate', though this didn't stop spokesmen for the IFPI referring to these releases as bootlegs to the press, or blurring the line between protection-gap CDs and those aimed at a more specialist market.

Edward Will [IFPI]: I don't care to discriminate between the two types of bootleg product ... because both kinds are the result of an illegal act: unauthorized recording, an activity specifically prohibited in the warning on the back of all concert tickets ... It is rubbish when the bootleggers say their product has no impact on regular sales. Some bootleg CDs sell to the dealer for as little as 6 marks [$4.30], and they can sell in quantities up to 100,000.[3]

Of course, the real cowboys were not content with the mark-ups they could make on protection-gap titles. They wanted to avoid paying any mechanicals at all and still be legitimately distributed. In December 1992, Italian police seized a truck loaded with 45,000 CDs and some 200,000 SIAE stickers. The cargo was apparently en route from Czechoslovakia. The problem of Eastern European pirate goods crossing into the EC had increased tenfold with the collapse of the Iron Curtain. Though there were few independent CD pressing plants in Eastern Europe, those few remained largely unregulated. They were also desperately in need of hard currency and, like many plants around the world, were running at well below capacity. As a deposition by a CD plant to a parliamentary sub-committee recently observed:

There has been for the last five years a glut of CD manufacturing in almost every developed country in the world, with supply always exceeding demand, and factories have been desperate to fill their plants at any price. Consequently there has, in my experience, hardly been a plant that has boasted of the profits it has made in CD manufacturing. To break even a plant operating at a normal 60 per cent capacity throughout the year (and this is a seasonal business with ups and downs) needs to be charging £1.50 per disc manufactured – a price not obtained by any of the plants since 1986.[4]

The reason the bulk of independent plants around the world were functioning at well below capacity was that the predicted explosion in CD ownership had simply not happened. Sure, the CD market had continued to expand, but not explode. The reason: the prohibitive price of CDs themselves. With plants desperate for business, just like the vinyl pressing plants of LA in the seventies and eighties, some were prepared to turn a blind eye to questionable product. If pressure was brought to bear on one particularly injudicious plant, whether in the Far East or Europe, then the underground producers would simply move on.

Rinaldo Tagliabue: I don't know if the record labels [apply any pressure] to CD factories, but I'm guessing they do. We expect [any given] record plant to refuse our production order, but there are now so many independent plants in Italy and Europe that this would not create a real problem for us.[5]

Mr Toad: There is no way to stop it. The plants are like every other industry, they wanna make money and you've got to keep these plants running twenty-four hours a day if you're going to make the best out of your equipment, your machinery and your employees, and they will make anything that anyone brings along. Yes, they're supposed to say, 'Do you have the rights to this music?' But at the end of the day, when you cough up the money and they export it, it's the problem of another country.[6]

The IFPI were also at pains to stop 'legitimate' titles illegally exported (with a little wholly illegal trade thrown in for good measure). If a Korean plant was making two Dylan bootleg CDs, one called *Friend to the Martyr*, the other *Going to Arlington*, it would have no idea which was the collection of studio outtakes from 1983 (the former) and which a legitimate German import of a live show from 1992 (the latter). In most cases, CD manufacture was entirely separate from artwork and design, so the pressing plant rarely knew what they were actually making, just that it was a Bob Dylan title for export to the EC.

Ian Haffey [IFPI]: It's difficult to prove that it's been done knowingly. 'Knowingly' is a term that doesn't exist in the laws of most [of these] countries.[7]

The irony of the protection gap was that it came at a time when various EC bodies were looking at ways of extending existing copyright. In 1987, a European Commission Green Paper on copyright within the EC seemed to take as its underlying philosophy what one critic called, 'a concern for copyright protection excluding the author'. At the centre of this Green Paper was the manufacturer-producer, not the author; the work was now 'a commodity to be exploited, rather than an intellectual creation'. Yet this was exactly what the protection-gap labels had been doing, exploiting a commodity and paying appropriate 'mechanicals' into the bargain.

One of the main areas that the Green Paper had assigned itself to consider was 'the excessive restrictive effects of copyright protection on legitimate competition in certain industrial activities'. One of its tasks was to come up with proposals to 'avoid copyright monopolies unduly broad in scope and lengthy in duration'.[8] It could be argued that the protection-gap labels were providing some long overdue competition in an area where copyright monopolies were certainly 'broad in scope' (i.e. covering all recordings of any given artist, whether or not they had been financed by his or her label) and 'lengthy in duration' (protection for sound recordings being fifty years in most EC countries).

Yet despite the laudable aims that the Green Paper took upon itself, the powers that be were looking to extend the 'restrictive effects of copyright', not curtail them. The European Commission was proposing not only an extension of copyright protection, but also introducing an EC-wide tape levy, against the wishes of at least four EC member states, and despite the failure to establish any moral foundation for this tax.

The inexorable process of copyright extension beyond the ken of authors into the Byzantine maze of 'neighbouring rights' was destined to continue. Ever since the Rome Convention of 1961, the whole direction of copyright reform has involved extending the rights of the manufacturer-producers, often at the expense of the artist. In 1988, Britain produced its most radical reform of copyright laws this century with a new Copyright, Designs and Patent Act. In it the First Copyright Owner was no longer the artist *per se* but rather anyone 'responsible for making arrangements for a recording to be made'. The act also provided, for the first time, criminal penalties for acts of piracy, previously deemed an entirely civil matter.

In order for a criminal act to be perpetrated, the offender needs to commit what is termed 'a primary infringement', primary infringers being 'those who a) themselves commit an infringing act [i.e. manufacture themselves]; or b) authorize another to commit an infringing act'. (Secondary infringers are broadly speaking, 'those who do not themselves infringe or authorize others to infringe but who deal commercially with infringing copies or articles or premises to be used for infringement [i.e. retailers] ... When a person imports infringing copies into the UK, otherwise than for private and domestic use, there is a liability for secondary infringement. As always with secondary infringement the infringer must know or have reason to believe that the copy is an infringing one.'9)

Britain's bootleggers had long abandoned manufacturing their titles in their homeland. The legal risks had always been too great and it was more straightforward to manufacture in Italy or Germany than risk running foul of the law. With the possible exception of a handful of live recordings since the beginning of 1993 which have made it on to bootleggers' stalls in three weeks or less – including a highly successful double-CD of Dylan's Hammersmith 1993 residency called *Apollo Landing* – there was little evidence that bootleg CDs were being manufactured in the UK. Since the 1988 Act considered the importation of 'infringing copies' as a secondary (i.e. wholly civil) infringement, there was little increased risk to bootleggers, even those like Mr Toad who were, shall we say, causing infringing items to be made. The evidence necessary to establish a primary infringement is always likely to elude the BPI, even when it finally establishes that a particular live CD is an infringing item.

The 1988 Copyright Act also gave the British consumer two important rights not previously tested in law. One was the right to import a single copy of any 'infringing item' for one's own personal use. Thus the situation that had occurred in America, where private collectors were being harassed by the authorities, could not happen in the UK. The second was a carefully worded right to record live performances, again for 'private or personal purposes'. In an article in the *Guardian* at the time of the Act, the scope of this right was rather exaggerated: 'From August 1 ... it will become legal to record musical performances for private or personal purposes without the permission of the musicians, the songwriters or whomever has been assigned these rights.'[10] In fact, the right to record live shows was certainly not absolute. The essential restraint remained the contract entered into when a concert ticket is purchased, which often explicitly prohibits any recordings of the performance:

> The contract's basic elements are the ticket itself and any conditions printed on it ... For a theatre-goer to be bound by such conditions, he must either have prior knowledge of the conditions, or they must be brought to his attention when he buys the ticket. Any subsequent notice, whether in the theatre or in the programme, is ineffective because the contract dates from the moment of ticket purchase.[11]

Even in a situation where a member of an audience is caught taping a show when strictly prohibited, the offence remains purely a civil one and the perpetrator is in no way obliged to hand over his (presumably incomplete) tape or give his name, though he could, of course, be legally (and quite probably forcefully) ejected from the venue. In reality there are usually so many people taping major shows with top-notch equipment that security can never hope to catch every one of these covert tapers.

At least the artist's rights were extended in one important way by the 1988 copyright revision. The Act introduced into UK law the concept of Moral Rights, thus complying with Britain's International Treaty Obligations (i.e. Berne). The rights now recognized included the author's right 'to have paternity (i.e. authorship) in the work properly acknowledged' and the right 'to maintain the integrity of the work'.

Britain had previously remained firmly in the Anglo-Saxon legislative tradition, in which:

the tendency has been for authors' rights to be regarded as equal to those of others involved in the production of intellectual property. This approach has been strengthened by technological and commercial changes in the film and music industries which are dominated by the financial resources of the 'producers' the studios and record companies. From the viewpoint of these organizations, the provision of moral rights to authors is often regarded as a threat to the full commercial exploitation of the work.[12]

The other EC member states, with the exception of the Netherlands and Eire, had traditionally based their copyright laws on more Gallic notions, and 'In the *droit d'auteur* tradition ... the position of an author as creator of works is prior to that of any other rights owner.'[13] With Britain's recognition of moral rights, the only G7 country to be more concerned with the full 'commercial exploitation of the work' than the author's rights was the USA, by far the most important economy to remain a non-signatory to the Rome Convention.

The irony is that the 'moral rights' of an author have recently become a useful method of attacking protection-gap outfits in the European courts. One test case involved an American artist in cahoots with an American label. With Warner *v.* Imtrat, Warners were seeking $180,000 in damages on the grounds of infringement of 'moral rights' for a live Prince CD released by Imtrat on the Live & Alive label. Since all countries in the EC were bound by the Berne Convention, they were all bound by article six of the Paris text of the convention, which stated that 'the author shall have the right to ... object to any distortion, mutilation or other modification of, or other derogatory action in relation to, the said work, which would be prejudicial to his honour or reputation.'[14]

The Live & Alive CD in question was certainly an insult to Prince's work, which was always rigorously supervised and approved by the artist himself. Even the majority of Prince bootleg

CDs – many Prince CDs, being studio recordings, are 'pure' bootlegs – came in ornate covers with beautifully designed booklets and picture-disc CDs (notably two rather elegant boxed-sets *Jewel Box I and II*). Yet it was Warners – the label that had refused to release Prince's triple-album *Camille* set, forcing him to edit it down to a double LP, *Sign of the Times* – who were taking this action.

Imtrat had little defence. Their artwork was universally appalling – equally mutilated representations of Bruce Springsteen, Talking Heads and others graced these terminally tacky Live & Alive releases, while their source information was vague to the point of obtuse. The case was decided in Warners' favour by a lower court in Hamburg and is awaiting appeal to the Supreme Federal Court, It seems inconceivable that Imtrat can win their case, or survive a more determined use of 'moral rights' by the other artists they have exploited.

In fact, Imtrat has become the IFPI's primary target in their ongoing battle with Europe's protection-gap merchants. If Swingin' Pig and Great Dane always sold their CDs at full price, and rarely sold more than 5,000 of each title, Imtrat were looking to sell tens of thousands of their titles, dumping them on the market at ludicrously low prices (around $6 retail), wholesaling them across Europe through newsagents, supermarkets and even corner shops.

Another test case involving Imtrat proved to be an even more important victory for legitimate record companies. *Phil Collins Live USA*, a 1983 concert, was the offending item this time around. The case, brought by Phil Collins and Warners together, was founded on the argument that, under Article Seven of the Treaty of Rome, any legal protection offered to a national in their own country must also be provided to any other citizen of an EC member-state. The anomaly in German law, that allowed absolute protection against unauthorized live-performance CDs of a German artist but only protected foreign artists for performances in Germany, seemed to contravene this clause of the EC's founding treaty.

Warner Music (Germany) first brought their action in a Munich court in March 1992. The Munich court adjourned the case, requesting a ruling from the European Court of Justice. It took until 20 October 1993 for the Luxemburg-based court to hand down its ruling, but, predictably, it judged in favour of Warners and Phil Collins. All EC artists were entitled to the same copyright protection in Germany as already given to German performers, with immediate effect. With the ruling, the constraints on protection-gap titles tightened considerably. Even an American artist recorded in America could be illegal under this new judgement if one of the musicians was European (so a 1992 Dylan CD was now illegal because it featured English drummer Ian Wallace). Berhand Roessle, managing director of In-Akustik and distributor of Living Legend, reflected a general feeling that the goldrush might now be over in a statement to *Billboard*:

We had been anticipating this decision, so we stopped distributing repertoire by European artists some time ago. I can't say at present whether we will continue to handle protection-gap repertoire by US artists, but it is possible that we will cease to distribute this product altogether.[15]

Oh Boy! had already shut down shop. Within weeks of the judgement, Flashback were seeking to dump much of their stock at the larger English record fairs. The other German labels were also severely affected by the judgement, which effectively ruled out any product by The Stones, The Beatles or Led Zeppelin, as well as U2, whose recent 'Zooropa' tour had been so heavily targeted. Also, two Supreme Court judgements, in cases based on the same legal premise, were pending against Perfect Beat and seemed destined to go against them.

The judgement also gave GEMA authority to begin refusing mechanical licences to some of these quasi-legitimate labels. For some time GEMA had been trying to establish a way of refusing a licence without breaching Articles 11 and 61 of German copyright law, which obliged it to license an unprotected performance.

They were already in discussions with the German IFPI group to see if it could refuse to license a recording of an American artist on the grounds that it may be prejudicial to the interests of the composer. Indeed, in December 1992 GEMA had actually ordered a company that was pirating (not bootlegging) early Beatles studio recordings to cease manufacture and distribution of these recordings on the grounds that they infringed the rights of the authors of the repertoire – John Lennon and Paul McCartney.

Of course, a CD could still slip through the net, even if GEMA refused it a licence. As has already been observed, the authorities often lacked the expertise to definitively establish whether mechanical rights had been paid, particularly if the CD had been imported. Parallel imports were an inevitable consequence of the lowering of trade barriers in Europe (though legitimate record companies circumvented one of the more worrying aspects of this practice by refusing British wholesalers accounts with continental sister-companies). The protection-gap labels had no such cartel.

The Collins judgement may have closed one onerous protection gap, but the decision had little bearing on the second largest underground CD market in Europe. All manufacturers of live recordings who paid the necessary royalties through SIAE were operating within Italy's legal framework. Yet the screws were even being applied in this most *laissez-faire* of EC economies. As *ICE* reported in April 1992:

Serious pressure is building for the first time from the official record companies to change [the] laws that make live CDs possible. The major labels are beginning to convince lawmakers that the abundance of live CDs has cut significantly into their overall sales, and they want something done about it . . . The source predicts that the manufacture of live CDs in Italy may be curtailed significantly by the end of the year.[16]

The prediction proved premature. Great Dane, KTS and Red Phantom continued to get their releases past SIAE, the latter two concentrating on artists that perhaps SIAE were not aware generated such considerable sales – bands like Nirvana, Pearl Jam and

Soundgarden, and other stalwarts of the annual 'Lollapalooza' jamborees.

It seemed that the only real way to close this most stubborn of protection gaps was a wholesale revision of EC copyright law. Not surprisingly, this was what the European Commission had in mind when submitting proposals for the 'Harmonization of the term of protection of copyright and neighbouring rights' to the European Parliament in January 1992. This draft directive attempted to fix a common level of protection at the highest set by a member state: i.e. seventy years after death for authors, and fifty years after 'first publication' for record companies and performers.

The proposals left unresolved the question of whether to reimpose protection for recordings that had already fallen into the 'public domain' in countries like the Low Countries and Luxemburg. According to IFPI legal advisor Alessandra Silvestro, 'Sound recordings published before 1 January 1993 and whose term of protection granted at national level expired before 31 December 1994 will remain in the public domain in that country, even if the term of protection for the same sound recording still runs in another EC country.'[17]

The European Commission was also looking to gain universal approval for an EC-wide blank-tape levy that would raise the obscene sum of $600 million a year, of which the main European 'producers' stood to carve up around $250 million between themselves. Thankfully, the UK managed to cajole Ireland, Italy and Luxemburg into opposing the levy at the starting post, though recent history has shown that the record industry is unlikely to abandon attempts to impose this uniform levy. Such a levy would not only apply to EC countries currently resistant to the so-called principle, but would involve a substantial hike in the current levy set in major markets like Germany (where the levy is a mere 2 per cent on software, 3 per cent on hardware).

Aside from the tape-levy, it did look as if the basic contents of the Commission's draft would be adopted. However, when the agreement was redrafted, minus the contentious tape-levy issue, there was a new intent to apply copyright protection retroactively to existing recordings. By June 1993 the IFPI was hoping for an EC-wide copyright harmonization that would make sound recordings 'enjoy revived protection in those territories which currently have protection for less than fifty years and gain protection where no protection currently exists.'[18]

This reversion threatens to become a logistical nightmare for all publishers and record companies with 'public domain' repertoires that would go back into copyright. Yet in July 1993 the council of EC ministers agreed a draft directive for copyright harmonization, which included retroactive protection for 'public domain' material. Four countries voted against the proposed harmonization – Eire, Portugal, Luxemburg and the Netherlands. The Dutch, who had only recently formulated their own 'neighbouring rights' legislation, were the most intransigent in their opposition, arguing that they saw no reason why an author's protection should be extended, as Germany was the only EC country to provide protection for seventy years after an author's death.

Should such legislation pass its final hurdle, it will almost certainly require a revision of the anomalous Italian position regarding live performances, particularly when taken in tandem with the marvellously named 'Directive on Certain Rights related to Copyright in the field of Intellectual Property'. This directive, parts of which were adopted by the EC's Council of Ministers on 19 November 1992, included a provision allowing performers and broadcasters the right to authorize or prohibit the 'fixation' of their performances and/or broadcasts.

The copyright noose is not only being tightened in the EC. Concurrent with all these EC directives was a draft agreement on Trade-Related Aspects of Intellectual Property Rights (TRIPS), formulated to be part of the GATT treaty provisions. TRIPS sought to bind all 107 member countries of GATT to the following:

(i) all works having a minimum term of protection of fifty years;

(ii) record companies being given full rights to authorize or prohibit the reproduction of sound recordings;

(iii) copyright and other rights holders being able to apply for customs personnel to detain imports suspected of being illegal. Governments must enable rights holders to inspect these goods.[19]

The signing of the GATT treaty by the 107 countries in December 1993 committed signatories to a timetable within which these reforms must be in place (though the US managed to insert a clause in TRIPS that allowed countries to exempt themselves from Article 6, the 'moral rights' clause, of the Berne Convention).

What all these reforms once again marked was the gradual passage of rights from author to 'producer'. TRIPS is not really about stopping performance CDs but about ensuring that the rights and masters remain with the record label long after the artist (not the record company) has paid for all the attendant costs of recording. As Simply Red's manager told the National Heritage Committee:

Elliot Rashman: An artist pays for everything. He makes a 25 per cent contribution to the manufacturing and packaging deduction costs, he pays for the [record] producer and he pays for the recording completely. And it is all recoupable. [Yet] the masters and the copyright are owned by the record company until fifty years [hence] ... The whole structure and how an artist is exploited by a record company is what is wrong.[20]

The European-wide fifty-year protection term and concomitant extensions of copyright in the Far East are about ensuring that a company like EMI continues to benefit from Beatles recordings – which even in the eighties constituted 3–4 per cent of EMI's total annual sales – as late as 2019. As one critic of the fifty-year term has written, 'the lengthy terms of protection given to neighbouring rights seem unduly long, since the rationale for protection is based not on an author's human right, but on the need to protect the capital invested in the work.'[21]

The IFPI has never actually addressed the issue of why its members are entitled to prohibit live recordings made more than twenty years ago, or been called on to explain the difference between Sony releasing The Beatles' *Live at the Star Club, Hamburg* without Capitol and/or The Beatles' permission (as they did recently, before legal action was taken to stop them) and a protection-gap label in Italy doing the same.

Noel Forth [managing director of an Australian protection-gap label]: The Beatles sued Sony for putting out what they said was a bootleg tape. [The managing director of Sony Australia] said by definition a bootleg is a recording made in secret, without the knowledge of the band, and released without the authorization of the artist or the record company. Well, 'King Size' Taylor recorded [the Hamburg tape]. The Beatles never knew it was happening. He claimed in court, when they tried to stop its release in the late seventies, that he'd given them a crate of booze. They couldn't remember getting a crate of booze. That was total nonsense. He later revealed that in fact he didn't ask them at all. Therefore, according to Mr Sony himself, Sony themselves are bootleggers because they put out a recording which was recorded without the authorization of the band and released without the authorization of the band or record company. So here they are pointing the finger but when they can make money out of a tape that the band doesn't approve of they [chose to] put it out.[22]

While European bureaucrats attempted to impose a modicum of logic on copyrights in the EC, the disintegration of the Iron Curtain has threatened to make the closing of Germany's protection-gap an irrelevance. The need for hard currency and a small and shrinking home market for high-tech media like CD has meant that the pressing plants in Eastern Europe have to export to survive. In many instances what they have been exporting has been of questionable legality, though straight piracy has always generated the largest returns. Poland, in particular, has been repeatedly re-exporting pirate CDs to Germany. According to the IFPI, pirate copies of *Tubular Bells II* were on sale in Germany two days after release, an astonishing turn-around time unless the plant had access to an advance copy. Likewise, when the SIAE seized 150,000 CDs bound for Italy from Czechoslovakia in December 1992, the items were all counterfeit copies of albums by Madonna, Zucchero, and so on.

It seems surprising, given the lack of supervision and the ambiguous copyright situation in Eastern Europe, that the bootleggers have not exploited the new confusion more enthusiastically. Save for Yellow Dog's early Hungarian connection, the protection-gappers have largely avoided Eastern European plants. Possibly, horror stories of consignments being hijacked or going astray on their way to the West had dissuaded them.

Certainly, before 1993, Poland seemed to offer the most lax of all European copyright structures. Despite amending the law in 1975, authors' works were protected for only twenty-five years after death, and performers and sound recordings were not protected at all. Romania also had a hole in its laws that bootleggers might have been able to drive a truck of CDs through. Though recordings were protected for fifty years after publication, performances were not protected at all, and Romania was not a signatory to the Rome Convention (Michael Jackson attempted to take action in 1992 against four separate German releases of a concert he had given in Romania, seemingly unaware of this fact). Hungary and Bulgaria also offered their own versions of a protection gap, giving protection to sound recordings for only twenty and twenty-five years respectively.

Obviously, if the IFPI was to succeed in closing Europe's copyright loopholes, it needed to pressure Eastern European states into revising their copyright laws in tandem with EC directives. Yet given the volatile situation in Eastern Europe, the IFPI was not really in a position to use the bullying tactics so successful in the Far East. Threatening trade sanctions against economies already brittle from the transition to capitalist ways would only prove counter-productive.

Of the four East European countries most susceptible to piracy, only Hungary and Bulgaria had even begun the process of making copyright revisions in 1992–3, as the rest of Europe turned to a new copyrighted sunrise. In August 1993 Bulgaria brought in a new copyright law, though protection for foreign owners of neighbouring rights was limited at best. While performers were to receive protection for performances given in Bulgaria – and such events were few and far between – producers of sound recordings were required to be resident in Bulgaria or have their headquarters there in order to be protected. The new law was a smart form of economic blackmail. Bulgaria also remained outside the Rome Convention, so its reciprocal obligations were limited at best.

In Hungary, which was more geared up for CD production than most of its neighbours, a more 'western' type of copyright reform was under consideration. However, the hoped-for extension of protection for sound recordings from twenty to fifty years had only reached the proposal stage by the spring of 1993. When a change finally came in May 1994, the extended protection was not applied retrospectively. It covered only future recordings and those still protected when the amendment comes into force. Recordings made before May 1974 will remain in the public domain.

Meanwhile the scale of piracy in Poland remains out of all proportion to that in any other Eastern European state. According to IFPI figures, of the 70 million album units sold in Poland in 1992, some 90 per cent were 'unauthorized product'. This was a market almost entirely driven by cassette sales, with the average cassette retailing for little more than a dollar (compared with an average CD price of over $11).

Though Poland continued to grant no neighbouring rights, the IFPI did make one significant inroad. As of 1993, the release of new product in Poland without a licence is treated as a trademark infringement and fraud. As a result of this, the IFPI, in cooperation with the Polish police, have been able to raid several suspected pirates. However, whether protection-gap labels would have any greater problem getting their product licensed in Poland (or Hungary or Bulgaria) than in Italy is a question the IFPI would prefer not to arise.

21 The House That Apple Built

THE UNAUTHORISED RECORDINGS . . .
This live recording and its release, has not been authorised by
MICHAEL JACKSON or his record company.

Michael Jackson
the king of pop (vol. 1)

UNAUTHORISED

LIVE WORLD TOUR 1987

THIS SOUND RECORDING MAY NOT BE OF THE SAME
QUALITY AS AN AUTHORISED RELEASE

Adrian Fitz-Alan [Sony Australia]: Why don't I go down to Madonna when she's playing . . . and take my little Walkman, shove it out there, tape [the show] and put it out on CD and make an absolute bomb myself? There's absolutely nothing to stop me.[1]

While the IFPI focused their anti-piracy activities on Europe and the Pacific Rim, the most prodigious bootleg manufacturer of the early nineties was an Australian, with a long-standing vinyl pedigree. Acting as both a courier – for those bootleggers who needed to circumvent even the quasi-legal protection-gap routes – and a producer of his own titles, 'Captain Cook' was able to pump out an enormous amount of product on Blue Kangaroo and other assorted 'coloured animal' labels.

Though Cook had been absent from the Bootleg Biz since 1987, most of his vinyl contacts had made the switch to CD by the time he re-entered the fray. In a frenzied blitz of bootlegging, Cook was responsible for over 150 titles in little more than a year. Inevitably, he could never churn out a gross of bootlegs in such a short span of time without ruthlessly pillaging the work of others. This did not unduly concern him. He had decided to move in, make his money and move out, to await new opportunities.

Mr Toad: [Captain Cook] copied a lot of [the Byrdman's]. [All] the Flying Discs, the Ghosts, Adam the Eighth . . . Captain Cook made 'em for nothing . . . We saw the bill [for some of his CDs] as part of the shipping paperwork when they were bounced into a bonded warehouse and back again, and it showed that he was charged 85 Yen a disc, 50p. You make 3,000 you get free glass mastering. He was making 'em and buying 'em, the finished discs for 50–60p a disc. He's making the covers for bugger all. The discs were coming in at less than a quid a go, and he was selling them for seventeen dollars. His advantage was, and this belies this myth that you can just put a tape in a Jiffy bag and send it to a CD plant in the Far East, he knew his way around the Far East. He speaks a bit of the language, so he got on all right ... He made 158 CDs and I reckon he made 3,000 of each to get them as cheap as that, so that's about half a million discs he made. They cost him a quid each. But it ended up that [one of the Japanese dealers] was not going to pay him. [He] owed him $300,000 and he was not going to pay him. [He] figured he'd paid him enough at $17 a disc. So [that] certainly slowed [Captain Cook] down. But I think he'd made it anyway.[2]

After legal problems in Australia had halted a lucrative vinyl operation, Cook was smart enough to ensure that all of his seriously dodgy CDs passed through a holding company in one of the Pacific Rim countries least prone to piracy. None of the CDs passed through his antipodean base.

The Australian market for bootlegs in the vinyl era had always been hard to gauge because of its small population base (barely 20 million people) and the insistence of certain American bootleggers that their product was coming out of Australia (honest, guv). However, there was a smattering of genuine Oz product in these years. A Dylan live double from Sydney in 1978 and a classic Lou Reed Sydney 1974 single album, *Blondes Have More Fun* (probably taken from an ABC TV broadcast), were collectors' items outside Australia. Both were rebootlegged by the West Coast fraternity. Also rebootlegged by one LA dementoid was the first Australian bootleg of an Aussie band, *Eureka Birdman*, a crunchy tape of punk harbingers Radio Birdman playing a fond farewell to Sydney's Paddington Town Hall. It sold well enough in Birdman's hometown in the wake of their premature disbandment. Its US counterpart, *Where the Action Is*, though, must qualify as one of the least eagerly awaited items to ever come out of an LA pressing plant.

Though Captain Cook had proved it was possible to make real money manufacturing genuine bootlegs, the bulk of underground releases remained inaccessible to Australian collectors. That is until the summer of 1993, when an Adelaide-based company decided to see if a protection gap similar to the ones uncovered in Europe might exist under Australian law. How Noel Forth and Robert Tansing, the two ostensible founders of Apple House Inc., raised the A$500,000 required to set up their protection-gap CD company remains a mystery, but they soon found a willing cohort in one Gary Turner, manager of Australian Compact Discs (ACD). Frost, ex-drummer with Adelaide's Vertical Hold, had originally worked for ACD but failed to generate any mainstream business for the CD plant and had been discharged. Clearly there was little love lost between ACD and the Australian record industry.

Noel Forth: Australian Compact Discs are actually an Adelaide company, and they set up a A$3 million plant and were doing a lot of local bands. [They] approached all of the major record companies, who completely snubbed them and gave them no work at all. So when I went to them and said, 'Look, I could do this in Taiwan or whatever but I'd rather do it here. Will you match the price?' They said, 'Sure' ... [I made it clear,] 'This product is unauthorized. You might just like to have a look at our catalogue before you commit yourself.' And they said, 'We don't care. Is it legal?' They checked up and they said fine. I said, 'The big companies are not gonna like this.' And they said, 'So! The big companies never gave us any work at all. So why should we care what they think.'[3]

In August 1993, Apple House Music announced plans to issue a substantial catalogue of live recordings by today's top artists, at A$20 each, around ten Australian dollars ($4) lower than the retail price of the premium official CDs. Apple House, like its European counterparts, fully intended to pay songwriting royalties. Sony and Michael Jackson, though, sought an interim injunction to restrain Apple House from launching their catalogue. What Sony accused Apple House of was 'a breach of the Trade Practices Act and South Australian Fair Trading Act for misleading and deceptive conduct' or, in plain English, leading consumers astray by implying that these were 'approved' releases. What was not at issue was the copyright situation. As Sony Music Australia's managing director admitted to *Drum Media*:

There was no copyright infringement alleged by us for the particular Michael Jackson recordings. This is because there is a 'gap' or 'loophole' in the present Copyright Act against the particular recordings being released by Apple House.[4]

In fact, as long as the live performance was recorded before 1 January 1992 – when new laws applied – Apple House were within their rights to issue any live recordings. Nevertheless, in an attempt to be legally fireproof, they sent copies of the CDs they intended for release to the relevant labels, asking them to furnish evidence in any instance where they felt they owned the rights to the recording.

Noel Forth: We sent them through to all the record companies and we asked them, 'Please, if you own the copyright to this recording, let us know, [provide evidence] and we will not issue them. Out of the 155 tapes, they only claimed about half a dozen [one of which was by Queen]. We have a Queen at Wembley concert and there is an EMI album which is live at Wembley. But the one we have is a different date, different show . . . They claimed they owned the [rights] but we knew they were wrong.[5]

Among the 149 tapes for which no claim was made were two Dylan titles, a 1964 show at the New York Philharmonic Hall and a 1966 show at Manchester's Free Trade Hall (aka the legendary Albert Hall bootleg), neither of which was made by some covert taper skulking in his seat, microphone in hand. According to Sony Australia's MD, 'Apple House's recordings are of nowhere near the same quality as an "authorized" release. Anyone can tape a performance or a radio broadcast for minimal cost. We and our artists spend a lot of time and money on providing the best recordings available.'[6] Unfortunately for Mr Handlin, both these Dylan tapes had been made by Columbia itself, for possible live albums. Indeed, as I write, Sony are readying the latter of these two recordings for official release – same tape, same show.

Apple House's Dylan CD was almost certainly just copied direct from Swingin' Pig's *Royal Albert Hall 1966* CD, complete with speed fault (though it still sounds several notches above The

Stones' official 1966 live album, *Got Live if You Want It*). Apple House were certainly not breaking new ground aurally. Their catalogue was actually a fairly miserable selection of previously bootlegged performances, all with nominal titles like *Live World Tour 1985* or *Live in USA 1992*.

No matter. On 18 August 1993, Sony's interlocutory injunction was refused by His Honour Judge Einfeld. Apple House, in a (successful) attempt to deflect Sony's accusations of hoodwinking consumers, had emblazoned in bold type at the bottom of each CD the legend, 'The quality of these sound recordings may not be of the same quality as an authorized release.' Also rammed across the passport-size photo of the artist on each CD cover was the word UNAUTHORIZED, writ large in rubber-stamper fashion. As the judge succinctly observed, it would be an extremely stupid young member of the public who concluded that such a CD was approved by the artist and/or his official label.

When Sony attempted an appeal to the Full Court, events took an even worse turn for them. The three Full Court judges unanimously upheld Judge Einfeld's judgement and Sony and Michael Jackson were ordered to pay Apple House's costs of appeal. Though a final hearing is due to be heard at some point in late summer 1994, Sony know they have little prospect of reversing the earlier judgements. Meanwhile Apple House began to aggressively advertise their CDs in the daily papers, taking upon themselves a mantle of radicalism that does not gel easily with their lack of new source material, stripped-bare packaging and dearth of information on each CD:

Apple House Music is a newly formed Adelaide business which is offering to the Australian buying public unauthorized live concert recordings of some of the world's biggest rock music acts. Although taping and release of recordings of these concerts have not been authorized by the performing artist or record company, they are legal to sell in Australia ... These are not 'bootleg' recordings, as 'bootleg' really means illegal ... The recommended retail price of these CDs is under A$20, which we feel is a more realistic price for CDs. This hopefully will help drive down the price charged by the major record companies who until now have had little or no competition ... We are music fans and we enjoy giving the Australian buying public a chance to buy and hear the excitement of real live performances at a competitive price. All CDs are made in Australia and profits remain in Australia and create jobs for Australians.[7]

However, Apple House had not as yet learnt all the lessons they could have from their European predecessors. As one astute Australian journalist noted, 'Having cracked the legal code for bootleggers, Apple House can expect a rash of imitators selling shoddier products at an even lower price.'[8]

Sure enough, in December one anonymous label shamelessly copied Apple House's versions of famous bootlegs. The copies came with 'Not Authorized' stamped across aquablue covers, and they retailed for ten bucks. Not only were Apple House now embroiled in a price war, but many record retailers were increasingly reluctant to carry their titles for fear of reprisals by the official companies. Though the Trade Practices Act 1974 prohibited anti-competitive conduct, there was little the courts could do to recompense a shop should their promotional supplies dry up or their discretionary 'special discounts' mysteriously disappear. Whatever their original intentions, Apple House were forced to become a modern-day antipodean Bulldog, retailing their titles at five bucks a throw through general-store outlets.

Noel Forth: We had an opportunity there from a large number of bargain-variety store chains to sell enormous quantities at reduced prices – they always come to you with a big order but they want a big reduction in price. It was the culmination of a number of factors – a lot of the smaller stores were only ordering very small quantities and we had to get into a bigger market. Now that we're in there we realize that's where we should have been all along. There were just far too many [record] stores that believed they might lose their supply.[9]

Of course, Apple House's change of tack only made the situation worse for the official companies. At A$20, the Apple House titles were probably still selling primarily to collectors and serious fans. With a A\$5 (£3) retail price, Apple House were highlighting – in very large letters – just what sort of margins the big boys were playing with when they charged A\$30 for a hot new title. Though this Adelaide label – like the vast majority of European protection-gap merchants – has quickly sunk to the level of lowest common denominator with its choice of artists, packaging and titles, the way remains open for any Aussie entrepreneur with higher aesthetic concerns to inhabit the same house that Apple built.

The Byrdman: You're putting a perfect master out on the market. Immediately, the first copy out there is a perfect master. That's not the case with the vinyl. So if you're spending money buying a tape you have to get the return back on the start-up investment, and with titles being so easily copied it presents an extra pressure on marketing boots because you want to try and have a couple of months where you can have the exclusive . . . And there's so many shitty titles out there. It's got into this point now that there is such overkill you can't collect Pink Floyd bootlegs now, you have to do so much research, there's 500 Pink Floyd CD bootlegs now, replicating the same material, chopped up so many different ways . . . It's very difficult for a person to know what to buy . . . Vinyl is more of a craft thing whereas a CD is mass-produced. You can always re-get the CD, and now they have home CD recording machines so people can always copy someone's CD and have, on CD, the artifact and copy the sleeve on a colour xerox and you've got something that's 98 per cent of the original. It can be easily replicated, so it doesn't have the artifact value. But it can be made 'artifact-ish' if you put in a booklet or a sticker or a pin [badge] or something to make it a fan-oriented release.[1]

Collectors and fans would be forgiven for thinking that the bootleg industry had, by 1994, transcended its American origins. The RIAA's own figures for bootleg CD seizures in the last three years have seen copies confiscated fall from 36,857 in 1991 to a trifling 965 in 1993. Evidently the problem had gone away of its own accord.

In fact, by far the most outstanding entrant to the CD arena in the last two years is operating out of the traditional West Coast home of bootlegs. Vigotone II assumed the moniker of another original West Coast bootlegger. Vigotone I, for a short period in 1990–91, had been responsible for a handful of interesting CDs, including a version of Lennon's *Imagine* compiled entirely from alternative takes, and an excellent version of Dylan's first solo concert at the Carnegie Recital Hall (*Acoustic Troubador*).

Vigotone II, though, entered the fray at a time when there was a shortage of 'golden age' bootleg material. The Europeans were far too busy churning out documents of modern-day Walkman technology. Retaining the sixties bias of its predecessor, Vigotone II had found the perfect way to devalue the inevitable pirated editions of their releases: producing the sort of CD packaging that would make their edition the one to collect (after all, no pirate was going to replicate slipcases and deluxe colour booklets).

Their two-CD set of *Smile* outtakes proved that there was still mileage in the old warhorse, despite the release of an official five-CD set with thirty-five minutes of the best of *Smile* incorporated. Vigotone's *Smile*, though, came in a slipcase with a full-colour, perfect-bound book of colour photos and notation. The material, while it largely duplicated a previous three-album vinyl version, was from a very good tape-source. A similar slipcase package accompanied their version of The Beatles' *Sessions*. Though it made no audio advance on existing CD versions, it was certainly enticingly packaged.

Vigotone's most impressive package to date, though, must be their CD version of the famous twelve-album *Get Back Journals*. The eight-CD Vigotone *Get Back Sessions* came in a hard case (complete with metal straps) with a full-colour reproduction of the entire 130-page *Let it Be* book (included with the first edition of the original vinyl Apple release). The 'repro' was so close to the original that at least one art director at an official record company shook his head in amazement at the sight. Each CD was organized in chronological order, and notation as to the circumstances of the sessions was also included in the set. *Get Back Sessions* was superior in packaging to any official Beatles CD and along with Great Dane's *Complete BBC Sessions* collected the bulk of worthwhile unreleased Beatles material on two well-packaged collections.

Vigotone have largely confined themselves to the pop end of the spectrum. However, between Vigotone Proper and their Spank subsidiary, they have been responsible for at least four lovingly compiled Dylan sixties volumes. *The Freewheelin' Bob Dylan Outtakes* even included an outtake shot from the original cover photo session, while *Seven Years of Bad Luck* gave Dylan CD punters their first hearing of parts of a Dylan hotel tape made in March 1966 in Denver and some predictably embarrassing *Self Portrait* outtakes.

Nor were Vigotone the only people concerned with reviving America's pre-eminent status in the world of rock bootlegging. At least two other US labels are concentrating on archiving sixties and seventies goodies. Whoopy Cat's initial run of hot items concentrated on Hendrix. They even issued a CD of a Hendrix soundcheck, though a double-CD of the May 1970 Berkeley shows, in truly 'best ever' quality, was a more worthwhile purchase. However, their most welcome release to date has been a Springsteen title. *The Lost Radio Show* was just that – a 15 ips reel of a March 1974 radio show in Houston, Texas, on which Springsteen and assorted E Streeters run through eight acoustic renditions of early faves like 'Fever', 'Growin' Up' and 'Does This Bus Stop at 82nd St?'. The artwork was also one of the first covers in many a blue moon to show a Stout-like wit.

The most diverse – and most erratic – of the new generation of American labels, though, has been Gold Standard. In their first rush of releases, in the winter and spring of 1993–4, were titles by Syd Barrett, The Move, Neil Young, The Beatles, The Faces, Cream, Led Zeppelin, Eric Clapton, Bob Dylan and Van Morrison. The Clapton and Zeppelin titles were predictably horrific (the Zeppelin tape was yet another sludge of sound from a 1972 audience tape); the Dylan title was pointless (mono mixes of *Highway 61 Revisited* and *Blonde on Blonde* from vinyl); The Beatles' *English Summer* was a 'knock off' of the impossible-to-find Japanese *Peter Sellers Tape* CD; while the Barrett, Move, Faces, Cream and Morrison titles were all essential documents of the artists concerned. The Faces' *That's All You Need* and The Move's *Black Country Rock* were firmly in the Scorpio tradition, documents of the best that the BBC vaults have to offer. The two Van Morrison volumes, *Laughing in the Wind* and *Naked in the*

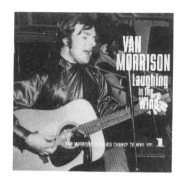

Jungle, were superb-quality collections of Morrison's (largely acoustic) Warners demos from 1969–70 and the mid-seventies 'Highway 101' demos (whose exact purpose remains a mystery). The Gold Standard may yet become a standard to which all bootleg CD makers can aspire.

On a retail level – despite the dent put in CD sales by the RIAA's 935-CD haul – the sheer volume of material available and the impact of a worldwide economic recession has begun to push prices down, at least on the East Coast and at record fairs, to around $20 retail. On the West Coast, for reasons that have more to do with lack of competition than lack of access, prices have held at around the $30–$35 mark.

In Europe, increasingly discriminating punters are making the retailers work harder for their margins. Prices have now nudged below those of official CDs, even for the so-called premium product of labels like Yellow Dog and Silver Rarities. This is largely a result of competition at the wholesale end of the market, rather than manufacturers cutting their margins. But it is also the inevitable result of the ease with which one can duplicate someone else's CDs – which may well include expensive artwork, colour photos and a purchased source tape among its start-up costs – and turn this pirated edition around in a matter of weeks. In particular, the various American CDs – many of which are barely distributed outside America and Japan – usually have their very own European pirated editions, certain Spank titles being turned around in less than two weeks.

The irony of labels like Vigotone, Whoopy Cat and Gold Standard is that they exist in perhaps the most legally unfavourable climate in the whole world. But in all three cases, those folding notes – nice as they are – remain subservient to the bootleg aesthetic and a love of the music. In Italy and Australia – where the legal climate remains entirely tolerant of live-performance CDs – it is the tastes of a jaundiced marketplace and the love of lucre that remain the driving forces behind the bulk of protection-gap kings. The CD revolution has uncovered a vast amount of wonderful archival material, but it has also poured more product out into

the world than the traditional bootleg market can withstand. But while the record industry cartel continues to maintain an artificially inflated price for official compact discs, the protection-gap will only grow wider and genuine bootlegs will continue to be lost in the shuffle.

Certainly, if the IFPI felt that, through their legal moves, the net was tightening around non-IFPI approved producers in Europe and the Far East, there was precious little evidence of it in the avalanche of new bootleg titles in the shops in time for the 1994 new year. With the advent of recordable CDs – albeit at artificially inflated prices to keep the machines out of the hands of consumers – and a general gearing up for the CD-ROM revolution, their chances of closing down every tinpot plant that needs the extra business are minimal. One central problem is that in so many markets in the world it is not illegal to manufacture these bootleg items, it is only illegal to commercially export them. No Korean plant is going to get a slapped wrist for making a live CD of REM and shipping it to an SIAE-licensed label in Italy or Apple House in Australia. The fact that it may end up in a rack of CDs in New York's Village does not make its manufacture illegal.

Of course, the biggest irony of all is that it is the USA's obstinate refusal to sign the Rome Convention for the Protection of Performers, Producers of Phonograms and Broadcasting Organizations that has kept so many areas of copyright law grey. And yet America has been the most belligerent of governments when it sees its corporations' rights being treated with contempt by other countries. During the GATT talks, US negotiator Mickey Kantor was demanding a share of European blank-tape levies for American copyright holders, funds that they are excluded from because they do not have 'reciprocal treatment', i.e. their own levy on analogue tapes. The tape issue will not go away.

America's hit-list of countries for the 'Special 301' treatment has also generated its fair share of protests, not just from those marked down for action, which now includes Japan, but from the EC. A European Commission report, 'Problems of Doing Business With the US', published in April 1993, accused the US of acting against

third-world countries 'without reference to, and often in defiance of, agreed multilateral rules'. After the GATT agreement, the US was supposed to give up the use of 'Special 301' in dealing with copyright issues covered by TRIPS (the relevant part of the GATT agreement). Yet, even after GATT, the Industry Functional Advisory Committee (IFAC-3) was still stressing the need to use 'Special 301' 'aggressively and creatively'.

The US government has been less hardy in defending the rights of its creative citizens. While there is a clear conflict of interest between 'producers' and 'artists' in international copyright law, the American government has consistently sided with the producers when matters have come to a head. The EC report mentioned above went to great pains to point out that the US government has refused to make moral rights available for authors despite the fact that this is a requirement of Berne, which the US finally subscribed to in 1989. In fact, US negotiators nearly caused the break-up of the GATT agreement in Geneva in December 1993 over the issue of 'moral rights'.

Though Britain's membership of the EC has forced it to make certain compromises to Anglo-Saxon notions of copyright, the US has consistently allowed fundamental rights to be transferred from the artists to the producers, whose sole concern, at the end of the day, is another buck in their pocket. It is because of this that artists have often been hamstrung by the companies and restricted in the material they are permitted to release.

In the sixties, labels required two albums a year plus four singles and a couple of provincial tours from their artists. The cycle of album releases has now reached the point where an album more than every two years is an extravagance and the world tour on the back of each album a requirement. That the official companies represent such intermittent output as reflecting the wishes of the artist shows how far removed they have become from the consumers who pay their bills. The bootleg industry is a necessary palliative to fans for whom such sporadic product is simply not enough. Consumers remain blithely unconcerned with how many days it took to get the drums miked up in the studio. Hence bootlegs.

Aesthetics

23 One Man's Boxed-Set (Is Another Man's Bootleg)

Harry [a Bootlegger]: In the Middle Ages, the church controlled all the artists. If some work of art didn't fit in with their religious doctrines, the church would put it away or destroy it. That's what record companies are doing.[1]

Record companies see commerce as a one-way street. Theirs is perhaps the most wasteful of all entertainment industries, slinging no-talent no-hopers at the wall and then into the street, hoping to find a U2, an REM, a Guns'n'Roses hiding amid such mediocrity. When they find that money-machine they hope to bind them with bonds of legal steel. The exclusive recording contract, signed by all recording acts, surely qualifies as the most unreasonable legal agreement in the arts today.

The standard contract given out to new artists by today's biggest record companies is onerous . . . The key to understanding why the contracts are so bad is the word 'recoupable'. In a standard agreement, most of the costs of making a record are to be repaid out of the artist's royalties rather than gross receipts. Items that are normally charged to the artists include manufacturing costs, recording-studio time, marketing, touring, packaging – in short, almost everything . . . The way contracts are structured, the record company can make a profit off an album while the artist's royalty account is still in the red. In fact, this is a frequent occurrence.[1]

Now if this was the end of the exploitation that would be bad enough, though many bands would presumably still sign away their future livelihood, hoping that they would be the exception, clearing all 'deductibles' and ascending to financial nirvana. In fact, even in this situation they find that they own very little.

Ed Bicknell [Dire Straits manager]: Once the recording costs have been recouped, we have a rather curious situation which is that the artist does not actually own the work that they have then paid for. It is still owned by the record company through life of [the] copyright ... The record industry relies for its profit to a very large extent on back catalogue ... If you look back to the history of popular music, to the fifties and sixties, there are artists still getting royalty rates that were 2 per cent of something in the UK and for the rest of the world it was half that.[3]

The record company's demands are still not over. The amount of control that the artist has over what the record company may choose, or more importantly choose not, to release is extremely limited, particularly in America where the artist does not even have the legal protection of a 'moral right' to his or her work. A record company can not only reject a finished album that an artist has toiled on for many moons, but can insist that the album they – of their own free will – rejected, does not constitute part of any stipulated minimum number of albums the artist is required to deliver. They can then offset the costs of making the 'rejected' album against any work released at a later date.

Yet the artist in question is still not permitted to take the 'rejected' album, which he or she will ultimately pay for (should the advances be cleared), to another record company without the original company's approval (for which they will almost certainly demand payment). The reason for this, as stated in *This Business of Music*, is that 'under the usual [recording contract] ... the artist is employed to render his personal services as a recording performer on an exclusive basis for the purpose of manufacturing phonograph records.' Because a recording contract is an employment contract, pure and simple, the artist retains no interest in the actual tapes, masters or copyright in the sound recordings. His sole claim is for contractual compensation and royalties – and even these royalties rarely stand up to scrutiny:

Don Engel [pop lawyer]: I would venture to say, except by accident, there isn't an honest royalty statement issued by any major recording company in the business today. That's my personal view, and I have a lot of evidence behind it. In one case, I deposed a man who had been audit manager for one of the biggest labels. I asked him, Did you ever in your career see an audit where there wasn't a shortfall to the performer? No. Did you ever see an audit where the performer was overpaid? Never. So these are not errors.[4]

When the royalties do match contractually agreed terms, they may still contain some highly questionable 'deductions', such as those made in the 'early years' of cassettes and CDs. These 'packaging' or R&D deductions range anywhere between 25 and 50 per cent, and were still being applied long after cassettes, and subsequently CDs, became the premier music-carriers. So what do these binding, pernicious contracts have to do with record companies' attitude to bootlegs? Well, Jon Pareles put it in a nutshell in the *New York Times* back in August 1991:

The issue is control. Recording companies don't want anyone else to sell [alternative] recordings; they don't get a piece of the action. They also don't want to admit that there are options; if listeners and musicians decided they didn't need 64-track studios and state-of-the-art computerized sound mixes, bands might not need recording company capital. The companies also want passive consumers who'll buy what's being marketed, not smart alecks who search out alternatives.[5]

In America, in particular, the companies want to control *all* imports, not merely those of dubious legality. Now that all bootlegs are on CD, and are therefore manufactured outside the USA, they have become part of a general embargo on imported 'phonorecords'. Despite much political rhetoric about free trade, the US has always been one of the most protectionist of Western economies, perhaps second only to France – and the record industry likes to think of itself as US-controlled (though in fact only Time-Warners of the Big Five has a US-based parent company).

The record companies' desire for control has increasingly encroached on the free will of artists – particularly when they display a prolific tendency. Columbia's disenchantment with Elvis Costello in the early eighties was apparently not down to the quality of his output or frequency of touring, but simply to the fact that he wanted to put out too many records, too often (between 1980 and 1984 there were six new Costello studio albums and one compilation of non-album tracks). The nineties music machine does not work like its sixties predecessor, when companies demanded a new single every two months, a new album every six months and a couple of greatest hits and live albums every few years for good measure. Now the hyping of every 'blockbuster' requires months of preparation, building the level of expectation to a point where disappointment is inevitable. Even priority releases will take a good six months from completion before they hit the racks (compare this with *Like a Rolling Stone*, which was in the charts five weeks after it was recorded).

The album-a-year artist has become almost a thing of the past, even when the number of songs he or she may churn out might warrant an annual résumé. For any prolific artist, the modern music-machine must be frustrating in the extreme. How Dylan would have convinced Sony nowadays to release *Bringing it All Back Home*, *Highway 61 Revisited* and *Blonde on Blonde* – two single albums and a double – in less than eighteen months, God only knows.

A bootlegger: The way it works at the moment is totally wrong; the way a record company can say to an artist, 'You can only release two or three singles this year as we don't want to flood the market.' As far as I'm concerned, if someone wants to put out a single every week, then why not? If people have got great music in them, then they should be allowed to get it out. Monopoly capitalists don't like to have the security of their monopoly threatened in any way. And that – basically – is what bootlegging is all about.[6]

Bootlegs operate within the same twilight as specialist labels. Just like bootleggers, these specialist labels have benefited greatly from the industry's greed in maintaining CD prices when production costs have plummeted. This has meant that the economics of small-run CDs (in the low thousands) is far more practical than similar runs on vinyl. However, the 'majors' have been notoriously reluctant to release 'rights' for long-deleted albums they own even though a CD reissue would probably generate sales below margins they consider acceptable.

As long ago as July 1972 John Hammond, director of talent acquisition for Columbia Records and the man who discovered Bob Dylan and Bessie Smith (and had just signed a Jersey boy called Bruce Springsteen to the label), told a Rutgers Institute of Jazz Studies seminar on the problems of piracy and bootlegging that the record industry had been 'terribly remiss' in their treatment of vintage jazz recordings. Many labels, he said, had held on to pieces that ought to be made available to the listening public, especially the collector. While he was careful not to condone bootleg operations, Hammond did wonder aloud whether labels did not have 'a moral, if not legal' obligation to release, or give up the rights to material they had, in many cases, held on to for over thirty years.

In fairness to Columbia, the belated formation of a separate archival division, Legacy, has corrected many of their most unacceptable oversights and led to some superb pre-rock & roll archival releases. (It is the pre-rock era which represents the greyest area of legitimate product, with legal rights often blurred by questionable original transactions, mysterious deaths and lost masters.) Classical companies – who in the sixties and early seventies looked the other way when pirated versions of deleted recordings appeared – began to reassert lapsed rights to these recordings as digital technology afforded them the opportunity to resuscitate the murkiest of tapes, and profit margins on CDs made small runs more attractive. Of course, the bootleggers had already successfully proved that an audience exists for such arcane recordings.

Only now are record companies with more popular fare starting to consider competing with the bootleggers, rather than trying to lock the vault doors after the fact. RCA, who were offered mid-fifties tapes of Elvis performing on the *Louisiana Hayride* radio show in the late seventies, turned them down on the grounds that it was not 'what the fans wanted'. They would not make the same mistake now. After the success of their eight-album *Elvis Aaron Presley* set, one five-CD set of fifties recordings and one six-CD set from the sixties, they have acquired a partial understanding of the fan mentality.

Of course, the edge that bootleggers will always retain is their ability to dispense with legal niceties. If The Beatles are too busy squabbling with each other about who is getting the higher royalty rate, the bootleggers have been happy to pay none of them royalties and issue *Sessions* anyway. A similar disregard for the internal politics of Pink Floyd has meant that the BBC sessions Floyd members apparently refuse to sanction for legitimate release are readily available in bootleg CD form. In certain cases, the bootleggers have issued what are really pirate compilations, derived from myriad bands and/or labels. When the idea has been copied by official companies, though, it has usually been with less spectacular results. *James Patrick Page* was a beautifully presented double-album collection of pre-Zep Jimmy Page sessions, compiled from a dozen different record labels. Two subsequent Page volumes with quasi-legit status – both called simply *Session Man* – only utilized neutered versions of this material. Likewise TMQ's *Who's Zoo* provided the genesis of the idea for MCA's *Who's Missing* and *Two's Missing* compilations and Polydor UK's *Rarities Volumes 1 and 2*. The attention to detail and loving care applied to some of these piratical albums has proved hard to replicate.

The appearance of bootleg versions of fabled live performances has also encouraged the legitimate release of recordings which otherwise might have been rejected. The inevitable bootleg CD versions of the nine-hour Monterey Pop radio broadcast in 1987 must have been a key factor in the belated Rhino release in 1992, though even this late in the day the Grateful Dead (thank God!) and Buffalo Springfield refused permission for their cuts to appear on the Rhino set, thus making at least one of the two Living Legend double-CD sets a necessary purchase for fans. Likewise, a 1987 bootleg of recently discovered Buddy Holly demos came from a tape that MCA, Buddy Holly's widow, the Holly family and the Norman Petty estate had been squabbling over for two and a half years. It seems that official companies still have to be forced to compete with bootlegs. They would prefer to just brand them pirates and leave it to collectors to hunt bootleg versions down.

Torsten Hartmann [Living Legend]: The record companies have reacted in a very ill-considered way. Why don't they release live material by their artists on cheap cassettes? If they did this, they could put us out of business.[7]

Bootlegs have also served as an important form of second take on albums bastardized by the artist or the record label. Thus a recent Pretty Things CD on Chapter One, *Pure and Pretty*, finally released seven tracks from the 1966 Pretty Things album *Emotions* without the overdubs that the record company had felt were necessary to 'sweeten' the Pretties' sound. The original, pre-fucked-up versions of Dylan's two finest albums in the last twenty years, *Blood on the Tracks* and *Infidels*, subsequently appeared as bootleg releases (as *Joaquin Antique* and *Down in the Flood* respectively).

Perhaps even more essential for fans of seminal sixties sounds was an Italian double-CD of the Velvet Underground at 'End of Cole Avenue'. Songs from these October 1969 shows comprised part of the 1974 live anthology, *1969*. However, Polygram had never gone back to the source tape but had relied on a dub of a dub (of the second night only) given by the engineer responsible to Velvets' manager, Steve Sesnick, back in 1970. A couple of Italians knew that there must have been more than the half a dozen cuts used on *1969* and, with the help of American Velvet aficionados, tracked down the man responsible for making the recordings in the first place. Sure enough, the taper in question, a sound engineer for a film company, had taped all four sets in Dallas, though the first was recorded at the back of the club. Only after this was he invited up front by the band's roadies, and he recorded the remaining shows with two mikes strategically placed on stage. The Italians purchased tapes of both sets from the second night, which they released in 1991 as a double-CD set wrapped in a velvet pouch. Two years later, having raised the necessary finances, they returned to purchase the tapes of the first night, sonically inferior but historically important, releasing another double-CD as *The First Night*, also in a velvet pouch.

Steve Hoffman [record producer]: When I hear 'From Me to You' on *Ultra Rare Trax* it sounds so great that I want to hear the real one. So I put on *Past Masters* and it sounds terrible; it's so filtered, like it's been strained through a flour sifter. That's depressing.[8]

Whatever illusions the various industry bodies may have about the sound quality of bootlegs, there seems little doubt that the fans prefer the Swingin' Pig *Atlantic City '89* to CBS's single-CD live album; and there is no competition between Columbia's sixteen basement-tape tracks (spread over two CDs) and the hundred plus (mostly stereo) basement-tape cuts found on the five 'Scorpio' CDs that make up *The Genuine Basement Tapes* series.

Instances where official releases have been put together in the spirit of a bootleg have generally worked best when the artist has had the humility to enlist the help of fans. Jethro Tull and Deep Purple have both produced lovely sets of archival material with the full input of their respective fan clubs. The four-CD King Crimson set *The Great Deceiver*, though not allowing of any input save Robert Fripp's himself, was also an example of how to produce a boxed-set with the mind-set of a bootlegger. *The Great Deceiver* was entirely composed of live recordings from 1973–4. The reason for its existence Fripp details in his introduction to the box:

There are currently 120 King Crimson bootlegs available in Japan [this is something of an exaggeration] from throughout the group's history. The bulk of the bootleg catalogue centres on 1973 and 1974. So, I am persuaded of a wide and continuing demand for live Crimson of this period. My personal collection of live KC recordings is extensive, and generally much better in quality than available on the black market, collectors' magazines, Japanese record shops or leather suitcases in Amsterdam record bazaars.

Most of the bootlegs are pretty rough but present an interesting perspective of what it is like to be in the audience – that is, the audience as performer with group as backdrop. Some of the bootlegs are quietly hilarious, with discussions and arguments between die-hard Crimheads and innocent *nouveau-audient* over some Crim-voyage into Unchartered Territory. Those who saw the shows know the unnerving power of this uneven outfit, but a younger generation has only the studio albums and the bootlegs.[9]

Ultimately, though, the record companies are not about to re-evaluate their long-standing anti-competition stance. It is down to the artists to convince them of the feasibility of projects like the Crimson boxed-set (two more volumes are scheduled to appear) or Jethro Tull's equally ambitious twenty-fifth anniversary four-CD boxed-set. It is also down to the artists to ensure that the rights to their old material revert to them and that the 'exclusive rights' that the record companies have historically insisted upon continue to be eroded (by actions like George Michael's against Sony). It is the artist, after all, who should have the primary rights – legal *and* moral. The role of the record companies? Well, I think Mr Rotten had it down when talking about A&M's sacking of the Sex Pistols:

A record company is there to market records – not dictate terms.[10]

24 Roll Your Tapes, Bootleggers

Lenny Kaye: I think that bootlegs keep the flame of the music alive by keeping it out of not only the industry's conception of the artist, but also the artist's conception of the artist. I think a lot of artists would like to keep the scruffy moments away. There's that self-editing thing and, with all due respect to great artists, a lot of times their own instincts aren't as righteous about the music as someone else. You might say, my guitar tone is so bad there, and yet you're playing something you've never played before and will probably never play again. You don't know, sometimes, what it is you've done that is good, bad or indifferent until years later . . . I'd rather have a lot of scattered stuff so that someday, maybe even in fifty years, someone will be looking at the work of, say, Bob Dylan and all of a sudden hear something that might have been lost forever had somebody not grabbed it somewhere and put it out.[1]

All art involves censorship – self-censorship. Few songs spring fully formed from one head, fewer songs still get cut in a single take at a single session. (Even the oft-mentioned 'first' take of 'Like a Rolling Stone' was in fact prefaced by at least three partial takes, during which the song went through a couple of key changes and its time signature switched from a waltzy 3/4 to a more orthodox 4/4.) Judgements about what to keep and what to discard are an integral part of what makes up the artistic bent.

And yet the artist may be the last person in the world who should be making judgements about his art. Too close to the creative act, the artist often lacks the perspective given to an objective observer. Unfortunately, the rock process is fraught with so many sycophants and yes-men that objectivity is sometimes hard to find. Even fans, who are wont to descend to 'everything Dave/Jimi/Patti does is great, really great or really, really great', are often poor judges. As for critics, well . . . 'Name me someone who's not a parasite and I'll go out and say a prayer for him,' to quote a phrase. In rock music, songs are usually created only semi-consciously, the result of a confluence of 'flukes', built around what may well be a highly derivative twelve-bar melody. A great song does not a great performance make, but a great performance can always make a song great.

The quest for this musical alchemy was an integral part of the studio experience in the sixties and seventies. (Sadly, many so-called 'rock' artists abandoned recording 'live' in the studio with the advent of sixteen-track technology in the early seventies.) As long as there remained a notional belief in the virtues of cutting tracks live in the studio (with vocals and guitar solos perhaps redubbed at a later date), the relationship between 'performance' and 'recording' remained at least partially intact. When that connection was eventually unplugged, studio 'recording' passed beyond rock, and 'alternative takes' (as opposed to alternative mixes) became largely a thing of the past.

The studio should be the most sacred preserve of the rock artist. It is here that he will either deliver the goods or fade from view. Closeted from all daily distractions, he sculpts his material, fleshes out fragments and coaxes their all from fellow musicians. Inevitably, what he discards at the end of the process he would like discarded for good. After all, it has been part of the process to lay aside this flotsam. Then some bastard bootlegger shakes down the engineer (not actually the way it happens) and suddenly all those artistic judgements are open to new scrutiny. How would you like it?

Steven D'Onofrio [vice-president of RIAA piracy division]: There are artists out there that are very concerned about this bootlegging . . . They hear their voice not as flattering as it is in the studio, being recorded and released permanently, and they don't necessarily like that. There are artists that spend weeks, months and even years in the studio – and you know them as well as I do – that are fanatical about what they release, and they'll see something live of them and it'll drive them crazy. Although they may have sounded that way in concert, they don't want that to be memorialized. You have to understand the perfectionism that some of these artists have.[2]

But then 'perfectionism' is the antithesis of what rock is surely all about. To wheel out my favourite Lester Bangs quote (again), 'Rock and roll is not an "artform". Rock and roll is a raw wail from the bottom of the guts.' Who is most akin to the spirit of rock & roll – the collector who chases down each audio tape in search of that 'moment' of inspiration, or the rock star who clocks up days of studio-time getting his solo just right? And how come there are so many more 'classic' rock albums recorded on four- and eight-track in a matter of days than ones recorded on twenty-four or more tracks in a matter of months?

Not surprisingly, the artists who have been most fanatical in attempting to quosh bootlegs have also tended to be those whose judgement has been called into question most often. Dylan's paranoia is justifiably legendary, but his description of bootleggers in the *Biograph* boxed-set (a glorified cut'n'paste effort, part bootleg, part greatest hits) bears little correlation with reality:

Bob Dylan: [They're] outrageous . . . you're just sitting and strumming in a motel . . . the phone is tapped . . . and then it appears on a bootleg record. With a cover that's got a picture of you that was taken from underneath your bed.[3]

But then who could blame Dylan for waking up in the morning and checking under the bed for a reel-to-reel or two? After all, he has been by far the most meticulously documented of all rock artists, even into the late eighties when his five-hundred-plus Never Ending Tour shows have been so thoroughly covered by fans that a mere dozen shows have passed them by (all in Central and Southern America – rock stars take note). Of course, Dylan's profligacy is only one reason that he has been so extensively documented. His choice of songs, takes and producers has constantly been called into question by the onslaught of studio tapes. And despite his professed anti-bootleg stance, Dylan has catered to the desire of his fans to hear his cutting-floor discards (*More Greatest Hits*, *The Basement Tapes*, *Biograph*, *The Bootleg Series*) more than any of his contemporaries – save perhaps for Frank Zappa.

Unlike Zappa, though, Dylan has not been personally responsible for any of the major archival digs through his and/or Columbia's vaults. In fact, the appalling results that his compilers (Robbie Robertson in 1975, Jeff Rosen in 1985 and 1991) have managed, is perhaps the best argument that archival releases should be left to bootleggers. *The Basement Tapes* represents the most extreme travesty, mixing stereo tapes into mono, including eight superfluous Band cuts recorded elsewhere and later, and leaving at least as many classic Dylan originals off the double-set as were included. *The Bootleg Series*, the 1991 boxed-set of outtakes that managed to outsell Dylan's last three studio albums, seemed an overt admission that, whatever Dylan's wishes at the time, the allure of hearing his rejects has not been dimmed by years of frustratingly unfinished albums. The title was, of course, a misnomer as so much of the material had never been bootlegged, and what had was not drawn from the bootlegs that created the legend in the first place.

Zappa's own bootleg series, on the other hand, was actually the genuine article. *Beat the Boots I and II* consisted of two eight-album boxed-sets that were simply counterfeits of existing bootlegs, dubbed direct from the original versions, complete with pops and crackles and original artwork. Zappa, though, was just as vehemently opposed to bootlegs as Dylan. The first volume even included one bootleg, *As An Am Zappa*, on which he is complaining about bootleggers who attend his concerts being able to release his newest songs before him. The *Beat the Boots* volumes were not intended to legitimize this part of his oeuvre but to undercut the bootleggers and make Zappa money from the bootleggers' industry (and make money they did). One bootlegger even threatened to sue Zappa for the artwork to *'Tis the Season to be Jelly*, which was, of course, copyrighted and which Zappa was illegally appropriating.

Interestingly enough, Zappa did not include in either set any part of the ten-album *Mystery Box*, which many fans considered superior to *You Can't Do That . . .* as an overview of his live career. The last thing Zappa wanted was for his own judgement to be called into question, however dubious some of his past 'calls' may have been.

The objections of rock artists like Dylan and Zappa are primarily about control. The record companies' concerns remain entirely different – the commercial exploitation of an exclusive output. It is interesting to note the choice of plaintiffs in recent cases against bootleggers in Europe. The pending cases in 1993 involved Phil Collins, Cliff Richard, Dire Straits and Michael Jackson, people who, to a man, have no understanding of the rock aesthetic. Presumably, then, their concern in these legal actions is not the presumptiousness of bootleggers – deciding what may or may not be dispensed to their fans – but the (largely illusory) financial losses that these releases are purported to involve. (In fairness to these acts, the motives of the so-called bootleggers in these cases has been equally dubious. 'Performance piracy' of acts for whom every performance is an attempt at reproduction not extension was largely unknown in the vinyl era, because the market was entirely collector-driven. Companies like Imtrat, and Perfect Beat in its latter days, are not interested in catering to such collectors.)

The financial argument against bootlegs – at least from the artist's point of view – is not remotely sustainable. The total 'losses' in royalties for every single one of the close-to-a-thousand commercial bootlegs by Dylan would still be a blip on the oscillo-scope compared with the sums deducted by Columbia from his royalties for CD research and design costs, despite having nothing to do with any aspect of compact disc's design or innovation. Frankly, if stars worth upwards of $50 million are starting to worry about lost royalties on items they never intended to release, then their sense of priorities is all to cock. Ultimately, the choice remains for the artist to put the item out officially and recoup his losses. Yet perhaps the two most famous bootlegs – Dylan's *Albert Hall* and The Beatles' *Get Back* – have steadfastly failed to appear (though *Albert Hall* is actually scheduled for an autumn 1994 release). In the case of The Beatles, the ability of one or more members to veto an official release has always halted any collection of Beatles outtakes. Back in 1984 EMI had hoped to release a single album of Beatles outtakes, *Sessions*, but at the last minute The Beatles pulled the plug. The result was an endless series of bootleg versions of the same set. Ringo Starr wanted *Sessions* to be officially released:

Ringo Starr: I always felt that what we put out was what we thought was the best. Then these bootlegs came out and there were enormous sales. I want to put out Beatles bootlegs by The Beatles. You know, instead of someone else putting them out, we should do it. Because it's out there anyway.[4]

It is interesting that of all the four Beatles the most crucial creative figure, John Lennon, should be an avid collector of his own bootlegs. McCartney, on the other hand, though he has released his own official bootleg, refers to standing 'with a bootleg in his hand' in 'Hi Hi Hi' and was responsible for one of the most bootlegged items of the eighties (*The Russian Album*), has remained antagonistic to those who recycle his past so creatively.

The one band presumed by most punters to be entirely pro-bootleg are The Grateful Dead. Yet they are among the most vehement in their opposition to commercial bootlegging. Their 'tapers' section' at concerts is partially an attempt to circumvent the more commercial aspects of bootlegging. In encouraging their fans to freely trade audio tapes of Dead shows, and to make tapes for other Deadheads without charge, they are giving fans the opportunity to collect their performances without having to line the pockets of bootleggers. In this they have had some success. Despite the free availability of boxes of superb audience and soundboard tapes, and their substantial (and fanatical) following, the Dead have never been bootlegged on vinyl and CD with any of the intensity of the Big Five. The Dead have also been known to police stores which sell bootlegs, and have made public statements requesting that their fans avoid such product.

Part of the irony of artists speaking out against bootlegs is that so many of them collect other artists' (or indeed their own) bootlegs. Thus Dylan can refer in an interview with one journalist to bootleggers hiding under his bed, and literally days later enthuse about a recently released collection of Hank Williams radio tapes to another journalist. These tapes had been recorded by a collector from the radio and circulated on bootleg for many years before some wily company made them legitimate. Richard Thompson, speaking to some of his fans at a folk festival, admitted to double-standards in his attitude to people taping his shows:

Richard Thompson: I like the general idea of it. I know that if Bix Beiderbecke was alive today then I'd want to hear every solo. I'm glad that that guy taped every Charlie Parker solo for two years – turned his machine on when he took a solo – on his wire recorder. I'm glad he did that. The problem is you don't always want people to hear the off nights, or to hear the outtakes.[5]

It is well known that there are many artists who go out of their way to collect all of their own bootlegs. John Lennon, Mick Jagger, Peter Buck of REM and Eddie Vedder of Pearl Jam are among those who have admitted to an abiding interest in their unofficial oeuvre. Indeed one tape that circulates among Stones collectors consists of Jagger buying bootlegs in a hotel room in New York in 1974.

Some artists have a different attitude to live bootlegs than to ones derived from studio outtakes. Certainly in the recent past, in certain countries, the law has treated live bootlegs in a very different way, as perhaps it should. Studio outtakes are perhaps the most intrusive of all 'acquired' recordings. They were usually recorded at great expense, are paid for by the artist and might reasonably be considered one's private preserve. A live performance, on the other hand, has historically been accorded a much lower level of legal protection. As long as the Rome Convention remains the only reciprocal international accord preventing 'performance piracy', live CDs will continue to be produced.

I would argue that there is no sound reason why live performances should not be commercially released by independent labels, without any legal requirement to gain the artist's agreement, as long as requisite songwriting *and* performance royalties are fully paid (the non-payment of performers by the protection-gap labels seems morally indefensible). The argument that this impairs the sales potential of studio product does not hold vodka. Nor is the argument that an artist should be able to control his live output. One would hope that what was good enough to warrant charging 70,000 fans £25 a head to witness might also justify a similar sum to provide the four or five thousand so inclined with a more permanent memento on CD. If not, then frankly the artist is a charlatan.

Yet unlicensed live CDs remain unacceptable to many artists, even those who are receiving mechanical royalties from such releases. This is partly because many bands hope to release a mass-market live album, sanitized by post-production to correct every bum note, intrusive whoop or flat vocal – i.e. all the moments that make one show different from the next. Perhaps there is an all too real fear that they might be shown to be a little less proficient, a little more shambolic than they are prepared to admit, once the music is stripped of all the pomp and ceremony that surrounds stadium-rock shows. Perhaps fans will hear just how lacking in real chops a band might be.

In fact, it is only as a live act that a rock band is in its element. If the dynamism inherent in a rock gig is lost on any given bunch of would-be musicians, then a rock band they are not. In this sense, at least, The Beatles were the worst of bands since they could never cut it live. But they came from an era, the sixties, and a town, Liverpool, where their audiences had no expectations to burn. If The Beatles were a functioning band today, and sounded like they did in the sixties, they would be lucky to make it as far as *Opportunity Knocks*.

Of course, there are plenty of rock artists who have little to be ashamed of, and are – or have come to be – grateful that their shows were so rigorously documented by fans.

Graham Nash: I specifically remember David and I talking long and hard about *A Very Stoney Evening*, the Crosby/Nash bootleg of a concert that we did in the Dorothy Chandler Pavilion in LA, and one of the reasons that we remember it so well is [because] that was one night when Crosby was really sick with flu. We nearly had to cancel the performance but he went to the doctor and the doctor gave him a bit of this, a bit of that, and he managed to do the performance but he was delirious, he was out there that night ... and we had a great night and it was very nice to see that performance captured.[6]

Lenny Kaye: Historical documentation is a very important thing and I personally know that if it weren't for the Patti Smith Group bootlegs there would be no live album. And for us the live thing was so important, in many ways it was more important than the actual recordings that we would make once a year or something like that. So I'm very happy that there are bootlegs out there that document us at various stages of our growth in a live setting.[7]

Plenty of bands whose reputations were founded entirely on live performances have no official live set to back up their renown, for example Television (there is just a double-play cassette, *The Blow Up*, compiled from two audience tapes originally bootlegged as *Arrow*) and Led Zeppelin (whose double-album soundtrack *The Song Remains the Same* they do not consider part of their recorded works). Ditto The Beatles with *Live at the Hollywood Bowl*. In Zeppelin's case both Plant and Page have implied that the bootleggers are doing a better job preserving their live performances than Atlantic could ever do legitimately.

The one band whose official live sets have most closely paralleled their bootleg releases has been Deep Purple. Purple were a band who never seemed opposed to the idea of fans hearing their live performances, good, bad and indifferent, right from the appearance of their very first bootleg, *H-Bomb*, back in 1970.

Ritchie Blackmore: I think we all were pretty flattered – but it was a shame that the technique of recording [on *H-Bomb*] was so bad. You see it was done at a concert in Aachen, and that night the stage caught fire. So for twenty minutes of the album there's just the sound of burning wood, no music at all. If we were bootlegged again, then I think I'd be just as flattered. I look on bootlegs as being collectors' items. If I was really into an artist, and I wanted to hear how he performed live, then I'd buy one.[8]

In fact *H-Bomb* was instrumental in convincing Deep Purple to release their own live set in 1972, the landmark *Made in Japan*.

The steady flow of official Purple 'In Concert' collections in the ensuing years (which now totals something like eleven volumes) has largely negated the point of collecting their bootlegs, especially for the Mk 2 (1970–73) and Mk 3 (1973–4) line-ups (the twenty-first anniversary triple-CD *Live in Japan* set, released in 1993, shows just how live sets catering to fans who buy bootlegs should be done).

Lenny Kaye: My perception is that most artists don't mind bootlegs. In fact they kinda like them; they might not like them when they're a few more years along, when they start to worry that the royalties are not going to their pockets, but when they're first bootlegged they kinda think they've made it. I know we were really excited when our first bootlegs came out, it was like we were popular enough to get bootlegged . . . I think it's a great tradition and keeps alive a lot of music that would ultimately be shut up in a vault somewhere and maybe painstakingly edited and extracted. I like the unexpurgated diaries, myself.[9]

Of course, in certain instances the bootlegger has genuinely come up with something 'unexpurgated'. Bootlegs have sometimes been rock's very own *It'll be Alright on the Night*. Some tapes have been deliberately leaked to bootleggers by disgruntled ex-employees. This has been the case with several Springsteen tapes, belying his reputation as a generous employer. A notorious tape of 'Hey Jude' performed by McCartney's Wings, with Linda McCartney's painfully atonal backing vocals isolated in the mix, was apparently circulated by a soundman sacked by McCartney. Mick Jagger's notorious 'Cocksucker Blues' could never be released officially.

Less embarrassing, but more personal, recordings have also leaked into the pit. Dylan's attempts to re-record *Blood on the Tracks*, deleting painfully naked versions of 'You're a Big Girl Now', 'If You See Her, Say Hello' and a radically alternative 'Idiot Wind', in favour of sanitized later versions, was a form of artistic cop-out not lost on the bootleggers, who had the original versions on the streets less than six weeks after CBS released the official album. This again raises the question of what qualifies as intrusion into an artist's life. But then, like most matters involving art, intrusion may well equal insight.

Graham Nash: If it was too personal, why the fuck did he write it in the first place and why the fuck did he record it? I think you're committed, I do, I truly do. I don't think that afterwards you can say, 'Well, no one's gonna hear this because it's too personal.'[10]

Since an artist is constantly acting as his own self-censor, he is usually the last person to catalogue and document all the ideas to fall by the wayside. Somebody needs to pick them up, and even sometimes throw them back. There is a story that Linda Thompson used to go through the wastepaper bins in which her then-husband Richard Thompson would often discard ideas, scraps of songs, and ask him why he had rejected such-and-such. (Is that why he divorced her?!)

The nature of modern recording technology allows a singer-songwriter to document virtually every process he goes through when writing a song, from genesis to (hopefully) revelation. As a result, the sheer scale of material required to fully document the art of a performing artist is out of all proportion to that of a writer who works entirely with the printed page. So who gets to document this material? Is the artist himself, or his hired lackey, the best choice? Are the record companies to be trusted to archive all the important recordings of one of their out-of-vogue artists? History suggests not.

25 Copycats Ripped Off My Songs

Andy Dodd [Simply Red road manager]: In the early eighties the music business was experiencing a major decline which was only stemmed by the introduction of the CD format. This allowed companies with back-catalogue of interest to reissue old vinyl titles at great profit given that the format was being subsidized by reduced artist royalties, if indeed these re-issues bore high royalty rates at all. It was the musical equivalent of re-inventing the wheel. The pressure was removed from the A&R departments to effectively find new talent, back-catalogue was king and the industry relaxed into its ongoing period of . . . blatant necrophilia.[1]

Since 1985, when the potential of a digital 75-minute music-carrier as a medium for collecting someone's work was first realized, the record companies have indulged in a grand parade of lifeless repackaging. At this point they belatedly realized the importance of maintaining their archives and the historical significance of much bootlegged material.

What Andy Dodd refers to as an 'ongoing period of blatant necrophilia' was largely the result of realizing that not only was the demand for 'new' product in steady decline, but that this decline was quite probably irreversible. Labels sprang up whose entire modus operandi was to reissue and re-configure material for CD. By a long way the best of these labels was Rhino Records, who came to their trade on the back of LA's most public retail outlet for bootlegs, the Rhino store (the original Rhino logo was the work of none other than William Stout).

The new importance of back-catalogue also came at a point when much of the material record companies had under-exploited for so long was passing into the 'public domain' in certain major markets. Japan did not recognize foreign rights until 1978 (retro-gressing to 1968 in 1991), while Germany – the third biggest market in the world – offered only twenty-five years' protection to foreign sound recordings, meaning that the first Beatles recordings would begin to pass into the 'public domain' in 1988.

Of course, the CD revolution gave the legitimate labels one important edge in that only they owned the master tapes required for remastering to CD – or did they? Most of the major companies had been notoriously lax in archiving their master tapes. Many (one may even say most) first-generation back-catalogue CD releases were taken from tapes a couple of generations removed from the studio masters. In perhaps the most embarrassing back-catalogue farce of the CD era, Columbia remastered Dylan's *Blonde on Blonde*, their most serious contender for finest rock album of all time, on three separate occasions from an equalized tape at least two generations down from the master. When they finally got around to issuing a CD version from the original tapes they impertinently charged $30 for the privilege.

Not only were the record companies accessing the 'wrong' tapes but they were coming to realize just how many tapes that they thought they owned were not where they were supposed to be. RCA were forced to hunt down copies of Elvis Presley's sixties soundtrack sessions that they had previously junked and which, according to legend, a janitor took home (eventually they found their way on to Audiofon's *Behind Closed Doors* boxed-set). Columbia had kept many master tapes from sessions in Nashville in storage. They failed to reclaim the tapes when the storage facility was shut down in 1990. The tapes were subsequently auctioned off to a private individual who has been locked in a, to date successful, battle to retain the tapes (hopefully for resale). The embarrassment to Columbia has far outweighed the actual commercial value of the tapes.

Perhaps the greatest windfall of studio tapes to have passed into private hands, though, was the Olympic Studios haul. These were rescued from a skip where all the various tapes from this legendary London studio, purchased by Virgin and due for a complete refurbishment, had been deposited. Clearly such people should not be in charge of a local children's library, let alone an archive of immeasurable historical importance.

Many creative artists have treated their archives far worse than the record companies. Dylan's office destroyed some ninety master reels of 1978 rehearsals recorded at Dylan's own Rundown Studios in Santa Monica. They presumably felt that they had no further need of them. Thankfully a couple of the band musicians had taken copies of certain favourite songs so that some documentation exists of Dylan's most extensive bout of rehearsing, though the bulk of recordings from these sessions are now irrevocably lost. Likewise, when tapes were accessed for the 1991 *Bootleg Series* set, the version of 'I Shall be Released' was clearly not taken from the master tape (it was in mono, to start with). Had Dylan's people not been able to access the original basement tapes? One is left to wonder what might have happened to the hours and hours of recordings at Big Pink if collectors had not followed stray leads back to something approximating to the source tapes in the late eighties.

Graham Nash: [The writer] Alan Wilson has the original acetate that The Fourtones did. Now The Fourtones was three years before The Hollies. It was me, Alan Clarke, and all those people. And I'm going, 'Wait a minute, how the fuck does he have this? Even I don't have a copy of this.' The point being that it wasn't important to us then, 'Let's go, we're busy recording.'[2]

Many rock artists from the sixties and early seventies have now enjoyed long, erratic careers. Yet awareness that CD boxed-sets might be the only realistic way to repackage their work was slow to dawn. It was Jeff Rosen's sprawling five-album, three-CD anthology of Dylan's first twenty years at Columbia, *Biograph*, that first hinted at the potential, and the potential hazards, of the 'retrospective' boxed-set. Rosen's collection was divided – two to one – in favour of previously released cuts.

It is a format that has been rigidly adhered to by the record companies, despite its patent unfairness to collectors. Like Hollywood, the Record Biz has a tendency – when it finds a winning formula – to stick to it, rather than seeking to refine it further. When *Biograph* became only the second multiple-album set in history to go Top Forty on the *Billboard* charts, the record companies decided that a dozen or so rarities, a 'historical' booklet with pretty pictures, and the promise of 'digital' remastering (as if there was any other kind for CD), were all that was required to clock up another 100,000 units.

The beauty of CD boxed-sets is that they require no major investment – a little studio time for mastering and mixing purposes, but no prohibitive recording costs – carry a substantial retail price (generally between $50 and $70), and have a guaranteed market, three factors absent from a first album by an untried act. They have also allowed record companies to trade on the status collectors have accorded certain bootleg recordings.

In fact, in most instances these boxed-sets have fallen well short of previous bootleg boxed-sets. Springsteen's disappointing live set, *Live 1978–85*, contained a healthy dose of cuts from his scintillating 1978 Roxy show. But they just don't sound right – drummer Weinberg is using that annoying mid-eighties 'gunshot' drum-sound, suggesting that some serious rejigging of the original performance had taken place. Dylan's *Bootleg Series* included a generous slug of outtakes (five) from Dylan's lost masterpiece *Infidels*, but the versions of 'Someone's Got a Hold of My Heart' and 'Blind Willie McTell' are a long way short of the dynamic versions in general circulation on bootleg.

And the last thing that these catch-all boxed-sets are is systematic. There is very little serious peeking behind the shades going on here. The unravelling of a particular song in the studio is rarely in evidence. With artists that have some input into their own sets – meaning most artists who are still alive – the same process of self-censorship that is to be found in their art, good or ill, is just as likely to be found on their boxed-set.

In a recent interview, Richard Thompson admitted that if he had compiled the lamentable triple-CD Thompson anthology, *Watching the Dark*, there would not have been anything prior to 1984, and that his only input had been censorial – to reject things that he disapproved of. Dylan apparently nixed the 1980 outtake 'Yonder Comes Sin' from his *Bootleg Series*, while Lou Reed was even more brutal with *Between Thought and Expression*, killing a psychotic first take of 'The Gun' and a magnificent 10-minute blast through 'Sister Ray' with his first post-Velvets pick-up band,

The Tots. To my mind it is a shame that artists like Thompson, Dylan and Reed are allowed any say in these overviews of their recorded work if it is only as a censor that they involve themselves.

So does the fan – who pays the bills – have any 'right' to hear (i.e. acquire) those recordings an artist rejects for public consumption? After all, it is not only the artist who is wrapped up in his or her work. It matters to many. If the industry perceives music as a commodity, a recording of a musical performance is not merely an item of commerce to those who appreciate it, it is 'an artistic document, and the public has an interest in its preservation, and perhaps in its availability as well'.[3]

Yet there remains a curious doublethink applied by many artists. They are often extremely nonchalant about who may have copies of private recordings and performances, yet are resentful when that material passes beyond their immediate circle of influence. Their success has presumably been dependent on making music that encourages people who hear it to 'spread the word'. So why the surprise when these 'private' tapes are played and copied by people? Isn't that the point? Or is it all about the filthy lucre? In this imperfect world, the privately distributed tape may well become a publicly sold CD. But then what is the alternative?

Lenny Kaye: Sometimes you don't want to see the stitches. On the other hand, some of that is really fascinating to me – to see less good work – because there are certain revelations into character or how somebody thinks. I can remember somebody playing me a 'work tape' of 'Good Vibrations' and how it grew. I've also heard an Elvis Presley 'Can't Help Falling in Love' and I never realized how big a part the steel guitar played. Listening to it, you can hear him find that part and later it tucks in and it's almost subtle and unnoticeable . . . To me it enhances an artist because you can see creation taking place before your eyes and that's the most exciting thing of all. Sometimes I'd much rather listen to the reach and the desire than the completed formal effort. As a record producer I enjoy being in the studio and [participating] in that moment much more than getting a copy of the finished record. It's always somehow less . . . It's gone . . . You gotta document it. You gotta have it preserved. So if you want to go back to it at some future date, it's there. It's a small price to pay for a record company losing a couple of sales here and there.[4]

It would be naïve to assume that the only type of collector who can, or should, have access to these recordings must be someone who has connections with industry boffins and/or has the time, money and inclination to trade, barter, browbeat and cajole friends (and other strangers) to part with items of interest. Figures like these are at the top of a steep pyramid, with tapes filtering down through the various gradations of collectors, finally reaching those who are unwilling to try and climb the pyramid but are happy to languish 'neath its weight, paying for the privilege with their bootleg cassettes, records and CDs. After all, perish the thought that one day all music will be under the thumbs of the same moguls that dominate the film industry. The idea that there is 'approved' music and 'unapproved' music is really quite scary.

Neal Schustack [bootlegger]: These are alternative recordings, and they aren't in competition with stuff that's out. That doesn't make it legal, but it does raise questions about the rights of collectors.[5]

Bootlegs represent no threat to the music industry. Only the most dedicated of fans is going to appreciate the 'point' of hearing all twenty-seven takes of 'Can't Help Falling in Love'. The real bootleggers – and there is no doubt that the protection gap in Europe in the last five years has blurred divisions – presume that the punter knows why he is buying this item. It presupposes dedication. The exception to this rule are the bootleg tapes (and now even CDs, when they can be on the streets in three weeks or less) that are a souvenir of a recently witnessed performance, surely an innocuous enough form of the rock & roll disease.

Lenny Kaye: I love it in England where you can go see a gig and then go to Camden Market and buy the gig the next day, but that's more of a souvenir. I would like to be able to go and buy a live performance of say, the Johnny Burnette Trio someplace, just some weird night . . . Sometimes, when it's put in a recorded product and conceptualized, it becomes more of an *objet* *d'art* than a peek behind the curtains from a small position backstage. Bootlegs tend to reveal more of the day-to-day of the musical experience. One of the charms of bootlegs is that when you get it you come to it with a mind-set that you're not listening for perfection. You're listening for something scratchy and of the moment, like a snapshot as opposed to a glossy painting, and when you're presented with a boxed-set with liner notes and official things, all of a sudden the scratchiness becomes annoying, all of a sudden you start expecting a different level of finesse. You start expecting your classic live album of today which is someone taking 24-tracks into the thing and polishing it up and if there's any bum notes replacing 'em and adding a little vocal harmony 'cos the lead singer was deaf that moment, or whatever.[6]

Of course, even if the legitimate record companies could compete, by turning tapes around in a short enough time to market good recordings of recent shows, they never would. By choice, they exist in the world of large-scale economics, and in such a world profits don't exist on the kind of runs bootleggers produce.

The Byrdman: No American record company's going to release [the Velvet Underground's] *Sweet Sister Ray*. [But] somebody who wants it should be able to listen to it . . . I mean *Sweet Sister Ray* will probably realize about $3,000. Only half have been sold at this point and interest is kinda slow, so it may not make any money. At this point it's in the red . . . So big deal if someone's hearing music from twenty-five years ago . . . If the companies or the bands aren't interested in it – put it out. Put it out, it's as simple as that. They don't want to put it out, but they performed it in front of an audience, people heard it . . . it's not an invasion of privacy.[7]

The sad thing is that the big companies won't even let their artists sanction small-run specialist releases, though they could never release such items themselves. They object to bootleggers yet refuse to countenance the sort of truly specialist, 'fan-club' labels that could genuinely fill the same niche.

Graham Nash: Why go through all the rigmarole of cutting and pressing and covers and advertising for something that's only going to sell a couple of thousand copies? It's just not worth it to [the major labels], but through that crack falls a lot of great music . . . There are certain things that should be out there, I feel, and if we don't do anything about them, they'll just never come out . . . I don't care what the source is, if the emotion of the song is on the tape I don't care where it comes from. I don't care if it was recorded on a tincan . . . Neil [Young] I believe is planning to use a tape of me and him singing 'Oh, I've Loved You So Long', from the Greek Theatre from an audience tape [on his boxed-set]. It's a beautiful performance, and regardless of the quality of the recording, I think it deserves to be out there, and so does Neil.[8]

Perhaps what it comes down to is this: How do you like your music? All music buffs start out assimilating those cherished studio albums, and many music fans – good luck to them – never advance beyond appreciating the finished article, preferring their artists to reproduce and remind, not stretch and transform. Theirs is a different aesthetic to that of the bootleg fraternity.

Bootleg punters are looking for something that is locked into the wellspring of inspiration, and the beauty of the musical interplay that rock music allows is that just such a moment can sneak up on you real quick and unexpected – and just as quickly be gone. Those magical moments are always live – even when they happen in the studio. They do not happen when you get that click-track just right. They do not happen when the bass has to be overdubbed because towards the end of a take the bassist gets so into it that he begins to drown out the guitarist. They can be found on the Velvet Underground's studio version of 'Sister Ray'; pretty much any live version of Television's 'Marquee Moon'; indeed they can happen any time you put great musicians together and get them to play some songs. It's called rock & roll and it's why people who saw The Sex Pistols live went out and formed bands. And it's to be found as easily in the off-key harmonies on 'Anarchy in the UK' as in the (oops, quick) tempo change in the intro to 'It's a Man's World'.

Lenny Kaye: A lot of the best moments are the ones that just happen within forty-five seconds of a song ... especially with [something like] 'Radio Ethiopia', twenty minutes of it could just be wandering around in the wilderness painfully and then all of a sudden, something would lock in and we'd be there. And we'd be there for a half-minute, or two minutes or five minutes or be able to rise through the rest of the set. But I wouldn't sacrifice those moments for a performance which is even, capable, proficient ... Sometimes you've got to scale the highs and lows. A lot of times in the framework of legitimate albums people don't have the patience ... There are a lot of people who regard music very casually. Maybe if you [only] sell 20,000 of an album like *Nuggets* the 20,000 who bought that album are really into it, and really cared about each note. If a million people bought it, you know a lot of people are not that deep into a thing. Bootlegs definitely appeal to the connoisseur. There's very few artists that I personally care about [enough] that I would even buy the bootlegs ... [but] I have Television recordings which are the way I heard 'em, night after night at CBGB's, and there is no real Television live album.[9]

Rock music is live music, and record companies do not like live music. What they desire are artists who believe that they are a necessary evil, a requisite part of recording and marketing a successful album, but whose advance remains permanently 'recoupable'. As for the artist and his or her perception of a live album, Jon Pareles again put it best:

After all their work, [bands] can't bear to think that a version of the song they belted out years ago in some nondescript arena might eventually show more passion, even if they missed a high note ... What bootlegs offer, and performers and companies are reluctant to let out, is testimony that the musicians are fallible – that they make mistakes ... they also challenge the notion that music belongs to big companies and can be doled out at their convenience.[10]

Anything that challenges that notion can't be all bad; nor can something which reminds us all that anyone can make live music, anyone can record live music and – if the legislators had any sense – anyone would be able to put out live music.

Record companies may need to convince bands that, yes, there is a reason why their last album cost a quarter of a million (recoupable) dollars to record, but what if it could have been recorded live in two nights at New York's Supper Club and sound just as good, nay better? What use the producer-manufacturer then?

> Steal a little and they throw you in jail,
> Steal a lot and they make you king.[11]

Glossary of Terms

ARRC Audio Recording Rights Coalition.

Berne Convention The International Union for the Protection of Literary and Artistic Works (1886). The most recent revision of the Berne Convention was 1971, the so-called Paris text.

BPI British Phonographic Industry.

CD–R A recordable CD. The current state of CD–R technology only allows these CDs to be recorded on once, but they can then be played in any conventional CD player.

Copycode The CBS-devised system for limiting digital copying, which was ultimately rejected by Congress and abandoned in favour of the SCMS system (see below).

DAT Digital Audio Tape.

DCC Digital Compact Cassette, a patently inferior digital system to DAT, based on the principle of data-compression. Destined to fail.

De-clicking The process by which noise from shellac and vinyl records is removed by computer before being transferred to CD.

EQ Equalization of sonic highs and lows to produce an enjoyable experience.

GATT General Agreement on Tariffs and Trade.

GEMA The German organization responsible for collection and clearance of 'mechanical' copyrights.

Geneva Convention The Convention for the Protection of Producers of Phonographs Against Unauthorized Duplication of their Phonograms (1971).

Glass master The master from which CDs are manufactured.

IFPI International Federation of Phonographic Industries.

Mechanicals The abbreviated term commonly used for 'mechanical' royalties.

Neighbouring Rights The subsidiary rights owned by producer-manufacturers and broadcasting companies to the works which they have participated in and/or financed.

NoNoise A computer-generated noise-reduction system which can 'de-click' (see above), reduce hiss or mask imperfections in recordings.

Protection gap A legal loophole which allows the legal manufacture of live-performance recordings provided 'mechanical' royalties are paid.

Public domain Material that has passed out of copyright owing to the passage of time or the anonymity of the author.

RIAA Recording Industry Association of America.

Rome Convention The Convention for the Protection of Performers, Producers of Phonograms and Broadcasting Organizations (1961).

SCMS Serial Copy Management System: an anti-copying device which is now included in all domestic digital recording equipment, SCMS allows a single digital generation of an encoded tape but prohibits further digital copies.

SIAE The Italian organization responsible for collection and clearance of copyrights.

Soundboard Sometimes referred to as 'board' or 'PA' or 'line' recordings, these are concert recordings that are recorded from the sound system rather than by a microphone from the audience.

Special 301 A form of trade sanction utilized by the US government against countries they consider to be providing inadequate copyright protection to American interests.

STEMRA The Dutch organization responsible for collection and clearance of copyrights.

TRIPS Trade-Related Aspects of Intellectual Property Rights (see also GATT).

Universal Copyright Convention The alternative copyright convention to Berne, this was enacted in 1952. Though it provides a measure of protection, its scope is considerably more restricted than Berne.

The Top 100 Bootlegs

A subjective list in alphabetical order

The Band *Live at The Hollywood Bowl* (LP)

Syd Barrett *Magnesium Proverbs* (CD)

The Beach Boys *Smile* (Japanese CD)

The Beatles *Get Back and 12 other songs* (LP/CD)

__ *Complete BBC Sessions* (CD)

__ *Ultra Rare Trax* (CD/LP)

__ *Unsurpassed Masters Vols. 1–7* (CD)

__ *Collector's Item* (LP)

David Bowie *Thin White Duke* (LP) [CD version: *Suffragette City*]

__ *In Person/In America* (LP) [now officially available on CD/LP as *Live at Santa Monica*]

Buffalo Springfield *Stampede* (LP/CD)

The Buzzcocks *Time's Up* (LP) [now officially available on CD]

Captain Beefheart *Another Chapter in the Life and Times* (LP)

The Clash *White Riot* (LP)

Elvis Costello *50,000,000 Elvis Fans Can't Be Wrong* (LP)

Cream *Secret History* (CD)

Crosby, Stills, Nash & Young *Wooden Nickel* (LP)

Deep Purple *H-Bomb* (LP)

Devo *Workforce to the World* (LP)

The Doors *Rock is Dead* (LP)

__ *Live Seattle 1970* (CD)

Bob Dylan *Royal Albert Hall* (LP/CD)

__ *The Genuine Basement Tapes Vols. 1–5* (CD)

__ *History/Dylan* (LP)

__ *Ten of Swords* (LP)

__ *Little White Wonder* (LP)

__ *You Can't Kill an Idea* (CD)

Fairport Convention *From Past Archives* (CD)

Peter Gabriel *At The Roxy* (LP/CD)

Genesis *The Lamb Lives* (CD)

The Grateful Dead *Dead in Cornell* (CD)

Jimi Hendrix *Studio Haze* (CD)

Jason and the Scorchers *Rock on Germany* (LP)

Elton John *Rainbow Rock* (CD)

Joy Division *Shadowplay* (CD)
__ *Warsaw* (LP/CD)
King Crimson *Une Reve Sans Consequence Speciale* (LP)
  [CD version: *Lament*]
The Kinks *Kollectable Kinks* (LP)
Led Zeppelin *Pure Blues Live* (LP) [LP/CD version: *Mudslide*]
__ *Secret History* (CD)
__ *Studio Daze* (CD)
__ *Plays Pure Blues* (CD)
Little Feat *Electric Lycanthrope* (LP)
__ *Rampant Synchopatio* (LP)
Groucho Marx *I Never Kissed an Ugly Woman* (CD)
Van Morrison *Pagan Streams* (CD)
__ *If You Don't Like It, Go Fuck Yourself* (CD)
The Move *Black Country Rock* (CD)
New York Dolls *Seven Day Weekend* (LP/CD)
Jimmy Page *James Patrick Page: Session Man* (LP)
Pearl Jam *Eddie Sings The Doors* (CD)
Pere Ubu *The U-Men* (LP)
Pink Floyd *Winter Tour '74* (LP)
__ *A Great Set* (LP)
Elvis Presley *Good Rockin' Tonight* (LP)
__ *The Burback Sessions Vols. 1 and 2* (LP)
__ *Behind Closed Doors* (LP)
Prince *The Black Album* (LP/CD)
__ *The Jewel Box I and II* (CD)
Radio Birdman *Eureka* (LP)
Lou Reed *Despite All the Amputations* (CD)
__ *Whatever Happened To Dick & Steve* (LP)
  [CD version: *Waiting For Lou*]
REM *The Trouble With Michael* (CD)
__ *From The Borderline* (CD)
The Rolling Stones *Brights Lights, Big City* (LP/CD)
__ *Brussels Affair 1973* (CD)
__ *Get Your Leeds Lungs Out* (LP/CD)
__ *LiveR Than You'll Ever Be* (LP/CD)
__ *Mad Shadows* (CD)
__ *The First Decade* (CD)
__ *Trident Mixes* (LP/CD)
Roxy Music *First Kiss* (CD)
The Sex Pistols *No Future UK* (LP) [Now officially available on CD]

__ *Indecent Exposure* (LP) [Now officially available on CD]

__ *Welcome to the Rodeo* (LP)

Siouxsie & the Banshees *Love in a Void* (LP)

Slade *Watch Out! Here Cum T'Nutz* (CD)

Patti Smith *Teenage Perversity & Ships in the Night* (LP)

__ *I Never Talked to Bob Dylan* (LP)

Bruce Springsteen *All Those Years* (LP/CD)

__ *The Saint, the Incident and the Main Point Shuffle* (CD)

__ *Pièce De Résistance* (LP/CD)

__ *Fire on the Fingertips* (LP) [CD version: *Forgotten Songs*]

Rod Stewart and The Faces *Killer Highlights* (CD)

Talking Heads *Memories Can't Wait* (CD)

Television *Double Exposure* (LP/CD)

Pete Townshend *The Genius Of* (LP) [CD version: *Lifehouse Demos*]

U2 *The Salome Demos* (LP/CD)

Velvet Underground *Sweet Sister Ray* (LP)

__ *The Wild Side of The Street* (CD)

__ *End of Cole Avenue* (CD/LP)

Tom Waits *Cold Beer on a Hot Night* (CD)

The Who *Tales From* (LP/CD)

__ *Fillmore East 1968* (LP/CD)

__ *Who's Zoo* (LP/CD)

The Yardbirds *Golden Eggs/More Golden Eggs* (LP)

Neil Young *Old Man's Fancy* (LP)

__ *Separate Ways* (CD)

Frank Zappa *The Mystery Box* (LP)

__ *'Tis The Season to be Jolly* (LP)

Various Artists *Monterey Pop Festival Volume 1* [Living Legend] (CD)

Bibliography

The bulk of information derived from printed sources has come from the music business and 'collector' magazines listed in the periodicals section. What other features and books I have drawn on are listed independently.

PERIODICALS

Billboard 1969–94
Music Week 1974–94
Record Business 1978–82.
ICE (International CD Exchange) Nos. 1–84
Music & Copyright Nos. 1–32
Record Collector Nos. 1–175
Hot Wacks Quarterly Nos. 1–12
Why a Pig? Nos. 1–3
Live! Music Review Nos. 1–9
Belmo's Beatleg News Nos. 1–12

BOOKS

Cable, Paul, *Bob Dylan: His Unreleased Recordings* (Scorpion/Dark Star, 1978)

Coover, James, *Music Publishing, Copyright and Piracy in Victorian England* (Mansell, 1985)

Cotten, Lee, and Dewitt, Howard A., *Jailhouse Rock* (Pierian, 1983)

Crowe, Cameron, with Dylan, Bob, *Biograph* (Columbia, 1985)

Dannen, Fredric, *Hit Men: Power Brokers and Fast Money Inside the Music Business* (Muller, 1990)

Dworkin, Gerald, and Taylor, Richard D. *Blackstone's Guide to the Copyright, Designs & Patents Act 1988* (Blackstone, 1989)

Flanagan, Erik, *You Can Look but You Better Not Touch* (Introduction) (privately published 1991)

Fripp, Robert, *The Great Deceiver* (Discipline, 1992)

Glemser, Kurt (ed.), *Hot Wacks IV–XI* (Blue Flake, 1977–85)

Green, Jonathon, *Days in the Life: Voices from the English Underground 1961–1971* (Heinemann, 1988)

Heylin, Clinton (ed.), *The Penguin Book of Rock & Roll Writing* (Viking, 1992)

Heylin, Clinton, *Gypsy Love Songs and Sad Refrains* (privately published, 1990)

Horn, Delton T., *DAT: The Complete Guide to Digital Audio Tape* (McGraw-Hill, 1991)

National Heritage Committe – *The Price of Compact Discs: Minutes of Evidence and Appendices* (HMSO, 1993)

Porter, Vincent (ed.) – *Beyond the Berne Convention* (John Libbey, 1991)

Read, Oliver, and Welch, Walter L., *From Tin Foil to Stereo* (Howard W. Sams, 1976)

Rey, Luis, *Led Zeppelin Live: An Illustrated Exploration of Underground Tapes* (The Hot Wacks Press, 1991)

Savage, Jon, *England's Dreaming* (Faber, 1991)

Schultheiss, Tom – 'Everything You Always Wanted to Know About Bootlegs, but Were Too Busy Collecting Them to Ask', in Charles Reinhardt (ed.), *You Can't Do That* (Pierian, 1981)

Shemel, Sidney, and Krasilovsky, M. William, *This Business of Music* (4th edition Billboard, 1979)

Walker, Bob (ed.), *Hot Wacks XII, XIII, XIV, XV* (The Hot Wacks Press, 1986–92)

Walker, Bob (ed.), *Hot Wacks Supplements I and II* (The Hot Wacks Press, 1993–4)

Wenner, Jann, *Lennon Remembers* (Penguin, 1972)

Williams, Paul, *Performing Artist: The Music of Bob Dylan* Volume 1 (Underwood–Miller, 1990)

US FEATURES

Anon., 'Bootleg Albums Hit England', *Circus* January 1971

Anon., 'Anti-Bootlegging Bill Becomes Law', *Rolling Stone*, 9 December 1971

Anon., 'Big Crackdown on the Bootleggers', *Rolling Stone*, 18 February 1971

Anon., 'Disc Firm Sues Over Bootleg Dylan Album', *LA Times*, 29 November 1969

Alverson, Charles, 'White Wonder Visits London', *Rolling Stone*, 19 March 1970

Chorush, Bob, 'Feds are Leaning on Bootleggers', *Rolling Stone*, 14 October 1971

Gleason, Ralph J., 'All the Quack Robin Hoods', *Rolling Stone*, 14 October 1971

Goldberg, Michael, 'Bootleg Bob: Dylan Creates a Stir, CBS not Amused', *Rolling Stone*, 10 April 1986

Harrington, Richard, 'Bootlegs Kick 'em Where it Hurts', *LA Times* 22 June 1986

Himes, Geoffrey, 'Bootleg Bonanza', *Crawdaddy*, May 1976

Hopkins, Jerry, 'New Dylan Album Bootlegged in LA', *Rolling Stone*, 20 September 1969

Hopkins, Jerry, 'Elvis Collector Item, for True', *Rolling Stone*, 29 April 1971

Kasindorf, Jeanie, 'Pop Piracy', *Entertainment World*, 27 March 1970

Marcus, Greil, bootleg reviews in *Rolling Stone*, 7 February 1970

Ressner, Jeffrey, 'Bootlegs Go High-Tech', *Rolling Stone*, 30 May 1991

Ross, Michael, 'A New Dylan', *LA Herald-Examiner*, 21 September 1969

Shaw, Breg, 'Bootleggers: Rock Robin Hoods or Commie Threat?' *Who Put the Bomp*, No. 20

Sullivan, Lorana – 'Piracy on the High Cs', *Wall Street Journal* 13 December 1969

Tiven, Jon, 'Godzilla's Revenge', *Rock* 23 April 1973

Van Ness, Chris, 'The Great White Wonder', *Entertainment World*, Vol. 1 No. 5

Wainright, Teddy, 'These Discs are a Real Steal', *Life*, 17 April 1970

Ward, Ed, 'The Bootleg Blues', *Harper's Monthly*, January 1974

UK FEATURES

Anon., 'Bootleg Bashing Begins', *Melody Maker*, 13 November 1971

Anon., 'Message from a Bootlegger', *Melody Maker*, 11 March 1972

Anon., 'BPI Tells Pirates to Leg It', *NME*, May 1975

Carr, Roy, 'Ruling the Airwaves', *NME*, 17 March 1979

Carr, Roy, 'Big Brother is Watching You', *NME*, 8 September 1979

De Whalley, Chas, 'Spunk Rock', *Sounds*, 29 October 1977

Ellen, Mark, 'Me and the Boys was Wondering About This Bootleg Business. . .', *NME*, 26 May 1979

Ellison, Mike, 'Profits of the Record Pirates', *Guardian*, 21 October 1993

Heylin, Clinton, '25 All-Time Greatest Bootleg Records', *Q*, July 1988

Hill, Dave, 'Slipping Out Discs', *Independent*, 2 June 1992

Humphries, Patrick, 'Roll Those Tapes', *Vox*, May 1992

Murray, Charles Shaar, 'Now the Boot's on the Other Leg', *NME*, 30 July 1977

Oldfield, Mike, 'Bootleg Blues' *Guardian*, 29 July 1989

Parsons, Tony, 'Blank Nuggets in the UK', *NME*, 21 May 1977

Rambali, Paul, 'Home Taping', *NME*, 12 July 1980

Tyler, Andrew, 'The Big Time Clown in the Bootleg Ring', *NME*, 2 August 1980

Williams, Richard, 'Well, What Can be Done to Stamp Them Out?' and 'The Essential Bob Dylan', *Melody Maker*, 19 June 1971

AUSTRALIAN FEATURES

Apple House Inc., 'Live CDs: An Ad', *The Age*, 8 October 1993

Cameron, Kirsty, and Warren, Matthew, 'Live and Scratchy', *Who Weekly*, 15 November 1993

Handlin, Denis, 'An Open Letter to Music Consumers', *Drum Media*, December 1993

Megalogenis, George, 'Pirates of the High CDs' *The Australian*, 3 January 1994

RECORD INDUSTRY MATERIAL

'DAT is a RAW DEAL for American Music' (pamphlet), Coalition to Save American Music

'Germany Caught in Bootleg Gap', by Mike Hennessey, *MIDEM News Daily*, 25 January 1993

Inside RIAA: Fall 1992, 1992

International Conventions & Copyright/Neighbouring Rights Legislation (IFPI, 1988)

International Conventions & National Legislation on the Rights of Producers, Performers & Broadcasting Organizations (IFPI, March 1993)

The World is Listening Vol. 1 – RIAA 1992 Annual Report

UNPUBLISHED MATERIAL

SADD pastiche insert (by HAR)

Archive/Brigand/Scorpio Catalogue

Hoffman Avenue Wholesale Catalogues

Richard Records Catalogue

Trade Mark of Quality Master Tapes File

Mandy Welles' Bootleg CD Discography of Labels and Artists

Apple House Music press material

FBI File No. LA 28-6852 (Re: Lou Cohan)

FBI File No. LA 28-7657 (Re: Michael Mess)

Final Judgment: Dwarf Music, B. Dylan & Columbia *v.* Beckman, Feldman, S & R, Goldman and Taylor.

Ex Tempore Judgment: Sony Music & Michael Jackson *v.* Apple House Music.

Notes

Introduction: A Boot by Any Other Name . . .

1 Cotton Mather, the eighteenth-century Puritan, preaching to pirates condemned to death.
2 Shemel and Krasilovsky, *This Business of Music*, pp. 93–4.
3 Interview with author.
4 Schultheiss, in *You Can't Do That*, p. 396.
5 Interview with author.
6 *Los Angeles Times*, 22 June 1986.
7 Shaw, 'Bootleggers: Rock Robin Hoods or Commie Threat?', *Who Put the Bomp*, No. 20.
8 Interview with author.

Artifacts

1 From the Bard to the Blues

1 St Augustine, *City of God*, Penguin, 1972, p. 139.
2 'Proposals for printing, by subscription, the dramatic works of William Shakespeare', 1756.
3 William Shakespeare, *Hamlet* (ed.) Bernard Lott, Longman, 1968, xliv.
4 *This Business of Music*, p. 109.
5 Dworkin and Taylor, *Blackstone's Guide to the Copyright, Designs and Patents Act 1988,* p. 104.
6 Porter (ed.), *Beyond the Berne Convention*, p. 94.
7 Coover, *Music Publishing, Copyright and Piracy in Victorian England*, p. vii.
8 ibid., p. 142.
9 ibid., p. 142.
10 ibid., p. 142.

2 The Custodians of Vocal History

1 A classical-music bootlegger quoted in *Stereo Review*, February 1970.

2 Read and Welch, *From Tin Foil to Stereo*, p. 418.
3 *You Can't Do That*, p. 399.
4 Quoted in *Hot Wacks Quarterly*, No. 5
5 *You Can't Do That*, p. 401.
6 Interview with author.
7 *Stereo Review*, February 1970.
8 ibid.
9 ibid.
10 ibid.
11 ibid.
12 ibid.
13 ibid.
14 ibid.

3 The First Great White Wonders

1 Interview with author.
2 Interview with author.
3 Interview with author.
4 Interview with author.
5 Interview with author.
6 Interview with author.
7 *Entertainment World*, vol. 1, No. 5.
8 *Melody Maker*, 19 June 1971.
9 Writ, courtesy of Dub.
10 ibid.
11 Copied from bootleg album.
12 Interview with author.
13 Morthland and Hopkins 'The Rock and Roll Liberation Front?', in *The Penguin Book of Rock & Roll Writing*, p. 472.
14 *This Business of Music*, p. 272.
15 *Wall Street Journal*, 3 December 1969.
16 Interview with author.
17 Interview with author.
18 'The Rock & Roll Liberation Front?', in *The Penguin Book of Rock & Roll Writing*, pp. 471–2.
19 ibid.

20 Jann Wenner, *Lennon Remembers*, p. 120.
21 Interview with author.
22 *Entertainment World*, 27 March 1970.
23 *Wall Street Journal*, 3 December 1969.
24 Interview with author.
25 *Rolling Stone*, January 1970
26 *Entertainment World*, 27 March 1970
27 Interview with author.
28 Interview with author.
29 Interview with author.
30 'The Rock & Roll Liberation Front?', in *The Penguin Book of Rock & Roll Writing*, p. 465.
31 Interview with author.
32 Interview with author.
33 Interview with author.
34 *Rolling Stone*, 14 October 1971.
35 ibid.

4   All Rights Reserved, All Wrongs Reversed
1 *Entertainment World*, 27 March 1970.
2 *Rolling Stone*, 29 November 1969
3 Interview with author.
4 Interview with author.
5 Interview with author.
6 Interview with author.
7 Interview with author.
8 Interview with author.
9 Interview with author.
10 Interview with author.
11 Luis Rey, *Led Zeppelin Live*, p. 51.
12 Interview with author.
13 Interview with author.
14 *Harper's Monthly*, January 1974.
15 ibid.
16 ibid.
17 Interview with author.
18 Interview with author.
19 Interview with author.

5   The Smokin' Pig
1 Interview with author.
2 Interview with author.
3 Interview with author.
4 Interview with author.
5 Interview with author.
6 Interview with author.

7 Interview with author.
8 Interview with author.
9 Interview with author.
10 Interview with author.
11 Interview with author.
12 Interview with author.
13 Interview with author.
14 Interview with author.

6   Going Underground
1 SADD album insert.
2 *New Musical Express*, 8 September 1979.
3 Interview with author.
4 Interview with author.
5 *Hot Wacks Quarterly*, No. 1.
6 *Bridgett's Album* insert.
7 *Hot Wacks Quarterly*, No. 12.
8 ibid.
9 Interview with author.
10 Interview with author.
11 Interview with author.
12 Interview with author.
13 Interview with author.
14 Dominique Roques – *Great White Answers*.
15 Dannen, *The Hit Men*, p. 49
16 Cable, *Bob Dylan: His Unreleased Recordings*, p. 6.
17 *This Business of Music*, p. 230.
18 Interview with author.
19 Interview with author.
20 FBI files, courtesy of Lou Cohan.
21 Interview with author.
22 Interview with author.
23 Interview with author.

7   Vicki's Vinyl
1 *Who Put the Bomp*, No. 20.
2 Interview with author.
3 Interview with author.
4 Interview with author.
5 Interview with author.
6 Cotten and DeWitt, *Jailhouse Rock*, p. xxvii.
7 Interview with author.
8 *New Musical Express*, 14 October 1978.
9 *Vox*, May 1992 (from a quote in a 1981 edition of *Creem*).
10 *Billboard*, 21 July 1979.
11 Interview with author.

12 *Hot Wacks Quarterly*, No. 6.
13 FBI report.
14 *Billboard*, 8 March 1980.
15 Interview with author.
16 Interview with author.
17 Interview with author.

8 White Cover Folks!
1 *Rolling Stone*, 19 March 1970
2 ibid.
3 Interview with author.
4 *A Day in the Life*, pp. 227–8.
5 Interview with author.
6 Interview with author.
7 *This Business of Music*, p. 21.
8 *Beyond the Berne Convention*, p. 18.
9 *Billboard*, 11 March 1972.
10 Interview with author.
11 Interview with author.
12 Interview with author.
13 *Jailhouse Rock*, p. xxiv
14 *Hot Wacks IV*, Introduction.

9 Anarchy in the UK
1 Interview with author.
2 *New Musical Express*, 30 July 1977.
3 'Spunk Rock', *Sounds*, 29 October 1977.
4 Interview with author.
5 'Spunk Rock', *Sounds*, 29 October 1977.
6 ibid.
7 ibid.
8 Jon Savage, *England's Dreaming*, p. 414.
9 *New Musical Express*, 26 May 1979.
10 *Hot Wacks Quarterly*, No. 6.
11 *New Musical Express*, 26 May 1979.
12 Interview with author.
13 Interview with author.

10 East/West
1 *Jailhouse Rock*, p. xxix.
2 Interview with author.
3 Interview with author.
4 Interview with author.
5 Interview with author.
6 Interview with author.
7 Interview with author.
8 Interview with author.
9 Interview with author.
10 Interview with author.

11 *The Get Back Journals*, sleeve notes.
12 Interview with author.
13 Album cover notes.
14 Interview with author.
15 Album cover notes.
16 Interview with author.
17 Interview with author.
18 Interview with author.
19 Interview with author.
20 Interview with author.
21 Interview with author.
22 Interview with author.
23 Interview with author.
24 Interview with author.
25 Interview with author.
26 Interview with author.
27 Interview with author.
28 Interview with author.
29 Interview with author.
30 Interview with author.
31 Interview with author.
32 Interview with author.
33 Interview with author.
34 Interview with author.
35 Interview with author.
36 Interview with author.
37 Interview with author.
38 *Guardian*, 2 January 1989.

11 Real Cuts at Last
1 San Francisco Press Conference [private video], 3 December 1965.
2 *New Musical Express*, 8 September 1979.
3 *Music Week*, 31 March 1980.
4 National Heritage Committee report, 1993, p. 112.
5 Interview with author.
6 *Billboard*, 8 September 1979.
7 *New Musical Express*, 2 August 1980.
8 ibid.
9 *Music Week*, 13 April 1981.
10 *Record Business*, 5 May 1980.
11 *Hot Wacks Quarterly*, No. 13
12 *Music Week*, 6 June 1987.
13 *Music Week*, 3 December 1988.
14 Interview with author.
15 Interview with author.
16 Interview with author.
17 Interview with author.
18 Interview with author.

19 Interview with author.

12 Complete Control
1   *Record Business*, 12 November 1979.
2   *Music Week*, 12 February 1983.
3   *Music Week*, 9 May 1981.
4   *Music Week*, 21 May 1988.
5   *Music Week*, 20 August 1977.
6   *Billboard*, March, 1979.
7   *Music Week*, 26 August 1978.
8   *Record Business*, 11 February 1980.
9   *Beyond the Berne Convention*, p. 72.
10 *Music Week*, 3 December 1983.
11 *Billboard*, 21 December 1985.
12 Peter Titus, 'The Man Can't Scotch Our Taping', in *The Penguin Book of Rock & Roll Writing*, p. 499.
13 *Billboard*, 9 November 1985.
14 *Music Week*, 7 November 1987.
15 *Beyond the Berne Convention*, p. 41.
16 *Billboard*, 4 July 1987.
17 *Billboard*, 8 August 1987.
18 Delton T. Horn, *DAT: The Complete Guide To Digital Audio Tape*, p. 168.

Audiophiles

13 Eraserhead Can Rub You Out
1   Paul Williams, *Performing Artist: The Music of Bob Dylan*, p. 8.
2   Erik Flanagan, *You Can Look but You Better Not Touch*, Introduction.
3   Interview with author.
4   *The Only Ones: The Peel Sessions*, sleeve notes.
5   *Billboard*, 8 August 1992.

14 It Was More Than Twenty Years Ago . . .
1   'Bootlegs Go Hi-Tech', *Rolling Stone*, 30 May 1991.
2   Interview with Erik Flanagan on behalf of author.
3   *Billboard*, 8 August 1992.
4   ibid.

15 Some Ultra Rare Sweet Apple Trax
1   *ICE*, June 1990.
2   Interview with author.
3   *ICE*, October 1988.
4   *ICE*, November 1988.

5   Interview with author.
6   Interview with author.
7   *ICE*, March 1990.
8   *You Can Look but You Better Not Touch*, Introduction.
9   *ICE*, February 1990.

16 They Said it Couldn't be Done
1   *Billboard*, 21 December 1985.
2   National Heritage Committee report, 1993, p. 33.
3   Interview with author.
4   Interview with author.
5   Interview with author.
6   *ICE*, May 1989.
7   Interview with author.
8   *ICE*, May 1989.
9   Interview with author.
10 Interview with author.
11 Interview with author.

17 It Was Less Than Twenty Years Ago . . .
1   *ICE*, December 1989.
2   Interview with Erik Flanagan on behalf of author.
3   *ICE*, December 1989.
4   Interview with author.
5   Interview with author.
6   Interview with Erik Flanagan on behalf of author.

18 The Third Generation
1   Interview with Erik Flanagan on behalf of author.
2   Interview with author.
3   *Billboard*, 8 August 1992.
4   Interview with author.
5   *You Can Look but You Better Not Touch*, Introduction.
6   National Heritage Committee report, 1993, p. 80.
7   Interview with Erik Flanagan on behalf of author.
8   Interview with Erik Flanagan on behalf of author.
9   Interview with Erik Flanagan on behalf of author.
10 Interview with author.
11 Interview with author.
12 Interview with author.
13 Interview with author.
14 Interview with author.

19 The First Rays of the New Rising Sun

1   Interview with author.
2   'Japanese Copyright Free for All', *Billboard*, 24 October, 1987.
3   *ICE*, November 1989.
4   Interview with author.
5   *Billboard*, 23 March 1991.

20 The Status Quo Re-established?

1   Interview with author.
2   *Billboard*, 8 August 1992.
3   ibid.
4   National Heritage Committee report, 1993, p. 137.
5   Interview with Erik Flanagan on behalf of author.
6   Interview with author.
7   *Billboard*, 8 August 1992.
8   *Beyond the Berne Convention*, p. 40.
9   Dworkin and Taylor, *Blackstone's Guide*, pp. 65–6.
10 *Guardian*, 29 July 1989.
11 *Independent*, August, 1989.
12 *Music & Copyright*, No. 12.
13 *Music & Copyright*, No. 12.
14 The Berne Convention (Paris text).
15 *Billboard*, 30 October 1993.
16 *ICE*, April 1992.
17 *Music & Copyright*, No. 13
18 ibid.
19 ibid.
20 National Heritage Committee report, 1993, p. 8.
21 *Beyond the Berne Convention*, p. 87.
22 Interview with author.

21 The House that Apple Built

1   *Who Weekly*, 15 November 1993.
2   Interview with author.
3   Interview with author.
4   *Drum Media*, December 1993.
5   Interview with author.
6   *Drum Media*, December 1993.
7   Apple House press release.
8   *Australian*, 3 January 1994.
9   Interview with author.

Aesthetics

22 Bringing it All Back Home

1   Interview with author.

23 One Man's Boxed-Set

1   'Bootlegs Go High-Tech', *Rolling Stone*, 30 May 1991,
2   *The Hit Men*, p. 143.
3   National Heritage Committee report, 1993, pp. 8–9.
4   *The Hit Men*, p. 144.
5   Jon Parales, 'Industry's Bane, Fans' Bonanza', in *The Penguin Book of Rock & Roll Writing*, p. 512.
6   *New Musical Express*, 26 May 1979.
7   *Billboard*, 8 August 1992.
8   *ICE*, November 1988.
9   *The Great Deceiver* album cover notes.
10 *Melody Maker*, May 1977.

24 Roll Your Tapes, Bootleggers

1   Interview with author.
2   *ICE*, February 1990.
3   *Biograph* booklet
4   'Bootlegs Go Hi-Tech', *Rolling Stone*, 30 May 1991.
5   Clinton Heylin, *Gypsy Love Songs & Sad Refrains*, p. 9
6   Interview with author.
7   Interview with author.
8   *Melody Maker*, 19 June 1971.
9   Interview with author.
10 Interview with author.

25 Copycats Ripped Off My Songs

1   National Heritage Committee report, 1993, p. 18.
2   Interview with author.
3   *Stereo Review*, February 1970.
4   Interview with author.
5   'Bootlegs Go Hi-Tech', *Rolling Stone*, 30 May 1991.
6   Interview with author.
7   Interview with author.
8   Interview with author.
9   Interview with author.
10 'Industry's Bane, Fans' Bonanza', in *The Penguin Book of Rock & Roll Writing*, p. 512.
11 Bob Dylan, © Special Rider, 1983.

Index